Front Endpaper

Left page, a color composite photograph of the New York–New Jersey area taken from ERTS–1 (Earth Resources Technology Satellite–1) at an altitude of 568 statute miles. Healthy crops, trees, and other green plants are shown as bright red. Suburban areas with sparse vegetation appear as light pink and barren lands as light gray. Cities and industrial areas show as green or dark gray, and clear water is completely black. The major geographical landmarks include: the Hudson River (upper left down to center right); New York City (center right); Long Island (upper right to center right); and Newark, Jersey City, and Elizabeth, New Jersey (center right). (NASA Photo)

Right page, a high-altitude aerial photograph of New York City showing Manhattan Island, Brooklyn, Governors Island, and the Statue of Liberty on Bedloes Island. (NASA Photo)

Introduction to Cultural Geography

Introduction to

Harcourt Brace Jovanovich, Inc.

New York   Chicago   San Francisco   Atlanta

Cultural Geography

Henry M. Kendall

Late of Miami University

Robert M. Glendinning

University of California, Los Angeles

Clifford H. MacFadden

University of California, Los Angeles

H. Craig MacFadden

Introduction to Cultural Geography

Cover photo: Nancy Palmer Agency

The globe on Plate I is reprinted by permission of Rand McNally & Company, © Rand McNally & Company, R. L. 73-GP-14.

The Geologic Time Scale in Appendix E was adapted from that of J. Lawrence Kulp in *Science*, April 14, 1961. Used by permission of *Science* and the author.

ISBN: 0-15-541670-7

Library of Congress Catalog Card Number: 75-30451

Printed in the United States of America

Preface

In recent times, the study of humankind's relationship with the earth's environment has become a matter of increasing practical importance. With human population growth placing ever-greater pressures on natural resources — in some instances, to the danger level — many people are beginning to recognize that this environment is not the inexhaustible gift of nature they had assumed it to be. As they awaken to the reality that the earth is not only a varied and ever-changing planet but a highly fragile and endangered one, people are also realizing that they must obtain a better understanding of their habitat if they are to restore and preserve it. There is, therefore, increasing public awareness of the need for additional research and study in those areas of the physical and social sciences that relate to human use of the environment. In geography, work involving the dynamics of culture has always been a major part of the discipline; today, this work is rapidly expanding into new areas and in new directions in quest of solutions to environmental problems.

Introduction to Cultural Geography responds to these new directions while carefully reflecting its parent volume's balanced coverage of the total human habitat. As an introductory textbook for today's college student, it addresses the expanding needs of many courses, old and new, in geography and allied fields involved with environmental structure and utilization. The focus of this book is on the relationship between cultural development and the natural environment: Chapters 1 and 2 present the basic concepts to be employed in the exploration; Chapters 3, 4, and 5 trace the origins and diffusions of human groups and their cultural institutions; Chapters 6 through 10 discuss human utilization of the earth and thus describe changing world patterns in the growth of agriculture, energy use, and industry; settlement types and the development of modern urban societies are the concerns of Chapters 11 and 12; Chapter 13 describes population trends and the modern world's spatial linkage systems; and some of the major adverse environmental impacts of modern societies are examined in Chapter 14.

Clarity, balance, and conciseness have been the watchwords in the planning and writing of this book; and while naturally presenting several important theoretical works, including those of Christaller, von Thünen, and Weber, we have usually sought to project the reader's thinking beyond the classroom to the facts and problems of the "real world." It is our hope that this approach will encourage people to view the study of geography as more than mere academic training in nomenclature—and thus encourage many more of them to become truly responsible guardians of this delicate planet and of its equally delicate human societies and cultures.

No extended listing of acknowledgments will be attempted here, but our thanks go to many colleagues and associates and to several staff members at Harcourt Brace Jovanovich (Joanne Daniels, Helen Faye, Harrison Griffin, Carolyn Johnson, Susan Joseph, and Harry Rinehart)—who have given us continuing encouragement, direction, and constructive editorial criticism; and to Richard F. Logan, who contributed materials for portions of two early chapters.

Robert M. Glendinning
Clifford H. MacFadden
H. Craig MacFadden

Contents

Chapter **3**   *Human Origins and Diffusions, 34*

Chapter **4**   *Race and Cultural Diffusion, 56*

Chapter **5**   *Societies and Political Order, 98*

Chapter **6**   *Mosaic of Agricultural Land-Use, 130*

Chapter **7**   *Agrarian Societies: Changes and Diffusions, 158*

Chapter **8**   *Societal Pacemakers: Energy, 182*

Chapter **9**   *Modern Societies and Agro-Industry, 208*

Chapter **10** *Industrial Societies: Diffusion and Regionalism, 228*

Chapter **11** *Settlement Types and Contrasts, 252*

Chapter **12** *Challenge of Urban Growth, 284*

Appendixes

PLATE I

THE PHYSICAL WORLD

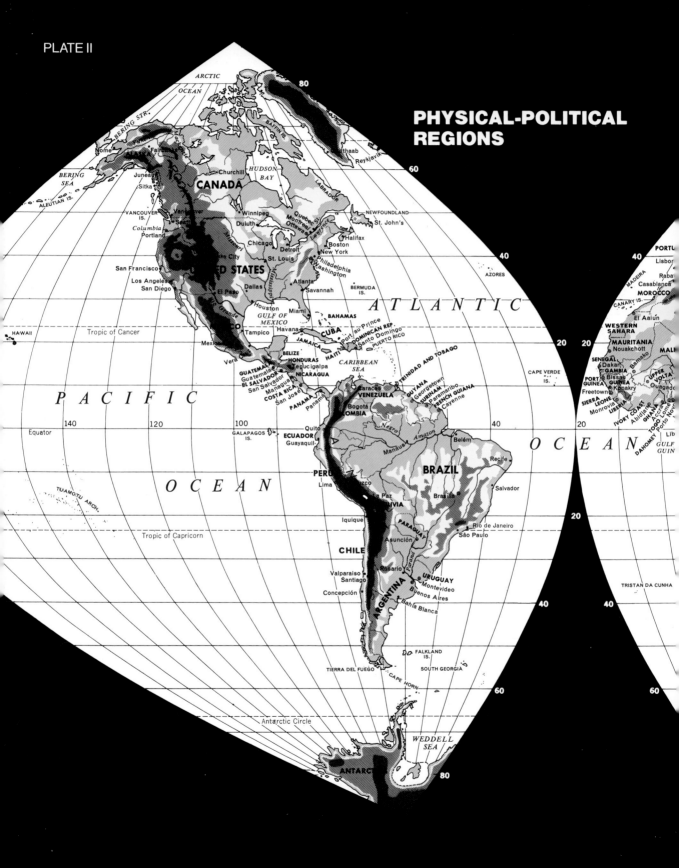

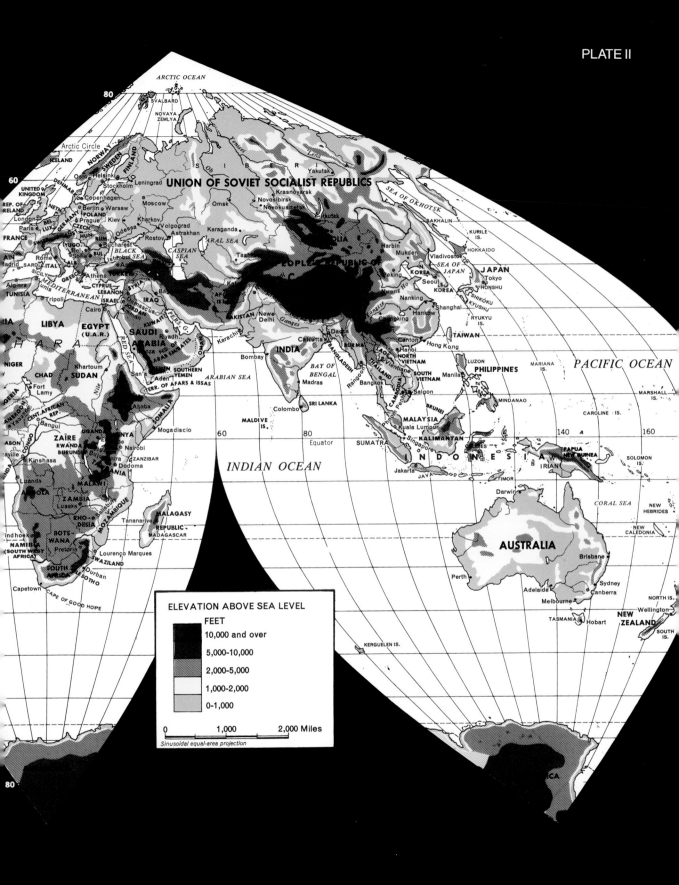

PLATE II

ELEVATION ABOVE SEA LEVEL
FEET
10,000 and over
5,000-10,000
2,000-5,000
1,000-2,000
0-1,000

0   1,000   2,000 Miles

Sinusoidal equal-area projection

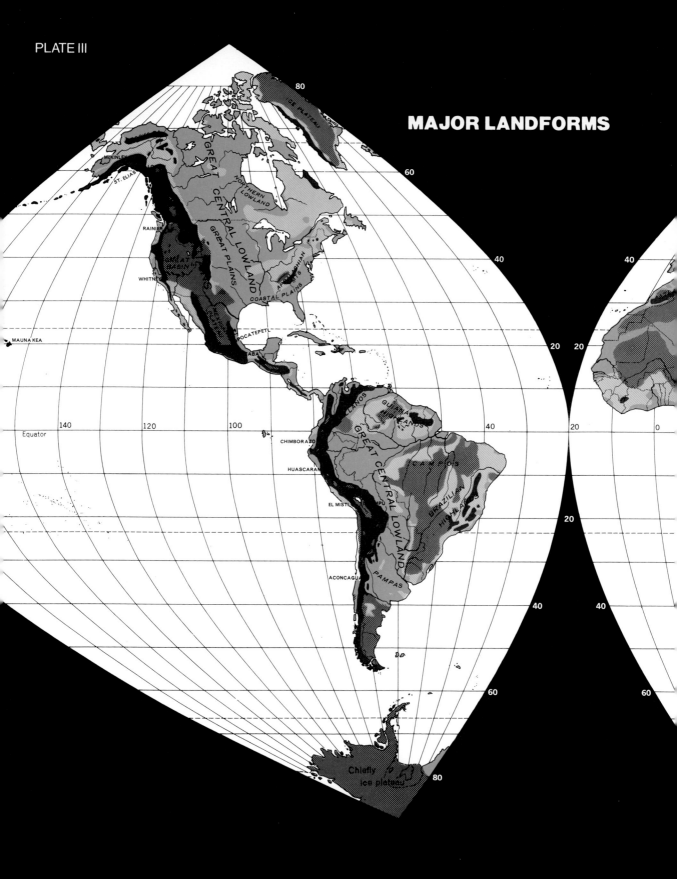

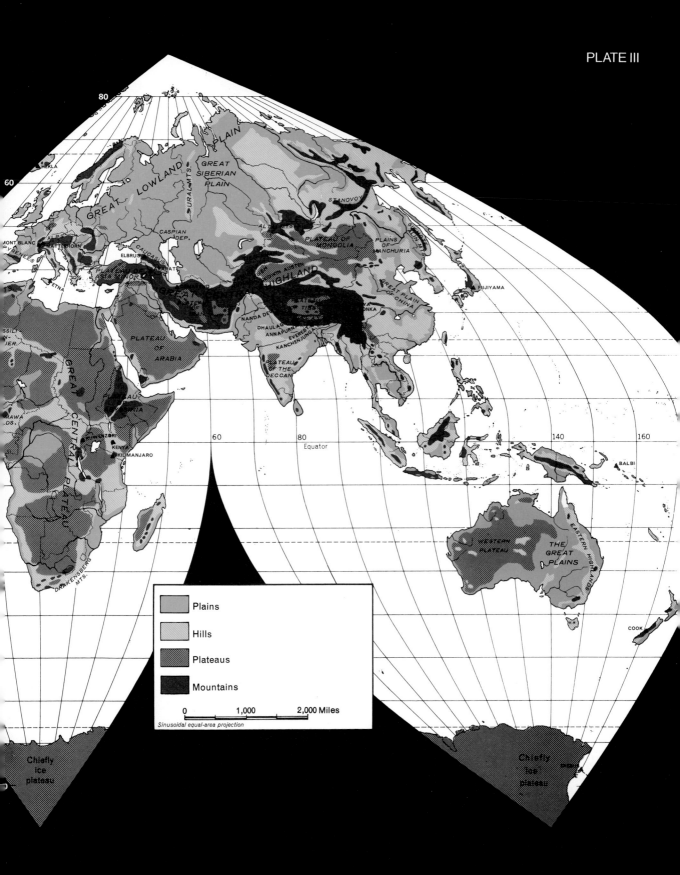

PLATE III

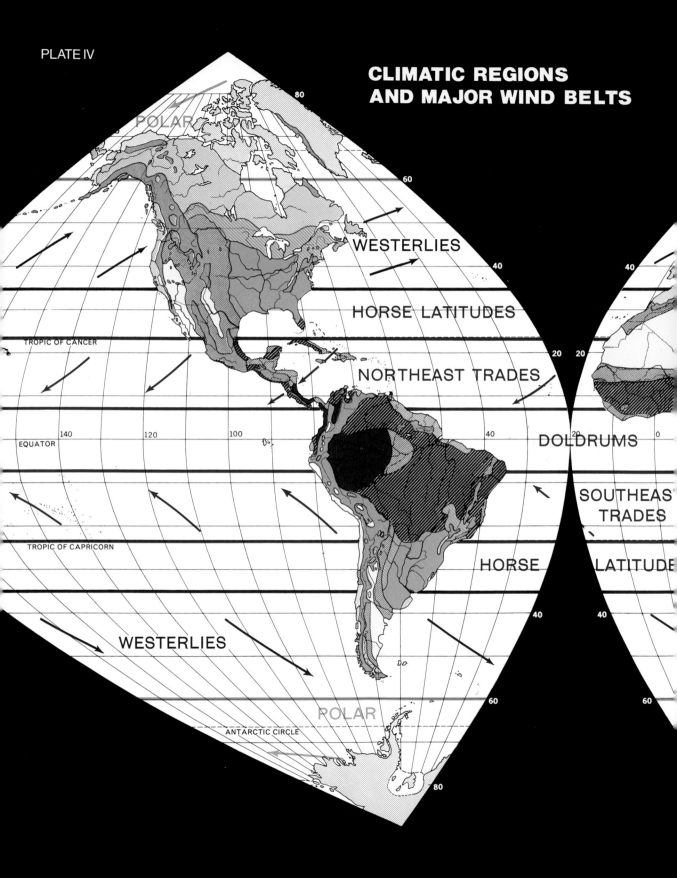

PLATE IV

CLIMATIC REGIONS
AND MAJOR WIND BELTS

POLAR

WESTERLIES

HORSE LATITUDES

TROPIC OF CANCER

NORTHEAST TRADES

140   120   100

EQUATOR

DOLDRUMS

40

SOUTHEAST
TRADES

TROPIC OF CAPRICORN

HORSE   LATITUDE

40

40

WESTERLIES

POLAR

ANTARCTIC CIRCLE

80

60

80

60

40

40

20   20

0

60

60

80

PLATE IV

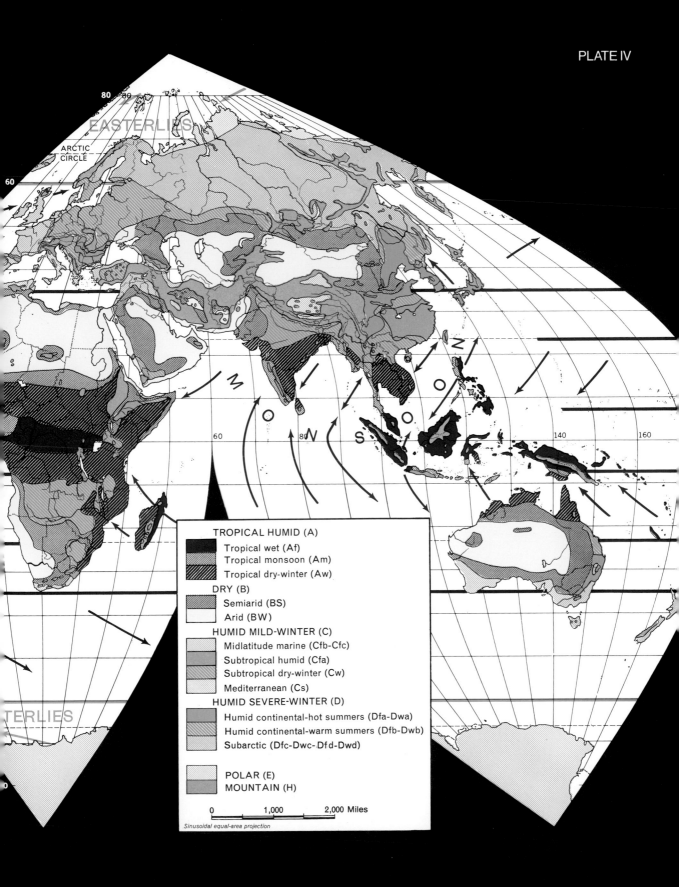

EASTERLIES

ARCTIC
CIRCLE

MONSOON

TERLIES

TROPICAL HUMID (A)
Tropical wet (Af)
Tropical monsoon (Am)
Tropical dry-winter (Aw)
DRY (B)
Semiarid (BS)
Arid (BW)
HUMID MILD-WINTER (C)
Midlatitude marine (Cfb-Cfc)
Subtropical humid (Cfa)
Subtropical dry-winter (Cw)
Mediterranean (Cs)
HUMID SEVERE-WINTER (D)
Humid continental-hot summers (Dfa-Dwa)
Humid continental-warm summers (Dfb-Dwb)
Subarctic (Dfc-Dwc-Dfd-Dwd)

POLAR (E)
MOUNTAIN (H)

0   1,000   2,000 Miles

Sinusoidal equal-area projection

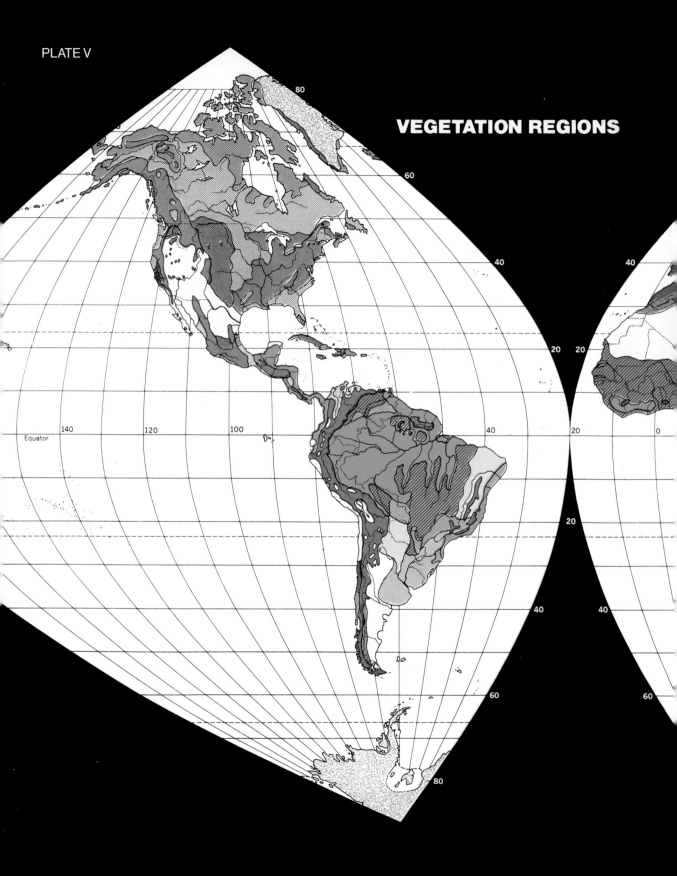

PLATE V

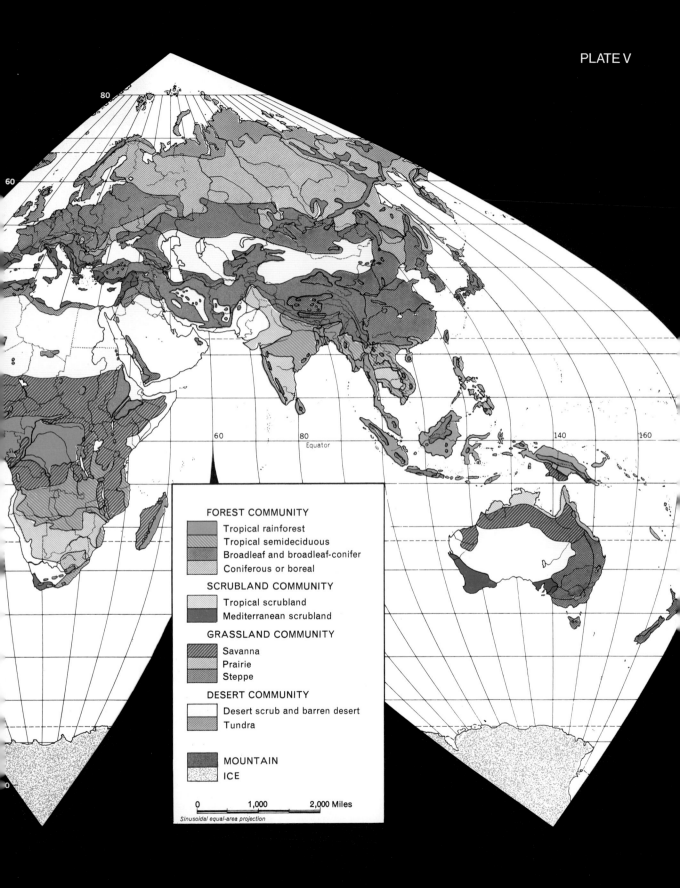

FOREST COMMUNITY
Tropical rainforest
Tropical semideciduous
Broadleaf and broadleaf-conifer
Coniferous or boreal

SCRUBLAND COMMUNITY
Tropical scrubland
Mediterranean scrubland

GRASSLAND COMMUNITY
Savanna
Prairie
Steppe

DESERT COMMUNITY
Desert scrub and barren desert
Tundra

MOUNTAIN
ICE

0   1,000   2,000 Miles

Sinusoidal equal-area projection

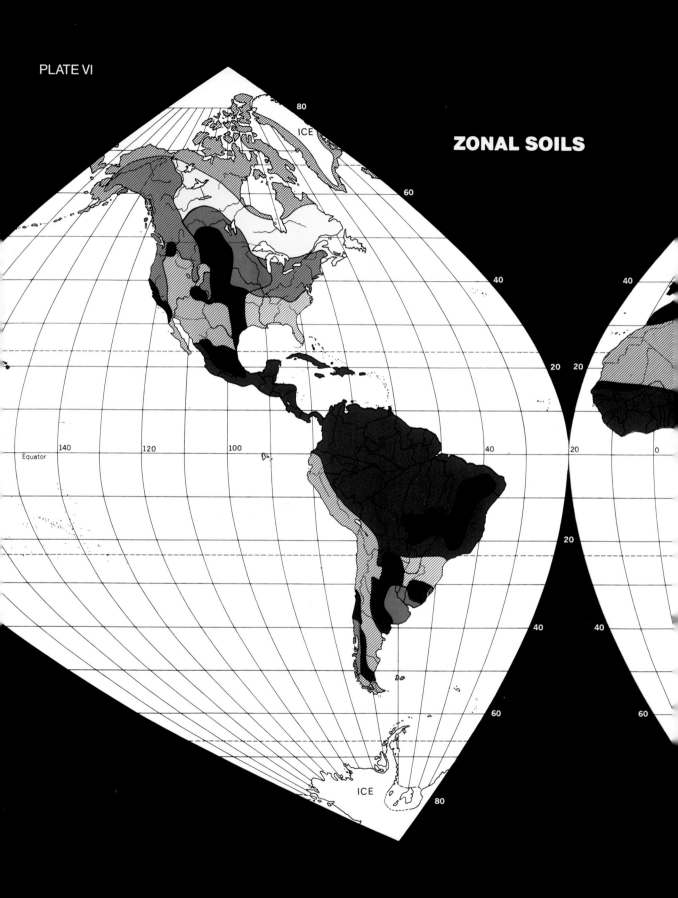

PLATE VI

ZONAL SOILS

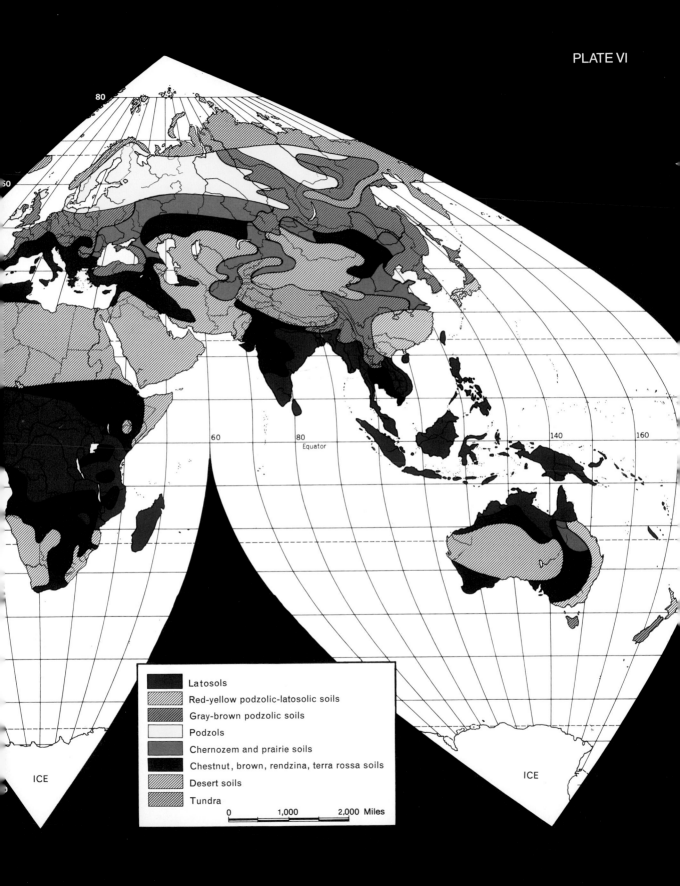

PLATE VI

Latosols
Red-yellow podzolic-latosolic soils
Gray-brown podzolic soils
Podzols
Chernozem and prairie soils
Chestnut, brown, rendzina, terra rossa soils
Desert soils
Tundra

0   1,000   2,000 Miles

ICE

ICE

80

60

80
Equator

140

160

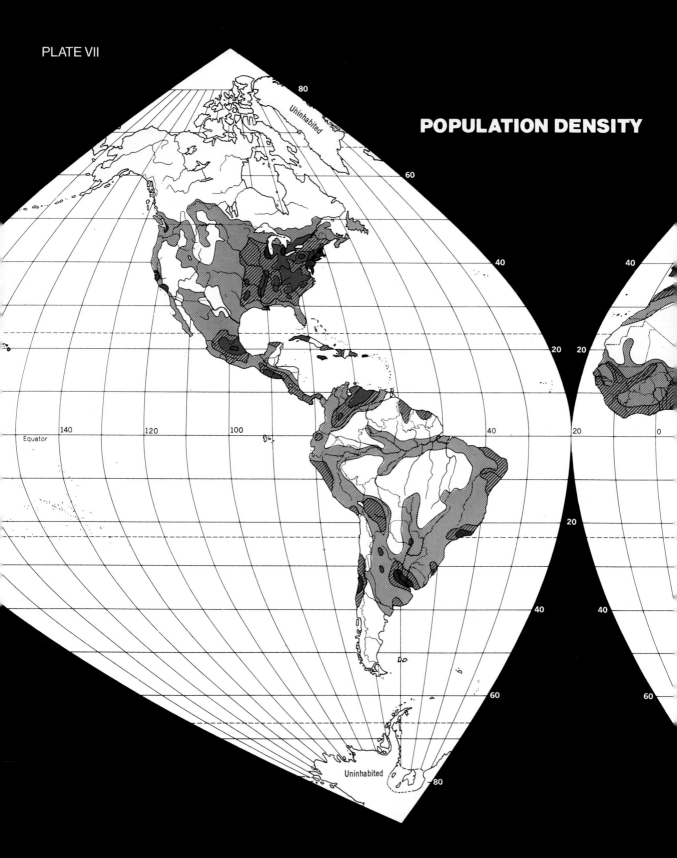

PLATE VII

POPULATION DENSITY

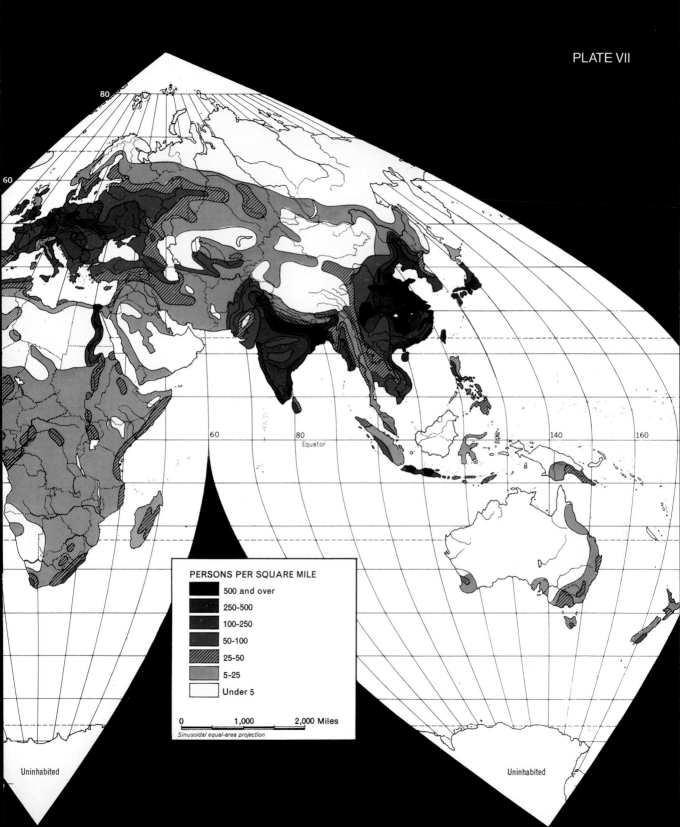

PLATE VII

PERSONS PER SQUARE MILE

500 and over
250-500
100-250
50-100
25-50
5-25
Under 5

0   1,000   2,000 Miles

Sinusoidal equal-area projection

Uninhabited

Uninhabited

PLATE VIII

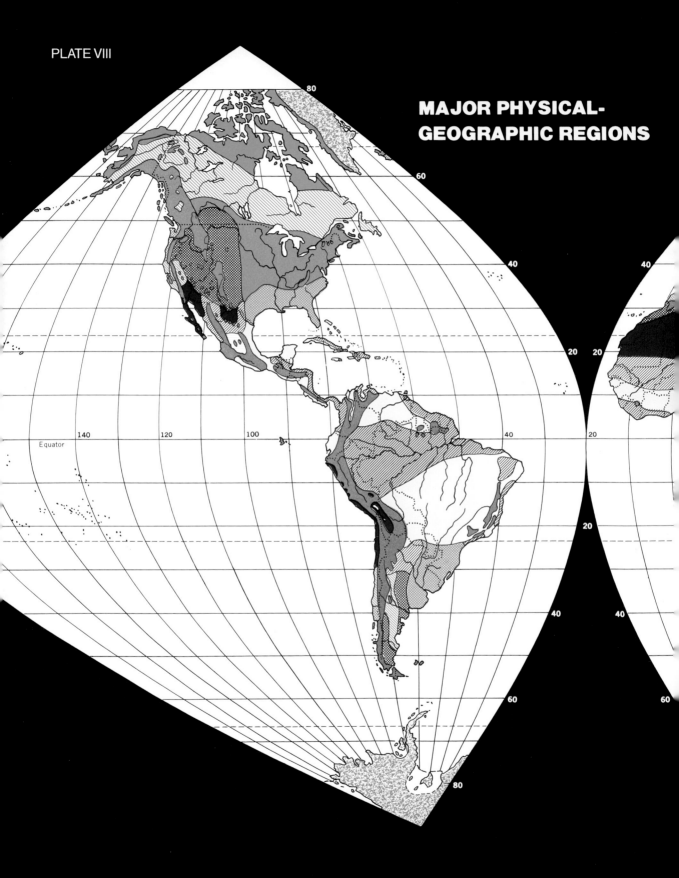

**MAJOR PHYSICAL-
GEOGRAPHIC REGIONS**

PLATE VIII

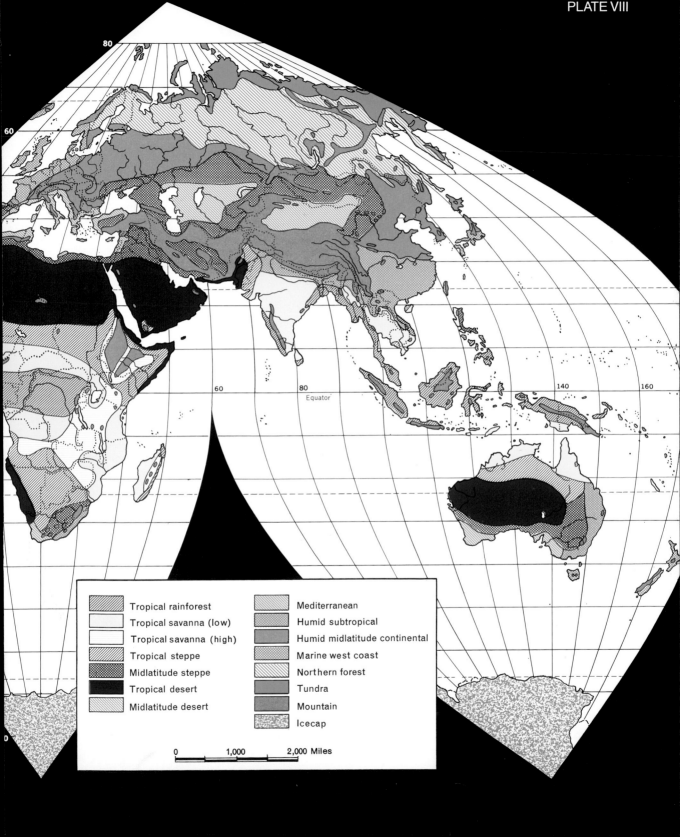

	Tropical rainforest	Mediterranean
	Tropical savanna (low)	Humid subtropical
	Tropical savanna (high)	Humid midlatitude continental
	Tropical steppe	Marine west coast
	Midlatitude steppe	Northern forest
	Tropical desert	Tundra
	Midlatitude desert	Mountain
		Icecap

0   1,000   2,000 Miles

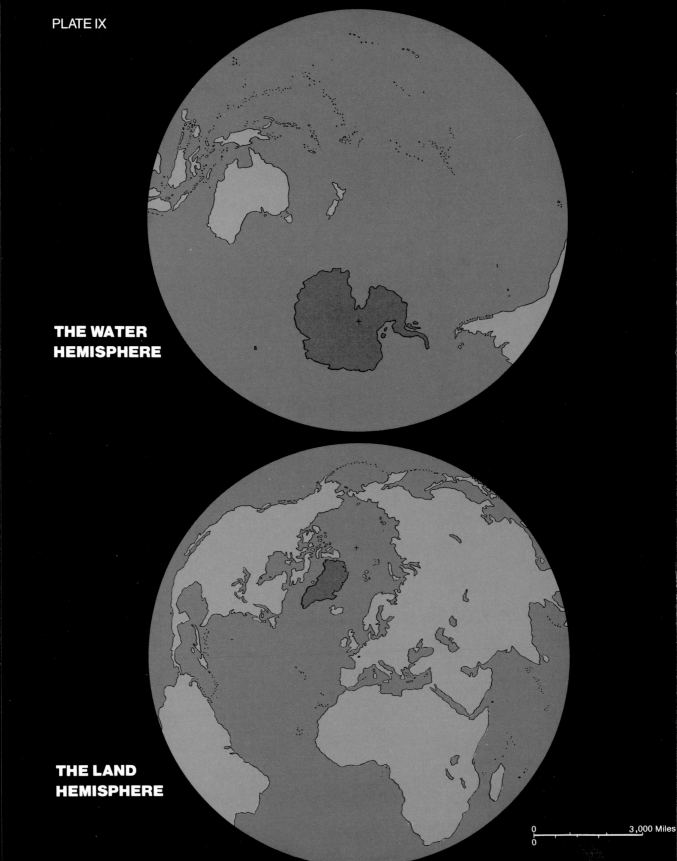

PLATE IX

THE WATER
HEMISPHERE

THE LAND
HEMISPHERE

0   3,000 Miles
0

Maps

Chapter **8**   *Societal Pacemakers: Energy*

Chapter **9**   *Modern Societies and Agro-Industry*

Chapter **10**   *Industrial Societies: Diffusion and Regionalism*

Chapter **11**   *Settlement Types and Contrasts*

Chapter **12**   *Challenge of Urban Growth*

Introduction to Cultural Geography

The city of Rio de Janeiro, nestled between the Atlantic Ocean and the highlands of Brazil. (Pan American)

1

The Cultural Complex

Cultural Geography

As human interdependence continues to grow, each human being alive today has a responsibility to understand the varied peoples who share this small planet. One means toward this achievement is the study of *cultural geography*, a branch of geography that deals with the relationships between human social organization and the environment.

In the very early periods of human history, human beings made use only of the resources found within their particular habitats. The world of each group was limited to the small area its members could traverse afoot in their constant search for the necessities of life, and each group was concerned with satisfying only its own needs for food and shelter. Thus its members lived or perished through their own efforts as food gatherers and hunters. These first human societies were small, and, owing to the limitations of primitive transportation and communication methods, contacts between them were infrequent.

Through the millennia, the human way of life became much less isolated and, with the domestication of animals and plants and, later, the utilization of metals, much less rigorous. More extensive and more effective use of the natural resources of most human habitats enabled them to support larger and larger settlements, and contacts between such groups became more frequent. Surpluses of food, clothing, building materials, and implements were accumulated, and *commerce* (the exchange of goods between human groups) came into being. Each group was no longer limited to seeking its basic necessities only within its own area but could now obtain many of them by trading with other groups at greater and greater distances. For the first time a settlement could specialize in one basic economic activity — such as growing wheat, raising animals, weaving cloth, or making tools — and then offer its product to the inhabitants of places ill-equipped for its production, in return for

3

FIGURE 1-1
Modern transportation and communication devices link almost every human group. Here, Big Nambas of the New Hebrides inspect a helicopter that has brought them visitors. (© Kal Muller, Woodfin Camp)

other items. Eventually, more extensive exchange of goods and the use of currency made it possible for some communities to specialize in the production of nonessential, or luxury, items while securing all or most of their essentials from other settlements.

Both a cause and a result of the growth of commerce has been the development of human transportation. The domestication of hoofed animals, employed originally as an aid in hunting, was humankind's first means of extending its range of travel. Navigation, even when confined to the use of rafts, provided new and faster routes as well as a method better suited to the transportation of heavy loads. The invention and application of the steam engine, in the mid-eighteenth century, significantly increased the speed with which human beings could travel on land and water. Steamboats made river travel more practical, and railroads cut to a fraction the time required for many overland trips. In the nineteenth century the introduction of the internal-combustion engine—first a conqueror of the land surface and then a conqueror of the skies—led to further refinements of human transportation, and today the whole surface of the planet is known to its inhabitants. No longer can any human group remain wholly isolated (Fig. 1-1).

Humans and Culture

Human beings, primates of the genus *Homo*, have existed on earth for over three million years. They appeared first in several species known collectively as "ancient man" and, later, in the only surviving species of the genus, *Homo sapiens*. This species, modern humanity, has inhabited much of the earth for the past fifty thousand years. Almost all of this period and, indeed, almost all of humankind's three-million-year existence, is considered prehistoric, for it is only within the last five or six thousand years that humans have learned to create written records of their ideas and activities. But while the lives of prehistoric peoples are not known to us directly through writing, many cultural advancements of such peoples have been recorded, in a more limited way, through their artifacts (Fig. 1–2).

The Meaning of Culture

The cultural achievements of our species are not simply matters of genetic inheritance but, rather, they are products of human creativity that have added new dimensions to human existence and survival. The basic meaning of the word *culture* is acquired behavior, behavior that is learned, exchanged, and passed from one generation to another through various channels. Human use of tools, fire, language, labor, and rites of birth, death, and marriage have all presented occasions for such behavior. Although we may never know precisely when these occasions first arose, all the evidence found to date suggests that the human capacity for cultural development has been demonstrated for hundreds of thousands of years. It may well be, in fact, that the evolution of human culture has proceeded throughout the entire life of the species.

Because of the great diversity in geographical locations and ideologies, there have always been a number of different human cultures. Each of these individual cultures has reflected the thoughts and activities of the *human,* or *cultural, groups* of which it was composed. A cultural group may be a small, isolated society or an extensive societal complex; in either case, however, it is composed of individuals who are joined together by a sense of belonging, by a dis-

FIGURE 1–2

Using earth and ash from the fire, early humans sometimes painted pictures on the walls of their caves. The painting below, on a wall of Lascaux, a cave in the Dordogne River Valley of southern France, records several types of ancient animals. The mural was probably executed over 170 centuries ago, and some of its animals are now extinct. (*The Hall of Bulls*, Colorphoto Hinz, Basel, Switzerland)

tinctive way of life, and, usually, by the occupancy of contiguous territory (Fig. 1–3). As a culture becomes more advanced and widespread, it may also become sufficiently established and enduring to be considered a civilization.

All cultures, whether simple or advanced, may be categorized by certain distinct *traits,* each of which describes the way the culture traditionally deals with some significant concept, occasion, or item. Marriage, one such occasion, provides an example of this. In some Eastern cultures, arranged marriages are traditional; while in most Western cultures, the choosing of one's own spouse is an equally ingrained cultural trait. Many cultural traits are often closely related and interwoven. For example, some nomadic groups of southwestern Asia who keep large numbers of cattle make animal products their basic diet and use animal skins in making their tents and garments. Wealth is measured by these people in terms of cattle, which are also used as a medium of exchange. Such a related set of traits, which may be operant within a single culture or within several cultures that are otherwise quite different, is referred to as a *cultural complex.* Different sets of cultural traits dominate different cultures, and the most important traits within a given culture are known as its *key traits.* The measurement of wealth in cattle practiced by the Asian nomads, for instance, is a key trait of their culture, for it directly influences and controls their dietary habits, their types of clothing and shelter, and even the basic economic system of their society.

Although no two cultures are exactly the same, they all have several characteristics in common: skills and tools (*technology*); standard means of expression (*communication*); material possessions (*resources-artifacts*); systems of livelihood (*production-exchange-consumption*); values and beliefs (*ideology*); and systems of social organization (*institutions*). The quality of these characteristics and the ways in which they are used by the different groups are what differentiates one culture group from another.

Cultural Change— Invention and Diffusion

Cultures are not static but exist in a constant state of flux. Within each culture there is a perpetual tug-of-war between the forces of *tradition,* which support the established ways of doing things, and the forces of *change,* which advocate new ways of doing things; the society's *mores*—that is, its established social and moral attitudes, which may often attain the force of law—tend to strengthen the forces of tradition. The proper balance between tradition and change must be established separately for each cultural group. Though some cultures seem to be more fixed than others, they all require some degree of change in order to advance.

Cultural change comes about in two principal ways—by indigenous *invention* and by *diffusion.* Scientific opinion is divided as to which of these two methods is the more influential. The most rational view is, perhaps, that the two generally work together, in proportions determined by the degree of isolation of the culture in question and the relative levels of inventiveness that exist within it. Those cultures that are almost totally isolated rely predominantly on change from within; while those that have more contact with other groups can rely more on cultural diffusion, or borrowing. The degree of isolation of any culture may vary with time, which can always affect the proportions of the two methods suitable for the culture's continued development.

Invention. Societies can either promote invention and imaginative enterprise on the part of their members or they can im-

FIGURE 1-3

Gregarious by nature, human beings tend to construct their homes in groups, even when there is ample space for isolation. Top left, an encampment of nomads in Algeria. (Klaus Francke from Peter Arnold) Top right, a Chavante village in Mato Grosso, Brazil. (American Museum of Natural History) Bottom left, the Pueblo Indian village of San Geronimo de Taos, in New Mexico. (Santa Fe Railway Photo) Bottom right, a village in Nigeria. (British Information Service)

pede it. Many inventions have suffered delayed acceptance because their recognition and use required technologies or concepts that were not yet fully developed and accepted by the population. This sort of occurrence is an instance of *cultural lag,* the postponed incorporation of a new technology or institution due to the apathy or resistance of its potential users. The initial public reaction to the plow is a good example of this concept, for there were many people who preferred to continue to use such relatively crude and energy-consuming tools as the dibble stick and mattock rather than learn any new techniques. Thus the receptivity of its potential users lagged far behind the time of the plow's invention.

Most inventions, even most of the seemingly revolutionary ones, are merely combinations and refinements of previous inventions; and, as such, they involve little truly original thought. This is not surprising,

7

since totally new ideas of any sort are rare. Many inventions, discoveries, and innovations attributed to one or two individuals actually evolved only after generations, or even centuries, of thought and experiment by others. And while a small number of inquisitive individuals in a society may chance upon new inventions without the aid of other people's ideas, a far greater number build on theories advanced earlier by other thinkers within their own culture or by those beyond it.

Diffusion. Diffusion is the transfer of cultural elements from one culture to another. There is no doubt that, when added to independent invention, it increases the efforts of change within societies by expanding the societal bases of dependence for thought and action. In past centuries, when the intermixing of peoples and ideas was

FIGURE 1–4

Two cultures blend on eastern Africa's wild Serengeti Plain as Sam ole Saitoti (left), a park ranger and guide, shares a photograph with two of his fellow Masai tribesmen. (© National Geographic Society, courtesy CBS Television Press Information; from the film *Man of the Serengeti*)

relatively restricted, the number of new developments within any given society was small, and, consequently, cultural progress and change were slow. Today, intricate communication systems interlink even the remotest parts of the earth, creating a great many more opportunities for cross-cultural exchange and profoundly accelerating the rate of cultural change.

Cultural diffusion requires a giver as well as a willing and capable receiver (Fig. 1–4). Because of the competitive and acquisitive nature of most human beings, concepts and artifacts are not always freely exchanged, either within or between groups; thus, for example, societies develop such restrictions as patents and copyright laws. In many instances, societies that are potential givers of cultural developments find it advantageous to use diffusion as a means of barter, offering their expertise in some field in exchange for political allegiance, a right-of-way, or a natural resource. Military technology, for example, is shared along political lines, as are those few applications of atomic energy that are not considered absolute national secrets.

Acculturation

The process of diffusion is followed by that of *acculturation*, the changing within a given culture as a result of its adoption of aspects of another. Whereas diffusion involves only the spread of cultural elements as different cultures come into contact, acculturation is the process through which those cultural elements are absorbed into the receiving culture; it results in the blending, or coalescing, of cultures.

In acculturation, as in diffusion, there is both a giver and a receiver. When, however, an exchange of cultures of this nature takes place, it is rarely an equal one, and the dominant culture in the relationship is usually the society that is more highly advanced. The degree to which a particular subordinate culture is acculturized, that is, transformed into the image of another culture, may vary from the adoption of a few simple traits to total assimilation. In the latter instance, a dominant culture may influence the individuals of a subordinate one to such an extent that their culture eventually disappears. Numerous cultures have been eliminated in this way. Soon after the arrival of European settlers in Australia in the early 1800s, the aborigines of Tasmania began to decline rapidly in number, the victims of the brutish newcomers. By 1876 the last of the native Tasmanian aborigines had died and, with them, most of the Tasmanian culture.

Less extreme degrees of acculturation are more common. Consider, for example, the changes that have come about in the lives of Australian aborigines since their first contacts with Europeans. Throughout most of their history the Australian aborigines had an unsophisticated hunting and gathering economy, an animistic religion, and an unwritten language—key elements of the culture that had satisfied their needs for thousands of years. The invasion of their lands by the British in the eighteenth and nineteenth centuries brought the aborigines into contact with a highly complex, materially advanced culture. Within the few subsequent generations, their own culture has been greatly modified, for they have adopted many facets of British culture, including its foods, clothing, religion, economy, and language. On the other hand, little of the aboriginal culture has been adopted by the British save some place names and the nouns applied to plants and animals common in Australia but lacking in Britain.

Another example of acculturation involves the Eskimos, whose life style has also changed drastically within a very short period. Before the arrival of European peoples in Greenland and Alaska, the Eskimos there were primitive hunters and fishers; their survival depended upon their skill in seeking out wildlife over long distances and with only a few crude implements. Through the Europeans the Eskimos were provided with firearms, which made their hunting easier for a time but eventually caused the kill rate to exceed the rate of wildlife reproduction. Other features of European culture were adopted as well, and the Eskimos' essentially mobile life gave way to more sedentary behavior. Whereas formerly a family group, or perhaps two or three such groups, would dwell alone at a given site, miles from other people, and remain there only so long as the supply of food within hunting distance was sufficient, there came to be larger and more permanent Eskimo settlements near points where contact with the Europeans could easily be made. Since the ability of the land and sea to support them had been impaired, the Eskimos now required imported goods for survival. It had become impossible for the Eskimos to exist in their traditional way.

Cultural convergence, or cultural blending, is a phenomenon of particular significance in the twentieth century. In the past, when contacts between human groups were few and difficult to make, distinctive cultural features were numerous and could be easily observed. Now, the differences are less sharp, for there are few human groups so isolated that their traditional way of living is not increasingly subject to outside influences. Throughout the world there is a blending of the various cultures.

While there are a great number of culture groups in the world, two great cultures stand out clearly in the world today: the culture of western Europe and the Americas—known as Western, or Occidental, culture—and that of eastern and southern Asia, known as Eastern, or Oriental, culture. Western culture is distinguished basically by its dependence upon the use of machines powered by chemical and electrical energy; Oriental culture, by the use of human power.

Largely through its use of machine power, Western culture has spread from its original European base throughout most of the world. First, it moved by colonization to the Americas and then through trade to Africa and the East. Advantages both in numbers of people and in equipment made it possible for the Europeans to achieve a rapid disruption of the culture groups they found in North America and a somewhat slower disruption of similar groups in South America. The effects on native cultures in Africa occurred even less rapidly and were less complete, largely because there was less attempt at actual colonization; the possibilities of trade were of prime importance and the effects of contact were largely observable only in the slow disintegration, rather than wholesale destruction, of many African ways of living.

Last of all, and well after industrialization had become the keynote of Western culture, colonialism spread to the centers of Oriental culture. Here, also, Western influences have altered the native culture, but in a profoundly different way than they did elsewhere. In the Orient, the West was superimposed upon an already complex culture. Orientals began to take enough prominent parts of what the Westerner offered to give a sem-

blance of complete absorption. Witness the industrialization of Japan from the late 1860s to the present.

Slowly the industrial way of life spread to other Oriental areas, to India, China, and even to parts of the East Indies. But Western ways have only been imposed upon the Oriental base, not substituted for it. Though eastern and southern Asia have felt the contact of the West, the underlying Oriental culture still remains.

Through the past several decades, cultural change has also been apparent within the Soviet Union, but it is not yet clear whether this change will result in an amalgam of Western and Oriental cultures or whether it is simply a phase in the evolution of Western culture. The way of life produced through this change has spread rapidly from the European Soviet over a large portion of the Eurasian landmass, and it may ultimately establish itself as a distinctive new culture, Soviet culture, with the same world significance now characteristic of the Occidental and the Oriental.

In the more isolated parts of the world — the interior forests of the Amazon Basin or the nearly unexplored interiors of Borneo and New Guinea, for example — the native culture still bears little imprint of the two dominant world cultures. But, in most areas, native cultures are playing smaller and smaller roles in human life. Many exist only as curious fragments from the past.

Humans and Nature

The discussion to this point has been concerned primarily with culture and culture groups *per se*. Each academic discipline, however, views culture from a slightly different perspective. In geography, culture comprises human behavior and the ways in

which such behavior influences and reflects the natural environment. One of the few disciplines concerned with human behavior and the natural environment, geography places special emphasis on the constant interaction between the two and includes among its basic premises the notion that everything in the environment, including humanity, is interrelated (Fig. 1–5). The study of ecology is based on the same fundamental premise, but approaches it from a purely physical point of view.

The term *ecology* is most commonly defined as the study of the interrelationships that exist between living organisms (plants and animals) and their environments. *Ecosystem* is the term applied to the interaction of specific plants and animals and the environments they inhabit. All ecosystems function as complete units, varying in size from a drop of water to the great Sahara Desert—and even the planet earth itself.

The projection of this ecological viewpoint outside the biological sciences to the physical and social sciences has resulted in greater interest in *human ecology*, the study of the place of human beings in the ecosystem. Human ecology represents a concern similar to the traditional geographic interest in the interactions between humans and their total environment, that is, their cultural as well as their natural biophysical surroundings. The relationship between human beings and the natural environment is extremely complex, and, in spite of their cultural accomplishments, the fact that humans are still only one small component of any ecosystem must always be kept in mind.

Cultural Landscape

Human dominance of the earth and its other species is the result of the human ability to conceptualize and to create the artificial structures that constitute a cultural framework. For thousands of years human cultural creations have been meshed with the natural (physical and biotic) environment. Once a portion of the natural environment has been altered by human influence, in any way, geographers consider it a *cultural landscape* and label its human-made features "artificial," since they would not have occurred in the environment without human intervention.

The artificial features that make up a cultural landscape may be thought of as "human shelters." All too often, this phrase is interpreted in material terms only, spawning images of simple lean-tos, tents, or even some of the more sophisticated enclosures human beings have constructed to temper the forces of nature (Fig. 1–6). However, the term neither should be nor can be confined to the inclusion of such tangible aspects of culture alone, for material constructs represent only some of the human shelters that delineate a given cultural landscape. Equally important, if not more so, is the wide array of intangibles, such as the inhabitants' ideologies, values, and beliefs. Such features are also human shelters in the sense that they have been constructed to temper the forces of nature that pervade and surround human beings in all aspects of their lives.

An understanding of a culture based solely on its material features would necessarily be incomplete, and often inaccurate. Two human groups having similar or identical material features may attach totally different meanings to them, and, conversely, two groups may also assign the same meaning to very dissimilar material features. The distinctiveness of a culture, therefore, depends both on its material features and on its values and beliefs.

The Human Habitat

Although the human habitat is now very much a composite of cultural and natural landscapes, human beings must still draw their lives from elements of the earth's natural environment: the *lithosphere* (land), the *atmosphere* (air), the *hydrosphere* (water), and the *biosphere* (the plant and animal life associated with the other three). While humans

FIGURE 1–5

The cultural honeycomb, a representation of the inextricable relationship between human behaviors and the major elements of the environment — vegetation, animals, climate, soil, water, and landforms. (Center, United Nations; and from upper left, clockwise, USDA; Royal Canadian Navy; USDA; Standard Oil Co., N.J.; Harry W. Rinehart; Union Pacific Railway)

have created various kinds of temporary, artificial environments, some more sophisticated than others, the survival of the species is still ultimately dependent upon the balances that presently exist between the various elements of the natural environment.

However, the natural environment is dynamic, not static, and undergoes constant change through time and space. Most of this change occurs at a rate so slow as to make it imperceptible within the human lifespan.

The environmental change that comes suddenly and violently—as droughts, tornadoes, dust storms, floods, earthquakes, and volcanic eruptions—usually involves only local, relatively small areas. Though they tend to be brought about by natural forces alone, these sudden, localized changes are sometimes helped along by human activ-ities. Because of the constant change occurring on the earth, there is great variety within the planet's natural landscape: the lithosphere includes many sorts of landforms; the atmosphere is divided into several different climatic and weather types, all given to rapid change; the hydrosphere, reflecting the land, comprises a variety of water forms; and the biosphere offers countless species of plant and animal life also subject to rapid change.

Environmental Perception and Behavior

Human perception, or mental comprehension, involves both the ability to "see" or sense and the ability to think and interpret

FIGURE 1–6

Human shelters—tangible and intangible. Left, a Bedouin's tent in Saudi Arabia. (Standard Oil Co., N.J.) Right, the intangible shelter of religion as represented by a Moslem mosque in Algeria. (© Marc Riboud, Magnum)

FIGURE 1–7

Different approaches to alpine living. Above, terraced rice paddies in the mountains of Japan reflect the pressure of human population on the land. When the food needs of the people exceeded the capacity of the small amount of naturally level land, it became necessary for the Japanese to begin to level the hills for cultivation. And since usable land cannot be wasted, many mountain villages in Japan, including the one shown here, are established at the base of high slopes too steep for terracing. (Courtesy Consulate General of Japan) Below, a mountainside in the European Alps, where, since there is abundant level land nearby, terracing is not necessary and pastoralism is the predominant way of life. (Albert Steiner, Black Star)

something on the basis of past experiences with similar or identical stimuli. Similarly, *environmental perception* involves both the way one senses elements of the natural environment and, more importantly, the way one interprets them.

No two societies perceive any natural environment in exactly the same way. Even when given very similar natural settings, different groups of people tend to create quite different cultural landscapes. Thus, for example, the alpine regions of Europe contrast sharply with physically similar areas of Japan. The European mountain range known as the Alps is an area where seasonal pastoralism, or transhumance, is a common cultural trait. In search of good grazing land, herdsmen move their livestock up and down the mountain slopes, shifting from the lowland valleys in winter to the alpine meadows in summer. The region's permanent settlements are found mainly in the valleys. Halfway around the world, in Japan, there is another such natural alpine environment. Although its steep mountain slopes and humid, midlatitude climates make it very similar to the European Alps, this area is used quite differently by the Japanese, that is, largely as farmland rather than as pasture. The sea-oriented Japanese culture includes little use of domestic animals, except for a few draft purposes. The raising of livestock for food and clothing being of much less importance in Japan than it is in Europe, many of the lower slopes of the Japanese mountains have been intricately terraced for intensive agricultural use (Fig. 1–7).

The contrasting ways in which these two societies have responded to their similar environments are due, in part, to the differences between their environmental perceptions. Individuals in a pastoral society tend to view the elements of their natural environment differently than do individuals in an agricultural society. The particular way

one interprets natural environmental elements is based on one's values, needs, and desires—factors generally influenced by one's societal group. Thus the cultural objectives and methods of any given society are important in the shaping of its needs and wants and, ultimately, in the shaping of its perception of the environment as a whole.

A society's objectives and technology determine which of the naturally occurring substances it will use and in what manner it will use them. Only those substances that are actually used by a society are considered its *resources*; thus, just as natural resources vary from one society to another, they also vary within any single society as its culture develops. For example, coal, once considered nothing more than black rock, became a natural resource only after people discovered its value as a source of energy. Similarly, while most people consider land an important natural resource, to the "boat people" of Hong Kong, who spend almost all of their lives on water, it is of little value (Fig. 1–8).

The manner in which it uses its natural

FIGURE 1–8

Homes on the water—sampans and junks in Hong Kong harbor. The way of life they represent is gradually disappearing, however, as many of Hong Kong's offshore dwellers are resettling ashore in the island's new high-rises. (Northwest Orient Airlines)

resources generally reflects the concern a society has for its environment. Resources can be used destructively or constructively, depending upon whether the society perceives the environment as an endlessly exploitable commodity or as a prerequisite for survival to be used judiciously and treated with respect.

There is no one way of living in a given physical setting, but rather as many different ways as there are cultures. Thus the characteristics of a given portion of the earth are determined, in part, by the culture of the group that inhabits it. Much of the individuality of any area is also related to the length of time it has been occupied — either by one group passing through different cultural stages, or by successive groups of different cultures, providing a *sequent occupance* of the area.

REVIEW AND DISCUSSION

1. The growing trend toward world interdependence reflects the fact that modern communication and travel systems allow no human group to remain wholly isolated. Discuss the relationship of this trend to cultural geography. How is it evident within your own cultural group?
2. Through what methods have modern peoples learned about the prehistoric cultural development of human beings?
3. In addition to values and beliefs (*ideology*), all cultures have several other characteristics in common. Discuss those you think are the two most important ones.
4. Some scholars are of the opinion that the prehistoric discovery of the usefulness of fire still represents the greatest contribution to human cultural development. Discuss the merits of this opinion.
5. Compare and contrast invention and diffusion with reference to specific examples. Which phenomenon is more instrumental in bringing about cultural change? Explain.
6. Explain the relationship between diffusion and acculturation. Describe two situations that illustrate the growing influence of the latter around the world.
7. List some of the outstanding differences between Oriental and Western cultures.
8. Discuss some of the probable reasons for the spread of Western culture over a larger portion of the earth than Oriental culture.
9. What is the basis for thinking that a new culture may be developing within the Soviet Union?
10. How does the cultural landscape differ from the natural landscape? What are their relationships to the human habitat?
11. Is the quality of change constant throughout the human habitat? From your own experience, give some examples that support your contention.
12. Describe two geographical areas that have essentially the same physical characteristics but are populated by human groups with very different ways of doing things.
13. Illustrate the meaning of the term sequent occupance by reference to the area in which you live or the one you know best. Explain in detail at least one major occupance "change" in your example.

SELECTED REFERENCES

Barrows, H. H. "Geography as Human Ecology." *Annals of the Association of American Geographers,* Vol. 13 (March 1923), 1–14.

Bresler, J. B., ed. *Human Ecology.* Reading, Mass.: Addison-Wesley, 1966.

Brookfield, H. C. "On the Environment as Perceived." *Progress in Geography, International Reviews of Current Research,* Vol. 1 (1969), 51–80.

Chorley, R. J., ed. *Water, Earth, and Man.* London: Methuen, 1969.

Clark, J. G., and S. Piggott. *Prehistoric Societies.* London: Hutchinson University Library, 1965.

Gould, P. R. *Spatial Diffusion.* Washington, D.C.: Commission on College Geography, Resource Paper No. 4, Association of American Geographers, 1969.

Henry, J. *Culture Against Man.* New York: Random House, 1963.

Ittelson, W. H., and F. P. Kilpatrick. "Experiments in Perception." *Scientific American,* Vol. 185 (August 1951), 50–56.

Jefferson, M. "The Geographical Distribution of Inventiveness." *Geographical Review,* Vol. 19 (October 1929), 649–61.

Kroeber, A. L., and C. Kluckholm. *Culture: A Critical Review of Concepts and Definitions.* New York: Vintage Books, 1952.

Lowenthal, D., ed. *Environmental Perception and Behavior.* Chicago: University of Chicago, Department of Geography, Research Paper No. 109, 1967.

Rodnik, D. *An Introduction to Man and His Development.* New York: Appleton-Century-Crofts, 1966.

Saarinin, T. F. *Perception of Environment.* Washington, D.C.: Commission on College Geography, Resource Paper No. 5, Association of American Geographers, 1969.

Shepard, P. *Man in the Landscape.* New York: Random House, 1967.

Smythies, J. R. "The Problems of Perception." *British Journal for the Philosophy of Science,* Vol. 11 (May 1960), 224–38.

Stoddart, D. R. "Geography and the Ecological Approach: The Ecosystem as a Geographic Principle and Method." *Geography,* Vol. 50 (July 1965), 242–51.

Theodorson, G. A., ed. *Studies in Human Ecology.* Evanston, Ill.: Row, Peterson, 1961.

Wagner, P. *Environments and People.* Englewood Cliffs, N.J.: Prentice-Hall, 1972.

Watt, K. E. F. *Ecology and Resource Management.* New York: McGraw-Hill, 1968.

Whittlesey, D. "Sequent Occupance." *Annals of the Association of American Geographers,* Vol. 19 (September 1929), 162–65.

A Bushman hunting gazelle in southern Africa's Kalahari Desert.
(N. R. Farbman, Time-Life Picture Agency)

2

Culture and Nature

In trying to understand the present natural environment, many people tend to mentally separate and juxtapose nature and humanity, as though human life could exist apart from the rest of the environmental complex. Among primitive peoples, who lived in close harmony with the natural environment, such a conceptualization would have been most unlikely. But today, less conscious of their dependent role in nature, many human beings think in terms of a struggle between themselves and nature and wonder when they will be able to maintain total control over the natural environment.

Influences of Nature on Human Activity

Environmentalism

A time-honored concept, *environmentalism* is the view that human attitudes and activities are variously influenced by the elements of the natural environment. Reflected today in many biological and social sciences, this concept has been receiving support since the time of Hippocrates (c. 460–377 B.C.), the "father of medicine." Environmentalists have tended to regard certain elements of the natural environment—for example, climate—as key factors in promoting or retarding cultural progress.

In its most extreme form, environmentalism is *environmental determinism*, the contention that the natural environment is the sole determining factor in shaping all human culture. The implication here is that human behavior is dictated by the natural environment and that humans are thus slaves to their surroundings. While the environment is unquestionably an influence on human activities, it seems doubtful that it is the only one; for, as discussed in the previous chapter, human groups inhabiting similar environments often develop quite different ways of life.

Possibilism

In the early twentieth century, in response to what they viewed as environmental determinism's overemphasis on the role of nature in human life patterns, many students of human social development gave their support to a more moderate doctrine known as *possibilism*. Expounded first in Europe and increasingly accepted in recent decades in the United States, possibilism maintains that, in any aspect of culture, nature presents human beings with a number of alternatives from which to choose and thus, in some sense, allows them to determine their own future.

While they agree that nature, at any given time or place, does impose some limitations on human development, the possibilists emphasize that, in the last analysis, human beings must be considered at least partly responsible for formulating their attitudes and activities. From their point of view, the environment is a much less domineering factor than the determinists claim it to be; for it does allow human choice some latitude, even if within rather strict limits. Further, the alternatives it allows are dynamic, in that they vary both from place to place and from time to time. Having its own objectives and ways of doing things, one societal group may discover possibilities within the physical complex that another group has overlooked or avoided.

Influences of Human Activity on Nature

During the relatively brief existence of human beings on this much older planet, they have become a force capable of exerting significant and far-reaching influence on its physical complex. Since they first began to implement the methods for their survival they have never inhabited any portion of that complex without modifying it, intentionally or not, in some measurable way. Even the most primitive peoples, living by hunting and gathering, modified the environment in which they lived, simply by utilizing, either partly or completely, various elements of the biotic life therein.

As human tools and methods have become more sophisticated, the potential for influencing the environment has expanded. In a brief moment of geologic time, modern societies have evolved to the point where they can exert as much influence on their local living spaces—constructive or destructive—as have all the natural forces of the past several million years (Fig. 2–1).

Since it may appear that today, more than ever before, human beings are capable of altering or retaining any environmental condition almost at will, it requires some effort to keep their role in nature in proper perspective. The popular notion is that, through their modern technologies, human beings have become "masters of the world" —a somewhat exaggerated claim, especially when viewed through the shadow of today's world energy crises, food shortages, floods, droughts, and global population explosion. On the other hand, as a broad but ultimately fair and useful generalization, it seems valid to say that, within relatively small geographic areas and short time spans, human influences on an environment tend to supersede those of nature; whereas, within larger areas and longer time spans, natural forces tend to predominate. It must be understood, however, that not even cultural or human forces within small areas can function in a manner completely independent of natural forces. For, in the final analysis, human influences, even within these areas, reside ultimately in the ability of humankind to modify and/or control the many constant processes of nature.

As human activities increase in quantity and complexity, they continue to alter the landscape more sharply and more extensively. All such activities invariably upset delicate balances established in nature over long periods of time, and, when these balances are upset, other natural forces and processes over which humans have little or no control are often set in motion. Most commonly, these forces have existed beforehand but have been held in check by other features

FIGURE 2–1

The building of a dike across Lake IJssel, in the Netherlands. The enclosed area thus created will be drained and eventually used as cropland. (Netherlands National Tourist Office)

of the environment. In any case, there is an ecological goal to which all peoples should aspire: they should attempt to understand the balances in nature well enough to maintain or alter them constructively, that is, for the long-term service of humanity.

Spatial Order and the Regional Concept

Spatial Variation

The cultural traits with which any given group of people identify manifest themselves in various and complex interrelationships with the physical environment. Much geographic inquiry serves primarily as a framework for studying this so-called *spatial variation*, the assumption being that some degree of order can ultimately be discerned by studying the seemingly chaotic associations of cultural and physical phenomena. The science of geography itself has even been broadly defined by some geographers as *the study of spatial variation on the earth's surface.*

A principal tool in the geographer's quest for greater insight into the subject of spatial variation is the *map*, which provides a simplified picture of spatial reality. Unless pertinent data are scaled down to a size suited to map presentation, the distributions and associations of cultural and physical phenomena cannot be fully appreciated.

Interlocking Spatial Concepts

Spatial location is the basic point of reference used in discussions of either physical or cultural variations; therefore, location, or place, is fundamental to most geographic thought. A full geographic understanding of an environmental feature comes only through knowing its precise location, or *site*, as well as its *situation*, or spatial relationship to other features (Fig. 2–2). Such concepts as *scale, pattern, density, distribution,* and *interac-*

tion are also all directly involved with the location of environmental features and with their interrelationship within the human habitat.

The Regional Concept

The *regional concept,* like the map, is a device, or tool, long used by geographers as a means of comprehending the arrangement of spatial variations within the human habitat. A geographic *region* is defined as any portion of the earth's surface that has been delimited, or recognized, for a particular characteristic. Other general terms that are used in a similar manner include *area, belt, zone, realm,* and *landscape.*

There are many different types of geographic regions, and they can be large or small, simple or complex. Regardless of its type and size, however, each region possesses some areally unifying element (or elements). These elements may be either cultural or physical ones or some combination of the two. An island nation, for example, can be considered a region by virtue of both its administrative scope and its shorelines. Most regions, however, do not have such clear-cut physical boundaries. The term *Moslem world,* for example, describes a cultural region distinguished by a single, well-established religion, but it does not represent only contiguous landmasses (Fig. 2–3). A smaller, and somewhat more clearly defined, cultural region is the Mormon "nation," an area centered on Salt Lake City, Utah.

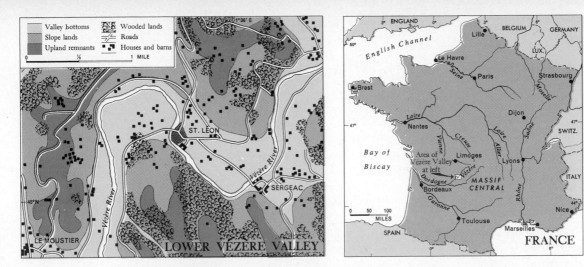

FIGURE 2–2

Site and situation. Left, the *site* of St. Léon: on the right bank of the lower Vézère River, midway between the towns of Sergeac and Le Moustier. Right, the *situation* of St. Léon (and the rest of the lower Vézère Valley): approximately 50 miles above the confluence of the Vézère and Dordogne rivers, on the west side of the Massif Central in southwest central France.

FIGURE 2–3

The Moslem world. Including most of northern Africa and southern Asia, this vast region extends, with some interruptions, from the Atlantic to the Pacific. Several of its countries share not only Islam's strong and long-established religious beliefs but many other cultural features as well.

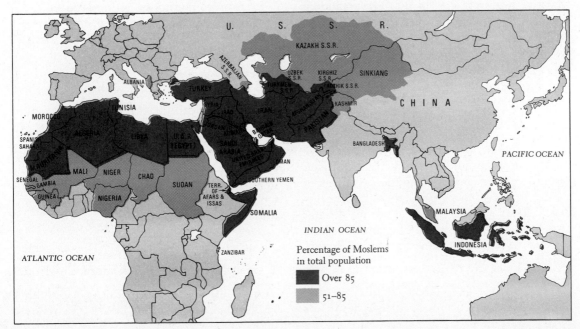

A Regional Study: The Dust Bowl

The following study examines the reciprocal influences of human beings and nature as demonstrated in the 1930s in a section of the Great Plains of the United States. The core of this area included coterminous parts of Colorado, Kansas, New Mexico, Oklahoma, and Texas (Fig. 2–4).

At one time, this vast steppe region supported a short-grass cover that served as a natural protection against extensive soil erosion by holding dry soils in place. However, with the overgrazing and inappropriate agricultural practices that followed the growth in human settlement in the region in the late 1800s, this grass cover completely disappeared, leaving the region's characteristic dry, fine-grained soils, which were no longer held in place, very susceptible to erosion. The erosion process actually began when strong westerly winds—wind being one of the chief agents of erosion—swept over the region during the dry-weather cycle that occurred in the 1930s. By 1934, great dust storms engulfed this dry-farming area and stripped it of most of its fertile topsoil. In this way stable steppeland suddenly became desertlike and barren.

The Original Landscape

Obviously, the effects of human activity in any area cannot be correctly appraised without first understanding the processes of nature at work there prior to human influences. Thus what follows is a brief discussion of the Great Plains region in its original state and a review of the geographical factors that operated therein.

Location. The Great Plains of the United States are a broad, flattish steppe, or short-grass, area sloping eastward from the Rocky Mountains toward the Mississippi River and straddling the 100th meridian, a theoretical line often used to demarcate the dry western portion of the country and the more humid eastern portion. This vast plains region was formed not as the result of one or two isolated geographic factors but rather by the long-term interaction of several such factors.

Precipitation. The Great Plains exhibit a progressive decrease in precipitation from east to west, with an annual average of 40 inches in eastern Kansas and 12 in eastern Colorado. When readings taken over several decades are averaged and plotted, those areas where the average precipitation is 20 inches align roughly with the 100th meridian; but in any particular year they may be areas hundreds of miles east or west of that line (Plate IV).

Annual rainfall variations on the order of 15 inches have been recorded in many parts of the Great Plains over long periods of time. Such variations are of little consequence in humid regions, but in semi-arid areas with, say, only 20 inches of rainfall annually, a 15-inch variation can have serious effects on the regional ecology. In these plains, as elsewhere, relatively wet- and dry-weather years tend to run in cycles of varying duration and intensity. It was the dry cycle of 1933–38 that helped to trigger the temporarily disastrous environmental conditions of that period.

The Rocky Mountains. The characteristically limited rainfall and dryness of the Great Plains is due, in large part, to the climatic influence of the Rocky Mountains. This range, rising high above the western edge of the region, serves as a barrier to the natural inflow of moist air from the Pacific Ocean and thus effects a rainshadow leeward over the high plains. As a result, the Gulf of Mexico, the Great Plains' other major source of moist air, becomes the dominant supplier of precipitation over the region. But since the air from the Gulf of Mexico tends to be deflected to the northeast by the Coriolis force, considerable moisture from these waters is supplied to the eastern Great Plains, while relatively little reaches the western portion of the region (Plate III).

Winds. The Great Plains are frequently plagued by a high-velocity westerly wind that descends the leeward side of the Rocky Mountains and moves eastward. Referred to as a *chinook,* or *foehn,* this wind is compressed and greatly warmed during its de-

FIGURE 2–4

The site of the Dust Bowl of the 1930s. (For its situation, see North America's Great Plains region on Plate III.)

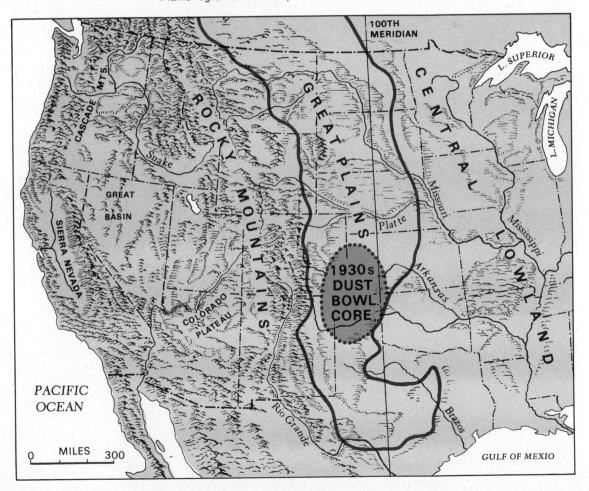

FIGURE 2–5

The flatness of the semiarid land of the Great Plains is illustrated by this area along the old Deadwood Trail, in southwestern South Dakota. Though, since the 1920s, most of the steppe of the Great Plains is usually covered by wheat crops, here one can still see the ruts created by stagecoaches and ox-drawn wagons as they took gold miners to the Black Hills in the 1870s. (South Dakota Department of Highways)

scent; at the same time, its relative humidity is greatly reduced. As it sweeps across the Plains, the chinook may cause surface temperatures to rise as much as 50 degrees in a few hours and, evaporating most available moisture, may cause the area to become almost desiccated.

Vegetation and Soil. Under natural conditions, the soils of the Great Plains were protected by a tough mantle of vegetation—primarily a grass-sod cover of prairie,

steppe, and buffalo grasses. Before the local introduction of beef cattle in the 1870s, luxuriant stands of these grasses supported great numbers of native grazing animals, particularly bison, and also helped protect the soil. The importance of the area's protective grasscover cannot be overemphasized: it served as a windbreak, and its relatively deep-root system was vital in keeping the soil in place and protecting it against rainwash and wind erosion. The threat of wind erosion is not very serious in the more humid eastern margins of the Great Plains, but it becomes more serious on the drier western borders (Fig. 2–5).

A Balanced Ecosystem. Before the introduction of farming to the Great Plains, the natural environmental factors in its ecosystem were in delicate balance: all functioned together in a precise system of checks and balances. Thus if even one of these ecological factors was disturbed, it would invariably upset and alter the entire balance.

Influence of Agrarianism

The natural characteristics of the Great Plains region foreshadowed the difficult future it was to face when subjected to extensive human settlement and should have been sufficient as a warning to those attempting to exploit the region to that end. The area's dry-steppe grasslands—especially their vegetation and soil types—indicated that there was a precipitation deficiency and that the land was most suited for limited grazing and, in its eastern portion, for crop farming.

However, most of the people who settled in the region were not well-acquainted with its characteristics nor with the techniques of semiarid cropping necessary to cope with its inherent limitations; in the main, they had migrated from more humid regions in the eastern states. Many of them saw in the region only a chance for easy exploitation and immediate financial return. After 1910, moreover, several new psychological influences and financial encouragements made themselves felt in the western part of the Great Plains (Fig. 2–6). High wheat prices during the war and postwar years, in combination with the development of the tractor, the combine, and other power machinery, resulted in a frenzied westward expansion of the wheat area.

Dry Farming and Grazing

The method of farming most widespread in the region during the 1920s and 30s is known as *dry farming*, which makes use of groundwater stored naturally in the soil. The practices employed to conserve as much of the vital groundwater as possible include: frequent cultivation to eliminate moisture-consuming weeds and to develop and maintain a dust mulch on the surface to break up capillarity; and the alternation of cropping and fallowing, with only one crop planted every second or third year. These methods were used in the region on the assumption that the amount of moisture stored in the soil during the fallow period would be enough to satisfy the moisture needs of the subsequent crop.

Dry farming is fine in theory and, in some parts of the world, it often succeeds in practice; but it was not employed with satisfactory results in the drier parts of the Great Plains, especially during the 1930s. During periods of low or no rainfall, the simple act of turning over the sod with a plow caused the soil to dry out excessively; and, as happens in any dry or semiarid region, the extremely fine-grained soil became very powdery when it dried (Fig. 2–7). Thus, overall, continued cultivation tended to make the soil even more susceptible to drying than it had been before. While the wheat and other crops that were planted had relatively low moisture requirements, they still used more moisture than the natural grasses they replaced. During periods when rainfall was abundant, the wheat thrived; but when precipitation was below its requirement, the wheat began to draw on the moisture contained deep within the soil. In addition, the stubble left when the wheat was harvested was not able to protect the soil against erosion; thus exposed, the soil became more vulnerable than under its natural grasscovers.

Even areas not plowed for wheat experienced major problems, particularly those used for grazing. Because of such factors as higher wartime prices and unusually lush pastures (the result of a wet-cycle period), most of the region's grazing lands had been overstocked. The most serious overgrazing occurred in areas that were naturally sparsely vegetated and arid or semiarid in climate, as, for example, the southwestern fringe of the region. The first livestock to be introduced into the area and raised in significant numbers were cattle; then came sheep and goats.

This order represented an increase in the destruction done to the area's grasscover; for while cattle eat only the uppermost part of the grass, sheep and goats often pull it up by the roots. The result was decided deterioration and, in extreme places, even complete destruction, of the original native grasses. Once it was stripped of its grasscover and binding root systems and exposed to constant trampling by livestock and direct sunlight, the soil soon became very loose and dry and thus highly susceptible to erosion by wind and running water.

FIGURE 2–6

The harvesting of a Kansas wheat field after World War I. During the postwar period, increases both in consumer demand and in food prices prompted a rapid expansion of the United States Wheat Belt. (Grant Heilman)

FIGURE 2-7

The drilling of winter wheat on a farm in the semiarid steppe of eastern Colorado in October 1939. Such dry farming is successful today in many parts of the world, including the Great Plains, but it was a dusty and often vain endeavor in the Dust Bowl states during the 1930s. (FSA, Library of Congress)

Dust Bowl Manifestations

Throughout most of the 1920s, a wet-cycle period in the region provided enough rainfall to protect the exposed steppe soils from scattering winds. But in the 1930s, the rainfall average dropped sharply, resulting in severe droughts in 1930, 1934, and 1936. Perhaps in its natural state the dry-steppe region could have survived this severe dry-cycle period with minimal injury to its landscape. However, because of the decades of poorly managed human activities, few areas were immune to the action of wind erosion. Whenever strong chinook winds from the west blew across the region, they shifted the soil's loose surface layers and carried away much of the topsoil (Fig. 2–8).

FIGURE 2-8

A shallow basin in northern Nebraska in 1936, one of the countless watering holes in the Great Plains that succumbed in the 1930s to wind erosion and overuse by livestock. (Monkmeyer Press Photo)

Throughout the early '30s, almost the entire ground surface of the Great Plains region was subject to *deflation* (the removal of surface materials by lofting into the air or rolling along the ground). In the heart of the Dust Bowl—southeastern Colorado, southwestern Kansas, the Oklahoma Strip, and the Texas Panhandle—more than one-third of the land was seriously affected by wind erosion.

Within a short period of time, the entire region was engulfed in severe dust storms, which appeared as great, dark, ominous clouds rolling along the ground and obscuring everything within their reach (Fig. 2–9). From Denver to Dodge City, quantities of good topsoil were carried to considerable distances—sometimes even as far as the eastern coastal states.

The continuous shifting of dry sand, dust, and other soil materials across the countryside often resulted in the formation of sand dunes that covered much of the artificially created landscape. Many fields, farm buildings, machines, and fences were buried; roadways were blocked; and water supplies were clogged (Fig. 2–10). In areas invaded by dunes, the original vegetation cover was seldom reestablished. Where a new cover did develop, it usually represented an ecologically retrogressed form, characterized by fewer and poorer types of perennial grasses, less nutritious annual grasses, weeds, and edaphically useless bushes—in sum, a completely new and less valuable vegetation cover.

Most of the native animal population of the region's rangeland was also either severely disrupted or completely eliminated. For example, when the natural ecology was intact, the area's rodents were kept in check by their natural predators. But with human

FIGURE 2–9

A dust storm approaching Springfield, Colorado, in May 1937. (U.S. Department of Agriculture)

hunting and land clearance and, eventually, the Dust Bowl conditions, many of these predators were eliminated, leaving such animals as the prairie dog, the jack rabbit, and the gopher to increase in number.

Conclusion

The ecological history of the Great Plains region shows that human activity over a relatively short period of time was instrumental in transforming a balanced natural steppe community into an artificially created, desolate, and desertlike environment. Droughts had come and gone in the area before human settlement, and the ecosystem had endured and recovered from them. But when careless human activity was added to natural disasters, a more cataclysmic situation arose.

It may seem, at first, that one area's loss was another area's gain, since the soil blown away from the Great Plains was deposited on lands farther east, making them more fertile. But there was no gain to any area that was capable of compensating for either the Dust Bowl's appalling loss of land and fertility or for the pain and tragedy of families displaced by the drought, dust, and economic catastrophe (Fig. 2–11).

The single positive result of the Dust Bowl experience was that it made the nation and its government aware—perhaps for the first time—of the great danger involved in the thoughtless manipulation of its ecosystem. In the ensuing years, the efforts made to rehabilitate the devastated area—most of them sponsored by the Soil Conservation Service—proved that people can sometimes repair the environmental damage they cause—albeit at great expense. Along with human efforts, nature provided its own ways of

FIGURE 2–10

An abandoned framstead near Guymon, Oklahoma, in October 1937, where windblown sand has all but engulfed a dump rake. (U.S. Department of Agriculture)

FIGURE 2–11

Migrants whose trek has been temporarily halted near Stockton, California. They were among the thousands of destitute farm families that left Oklahoma and other drought-ravaged states in the 1930s. (FSA, Library of Congress)

repairing itself. Thus the productivity of the Dust Bowl region was only temporarily interrupted. Beginning in the late 1930s, with the return of more favorable environmental conditions (particularly a more normal precipitation pattern), settlers in the region were gradually able to resume farming and livestock-raising activities. And, with the knowledge gained through experience, along with the assistance of expert agriculturists, these activities were controlled by a far more enlightened form of management. Even today, however, the threat of another "Dust Bowl" still confronts many agrarian developments located in similar semiarid transitional lands, whether in the United States or in the desert fringes of Eurasia, Africa, Australia, or South America (Plates IV, V, and VI).

REVIEW AND DISCUSSION

1. Support or refute the statement that "the natural environment is the sole determining factor in shaping all human culture."
2. Give an illustration, from your own area, of the limitations imposed upon cultural development by climate.
3. Are the limits of the human habitat fixed permanently, or can they be altered? If alteration is possible, suggest how it might be accomplished. If it is impossible, explain why.
4. Is it fair to characterize the relationship between human beings and nature as one based on conflict, or is the relationship more often a harmonious one? Cite at least three societies that have different relationships with their natural environments and explain these differences.
5. Do human beings themselves actually effect changes in the natural environment, or do they simply trigger natural forces that eventually bring about such changes? Explain your opinion.

6. Give examples of three different types of regions. Compare and contrast the Moslem world and the Mormon "nation" as cultural regions.
7. Which of the major geographical factors operating in the Great Plains region in its original condition had the greatest influence on the arrival of Dust Bowl manifestations? How was that influence exerted?
8. Assess the role of human activities in creating the Dust Bowl conditions in the Great Plains. From an ecological point of view, in what way was the area perceived incorrectly? Explain how it was particularly mismanaged agriculturally in the 1920s and '30s.
9. How is this Dust Bowl region perceived today? What steps have been taken to prevent another ecological disaster?
10. Dust Bowl conditions are not unique to the Great Plains area of the United States. Under what circumstances have similar conditions developed in other regions of the world?

SELECTED REFERENCES

Bailey, R. W. "Land Erosion—Normal and Accelerated—in the Semiarid West." *Transactions of the American Geophysical Union* (1941), 240–50.

Bates, M. *Man in Nature.* Englewood Cliffs, N.J.: Prentice-Hall, 1961.

Bennett, H. H. *Soil Conservation.* New York: McGraw-Hill, 1939.

Davis, D. H. *The Earth and Man.* New York: Macmillan, 1950.

Golomb, B., and H. M. Eder. "Landforms Made by Man." *Landscape,* Vol. 14 (Autumn 1964), 4–7.

Heathcote, R. L. "Drought in Australia: A Problem of Perception." *Geographical Review,* Vol. 59 (April 1969), 175–94.

Hewitt, K., and F. K. Hare. *Man and Environment.* Washington, D.C.: Commission on College Geography, Resource Paper No. 20, Association of American Geographers, 1973.

Huntington, E. *Civilization and Climate.* New York: Harper & Bros., 1920.

Jacks, G. V., and R. O. Whyte. *The Rape of the Earth.* London: Faber, 1939.

_____. *Vanishing Lands.* New York: Doubleday, Doran, 1939.

Johnson, V. *The Dust Bowl Story.* New York: Farrar Straus, 1947.

Lewthwaite, G. R. "Environmentalism and Determinism: A Search for Clarification." *Annals of the Association of American Geographers,* Vol. 56 (March 1966), 1–23.

MacFadden, H. C. "The Dust Bowl." Unpublished manuscript, 1975.

Meggers, B. T. "Environmental Limitations on the Development of Culture." *American Anthropologist,* Vol. 56 (1954), 801–24.

Meinig, D. W. "The Mormon Culture Region: Strategies and Patterns in the Geography of the American West, 1847–1964." *Annals of the Association of American Geographers,* Vol. 55 (June 1965), 191–220.

Semple, E. C. *Influences of Geographic Environment.* New York: Holt, 1911.

Tatham, G. "Environmentalism and Possibilism." In G. T. Taylor, ed., *Geography in the Twentieth Century.* London: Methuen, 1957.

Thomas, W. L., Jr., ed. *Man's Role in Changing the Face of the Earth.* Chicago: University of Chicago Press, 1956.

Wagner, P. *Environments and People.* Englewood Cliffs, N.J.: Prentice-Hall, 1972.

Whittlesey, D., et al. "The Regional Concept and the Regional Method." In F. E. Dohrs and L. M. Sommers, eds., *Introduction to Geography: Selected Readings.* New York: Crowell, 1967.

Huge ancient monoliths on Easter Island in the South Pacific. (Eugene Gordon)

3

Human Origins and Diffusions

The Beginnings of Human Life

While its earliest beginnings cannot be located precisely, the human race seems to have evolved in the portion of the earth known as the "Old World" (or, more formally, the Eastern Hemisphere) and to have been centered initially in several locations, ranging from eastern Asia to southern Africa. The first year of human existence is, of course, impossible to determine. But it is known with some certainty that as far back as three million years, several humanlike forms were already evolving in portions of eastern and southern Africa. Among these beings were a number of short, humanlike apes of the genus *Australopithecus.* Members of this genus are thought to have walked erectly and thus represent a critical evolutionary development. Inhabitants of savanna areas, these apes, who had binocular vision, once walked on all four feet. But this posture, which limited their viewing angle, caused them to experience great difficulty in seeing

predators amid the savanna's clumps of vegetation. Their need for self-preservation led them to discover that they could obtain a much better view by rising erectly on their hind legs while swivelling their heads to survey the countryside. Eventually, they learned to walk upright, and this new posture freed their forelimbs for use in other activities.

Early Tools and Social Units

About a million years ago, certain primate groups began making simple tools, which they used for such purposes as cutting meat. While various primate groups are known to use wood and stone as implements, the intentional manufacture of tools requires intelligence, planning, and foresight and is thus usually considered one of the traits that distinguish humans from all other animals (Fig. 3–1). Most of the tools at-

35

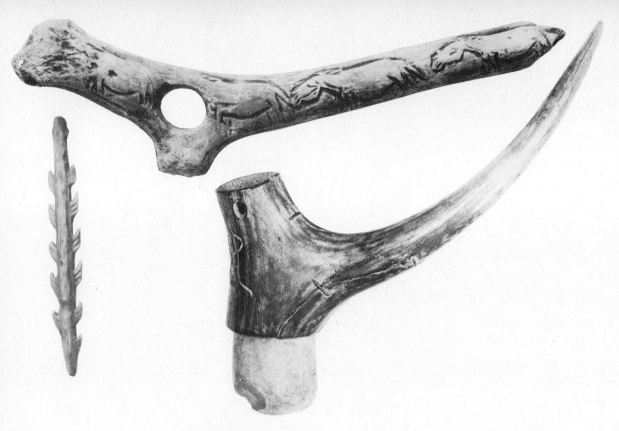

FIGURE 3–1

Some tools made and used by early human inhabitants of Europe. From the Late Paleolithic, or Old Stone Age: top, a *baton de commandement* carved from a reindeer antler and, left, a harpoon. Right, from the Neolithic, or New Stone Age, a pointed axe. (American Museum of Natural History)

tributed to these ancient human types, or *hominids,* were made of stone. Consequently, the first phase of human culture is called the Old Stone Age, or, borrowing from the Greek, the Paleolithic period.

Also about a million years ago, hominids began to form social units and to make sounds that gradually evolved into words and, eventually, into patterned speech. Such applications of intelligence increased in number and complexity as they proved to be invaluable aids to survival. The use of tools, weapons, and clever thinking was the only way the hominids could elude their enemies and obtain sufficient food; they had no sharp claws, no teeth or tusks, nor did they possess superior strength or fleetness of foot.

The Recent Ice Age

The development of the genus *Pithecanthropus,* earliest of the hominids, coincides roughly with the early stages of the Pleistocene Epoch, the geologicage comprising the greatre part of the last million years. The most recent ice age, the Pleistocene Epoch, is divided into four periods of large-scale glaciation, during which massive ice sheets covered much of northern Europe and the northern part of North America (Fig. 3–2). Three interglacial periods are also included in this epoch, the climate of at least one of which is thought to have been warmer than the present period. It is quite possible that the radical changes in climate during

Pleistocene times and the accompanying changes in vegetation and animal life through forced adaptation played a significant role in human evolution.

As early as 200 thousand years ago, there were some species that became very much like present humans in both appearance and action; thus, they have been included in the genus *Homo.* One of these visibly human species is known as *Homo sapiens neanderthalensis,* that is, intelligent man from the Neander Valley (a valley near Düsseldorf, Germany, where relics of the species were first discovered in a cave in 1857). Neanderthalers are believed to have evolved about 100 thousand years ago, in western Asia and Europe. They were rather brutish in appearance, with eyes deep-set under overhanging brows, protruding upper jaws, massive but chinless lower jaws, and stocky, sturdy bodies. They were also intelligent and sensitive, as evidenced by the development of a rudimentary religion, the careful burial of their dead, and the demonstrating of a technology (especially in the making of stone tools) far more advanced than that of their predecessors.

The emergence of the Neanderthalers was more-or-less synchronous with the beginning of the last interglacial stage—a

FIGURE 3–2

The areas in which the first human beings developed were widely separated areas of the Eastern Hemisphere, all far removed from the portions of the earth subject to long periods of glaciation.

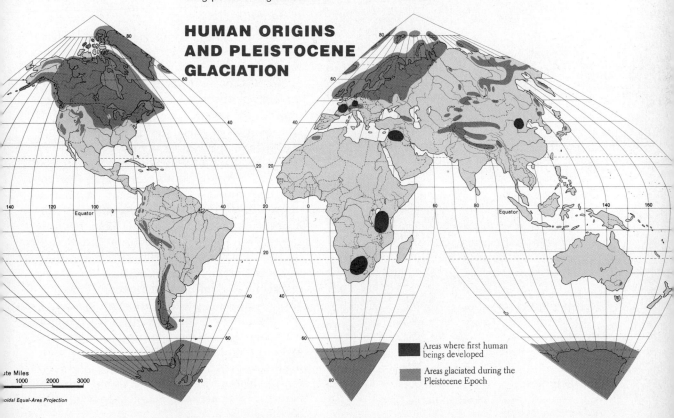

HUMAN ORIGINS AND PLEISTOCENE GLACIATION

Statute Miles
1000   2000   3000

oidal Equal-Area Projection

■ Areas where first human beings developed

■ Areas glaciated during the Pleistocene Epoch

FIGURE 3-3

Neolithic paintings from caves in the Sahara. (Jean-Dominique Lajoux)

period characterized by warmer winters and longer summers than those of the present, and by melting ice sheets, to which was related the northward migration of most plant zones in Europe and Asia. Under these mild conditions the race prospered, developing new technologies and spreading out widely over Europe and Asia. About 70 thousand years ago, the climate began to reverse itself again, bringing lower temperatures and greater snowfall. As these glacial conditions returned to northern Europe and Asia, however, the Neanderthalers, rather than retreating to warmer climates farther south, made use of their newly acquired technological skills and found ways to survive, even in the more northerly regions, which often were in relatively close proximity to the ice front.

The Emergence of *Homo Sapiens*

The present-day human species, *Homo sapiens,* first appeared in parts of Europe and the Middle East during the last glacial stage, about 50 thousand years ago, and gradually replaced or absorbed the last of the Neanderthalers. In several major aspects the new species represented the highest developmental level reached by the genus: first, their brains were larger than those of their ancestors, with frontal lobes, the centers of intelligence and reasoning (nearly nonexistent in earlier species), particularly well-developed; second, the newcomers possessed and applied greater intellectual ability, as demonstrated, especially, by their achieving of ways to communicate over long distances and with permanence; third, they also exhibited greater manual dexterity, which enabled them to produce finely made weapons, tools, and clothing. Among the early achievements of the new species were the development of spear throwing, the carving of designs in ivory and stone, and the painting of remarkable likenesses of animals on the walls of caves (Fig. 3-3).

The Peopling of the Earth

Semitropical Asia and Africa

It has been determined that the initial development of the human race occurred in the tropical and semitropical areas of Asia and Africa, where the climate is characteristically warm at all times of day throughout the year. Sometime later in the race's history, with the utilization of fire, it became possible for humans to move into the colder parts of the world. And 100 thousand years ago, human settlements were spread over most of southern and western Europe, most of southern Asia, and much of Africa. It was not until about 30 thousand years ago, however, that the first people occupied areas in the Americas and Australia.

The Americas and the Pacific

At the time of the first peopling of the Americas, Siberia and Alaska were joined by a strip of land that separated the Arctic Ocean and the Bering Sea; this land bridge has since been replaced by the Bering Straits (Fig. 3–4). Thus the first humans to settle in the Americas simply drifted across this land bridge from Asia, without realizing that they had entered another hemisphere (Fig. 3–5). In the same way, the descendants of these

FIGURE 3–5

The probable migration routes of the first human groups to inhabit the Americas. These nomads are thought to have entered the Western Hemisphere from eastern Asia and gradually expanded their hunting ranges southward and eastward.

FIGURE 3–4

The probable location of an ancient Asia–North America land bridge. The similarity of many fossil and living animals and plants found in the two continents contributes to the belief that such a path existed throughout much of the Pleistocene Epoch.

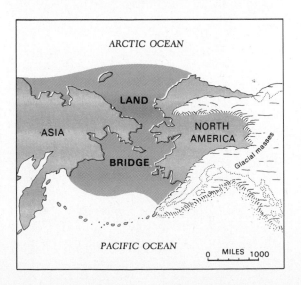

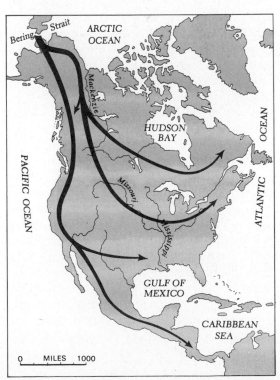

nomads gradually expanded their hunting ranges farther and farther into the new land, and, from time to time, they were followed by new groups from Asia. Eventually, after some thousands of years, the Americas—from Alaska to Tierra del Fuego and from the Pacific to the Atlantic—were populated by many separate groups.

In most cases, then, the settlement of the world was accomplished by people traveling afoot. The habitation of certain remote island areas, however, was accomplished only after the development of relatively so-phisticated seagoing vessels. The farthest removed islands of the Pacific were thus among the last parts of the world to be peopled. In large sailing canoes, which were constructed on the outrigger principle and capable of carrying fifty or more people and supplies for a month, Polynesians sailed from island to island, gradually extending the portions of the inhabited world eastward. They appear to have lived in Samoa and Tonga as early as 500 B.C., to have reached Tahiti in about A.D. 200, and Hawaii, in about A.D. 1000.

Early Migrations and Invasions

Relocations and Resettlements

Even after the peopling of virtually all areas of the earth's surface was accomplished, resettlements of many groups continued. Although it has often been said that a person's greatest desire is to have a stable and secure home, wanderlust has often affected whole tribes and nations. This desire, then, must almost certainly be the stronger of the two, as evidenced by the fact that, throughout history, the large-scale relocation of people has been almost continuous in most parts of the world.

There have been some resettlements, of course, that were undertaken out of desperation, motivated by such things as war, oppression, famine, or overpopulation—forces that tend to "push" people from an area. But, more often, there is no extreme propelling force; other fields simply look "greener," offering (or apparently offering) more fertile land, milder climates, or some particular freedom or economic opportunity. Such advantages are the things that "pull" people from one land to another.

Some generalized relocations of people have been the warlike thrusts of highly militarized tribes or nations. Others have been gradual, peaceful migrations of simple farmers and herders. Some have been planned, well-financed colonizations of distant lands. And some have been the separate, unplotted movements of rather poor families. In both large-scale and individual migrations, the pressures of population growth are often found to be a contributive factor.

Routes for Invasion and Travel.   Steppe and prairie lands have been the areas most continuously affected by migration, and the ones most commonly occupied by nomadic peoples. Before modern technology, the alternation of plentiful rainfall and drought in such areas resulted in great fluctuations in their life-sustaining capacities. In wet years, the flocks, herds, and human populations expanded greatly. In dry years, they faced hunger and starvation. It was during such periods of drought that some groups would set out to search for food and water elsewhere. The better-watered lands nearby were usually already occupied by sedentary farming peoples. Wanting to secure those lands for themselves, the nomads often violently attacked these less war-ready people, slaughtering, enslaving, or driving them away and occupying their lands, sometimes on a permanent basis. Thrust out of their homes, the displaced farmers displaced others in turn, setting off a chain of events that affected a great number of people over great distances. Such situations occurred repeatedly for over two thousand years, across the area between central Asia and western Europe, and came to a halt only in the last century. These mass movements involving millions of people are sometimes referred to collectively as the *Völkerwanderung* (German for the folk-wandering).

Consider, for example, the invasions by the Huns during the fourth and fifth centuries (Fig. 3–6). In A.D. 370 those nomadic pastoral people, who lived originally in central Asia, far beyond the Caspian Sea, suddenly appeared near the Volga River on the border between Europe and Asia. A great, warlike horde, they overthrew the Alani, a pastoral people settled on the grassy plains between the Volga and the Don rivers, in present-day European Russia. Surging westward, the Huns then quickly overthrew the

empire of the Ostrogoths, in the Ukraine between the Don and the Dnestr rivers, and by 376 had defeated the Visigoths and, taking most of Rumania, reached the Danube, the frontier of the Roman Empire, then at its zenith.

For the next fifty years, the Huns were relatively quiet in their new lands, their military involvements consisting only of minor border skirmishes. In 441, however, under their powerful leader Attila, they attacked the Roman Empire itself. By 443 they had defeated the Roman armies in southeastern Europe and had surrounded Constantinople (now Istanbul). In 451, they invaded France, and, in the following year they reached northern Italy, thus pushing right into the heart of the Roman Empire. When Attila died in 453 the contest for leadership between his sons caused fighting within the tribe, and, as a result, its military power sharply declined. By the end of the century the Huns had lost their unity and much of their identity and were being absorbed into the local populations throughout eastern and southern Europe. Once a nomadic dry-lands people living in tents pitched wherever there was grass and water for their herds and flocks, the Huns were now settled as farmers in relatively humid lands and harvested the same

FIGURE 3–6

The route taken by the Huns, during the fourth and fifth centuries, in their advance on Europe. The invasion of central Europe by the Mongols in the thirteenth century took a similar route through the steppe and prairie areas of western Asia.

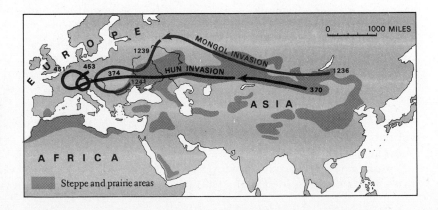

crops in the same fields generation after generation. In less than a century a whole tribe had been transplanted from semiarid desert borderlands to humid lands a few thousand miles away.

Reports of the ferocity of attacks by the Huns caused many groups to flee their lands even before they were invaded. Their flight started several relocations that were as significant as the movements of the Huns themselves. The Ostrogoths, fleeing the Ukraine, eventually settled in northern Italy. The Visigoths, displaced in Rumania, raided much of the Balkans, ravaged Italy, and took over much of southern France and Spain. The Vandals, originally residents of the area that is now eastern Germany, were also pushed westward. Mounting their own great, warlike drive, they crossed the Rhine and fought their way across France and Spain, eventually settling in North Africa and, in 455, attacking Rome (the term *vandalize* recalls their pillage of the sacred and temporal relics of that city). The Franks, another Germanic tribe, crossed the Rhine and settled in France, giving it its name. The Angles, the Saxons, and the Jutes, all peoples of northern Germany and Denmark, crossed the North Sea and settled in England (German for land of the Angles) and other parts of Britain.

Throughout Europe in the fifth and sixth centuries, tribes pushed from their homelands moved small or great distances and fought bloody battles to settle eventually in some new land. Often they were absorbed into the very population they had conquered, so much so that after several generations their distinctive features and habits were scarcely discernible.

Southern Britain. Southern areas of Britain were first populated 15 thousand years ago, when glaciers were still present in its central and northern regions. At that time, Britain was still attached to the continent of Europe by a land bridge, rather than separated from it by the Straits of Dover and the English Channel. The first people to cross this strip of land into Britain were a short, rather dark people who sustained themselves by hunting and fishing and by gathering wild plants. They lived in small groups, had no domesticated plants or animals (except, perhaps, the dog), and used the very simple tools and weapons of Paleolithic times (the Old Stone Age). Their language was unlike any spoken today.

About five thousand years ago, Neolithic (New Stone Age) farmers and herders began to arrive in Britain from continental Europe, bringing with them flocks of sheep and herds of cattle as well as a good deal of experience at growing wheat and barley. They took over the area's best lands and crowded its previous occupants into the less desirable areas—forested lowlands, rugged mountains, and peninsulas where the soils were thin, the skies overcast, and the temperatures cool even in summer. Lacking effective tools—they made no use of iron —these newcomers had great difficulty in felling trees. Hence, the "best" lands, from their point of view, were those of the *downs*, treeless, chalky uplands, where they could plant their crops most easily. These farmers avoided—in fact, they actually feared—the dense forests that covered the lowlands. This fear was probably reinforced by the presence there of bands of the short, dark people who had been the first group to settle in Britain. British folklore is full of references to the "Little People," "Bogey Men," and "Dark Ones"—each phrase probably an allusion to these primitive people, who long existed around the fringes of the settlements of more progressive groups.

By the fifth century B.C., Celtic tribes from Spain, France, and southern Germany had begun to invade Britain, and they continued to arrive in recurrent waves until the

FIGURE 3–7

Hadrian's Wall, a wall of defense in northern Britain constructed by order of the Roman emperor Hadrian (A.D. 117–138). This reminder of the Roman conquest of Britain extends approximately 73 miles, from Solway Firth to the mouth of the River Tyne. (Reece Winstone)

first century B.C. The people taking part in the earlier of these Celtic invasions were speakers of the Gaelic language; the later groups spoke Welsh. The name of one of the Welsh-speaking groups, Brythons, is the source of the appellations *Briton* and *Britain*.

Technologically, the Celts were relatively advanced, using iron tools and possessing both an agricultural technology and a military strength far superior to that of their predecessors in Britain. With their iron tools, they began clearing the lowland forests and transforming them into agricultural areas. They also drove all the earlier settlers into the mountains and the western peninsulas. Some of these peoples, such as the Picts, eventually banded together and, for several

centuries, offered the Celts considerable military resistance.

Although the Romans had conquered Britain by A.D. 43 and held it for about four hundred years, the Roman occupation was only a military and administrative one. It did not involve the mass resettlements characteristic of other invasions of Britain in ancient times (Figs. 3–7 and 3–8).

When the Roman forces withdrew, due to military concerns elsewhere, raids by seafaring peoples of northern Germany and Denmark (Angles, Saxons, and Jutes), which had begun around A.D. 300, developed into full-fledged invasions. The legends associated with King Arthur are based upon the attempts of the various Celtic groups to thwart these invasions. Despite their efforts, however, the Celts were gradually pushed into the mountains and peninsulas to the west, just as they had pushed the Picts a few centuries earlier. By A.D. 500, the Anglo-Saxons had occupied all of the eastern lowlands of Britain; many of the Welsh-speaking Britons of southern England had fled across the Channel into northwestern France, where they occupied and named such regions as Brittany; the remainder of the Celts had retreated into southwestern England, Wales, and southern Scotland; the Scots (an early Celtic group) had been occupying Ireland and southwestern Scotland for some time; and the Picts still held the Highlands of Scotland.

FIGURE 3–8
The network of major roads built in Britannia by the Romans during their long domination of western Europe. Antoninus' Wall, built about A.D. 142, marks the northern extent of the Roman military conquests.

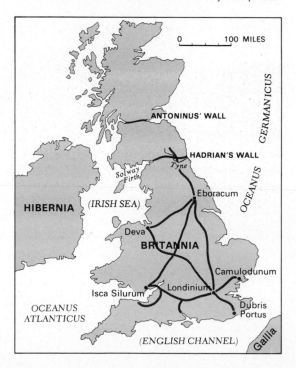

Eventually, the Anglo-Saxons were also faced with an onslaught by invaders from over the sea. Early in the ninth century, the Norsemen, or Vikings, of Norway and Denmark began looting the British coasts and soon thereafter had established a series of bases along the northern shores. By the end of that century, they had pushed their forces well into the interior of the north, either displacing the Celts and Anglo-Saxons living there or coexisting with them.

Another group of Norsemen had conquered part of northwestern France and had settled there in large numbers. They were generally called *Normans,* and the land they settled became known as Normandy. In time, they made many concessions to their new environment, adopting the French language as well as a wide range of French customs.

The last military invasion of Britain took place in 1066, when the Normans attacked and defeated the Anglo-Saxons at Hastings, on the southern coast of England, and took over most of Britain (Fig. 3–9). The Normans had a profound influence on all aspects of the country; they altered its language and introduced a new form of government as well as new customs and styles.

African Migrations and Invasions

Large-scale migrations have not been limited to the Eurasian world alone. For many centuries, for example, Bantu tribesmen had been migrating southward from their main homeland in the northeastern part of Nigeria (Fig. 3–10). Tall, able warriors, equipped with iron-headed spears and tough cowhide shields, certain of these tribes, perhaps, especially, the Zulus, were practically undefeatable; in gaining control of an area, they drove out the weaker tribes, or they killed or enslaved them. The warriors' relatives and possessions always followed close behind the battlefront.

FIGURE 3–9

A scene from the Bayeux Tapestry (eleventh century) depicting the military battle that occurred near Hastings, England, in October 1066. The invading Norman cavalry vanquished the infantry of the Saxon king Harold II. Harold was slain, and William, Duke of Normandy, succeeded him as King of England. (Giraudon)

A Bantu tribe often continued such onslaughts for several years, usually through the will of some powerful and energetic chieftain. But, eventually, it would settle down—at least for a time—and begin clearing fields, raising crops, and building homes and villages. This activity would continue until, suddenly, a new, warlike chieftain would arise and impel the tribe to again surge forward in a wave of conquest. In much the same way, during the centuries before European colonization, various other African tribes moved southward, traveling from areas in present-day Kenya and Tanzania south to the central part of Namibia (South West Africa), Botswana, and the vicinity of East London, in South Africa. In this area, they almost completely replaced the Bushmen and Namas (southern African tribes belonging to the larger group of people known collectively as the *Hottentots*), who had occupied it throughout time immemorial. In the nineteenth century, the Bantu were still pushing southward, but their advance was abruptly halted because of colonization by the Dutch in South Africa and by the Germans in South West Africa. Were it not for

FIGURE 3–10

The diffusion of Bantu-speaking peoples from the first century to 1000. The principal homeland from which these groups moved was in the area that is now northeastern Nigeria; by 1000 they had migrated westward and also conquered most of Africa to the south and east of their original sites.

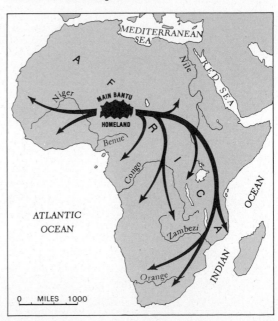

FIGURE 3-11

The siege of Jerusalem in 586 B.C. by the forces of the emperor Nebuchadnezzar of Babylonia. The destruction of this capital city marked the end of the Judean kingdom and the beginning of the Babylonian Captivity, a period in which many Jews were taken to Babylon as captives. (Frank J. Darmstaedter, Photographic Archive of the Jewish Theological Seminary of America, New York)

this outside intervention, it is likely that the Bantu would have reached the Cape of Good Hope early in the twentieth century and totally destroyed the original Nama and Bushman populations.

The Plight of the Jews

In marked contrast to these violent and warlike resettlements are the migrations of the Jews, known collectively as the *Diaspora*. From 586 B.C. — when they were made captives in Babylon by the emperor Nebuchad-

nezzar — to the present, the Jewish people have had to flee religious persecution and seek out new homes (Fig. 3–11). Such movements have always been domestic, that is, undertaken by an individual family or by groups of closely related families.

The many expulsions of the Jews from their traditional homeland (variously known as Canaan, Palestine, and Israel) and their first resettlements have caused them to be spread widely over the world. Since the first century, Jewish colonies have developed in most of the cities near the Mediterranean Sea and, in the Middle East, as far as Iraq. In each of these areas, Jews have played important roles in trade and commerce, in finance, and as patrons of the arts.

In the fifteenth century, the Spanish Inquisition caused the large Jewish population of Spain to be dispersed over much of the Mediterranean area. They formed settlements in North Africa (Tunisia, Algeria, and Morocco), in southern Europe (southern France, Italy, and Greece), and in the Middle East (mainly in Turkey, Lebanon, and Palestine). These people are known as the *Sephardim,* or Sephardic Jews (Hebrew: *s'pharadh* = Spain), and their vernacular language, Ladino, is a mixture of Hebrew and Spanish.

During the Middle Ages, other Jewish groups migrated to the cities of northern Europe. There, they gradually developed a distinctive language known as *Yiddish* (German: *jüdisch* = Jewish) — a mixture of Hebrew, German, and Slavic words written in Hebrew characters. These migrants are known as the *Ashkenazim* (Hebrew: *Ashk'naz* = Germany), and were centered primarily in Germany, Poland, and Russia.

Greek and Chinese Dispersals

Similar long-term migrations to distant lands include the two-thousand-year movement of Greeks into the towns and cities of the Mediterranean area and northern Africa. Greece, a country with few valuable mineral resources and little arable land, has been

	Number of Chinese	Percentage
Asia	15,859,820	96.6
United States and Canada	295,489	1.8
Latin America	148,709	.9
Oceania	52,572	.3
Africa	43,734	.3
Europe	20,586	.1
Total	16,420,910	100.0

FIGURE 3–12

The worldwide distribution of Chinese in lands other than China, as of 1963. Most of the large majority residing in other parts of Asia is located in the southeastern portion of the continent.

faced with overpopulation for much of its history; the main source of relief from the resultant grinding poverty has been migration to other lands.

The traditional flows of Chinese emigrants have come mainly from southern China, especially southern Fukien province and Kwangtung province, which includes the port city of Canton. Since the mid-seventeenth century, some 15 million people have migrated from these largely rural provinces to about 100 different countries throughout the tropical and subtropical world. There are now Chinese populations of over 3 million in Thailand and Hong Kong, over 2 million in Indonesia and Malaysia, and over 1 million in Singapore and Vietnam; sizable Chinese populations also exist in such non-Asian countries as the United States, Cuba, and Australia (Fig. 3–12).

The Age of Colonization

The Western world (the part of the earth whose present inhabitants are descendants of people who came from northwestern or Mediterranean Europe) has experienced two long-lasting periods of massive migration. The first was the *Völkerwanderung,* which was discussed earlier in this chapter. The second, which occurred from about 1500 to 1900, will be discussed here as the *Age of Colonization.*

Precolonial European Life

Throughout the Middle Ages (from approximately 500 to 1500), living conditions in western Europe were arduous. An extremely high birth rate was offset by an equally high death rate; life expectancy was short, averaging about thirty years. The high incidence of disease reflected the period's lack of adequate sewage systems, limited medical knowledge (including an ignorance of germ theory), and futile attempts to find ways of preserving food. Infant mortality was particularly high, with a very large percentage of babies dying in their first year.

With little long-distance trading, extensive crop failures often led to famine and widespread malnutrition, which made the population extremely susceptible to disease. During the winters, especially, most people suffered serious dietary imbalances, due to the absence of ways to preserve vitamin-rich foods.

Farming equipment was crude, planting methods were simple and inefficient, and crop yields were correspondingly low. By the end of the fifteenth century, the population of western Europe was very close to the carrying capacity of the land. In fact, had not the ''Black Death'' (the outbreak of bubonic plague that swept through Europe from 1347 to 1350) greatly reduced the population, widespread famine would probably have occurred (Fig. 3–13). It was thus fortunate that, early in the fifteenth century, the Portuguese and Spanish began the series of explorations that led to the discovery of the full extent of the African continent, a sea route to Asia, and the continents of North America, South America, and Australia.

Migrations to New Lands

The discoveries mentioned above opened up a vast new world to the over-

FIGURE 3–13

Detail of a contemporaneous illuminated manuscript that depicts the burning of infected clothing during the Black Death, the epidemic of bubonic plague that ravaged Europe's urban populations in the fourteenth century. (Bodleian Library, Oxford)

crowded inhabitants of Europe. Asia was already well-populated, highly civilized, and under the rule of strong local governments, and it was thus not open to any large-scale settlement and colonization by Europeans; Australia, southern Africa, and the Americas, however, provided a situation that was quite different. In those lands, population densities were low, and, in most cases, the level of material civilization was equally low; the few capable governments in existence, such as those in Mexico and Peru, could be overthrown far more easily than could those in Asia by European military might (due, especially, to their superior weaponry).

Great numbers of Europeans flocked to these new lands to administer and control, to trade and, especially, to farm. The majority of those who set out were youths; frequently, the journey was made by whole families; and, usually, they all shared the same intention—to make new homes for themselves. The new lands they reached were productive and provided raw materials that could be traded for goods manufactured in the homeland, thus stimulating its economy.

There was, of course, a tendency for settlers to emigrate to the lands controlled by their native countries. Portugal colonized Brazil, and Spain controlled most of the rest of the Americas from Mexico (even California for a time) southward. The French became established in Canada and northern Africa; the Dutch, in New York, the East Indies, and South Africa; and the British, in North America, eastern and southern Africa, and Australia. In each of these places today, the influence of the early European population is still strong, even though many of the areas have gained political independence, some as much as two centuries ago; in each, a significant portion of the population, the language, and many other aspects of local culture are all derived from the European country that first, or most lastingly, exercised control.

Not all of the countries of Europe were involved in the exploration and colonization of the New World. Many portions of the continent had not yet developed a national consciousness and, hence, were not up to the task of developing colonies. Germany and Italy, for example, were still fragmented into numerous independent, or quasi-independent, principalities, duchies, and the like. Eastern European countries in this era appear to have had no aspirations beyond their own local spheres. However, certain individuals and groups from these areas did emigrate to colonies of other nations and were gradually absorbed into their populations.

The gradual movement of individuals and families from Europe, for the purpose of colonizing and developing the newly found areas of Australia, southern Africa, and the Americas is, perhaps, the most significant migration of all time. And, while the term *colonization* has acquired many negative connotations, when this migration is viewed in context, its accomplishments are impressive, and there is much to be said in its favor.

Modern Human Distributions

Despite all the migrations throughout the centuries, the way in which the human population is distributed over the surface of the earth is still very uneven. This is due, mainly, to the uneven distribution of arable land and other natural resources and, increasingly, to the esthetic appeal of certain areas to mobile populations.

FIGURE 3-14

Mountains in the Arctic fringe of the Canadian northwest—cold, barren, and desolate. (Canadian Department of National Defense)

The Empty Areas

Even with the high density of population in many parts of the world and the rapid increase in its total population, some sections of the earth still remain devoid of human inhabitants (Plates II, IV, and VII).

Water Bodies. Obviously, the largest of such areas are the water bodies—the oceans, seas, and lakes. Aside from the people living on boats in such places as Oriental harbors and American marinas, and the fishers, sci-entists, and sailors on long-voyage vessels, the water bodies of the world are virtually unpeopled.

Arctic Fringes. The extreme cold of winter, the shortness of summer, the impos-sibility of producing crops by normal agri-cultural methods, and the lack of available sources of water throughout much of the year have all militated against the development and peopling of the more poleward parts of the earth. But the exploitation of their valu-able mineral resources—coal in Spitsbergen, uranium in northern Canada, iron ore in Labrador, and petroleum on the Alaskan North Slope, for example—has resulted in localized human settlements wherein miners and oilers live under comfortable but artificial conditions, their necessities and luxuries imported from afar, often at great cost. Similar situations exist at many of the military bases that various countries have established in the more remote of these places. In Arctic areas, where open water seasonally occurs along the coast, a scattering of primitive hunters, such as the Eskimo, also eke out a bare existence.

Otherwise, the Arctic tends to be quite empty. The interior of Greenland is totally uninhabited, as is the whole of Antarctica.

Except in mining areas, population density is very low throughout northern Canada, Alaska, and the northern part of the Soviet Union (Fig. 3–14).

Desert Lands. Owing to their critical shortage of water, deserts are usually occupied only where water is available in quantities sufficient for irrigation; where mining is profitable; and along border areas where, in rainy years, nomadic herders may temporarily graze their animals. Elsewhere, desert areas are either empty or sparsely populated, chiefly by primitive hunting-and-gathering peoples. Such areas include the interior of Australia, the Sahara, the deserts of Saudi Arabia, Iran, and Afghanis-

FIGURE 3–15

Sand dunes in a desert area of Saudi Arabia. The oasis in the background offers the wayfarer some relief from the dry and barren terrain that surrounds it. (Standard Oil Co., N.J.)

tan, large portions of central Asia, the coastal desert of Namibia in southwestern Africa, and, in the United States, parts of New Mexico, Arizona, and Nevada (Fig. 3–15).

In the United States, rapid growth of large urban concentrations on the desert borders and technological advances (in air conditioning and specially designed vehicles, for example) have helped to engender great interest in deserts as areas for both recreation and retirement. Particularly in the southern parts of California, Nevada, and Arizona, desert areas have experienced a rapid growth in population. They are frequented, on a short-term basis (that is, weekends and short vacations), by residents of the nearby metropolitan areas and, on a long-term basis, by vacationers and retirees from the colder parts of the United States.

Mountains and Plateaus. For a number of reasons, high mountains and plateaus are often areas of low population density. Among these reasons are: the diminished supply of oxygen at high altitudes, which necessitates certain physiological adjustments, often difficult for humans; the lower temperatures, which reduce the length of the growing season; and the frequent shortage of flat land suitable for cultivation. The few inhabitants of these areas are likely to be herders and miners. In recent years, selected areas in Norway, the Alps, the Sierra Nevada, and the Rockies have become important ski resorts as well as successful summer retreats.

Included among the empty, or sparsely populated, mountain-and-plateau areas are Tibet, the altiplano of Bolivia, the Andes in southern Chile and Argentina, large portions of Norway, and much of South Island, New Zealand.

Tropical Forests. In the dense forests of tropical-humid and equatorial regions,

leached soils, high humidity, and endemic diseases have acted to retard development; these areas remain sparsely populated. This is illustrated by the emptiness of much of the interior of Brazil, parts of central Africa, and most of Borneo and New Guinea.

The High-Density Areas

There are basically two types of areas that today possess dense populations—the agricultural areas in emerging countries, and the highly urbanized and industrialized portions of more advanced nations (Plate VII).

Agricultural Areas. On alluvial plains in tropical and subtropical areas with heavy rainfall, intensive agriculture, supplemented, as needed, by irrigation can usually produce such a high-food value cereal crop as rice; such a crop can be grown in quantities that will support high densities of people. In Java, where the richness of the alluvial soil is amplified by recent volcanic materials, the density of the population dependent upon agriculture alone may exceed 2,000 persons per square mile. Other areas of very high density include the agricultural areas of Japan, China, India, Bangladesh, Korea, Vietnam, Cambodia, Thailand, the Philippines, and the United Arab Republic (Egypt).

However, despite the richness of the soil, the fact that there are so many people dependent upon the land results in a *per capita* yield that is, necessarily, very low; the people live on a very limited diet, and cash income is meager. Any slight reduction in the yields—due to plant disease, inclement weather, or war, for instance—may cause widespread hunger, if not outright famine. Today, some hundreds of millions of people in these overcrowded parts of the world live a precarious existence, the threat of starvation being with them always.

FIGURE 3–16

The city of Tokyo, in central Japan. Like most of the world's high-density urban areas, it is a center of industry and trade, served by a complex of modern transportation systems. (Japanese Information Service)

Urban-Industrial Areas. Due to modern means of transportation, it is possible for large numbers of people who do not produce their own food to live in one area and still be well-supplied with food. Airplanes and trucks make it possible to provide urban areas with raw materials for industry, with great amounts of energy, and with adequate markets for their manufactured goods. Thus it was not until the present technological age that urbanization has been possible on a grand scale.

Large-scale modern urbanization is based upon industry and trade, both of which, in turn, are based upon the availabil-

ity of several resources; fuel and energy, skilled labor, transportation facilities, and a stable political environment. These have been fully combined on a long-term basis most successfully in the northeastern part of the United States, northwestern Europe, the western part of the Soviet Union, and, recently, central Japan (Fig. 3–16).

In these regions, urban population densities are often very high; but this does not necessarily mean poverty or the threat of starvation. Due to the value of manufactured products, the income from their sales and related trading activities, urban populations are usually fairly affluent. Japan provides an excellent example, for the marked increase in its population density over the past few decades has been accompanied, not by increased poverty, but rather by an obvious rise in the standard of living. This economic change has been caused, in part, by the country's shift from subsistence agriculture to large-scale industrialization. Many of Japan's new workers were formerly farmers dependent upon the yield of small rice fields; as wage earners, they now have cash incomes with which to purchase a wide variety of foods and goods.

The Moderate-Density Areas

The population density found in most areas of the world, however, is more modest, falling somewhere between the extremes discussed above. Generally speaking, densities are fairly low in areas where the economy is based on large-scale forestry, livestock raising, or the cultivation of grains (see Plate VII). For such agricultural regions, it seems that one rule of population density—the more fertile the soil, the denser the population—is countered by a second—the higher the degree of mechanization, the lower the density—and, sometimes, by a third—the longer the history of settlement, the denser the population. Thus India, for example—with fertile soil, little mechanization, and a very long history—has a high population density; while the Corn Belt in the United States (mainly the states of Iowa, Illinois, Indiana)—with fertile soil, a short history of settlement (150 years), and a very high degree of mechanization—is an area of moderate population density.

REVIEW AND DISCUSSION

1. What advantages did the earliest human beings have over lower animals in the struggle for existence?
2. What major evolutionary changes has the human race undergone over the past three million years or so?
3. According to most researchers, in what order were the various parts of the world peopled? What major technological innovation is believed to have allowed humans to move into the colder parts of the world?
4. Why has the large-scale relocation of people been almost continuous in most parts of the world? What are some of the forces that tend to "push" people from an area? What forces "pull" them to another?
5. In what specific ways has the natural environment influenced human migrations?
6. Compare and contrast the migrations of the Jews with the migrations of such other groups as the Huns, Celts, and Polynesians.
7. Which areas of the world were most open to the large-scale colonization and settlement begun by Europeans in the fifteenth century? Explain some of the reasons for their suitability.
8. "Despite all the migrations throughout the centuries, the way in which the human population is distributed over the surface of the earth is still very uneven." Discuss and evaluate the implications of this statement in terms of both the physical and cultural factors.
9. Which parts of the world constitute the "empty areas"? Why are these areas relatively devoid of people? Do you feel that some day large concentrations of people will be living and working in any or most of these areas? Explain.
10. What are the major characteristics of the world's moderate-density areas?

SELECTED REFERENCES

Braidwood, R. J. *Prehistoric Men,* 7th ed. Glenview, Ill.: Scott, Foresman, 1967.

Brodrick, A. H. *Man and His Ancestry.* London: Hutchinson University Library, 1960.

Butzer, K. *Environment and Archeology: An Ecological Approach.* Chicago: Aldine, 1971.

Campbell, B. G. *Human Evolution: An Introduction to Man's Adaptations.* Chicago: Aldine, 1966.

Carter, G. F. *Man and the Land, A Cultural Geography.* New York: Holt, Rinehart and Winston, 1968.

Clark, Sir W. E. Le Gros. *The Antecedents of Man.* Chicago: Quadrangle Books, 1960.

———. *History of the Primates,* 4th ed. Chicago: University of Chicago Press, 1963.

Dobzhansky, T. *Mankind Evolving: The Evolution of the Human Species.* New Haven: Yale University Press, 1962.

East, G. *The Geography Behind History.* London: Nelson, 1940.

Hawkes, J., and Sir L. Woolley. *History of Mankind: Cultural and Scientific Development,* Vol. 1. London: Allen and Unwin, 1963.

Hoebel, E. A. *Anthropology: The Study of Man,* 4th ed. New York: McGraw-Hill, 1972.

Hooton, E. A. *Up From the Ape.* New York: Macmillan, 1960.

Howell, F. C., and the editors of Time-Life Books. *Early Man.* New York: Time, Inc., 1965.

Howells, W. W. "The Distribution of Man." *Scientific American,* Vol. 203 (September 1960), 113–27.

Korn, N., and N. R. Smith, eds. *Human Evolution.* New York: Holt, Rinehart and Winston, 1963.

MacFadden, C. H. *An Atlas of World Review.* New York: Crowell, 1940.

Montagu, A., ed. *Culture and the Evolution of Man.* New York: Oxford University Press, 1970.

Outhwaite, L. *Unrolling the Map.* New York: Reynal & Hitchcock, 1935.

Pfeiffer, J. *The Emergence of Man.* New York: Harper & Row, 1972.

Piggott, S., ed. *The Dawn of Civilization.* New York: McGraw-Hill, 1961.

Simons, E. L. "The Early Relatives of Man." *Scientific American,* Vol. 211 (July 1964), 50–62.

Washburn, S. L., ed. *Social Life of Early Man.* Chicago: Aldine, 1961.

———, ed. *Classification and Human Evolution.* Chicago: Aldine, 1963.

White, L. *Medieval Technology and Social Change.* Oxford: Clarendon, 1962.

Willey, G. R., ed. *Prehistoric Settlement Patterns in the New World.* Publications in Anthropology No. 23. New York: Viking Fund, 1956.

Masai of central East Africa. (Maxwell Coplan, DPI)

4

Race and Cultural Diffusion

The peoples of the world are by no means all alike. Their many differences are both physical and social. Often the average members of two different human groups show obvious differences in such traits as height, build, hair form and color, skin color, and shape of eye and nose. They may also speak differently, worship in different ways, and utilize different clothing, foods, tools, and art forms. The first areas of difference, those involved with physical attributes, are passed on genetically, and thus are considered substantially racial. The others are char-acteristics acquired after birth, through inadvertent imitation or through deliberate education and training; these are considered cultural.

The early part of this chapter will examine the racial differentiation of humankind. Then it will consider certain highly visible aspects of culture and their spatial distributions. The latter part of the chapter will be devoted to several specific cultures—to their major characteristics, areas and modes of development, and diffusions into other regions of the world.

Racial Groups

A *race* is a segment of humankind whose members possess a set of physical characteristics so distinctive as to differentiate them from the rest of humanity. Most often these distinguishing characteristics relate to physical stature, shapes of facial features, eye and skin color, hair texture and color, and blood type. All are inherited characteristics or traits transmitted genetically from generation to generation. Since humans have been extremely mobile over the millennia, and the intermixing of both greatly contrasting and similar groups has occurred almost everywhere, there are no pure racial groups—nor is it likely that any have ever existed. Descriptions of racial groups are thus generalizations; the races cannot be differentiated by means of sharp lines. They blend.

Classification

Nonetheless, anthropologists endlessly make attempts to delineate the human races, providing nearly as many racial classifications as there are experts. Within this array the best primary classification is one that divides humankind into three groups: Caucasoid, Mongoloid, and Negroid—each having several subdivisions.

The Caucasoid race is characterized by light skin coloring, light eyes (blue, green, gray, brown), light wavy hair, thin lips, and prominent, narrow noses. The Mongoloid race exhibits light-brown to yellowish skin; brown eyes beneath epicanthic eye-folds, the so-called "almond eyes"; flat noses with rather depressed bridge areas; high cheekbones; broad flat faces; and straight, thick, dark hair. The Negroid race is characterized by light brown to very dark brown skin, dark woolly to kinky hair, eyes with dark brown irises and often brownish pigmentation in the sclera, broad and flattish noses, prominent lips, and forward jutting jaws.

Origins and Diffusions

It is commonly assumed today that humankind was once a single homogeneous population and that racial differentiation occurred during the late Pleistocene, when some groups, having drifted away from their common "nursery," became isolated by environmental phenomena. Thus the present Mongoloid group was cut off from the others by the glaciers of the Alpine-Himalayan mountain chain; the present Negroid group became separated by the increasing dessication of interior North Africa; and the present Caucasoid group was also separated. Genetic changes occurred, gradually, in *all* the groups, partly by natural selection and partly by mutation, and the groups grew less and less alike in physical characteristics.

The Negroid and Mongoloid races developed in areas of bright sunshine; the former in the savannas and steppes of sub-Saharan Africa, and the latter in the steppes and deserts of central Asia. Their more heavily pigmented skins and dark eyes probably represent an adaptation to the effects of bright sunlight and glare and excessive amounts of ultra-violet radiation. By contrast, the Caucasoid race (despite the eastern associations of its name) may well have developed in the cooler, moister climates of western Europe, under less sunny skies and often in the partial shade of the forests.

Current Distribution

Today the Negroid race is still most dominant within its original abode, the major part of sub-Saharan Africa (Fig. 4–1). Variant groups within this area include: the Bantu, long-time residents of central Africa and relatively recent arrivals in southern Africa, with dark brown skin, and slightly broad noses and protruding jaws; and the Nilotic Negroes of southern Sudan and adjacent parts of Uganda and Kenya, taller and slimmer, with thinner lips and narrower noses.

For thousands of years, Negroes were abducted in various parts of sub-Saharan Africa and sold as slaves in distant parts of the world. In the United States, from the seventeenth to the mid-nineteeth century, the labor of black slaves was an important factor in the functioning of the plantation agriculture of the South. Proclaimed free in the

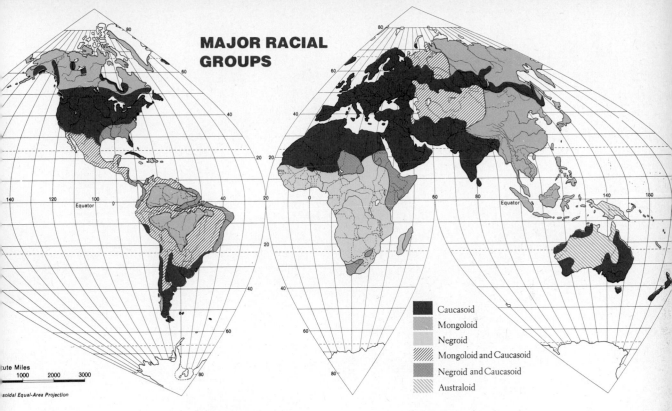

MAJOR RACIAL GROUPS

Legend:
- Caucasoid
- Mongoloid
- Negroid
- Mongoloid and Caucasoid
- Negroid and Caucasoid
- Australoid

FIGURE 4–1

Caucasoids comprise about 55 percent of the world's people; Mongoloids, 37 percent; Negroids, 7 percent; and Australoids, 1 percent.

1860s, many former slaves remained in the South; but others resettled in the northern states and western territories. And since the 1900s, and especially since the mid-1940s, large numbers of Southern blacks have migrated to the industrial cities of the Northeast and Middle West and to the urban areas of California. The enslavement of Africans is an historical fact elsewhere in the hemisphere as well. Descendants of former slaves comprise significant portions of the populations of coastal Brazil, French Guiana, Surinam and Guyana, the West Indies, and the Caribbean coasts of parts of Central America. Blacks were also transported as slaves to Arabia, where they now form an important part of the population of many of the coastal areas to the east (Fig. 4–2).

The Mongoloid race is well developed in its central Asian nursery and, with only minor variation, over most of the Asian continent north of the Himalayas. The great treks of the *Völkerwanderung* brought Mongoloid groups well into eastern Europe, the latest and most conspicuous of the invading groups being the Magyars, who settled in Hungary, and the Finns and Lapps of Scandinavia. The American Indian, both North and South American stocks, and the Eskimo are usually thought to be Mongoloid peoples who migrated, at different times, across the Bering Strait and along the Aleutian Island

FIGURE 4–2
Negroids of: above left, southern Sudan; above right, Ethiopia; bottom, Jamaica. (All, United Nations)

60

FIGURE 4–3

Mongoloids of: left, China (Mutual Security Agency); right, Indonesia (Eugene Gordon); bottom, the Cheyenne nation, western North America (Robin Engh, Photo Researchers)

chain; the Eskimo is considered the more recent arrival (Fig. 4–3).

The Caucasoid race is most clearly discernible in Europe, where three principal subdivisions are commonly recognized: Nordic, Alpine, and Mediterranean. The Nordics, providing the image of the typical Scandinavian, are blue-eyed and light skinned, with wavy to curly blond hair, narrow noses, and thin lips. This physical type is representative of Scandinavia, the Low Countries, northern Germany, and Britain; but it is not the sole type in any of these areas. Long histories of migrating invaders have brought with them many other physical character-

istics; thus, while predominately Nordic, these areas are genetically complex.

The Alpines are a physically stockier group than the Nordics, with straight to wavy brown hair, darker eyes, and broader heads. As their name implies, their area of greatest concentration is in central Europe, with an extension west across France and east toward central Asia. The Mediterranean Caucasoids occupy most of the Mediterranean basin from Portugal to the Middle East, and thence onward to India. They are distinguished from the other branches of the stock by larger noses, darker eyes, skin colors ranging from olive to light brown, and straight to wavy brown or black hair. In India, particularly in the south, the skin coloring is often very dark (Fig. 4–4).

None of these Caucasoid groups is "pure." In the core area occupied by each group the physical characteristics by which it is known may be in the majority, but they become increasingly mixed with the characteristics of other groups as one ventures outward toward the periphery. Thus there are many brown-haired, brown-eyed Scandinavians with light-brown skin — quite in contrast with the features of the typical Nordic person.

Since the beginning of the sixteenth century the Caucasoid race has spread itself widely over the world, partly through the large-scale colonizations undertaken by various European nations, and partly through the overseas migration of great numbers of European citizens on an individual basis. As a consequence, Caucasoids, mainly Nordics, comprise a large proportion of the population of places very distant from Europe — Australia and New Zealand, for example; in the United States and Canada, closer European settlements, they are the basic matrix of the population. Although Nordics predominate among the Caucasoid peoples of the United States, the country's population includes significant numbers of Mediterraneans, chiefly in the urban areas of the northeastern states, and a considerable population of Alpines, in the same areas and in the Middle West. Large numbers of Mediterraneans also live in the eastern and southern parts of Brazil, where they are the major Caucasoids and have been intermingled with Negroids from Africa. Argentina is another South American country occupied largely by Mediterraneans, with scatterings of Alpines and Nordics in the cities. Populations in the rest of Latin America are a blend of Mediterranean Caucasoids and native Mongoloids (American Indians) — a mixture termed *Mestizo*, or "mixed blood."

The eastward expansion of the Soviet Union has sent great numbers of Alpines from the European Soviet far into Asiatic Siberia, where they have settled on the agricultural lands of the steppes and in the cities along the Trans-Siberian Railway. They present a striking contrast to the indigenous inhabitants of that Mongoloid source area.

Unclassified Groups

Many groups of people do not fit into the classification of major races presented here, and thus in most studies are appended to it as unclassified populations. One such group is the Khoisan people of southern Africa; others in the same area include Bushmen and the Namas, or Hottentots. A short people with yellow-gray skin, the Khoisan have many other Mongoloid traits: pronounced development of the epicanthic eyefold, high cheekbones, V-shaped faces with small pointed chins, and a high incidence of the Oriental birth-patch (a highly pigmented patch of skin at the base of the spine, conspicuous at birth but disappearing in early childhood). Khoisan hair, on the other hand, grows in "peppercorns" (tiny, tight, spirals

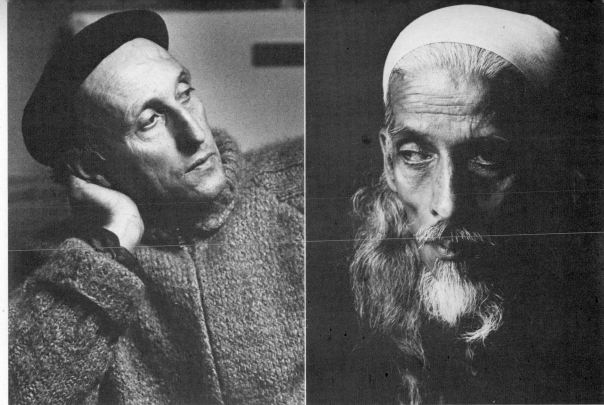

FIGURE 4-4

Caucasoids of: left, France (Mark Antman); right, India (Alan Keler, EPA); bottom, Saudi Arabia (Standard Oil Co., N.J.)

of hair separated by bare scalp), and the women exhibit pronounced steatopygy (storage of fat in the buttocks); neither of these traits is associated with any Mongoloid group. The Khoisan formerly occupied nearly all of southern Africa, but were first pushed southward by Bantu invaders and then displaced and partly absorbed by recent European settlers. They remain in a relatively pure form in Namibia (South West Africa). Many theories have been advanced as to the origin of these peoples, but none being conclusive, their place in any racial classification is still uncertain.

The place of the Australian aborigines is equally confusing. A very dark-skinned people with Caucasoid facial features, they have been called Australoid, or "Archaic

Caucasoid,'' by some authorities. Among these are those who account for the aborigines by hypothesizing that a Caucasoid group found its way into Australia and absorbed a small Negroid population that had preceded them—when the first modern Europeans visited Tasmania, the island south of Australia, its inhabitants were dark-skinned peoples.

Languages

Languages are one of the most vital aspects of culture, for they are the means by which ideas and concepts are transmitted from generation to generation and from group to group, the medium through which much of human experience is preserved, transferred, and expanded. Each language is a group of sounds and symbols; it may or may not be written, and may even include body movements or gestures (Fig. 4–5).

While repetition tends to stabilize elements of a language, use also allows a language to be a dynamic entity, changing with the times and conditions. Commonly, too, the implementation of a language varies considerably from region to region and from one social level to another in a given area. Such variations represent *dialects* and usually involve differences in pronunciation, grammar, and choice of words. The English language, for example, adapted liberally throughout the world, is even spoken variously in different parts of Great Britain, where it is represented by such dialects as London Cockney, Yorkshire, and Scottish.

History indicates that spoken languages preceded their written versions, and even today a large number of people speak languages that either have no written form or have acquired one only recently through the

FIGURE 4–5

A Bushman storyteller and his audience. (N. R. Farbman, *Life* Magazine, © Time, Inc.)

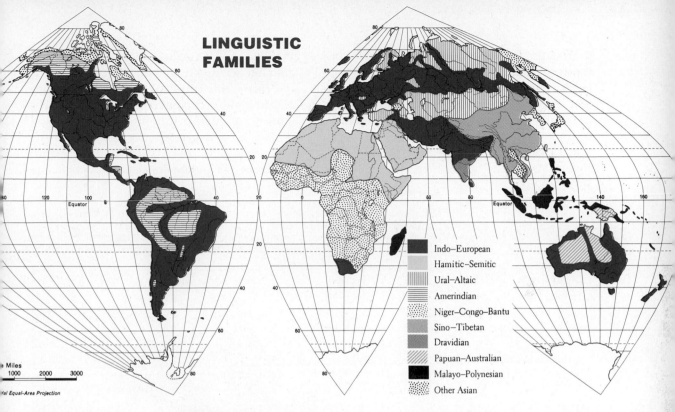

LINGUISTIC FAMILIES

Legend:
- Indo–European
- Hamitic–Semitic
- Ural–Altaic
- Amerindian
- Niger–Congo–Bantu
- Sino–Tibetan
- Dravidian
- Papuan–Australian
- Malayo–Polynesian
- Other Asian

Miles
1000 2000 3000

Val Equal-Area Projection

FIGURE 4–6

The Indo-European languages serve about 49 percent of the world's people, and the Sino-Tibetan, about 24 percent; each of the other major linguistic families accounts for less than 5 percent.

efforts of foreign linguists or missionaries. Berber, the language of some ten million Caucasoid inhabitants of North Africa, is written only in an Arabic script, never having generated a written form of its own. No Negroid African group has created a written language, and only among the Aztecs and Mayas of Mexico did there exist any semblance of a written language in pre-Columbian America.

Linguistic Families

Languages change gradually through time, and, in many cases, a dialect diverges so far from the parent tongue as to eventually constitute a separate language. But even when so separated, a language and its dialects can usually be related through a comparison of their vocabularies, grammatical structures, and distinctive sounds. A group of languages so interrelated is called a *linguistic family*.

The several thousand languages used by today's general populations can be variously grouped into linguistic families. For the purposes of this geographical survey, they can be divided conveniently into nine language families—Indo-European, Ural-Altaic, Sino-Tibetan, Malayo-Polynesian, Papuan-Australian, Hamitic-Semitic, Niger–Congo–Bantu, Amerindian, and Dravidian—and a group of miscellaneous Asian languages (Fig. 4–6).

Indo-European Languages. The Indo-European family includes nearly all of the languages of Europe and the Americas, the Soviet Union, Iran, and a good part of the Indian subcontinent—in all, the languages of nearly one-half the world's people. The western region of Europe alone has generated several language groupings; chief among them are the Celtic, Romance, and Germanic language groups (Fig. 4–7).

The Celtic languages, remnants of a language that once prevailed over much of France, Spain, and Britain, are now spoken by only a relatively few people in the westernmost extremities of Great Britain, Ireland, and France. The last speaker of *Cornish,* the

FIGURE 4–7

Major languages of the European nations. Although the staunch advocacy of one language is a common expression of nationalism, attempts to draw language boundaries in exact conformity with national political boundaries are all but futile. Such maps as this on language distribution are necessarily generalizations.

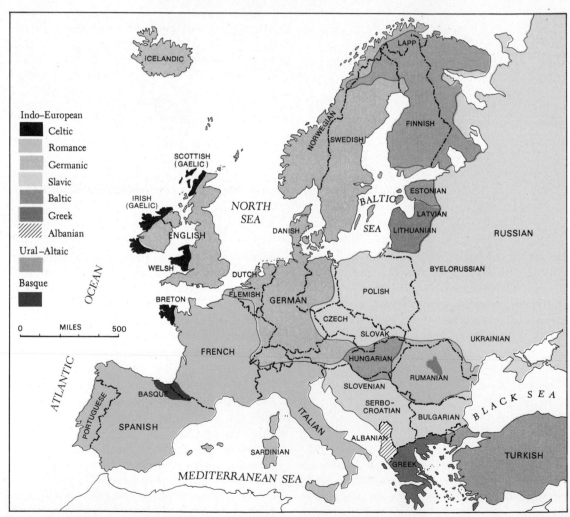

ancient Celtic language of southwestern England, died in 1840; and the last speaker of *Manx,* once the dominant language on the Isle of Man, died early in the present century. *Scottish Gaelic* is limited to northwestern Scotland and the adjacent islands of the Hebrides; and *Erse,* or *Irish Gaelic,* while the official language in the Republic of Ireland, is commonly spoken only in the western part of that country. *Cymric,* or *Welsh,* is spoken chiefly in remote areas of Wales, but it has acquired some prominence recently as part of a Welsh nationalist movement. And in Brittany, the northwesternmost peninsula of France, *Breton* is being gradually replaced by French.

The other major Indo-European language groups are now much more widespread than the Celtic. The Romance group, based upon Latin used two thousand years ago within the Roman Empire (and today as the official language of the Roman Catholic Church), includes Spanish, Portuguese, French, Italian, and Rumanian, the languages of most of southern Europe and virtually all of Latin America. The Germanic languages include German, Swedish, Norwegian, Danish, Dutch, and English, which is the primary language of such former British territories as the United States, Canada, Australia, and New Zealand and the "second language" of much of the world's remaining landmass. Although classified as Germanic, modern English is actually an admixture of Germanic and Romance languages. The English language has not been purely Germanic since A.D. 1066, when, with the Norman conquest of Britain, a large number of French words began to find their way into the vocabulary.

The eastern region of Europe has generated an even larger number of languages than the western region—among them Greek, Albanian, Baltic, and the very large group of Slavic languages. The latter dominate most of eastern Europe, and include such languages as Czech, Slovak, Slovene, Serbo-Croatian, Bulgarian, Macedonian, Polish, Byelorussian, Ukrainian, and Russian. Today the dominant language of the whole Soviet Union, Russian is thus also Asian, having been diffused eastward across central Siberia to the Pacific.

The major southwest Asian extensions of the Indo-European languages are the Iranic and Indic language groups. Included within the Iranic is Persian, a medieval language spoken throughout Iran in a number of local dialects and a large number of minor languages spoken by rather isolated societies in the Caucasus Mountains and in mountainous areas of Iran, Afghanistan, Baluchistan, northern Syria, and eastern Turkey. Most of the Indic languages are obvious derivatives of Sanskrit, the language of northern India in ancient times and very likely the source of *all* the Indo-European languages. In India today, a great number of languages are used—a fact that poses a major problem in the unification and administration of the country. *Hindi* is the official and by far the leading language of India; yet it is the language of only one-third of the population, mainly those who live in the north central states of Uttar Predesh, Madhya Predesh, and Bihar (Fig. 4–8). Its official status is resented by many Indians who speak one of India's twelve other major languages, most of whom have no command of Hindi. Among these tongues are *Urdu,* a Hindi dialect much used in parts of northwest India and in nearby Pakistan, and *Bengali,* the major language of Bangladesh and parts of eastern India.

Ural-Altaic Languages. The Ural-Altaic languages apparently originated in Siberia, but were carried into eastern Europe with the great migrations of the *Völkerwanderung.* Prominent among them is the Finno-Ugric

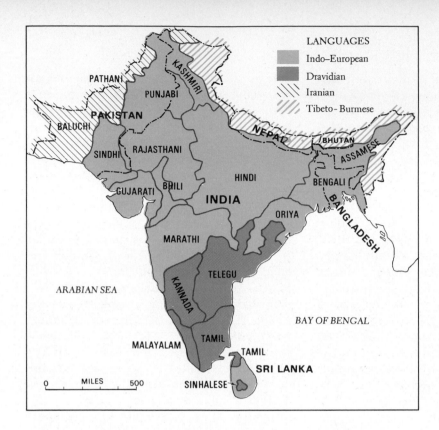

FIGURE 4–8

The languages of India. Since 1947 India has made major changes in its state boundaries in order to have them reflect the nation's pattern of languages.

group, which includes *Magyar,* the Ugrian language carried far into eastern Europe when the Magyars invaded Hungary at the end of the ninth century; and it still exists as a linguistic enclave surrounded by Romance, Germanic, and Slavic languages. Other major languages of the group are *Finnish,* spoken in Finland; its close relative *Karelian,* used in parts of the Soviet Union adjacent to Finland; and *Estonian,* spoken in the area across the Gulf of Finland to the south. The Lapps, reindeer-herding nomads of the mountains of Norway and Sweden, and of the tundras of northern Finland and the northwestern Soviet, also speak a Finno-Ugric language.

Since it is impractical here to describe all the languages of the world, Figure 4–9 gives a general classification of the major languages and their principal countries of use. The world map in Figure 4–6 should also be consulted at this point, for it portrays the spatial arrangement of modern languages.

Bilinguality

Bilinguality, the ability to speak two languages with nearly equal facility, occurs in several types of situations. For example: the language group finding itself under the political, economic, or cultural domination of another may retain its own language for use in private conversation and correspondence while employing the host tongue in broader social contacts and governmental activities. Such is the case in Quebec, a French-speaking province in otherwise English-speaking Canada. So strong is the French feeling and influence that Canada is officially bilingual, with even the postage stamps employing the two languages.

In other cases, two languages share linguistic dominance in the country. Such is the case in South Africa, where English and Afrikaans (a form of Dutch) are both widespread and exist without exclusive terri-

INDO-EUROPEAN
English:	United Kingdom, United States, Canada, New Zealand, Australia, Ireland
Spanish:	Spain, Latin America
Hindi:	North-central India
Russian:	Soviet Union
Bengali:	Bangladesh
Portuguese:	Portugal, Brazil
German:	West Germany, East Germany, Austria, Switzerland

French:	France, Belgium, Switzerland, Canada
Italian:	Italy, Switzerland
Ukrainian:	Ukraine (USSR)
Marathi:	Maharashtra (India)
Polish:	Poland
Punjabi:	Punjab (India)
Rajasthani	Rajasthan (India)
Sinhalese:	South Sri Lanka

HAMITIC-SEMITIC
Arabic:	North Africa, Middle East
Berber:	North Africa

URAL-ALTAIC
Finnish/Komi/Samoyed/Yakut:	Northern Eurasia
Tatar/Kazakh/Khalka/Turkaman:	Central Asia
Hungarian (Magyar):	Hungary, Central Rumania
Turkish:	Turkey

AMERINDIAN
Athabascan/Algonquin:	Northern North America
Arawak/Carib/Quechua/Aymara:	Amazonia

NIGER-CONGO-BANTU
Mandingo/Yoruba/Mossi/Ibo:	Western Africa
Kanuri:	Central Africa
Fang/Bulu/Congo/Swahili/Mbundu/ Makua/Bushman/Hottentot/Zulu:	Southern Africa

SINO-TIBETAN
Chinese Mandarin:	China, Taiwan, Southeast Asia
Cantonese:	South China
Fukienese:	South China
Tibetan:	Tibet

DRAVIDIAN
Tamil:	Tamil Nadu (India), North Sri Lanka
Telegu:	Andhra Praedesh (India)
Kannada:	Mysore (India)

PAPUAN-AUSTRALIAN
Australian:	Papua, Central Australia

MALAYO-POLYNESIAN
Indonesian:	Indonesia
Malagasy:	Malagasy Republic

OTHER ASIAN LANGUAGES
Japanese/Korean/Cambodian/Lao/Eskimo

FIGURE 4–9

Selected languages in the world's major language families and some of their territorial occurrences.

tories. The regional separation of national languages is found in Belgium, for example, where Flemish, a Germanic language closely akin to Dutch, is spoken in the northern half of the country, and Walloon, a French dialect, prevails in the south; it occurs also in Sri Lanka (Ceylon), where Tamil is spoken in the northern third of the country and Sinhalese in the southern two-thirds.

Even if it is too small a portion of the total population to secure official bilinguality, a minority group may still persist in the use of its language in a local area, thus creating an unofficial bilinguality. The Cajuns of Louisiana, for instance, speak a *patois* (dialect) of French that has nearly the same currency as English in their areas and that influences speech in other areas of the state as well.

Two countries are officially trilingual. In Switzerland, German, French, and Italian are used, but in three different regions; and in Namibia, Afrikaans, English, and German are thoroughly intermixed.

Lingua Francas

In some parts of the world, so many different languages are spoken within a relatively small area that traders and others who travel from place to place can seldom become fluent in all of them. Consequently, a *lingua franca*, or common language, sometimes develops; it is usually not an existing language but rather one composed anew of fragments of several tongues. In the southwest Pacific, from southern China to Samoa, Pidgin English is the prevailing language of trade (*pidgin* being a Chinese corruption of the English word *business*); it consists chiefly of English words that are badly mispronounced and arranged in Chinese word order. A similar jargon with a French base is widely used in parts of the southwest Pacific, where it was named *Bêche de mer* after a sea cucumber that is caught on the sea floor, dried in the sun, and exported to China and other countries in great numbers for use in Chinese cooking; it was the brisk trade in *Bêches de mer* between the Pacific isles and China that gave rise to the language.

In the gold-mining areas of South Africa, Bantu workers representing a dozen countries and scores of languages communicate with each other and with their European foremen in *Fanagalo*—a *lingua franca* in which English, Afrikaans, Portuguese, and Bantu words are combined in an essentially Bantu matrix. Similar languages have developed in the Caribbean—among them *Papiemento,* with a vocabulary borrowed from Spanish, French, Dutch, English, Carib Indian, and West African dialects; and in East Africa—most notably *Swahili,* which is composed of Arabic and Bantu words with a Bantu grammar.

Religions

Religion has become one of the most pervasive factors affecting social and political relationships. It can unite people of different languages and regions and it can help to bring about the alienation of neighbors who speak the same language. For some, values and priorities in all areas of life are governed, in varying degrees, by religious beliefs and taboos. And different religions often have very different sanctions on the same human activities. Thus Moslems eat no pork, and Hindus eat no beef; Jews refrain from labor on Saturday, and Christians refrain from labor on Sunday.

It is likely that religions have grown somewhat in response to the needs of human beings to have a place and purpose in the world and to transcend the frustrations and monotony of daily needs—individual and societal. Primitive tribal peoples worshipped many animate as well as inanimate objects: animals, the sun, and numerous images fashioned of stone and wood in both human and animal form. Such *animism* still prevails throughout much of central Africa, parts of Indonesia and Australia, interior Brazil and Peru, and in northern Siberia (Fig. 4–10).

But gradually in most areas, such direct nature-god worship has been transformed into more abstract worship and complex philosophies. The most advanced religious societies have also developed complex hierarchies to formalize the worship, guide the worshippers, and administer the faith's physical property.

Compared with its languages, the major religions of the contemporary world are relatively few in number. Five religions accommodate perhaps three-fifths of the world's four billion people (Fig. 4–11). Three of these five—Christianity, Judaism, and Islam (Moslem)—are *monotheistic* religions, for their doctrine contends that there is only one god; the others—Hinduism and Buddhism—are *polytheistic* religions, for their doctrine supports a belief in more than one god.

FIGURE 4–10

Animistic funeral dancers near a Dogon village in Sangha, Mali. (Eugene Gordon)

Monotheistic Religions

The major monotheistic religions, Christianity, Judaism, and Islam, all originated within the same small Middle East region: in arid and semiarid parts of Palestine, Jordan, and Syria (Christianity and Judaism) or in western Arabia (Islam) (Fig 4–12). In addition to this cradleland, they also share parts of the same religious tracts, such as the Old Testament. However, they still have many differences. For example, the Christians recognize Christ as the long-awaited Messiah, while the Jews recognize Christ as merely one of several prophets and await the true Messiah; the Moslems (Islams) also await the true Messiah but recognize Mohammed as the greatest of the prophets.

Since their place of origin is the arid environment of the Middle East, these three religions all have histories among the pastoral nomads and agrarian-herders of its barren steppe-lands. It is even quite possible that the monotheism of the religions was influenced by the harshness of these lands. They were demanding, and, in order to survive, their human inhabitants may have had need of a philosophy that stressed strength and discipline and provided strong leadership in their own image. Judaism, Christianity, and Islam are all decidedly patriarchal: in each, God is a male, the holiest followers are males, and women play only minor roles—circumstances that reflect the *pastoral nomadic societies* in which these religions developed.

All three monotheistic religions (and Buddhism as well) are traditionally dynamic,

having extended their influence far beyond their small bleak cradlelands. Christianity, born in Palestine, has spread over the world and is today the dominant religion in four of the six inhabited continents. Judaism, born in the same locale as Christianity, has taken hold in all the continents, even though its followers have seldom enjoyed the power or favor of rulers. And the followers of Islam have carried their religion from Arabia across North Africa, eastward through the Middle East, and far overseas into maritime southeastern Asia.

Christianity. With the preachings of the apostle Paul in Greece and Rome, Christianity passed out of its cradleland in Asia and into the lands of Europe. Christianity

FIGURE 4–11

The three major monotheistic religions comprise approximately 41.5 percent of the human population; and the two major polytheistic religions account for approximately 19 percent.

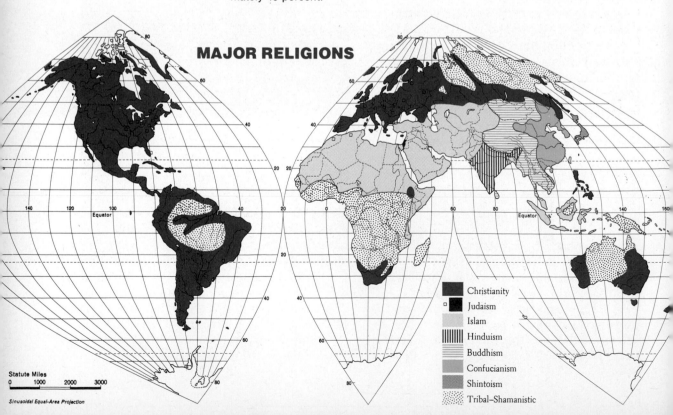

MAJOR RELIGIONS

Christianity
Judaism
Islam
Hinduism
Buddhism
Confucianism
Shintoism
Tribal–Shamanistic

Statute Miles
0   1000   2000   3000

Sinusoidal Equal-Area Projection

grew with Europe, and vice versa, and Europe has long since become the modern fountainhead of Christianity's three major subdivisions: Catholicism, Protestantism, and Eastern Orthodoxy (Fig. 4–13). *Catholicism* is dominant throughout most of western and central continental Europe, from beyond the English Channel to the Mediterranean to the Baltic Sea—in ten countries and adjoining country border areas. Catholicism also prevails in all the European-settled regions of Latin America and throughout French-speaking Canada (especially Quebec); and it is well represented in the northeastern, midwestern, and southwestern parts of the United States. As it has been for centuries, the Catholic Church is presided over by a Pope, who lives in Vatican City, an indepen-

dent territory within Italy's capital, Rome (Fig. 4–14).

In the early sixteenth century the German monk Martin Luther posted 95 theses attacking the established papal authority of the Roman Catholic Church. Luther protested that true Christianity lay not in a hierarchy headed by a Pope but in the humble layman's belief and direct communion with God. In the 1530s a strong German Lutheran Church was established; the Church of England had previously broken with the papacy, and many other dissident sects followed Luther's. Today, *Protestantism* is the dominant religion in central West Germany, East Germany, Denmark, the United Kingdom, and Scandinavia; and it has spread overseas to dominate the United States and most of

FIGURE 4–12

Cradlelands of the world's major religions.

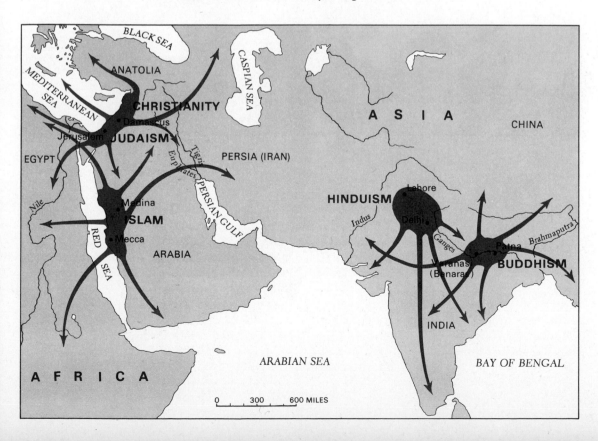

FIGURE 4–13

The dominant religious affiliations of European countries. (Modified from Karl Wenschow, *Weltatlas*.)

Canada, as well as to South Africa, Australia, and New Zealand.

The third largest branch of Christianity is the *Eastern Orthodox* Church. The Orthodox religion began in the Holy Land before there were any Christians in Rome, and its followers consider Jesus its founder. Constantine shifted the Roman Empire throne to Constantinople in A.D. 330; and thereafter Rome, headed by the Pope, and Constantinople, headed by its Patriarch, competed for converts. Seven centuries later they excommunicated each other, and the Great Schism began; it still persists. Today, while Roman Catholicism continues to dominate western Europe, the Eastern Orthodox religions have spread across all the Balkan countries, and the whole expanse of the Soviet Union.

FIGURE 4–14

The celebration of a Catholic mass. (*Ebony* Magazine)

Judaism. While the fundamental precepts of Judaism have not changed for thousands of years, new and differing views on the value of ritual and tradition give the religion its three subdivisions—Orthodox, Conservative, and Reform. Orthodox Judaism strictly observes all traditional Jewish laws and traditions; Conservative Judaism believes that the concept of revelation is open to "reasonably varied" interpretations; and Reform Judaism believes that each new generation has the right to accept or reject the traditions it inherits. Today, Judaism is well established in the new State of Israel and in many urban centers of the Middle East, North Africa, Europe, and the Americas (Fig. 4–15).

Islam. Islam is the youngest of the major religions, having emerged in the desert lands of western Arabia over 500 years after the death of Jesus. Its founder, Mohammed, explained himself as the best-informed of several prophets (among them Jesus), as a

FIGURE 4–15

The passing of the Torah, or written Jewish law, through a congregation. (Israeli Ministry of Tourism)

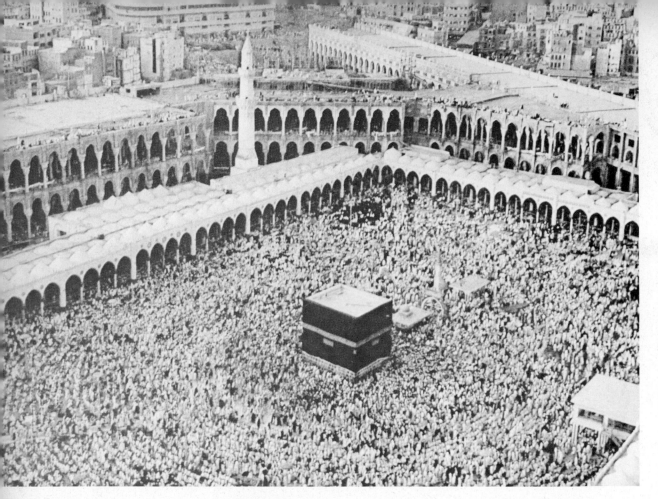

FIGURE 4–16

The Holy Mosque at Mecca, with thousands of devout Moslems performing the Tawaf, or circling ceremony, around the Ka'bah, the most sacred of all Islamic shrines. (Saudi Arabian Consulate)

common man through whose lips God spoke to the believers. Within a century after Mohammed's death (in A.D. 632), the Islamic influence extended from Gibraltar to the Himalayas. Today it spreads across northern Africa and the Middle East to South Asia's Pakistan and Bangladesh and has significant acceptance in northern India and the Malayo-Indonesian archipelago: from Morocco to the Malacca Straits. The teachings of Mohammed, reflecting aspects of Judaism and Christianity, comprise the Koran, the sacred text of the world's Moslems; Mecca, his home, is their holy city (Fig. 4–16).

Polytheistic Religions

Hinduism. Hinduism, the oldest contemporary religion and the dominant one in India, emerged in the broad fertile plains of the Ganges Valley of northern India, near the now sacred Ganges River (see Fig. 4–12). It has no known founder, no hierarchy, and no rigid moral code. A polytheistic religion, Hinduism embraces a great number of gods and goddesses and many lesser deities; they occur in human form and as animals, and others are resplendent combinations of human and beast or humans with many limbs (Fig. 4–17). The best known of the more recent Hindu leaders include Shankara (ninth century A.D.) and Ramanuja (eleventh century).

During its long and loosely structured history, Hinduism has suffered the rise of many splinter faiths. In the sixth century B.C., the sect known as *Buddhism* was founded in protest against the established Hindu caste system and adherence to ancient Hindu laws and doctrines. Other derivatives of Hinduism include *Jainism* (also sixth century B.C.) and *Sikhism* (sixteenth century A.D.). As it has grown stronger through the centuries, Hinduism has absorbed most of its splinter faiths and their reforms. However, it has not been a dynamic religion in other respects; for example, it has not spread to neighboring or distant lands and societies. By far the majority of the followers of Hinduism are located within a single national and cultural unit, India. Even within Asia other Hindu territories are few in number; and like the small island of Bali, east of Java, such areas exist in a vast sea of Islam.

Buddhism. When disagreement with the practices of Hinduism led to the founding of Buddhism in the sixth century B.C., the Hindus responded by appointing the leader of the new movement, philosopher Gautama Buddha, to the Hindu pantheon and by accepting many of the Buddhist protests. Consequently, Buddhism languished for a time as a movement without a cause. But Gautama Buddha continued his teachings, and, after his death, in the early fifth century B.C., they spread rapidly across India and were accepted by a majority of the Indian people, most of them formerly Hindus. Later, a reformed and rejuvenated Hinduism absorbed Indian Buddhism — and thus the Buddhist life-cycle in India came full circle.

But by then Buddhism, unlike Hinduism, had spread extensively within lands beyond India. In the third century B.C. Buddhist missionaries carried the faith to Sri Lanka, where it became the dominant religion; and, in the same way, it reached China by the first century A.D., Korea by the fourth century, Japan and Burma by the sixth century, and Tibet by the seventh century (Figs. 4–18 and 4–19).

FIGURE 4–17

A statue of Siva, the god representing destruction in the great Hindu triad of gods. Brahma, worshipped as the Creator, and Vishnu, the Preserver or Renewer, complete the triad, which is known as the Trimurti. (Leslie Holzer)

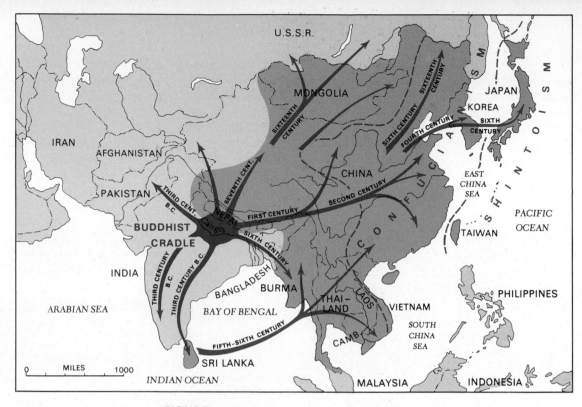

FIGURE 4–18

The early diffusion of Buddhism—from India throughout several countries of southern and eastern Asia.

FIGURE 4–19

The altar of a Buddhist temple in Chieng Mai, Thailand. Its dominant statue is a large representation of Gautama Buddha. (Steve Hershey)

Two schools of Buddhist doctrine have developed through the millennia. Hinayana Buddhism, the "Lesser Vehicle," exalts individual austerity and has its contemporary following mainly in Asia's southeastern countries—Sri Lanka, Burma, Thailand, Laos, Cambodia, North Vietnam, and South Vietnam. Mahayana Buddhism, the "Greater Vehicle," stands for individual salvation by faith and has its largest following in eastern and central Asia—in China, Taiwan, Mongolia, Tibet, Korea, and Japan. In several of these countries, local philosophies, such as Taoism, Confucianism, and Shintoism, blend with Buddhism, giving this religion a slightly different tone in different parts of the Eastern world.

Secularism

In many societies today, there is a drift away from organized religion on the part of a sizable segment of the population. Usually, this noninvolvement is on a purely personal basis, often reflecting the preoccupation of the individual with material concerns. However, in the Soviet Union and in China, Marxism and Communist ideology have made the minimization of religion a matter of national policy.

Early Culture Hearths

Many of the cultures the world has known have been very short-lived and have influenced only a handful of people. Others have been more long-lasting but equally localized; those that persist today are often described as "curious, unique, and exotic" by travel brochures offering expensive "journeys into yesterday." Some cultures, on the other hand, have been widespread and highly influential; and, by enduring through centuries and even millennia, have become the basis of modern civilizations. Each of these cultures originated in a particular region and, while it may have since spread widely over the surface of the earth, is still associated primarily with that source region, or *culture hearth*. The Old World comprises several such culture hearths, most notably: Mesopotamia, Egypt, Palestine, Crete and Greece, the Indus Valley, and North China. Within the New World there are two of comparable significance: Middle America and the Andes (Fig. 4–20). These areas have certain features in common: each has long been either a focus of trading or a crossroads of trade routes; each is, or lies close to, an area of early plant and animal domestication; and each possesses a climate that presents a certain challenge (a pronounced alternation of wet and dry seasons, a need for irrigation, a need to store food for use in a cool season), which in turn fosters planning for the future and organized group activity.

Old World Hearths

Mesopotamia. Mesopotamia, "the land between the rivers," is situated between the Tigris and the Euphrates rivers, in modern Iraq. In ancient times in the adjacent hilly lands to the northeast, a number of plants were domesticated, among them: wild grasses that evolved into wheat, barley, oats, and rye; legumes that were developed into peas, beans, and lentils; several kinds of nuts and such fruits as apples, peaches, pears, plums, cherries, and grapes; and a number of

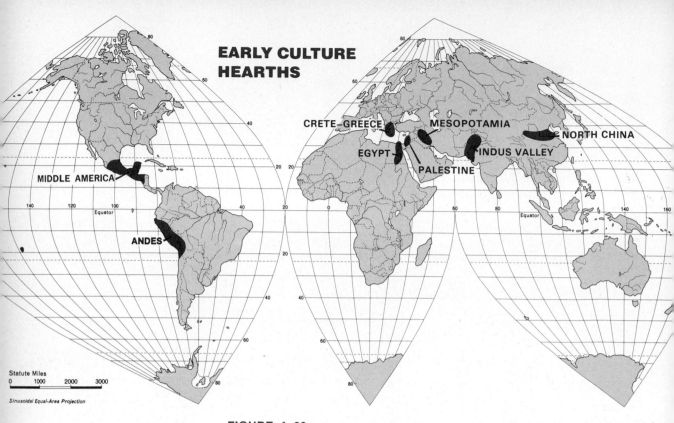

EARLY CULTURE HEARTHS

CRETE–GREECE

MESOPOTAMIA

NORTH CHINA

EGYPT

INDUS VALLEY

PALESTINE

MIDDLE AMERICA

ANDES

Statute Miles
0   1000   2000   3000

Sinusoidal Equal-Area Projection

FIGURE 4–20

Each of the eight areas considered among the world's early culture hearths was, by nature, a center of agriculture or trade.

root crops. The animals domesticated in the region include cattle, sheep, goats, and pigs.

With a reliable food source thus under their direct control, some human groups in Mesopotamia were able to give up their nomadic hunting existences and become sedentary farmers, living in a fixed abode and tending their crops and herds. Thus as early as 10,000 years ago, many of the area's people lived in agricultural villages.

These people were not isolated in their land. From time to time, barbaric, militarily powerful peoples attacked and conquered Mesopotamia. At other times, victorious Mesopotamian armies brought home large groups of conquered peoples, to serve as slaves. And continuously over the centuries, outside groups migrated into the area, attracted by its food supply. Each of these groups—conquering armies, captured slaves, and peaceful migrants—adopted the Mesopotamian culture and added to it technique, language, and philosophy from their own.

Out of all this a civilization was eventually forged—the first great civilization in the world. The first written language probably evolved in Mesopotamia—a *cuneiform* script with wedge-shaped or arrowhead characters, usually engraved into clay tablets (Fig. 4–21). There the first multistoried buildings were constructed, and communities with public buildings and organized street patterns first appeared. This civilization persisted through three millennia, in spite of invasion and conquest, linguistic and ethnic change, and economic transformation.

From this early culture hearth, the most ancient center of civilization, innumerable cultural traits were passed on to other peoples. This transfer was accomplished in many ways. The conquest of other lands by Mesopotamian armies, the migration of Mesopotamian civilians into other countries, and, above all, the movements of traders from country to country spread both the material culture and the ideologies of Mesopotamia to near and distant places. By 3000 B.C., aspects of Mesopotamian culture had been diffused to the southeast into southern Iran, to the northeast into Central Asia, westward across the Anatolian Plateau of Turkey to the Aegean Sea and on to Greece, by way of Syria and Lebanon to the Mediterranean, and southwestward across Palestine into Egypt.

Egypt. In contrast to Mesopotamia, ancient Egypt was somewhat protected from invading armies by its vast surrounding reaches of desert. It developed a strong and highly ritualistic culture that resisted all change for literally thousands of years. One element of this culture was a written language composed of *hieroglyphics,* or pictorial symbols. These were carved on the rocky walls of buildings, monuments, and tombs or were written on papyrus, a form of paper produced from a plant that grows abundantly along the Nile (Fig. 4–22).

Today, ancient Egypt is best known through its massive architectural constructions and statuary: the Sphinx and the pyramids, the temple of Karnak, the tombs of the Valley of the Kings, and the massive carvings of Abu Simbel. Because of the enduring nature of the rock from which they were made and the aridity of the climate, such structures have been beautifully preserved. They are not representative of most construction in ancient Egypt, however. The dwellings of ordinary people were usually made of a hard-

FIGURE 4–21

A Babylonian boundary stone (thirteenth to tenth century B.C.) that bears examples of *cuneiform* writing. (© British Museum)

ened mud much like the adobe used by Indians of the southwestern United States; these structures have succumbed to wind and rain. What is known of the life of the people has been learned from the paintings, stone carvings, and hieroglyphics that graced their places of worship and the homes of their leaders, and from the objects buried with them in tombs.

Ancient Egypt was visited occasionally by outsiders, mainly traders, who carried elements of its culture back to their homelands. The influence of this civilization is

FIGURE 4–22

Hieroglyphics, or pictorial writing, on pillars of an ancient temple at Karnak in southern Egypt. (Courtesy TWA)

thus detectable in contemporaneous and subsequent cultures of Palestine, the Middle East, Crete and Greece, and Rome.

Palestine. In many regards—physical geography, ethnic groups, historical developments—the Palestinian culture hearth was more complex than either the Mesopotamian or the Egyptian. Palestine, known also as Israel, the Land of Canaan, and the Holy Land, comprises a narrow strip connecting Mesopotamia and Egypt; it is hemmed in on the west by the Mediterranean Sea and on the east by the Arabian deserts. Through it, over thousands of years, has passed an endless procession of traders, nomads, armies, and whole nations. Its inhabitants have been conquered by several groups of outsiders, each affecting the area's landscape, genetics, customs, and ideologies.

Unlike Mesopotamia and Egypt, Palestine is not, and never has been, a fertile land easily capable of large-scale agriculture. Its great importance in ancient times reflected its position on the land bridge between Asia and Africa, not natural wealth or fertility. The principal "port-land" of the Middle East, it was a place for the cross-fertilization of cultures, a land of contrasts (maritime versus land-bound, sedentary versus nomadic, agricultural versus pastoral, conservative versus liberal) and endless change. Consequently, the culture it produced became the very antithesis of the unchanging Egyptian culture.

Thus it is not surprising that it was in Palestine that the world seems to have had its first town (as distinct from village), and that that town was founded at least in part on trade. By 6850 B.C., Jericho, located in the Rift Valley near the northern end of the Dead

Sea, was a flourishing settlement, existing partly on intensive agriculture and partly on trade in locally produced salt, sulphur, and asphalt.

In the following millennia, a regional settlement pattern evolved based upon a number of fortified towns and ports, each developing on a spot with natural protection (such as a hilltop), with defensive walls of stone, and houses of mud. While the walls persisted, defying invaders and the elements alike, the mud houses melted down in the rains or were destroyed in the invasions; at some later date, new houses (also of mud) were constructed on the ruins of the old, only to be eventually destroyed themselves. Thus layer accumulated upon layer (in most cases at least a dozen of them), each representing a different period of peace. Today, such sites can be clearly seen, even from a distance, as conspicuous mounds of earth rising well above their surroundings and disclosing, upon close inspection, shards of pottery, fragments of bone, and an occasional bead. This is a *tell,* an artificial hill where there was once, for a thousand years or more, a thriving community.

All the ancient empires of the Middle East exerted influence upon Palestine. Mesopotamia and Egypt both controlled it at times. So did the Hittites, a people of the Anatolian Plateau, whose capital was near the site of Ankara, in modern Turkey; the Assyrians of Kurdistan, with their capital at Ninevah across the Tigris in modern Iraq; the Babylonians, whose chief city was on the Euphrates south of Baghdad; and the Persians, from present-day Iran, who controlled all the area from India to Ethiopia, then the greater part of the "known world." And in addition to direct military and administrative control, these and other nations exerted influence upon Palestine through trade and commerce.

Many commodities were produced in Palestine for shipment to markets near and far—wines and figs, and olives that provided food and oil for cooking, cosmetics, and lamps. But most of the products traded there were produced elsewhere and used elsewhere. Goods brought from other lands, by camel caravan and by sailing vessel, were sorted, reworked, and sold in Palestine, then shipped away to still other destinations. Ports were developed by various groups, but especially by the Phoenicians, who carried on commerce with all parts of the known world. From the south, from Ethiopia, Sudan, the Red Sea and adjacent parts of Arabia, and from Egypt, they brought slaves, pearls, ivory, gold, gum arabic, frankincense, myrrh, perfumes, and cotton cloth. From the east, from Babylonia by camel caravan and even from India to Babylonia by sea, came handicrafts in metal, leather, and cloth, as well as pearls and exotic spices. Afoot from the north came herds of cattle and horses, flocks of sheep and goats, and caravans transporting wines, wool and woolen cloth, and garments. From the shores of the Mediterranean came a rich purple dye made from a type of snail, as well as wine and olive oil, and copper ore from Cyprus and timber from the mountains of Lebanon, Cyprus, Crete, and Greece. And from far away Cornwall, the southwesternmost extremity of England, by way of the Atlantic and Straits of Gibraltar, came tin ore that was mixed with copper to produce bronze, the wonder metal of the pre–Iron Age.

Many cultures developed in this area, ran their course, and disappeared. Many languages were spoken, and many gods were worshipped. The Judaic religion and the Christian religion both had their origins in this area of the world.

Crete and Greece. Because of their geographical proximity, and because their developments represent an historical continuum, it is logical to consider Crete and Greece together in this discussion. An amphibious landscape dominates each of these areas: long, rugged promontories separate deep, sheltered bays, and the sea is dotted with islands; on a clear day, even in the midst of the sea, land is always in sight. This setting inspired its early inhabitants to maritime interests: there was always a new land beckoning; always a cove to run to for safety, with a sandy strand at its head on which to beach a boat; always warm navigable waters; and always fish to be sought as food. With three continents contributing to its growth, this was a place, too, for the development of a new civilization.

At its peak, from 2000 to 1400 B.C., Cretan (or Minoan) civilization was on a level with the greatest periods of ancient Egypt or Mesopotamia. Its craftsmen produced exquisite pottery, glazed earthenware beads, finely wrought gold jewelry, and polished stone vases of flawless white marble. Architects and builders created great open palaces that could receive the sea breeze on hot summer days; these structures were equipped with running water and sewers and decorated with wall paintings whose elegant colors and flowing lines portrayed graceful animals and children amidst fields of flowers. There were no fortifications; the towns and the palaces were open and unprotected, perhaps because of the relative isolation of the island and the strong naval power of the government. The city associated with the chief palace, Knossos, probably included as many as 100,000 persons—a very large number considering the small size of the island of Crete, its even smaller area of arable land, and the difficulties of transporting food for so many people by sailing vessel and primitive land conveyances. The island's system of writing (still undeciphered) was both inscribed on clay tablets and written in ink on clay and on papyrus.

Cretan civilization came to an abrupt end about 1400 B.C., when the island of Thera (also called Santorin), about 75 miles north of Crete, literally exploded in a vast volcanic eruption. Knossos was instantly destroyed, very likely by the resultant tidal wave and fall of ash.

Well before catastrophe overwhelmed Crete, a strong culture had developed on the mainland of southern Greece, at Mycenae in the area called the Peloponnesus. It was a military culture and thus a marked contrast to the peaceful, artistic Minoan civilization. Its cities were hilltop fortresses; its people the aggressive warriors immortalized centuries later by Homer in his two epic poems, the *Iliad* and the *Odyssey*. At its peak, this culture held sway over all of Greece and the Aegean; but like many another civilization, it eventually mellowed, weakened, and was overthrown by an invading force.

The invaders were the Dorians, nomads from the Balkans who swept southward into Greece about 1100 B.C. They were acquainted with methods of smelting iron, and their weapons of that metal were far superior to the bronze ones of the Mycenaeans. Their attack initiated a period of chaos that lasted for three hundred years, during which time Greece came to be divided into many small, autonomous city-states. Some were Dorian, having been taken over by the invaders; others remained Mycenaean, having either resisted the invaders or worked out a shaky peace with them. In addition, there were Ionian settlements, colonies founded on the Aegean islands by former Mycenaeans.

These city-states would very likely have remained isolated and independent rather indefinitely had not a common enemy appeared. In 480 B.C. a large Persian army attacked the Greek mainland and occupied Athens. Faced with annihilation, some of the city-states unified to combat the Persians and, in 479 B.C., defeated them. Following this unification, Greek (or Hellenic) civilization achieved its Golden Age.

During the brief fifty years of their Golden Age, the Greeks attained one of the highest levels of culture the world has experienced. A new Athens was built on the ruins of the old. The Acropolis, long the citadel above the city, became the religious center; and it remains an architectural model to this day (Fig. 4–23). Knowledge and learning were revered, and the philosopher ranked in importance with the priest, the governor, and the financier. Poetry, literature, drama, sculpture, logic, and science flourished; and democracy, which had its beginnings in Greece, continued—still greatly qualified, however, by the denial of the franchise to slaves and to women.

Seeking to control trade and ease the overpopulation of their homeland, the Greeks established colonies in all parts of the Mediterranean, from Spain to Egypt and the far reaches of the Black Sea. From them, they imported grain and timber and ores; to them, they exported wine, olive oil, and pottery, jewelry, and carvings. And most important of all, they exported their laws, philosophy, and ideals. In this way, Greek culture became the foundation of Roman civilization, and later of European civilization, and eventually all the Western world.

Indus Valley. Pakistan, the country that comprises the Indus Valley, is a fairly new political entity, but its cultural roots lie deep in antiquity. The recent discoveries of the ancient cities of Mohenjo-Daro, in the lower valley, and Harappa, in the upper valley, suggest that, between about 5000 and 1500 B.C., a highly developed civilization

FIGURE 4–23

The Acropolis, Athens, Greece. This flat-topped hill, once a fortified retreat, bears the remains of temples built in the fifth century B.C. Its most prominent structure, the Parthenon, has inspired such relatively recent constructions as the Lincoln Memorial. (Courtesy TWA)

flourished in this arid but once fertile north-western part of the Indian subcontinent; this was a pre-Aryan culture, created by a people whose name is not now known. Mohenjo-Daro lies buried 40 feet below the sandy plains of the Sind Desert, and attempts to excavate it were first made over 30 years ago. They have now been halted, by order of the Pakistan government, because groundwaters rising in the diggings threaten the mud bricks of the buried structures; it is feared that, if the excavation continues before the water recedes, parts of Mohenjo-Daro may be lost forever. The portions of the city uncovered thus far include wide aligned streets with elaborate drainage systems and multi-story buildings with spacious courtyards.

The people of this ancient civilization apparently worked in bronze and utilized an alphabet, which has not yet been deciphered but seems to have influenced many of the languages of Asia and Europe. Sumerian seals of terra cotta found in the excavations of Mohenjo-Daro and Harappa are strong evidence that the Indus Valley people traded with peoples of Mesopotamia. Exactly why the civilization of the cities came to an end about 1500 B.C. is not known, but the decline and fall of the civilization may have been prompted by the invasions of Aryan nomads from southwest Asia—ancestors of present-day Hindus. The Aryans did adopt much of the religion of the Indus people, a religion that is thought to be the basis for modern Hinduism.

North China. Around 1500 B.C.—about the time of the decline of the Indus Valley civilization—another civilization arose in the valley of the Yellow River (Huang Ho), in North China. Like the Mesopotamian and Indus peoples before them, the North China people built large cities, with palaces of wood; one such site has been excavated near Anyang, in northern Honan province. These people also cast fine bronze vessels and inscribed, on bits of bone, the most ancient examples of Chinese writing that have yet been found. This early North China civilization diffused widely, influencing areas from Central Asia to Japan and the Vietnamese shores far to the south. It is perhaps most important to note that North China is the only major cradleland that has a clear cultural continuity through several millennia to the present.

New World Hearths

One of the most remarkable aspects of the ancient American civilizations was their development completely apart from the civilizations of the Old World. Early inhabitants of the Americas apparently did not suspect that the rest of the world existed, and there seems to have been no knowledge of their existence on the part of Europeans and Asians.

Middle America. It is very likely that the peoples of Mexico began growing a few vegetable crops to supplement their hunting and gathering as early as 7000 or 8000 B.C. By 1000 B.C. large ceremonial buildings had been constructed in the area, and by 300 B.C. large cities were developing. Under the Toltecs, the city of Teotihuacán, in the Valley of Mexico, where Mexico City now stands, was the principal scene of such cultural activities as crop-raising and the building of stone pyramids. By 1519, when the Spanish conquistador Cortes arrived in the Gulf of Mexico, Aztecs had supplanted the Toltecs and, controlling much of central Mexico, ruled a formidable empire.

The Indians in northern Guatemala and Yucatán also developed a strong civilization—the Mayan, which reached its peak about A.D. 700. The Maya grew crops, built limestone temples, and created fine paintings and pottery. They also developed a complex calendar, a system of hieroglyphic writing, and several advanced mathematical concepts.

Andes. Excavations along the Andean coasts of northern Peru have revealed evidence that village societies existed there perhaps as early as 2500 B.C., or before. The most enduring of these was the Incan, whose ancient peoples probably lived mainly by hunting and gathering and only secondarily cultivated such crops as squash, beans, potatoes, and maize. Cities developed in the area, but probably no earlier than A.D. 800; and road networks and suspension bridges no earlier than A.D. 900. The early Incas also cast vessels of bronze, gold, and silver, and their weavers made fine textiles of cotton and alpaca wool. Ancient stone walls built, without mortar, of huge fitted blocks still stand within the lands of the Incan Empire as one of humanity's early great structural achievements (Fig. 4–24). The empire itself remained intact until the sixteenth century, when it was destroyed in the Spanish conquest of the Americas.

FIGURE 4–24

Machu Picchu, the "lost city" of the Incas, an ancient stronghold that sprawls along a ridge 2,000 feet high in the Andes Mountains. Its gabled granite-block structures—including palaces, temples, barracks, and houses—cover more than 100 acres and testify to the ingenuity and hard work of their builders. (Eugene Gordon)

Modern Culture Realms

A *culture realm* is a region occupied by a group of similar, interrelated cultures, these usually sharing a multitude of elements, particularly language and religion. But no two authorities will ever agree *in toto* on the criteria to be applied in differentiating culture realms or on their boundaries. Furthermore, any possible classification can become invalid as time passes, even on the basis of its own criteria.

The modern world is usually divided into six major culture realms: Occidental (European), Islamic, Indic, East Asian, Southeast Asian, and African (Fig. 4–25). Each of these can be subdivided and is named for its core area, the region in which its set of distinguishing features first occurred; some contemporary cultures have expanded into areas very far removed from their original locales.

FIGURE 4–25

The most widespread of the six major culture realms is the Occidental, which has several subrealms: 1) the Northwest European, 2) the Mediterranean, 3) the Central European, and 4) the Russian. Two of these subrealms have shaped the present culture of large territories beyond Europe; such territories are indicated on the map as **a** areas.

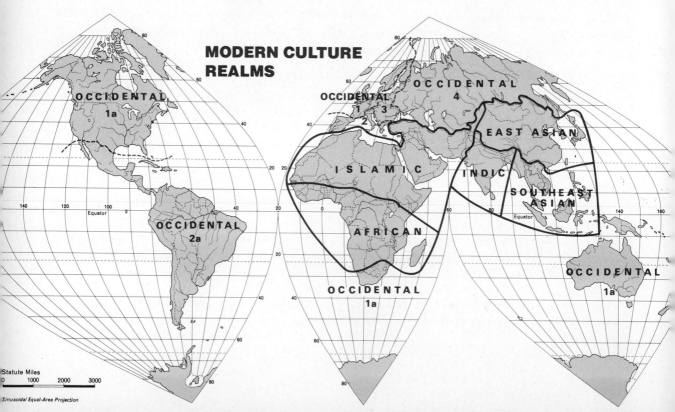

FIGURE 4–26
An evening street scene in Brussels, Belgium. (© Lynda Gordon)

Occidental Culture Realm

The Occidental (European) realm can be broken down into four subrealms: Northwest European, Mediterranean, Central European, and Russian. The first two of these comprise not only a portion of the European continent but overseas appendages.

Northwest European Subrealm. The homeland of the Northwest European subrealm includes the British Isles, the Benelux countries, West Germany, Switzerland, France, and Scandinavia. And, beginning in the seventeenth century, steady emigrations from this area have resulted in the development of large overseas outliers in the United States, Canada, South Africa, Australia, and New Zealand.

The Northwest European subrealm is characterized by adherence to Protestant and Roman Catholic Christianity and by the use of Germanic and Romance languages. Its governments are, for the most part, democratic and stable, and they possess an international outlook and exert great influence upon the international community. The individual cultures within the realm have long written histories, and their present populations are, overall, highly literate and well educated and have substantial access to the fine arts. These cultures have achieved the world's highest degrees of technological knowledge and thus high levels of industrialization and very high *per capita* incomes. Their diets are relatively high in protein, placing strong emphasis on meats and dairy products, and they utilize wheat more than any other grain and large quantities of vegetables and fruit—thus providing the world's most balanced diets and its healthiest populations (Fig. 4–26).

Mediterranean Subrealm. The Mediterranean subrealm includes Portugal, Spain, Italy, Crete-Greece, the island of Cyprus, and Israel—and its influence has spread overseas to most of Latin America. This Occidental subrealm is characterized by adherence to the Roman Catholic and Eastern Orthodox churches and by the use of Romance and Greek languages. Its countries' governments are at times relatively unstable, being prone to coups d'état, revolutions, dictatorships, and military juntas; and their present interest in international affairs is, for the most part, only regional. The subrealm has an extremely long written history, and maintains a fairly high rate of literacy. Most technological developments are known here, but there is still widespread dependence on manual labor—especially in agriculture and the many cottage industries. On a world scale, *per capita* income is moderately high in the more progressive areas, such as northern Italy, but extremely low in many rural agrarian areas, including large parts of Spain and Greece. In certain circles in the urban areas, there has been a large-scale development of the performing arts, art, literature, and music, but a great portion of the rural population lives with access to only the simplest arts and crafts. Most diets within the region are low in meat and dairy products and high in starches, especially wheat; seafood is plentiful, and there is much use of the olive, the grape, and spices.

Central European Subrealm. The Central European subrealm consists of the Balkan-Slavic cultures that lie between Germany and the Soviet and north of Greece. While many individuals from these cultures have migrated to other parts of the world, Balkan-Slavic peoples have never constituted a dominant population in any country beyond Europe.

The cultures of this realm are characterized by their adherence to the Roman Catholic and Eastern Orthodox churches and by a use of Slavic languages—although a Romance tongue predominates in Rumania and a Ugrian tongue in Hungary. Their governments, long monarchial and retaining many elements of feudalism until well into this century, have now come largely within the Communist sphere of influence; political involvement is largely regional in nature. These cultures have long written histories and, in recent times, fairly high literacy rates. With modest records of technological development, they have achieved a fair degree of industrialization and moderate *per capita* incomes. While the arts are highly evolved in this subrealm, a very large portion of the population lives in areas far removed from any artistic center and, therefore, encounters only rustic arts and crafts. The typical human diet in the subrealm is high in starches derived from potatoes, maize, wheat, rye, oats, and barley, but also contains moderately high amounts of proteins, from meat and dairy products, and root crops and leafy vegetables.

Russian Subrealm. The Russian subrealm once included only the area of the present Soviet west of the Urals. However, it gradually extended eastward during the eighteenth and nineteenth centuries and, since the 1930s, has vigorously encompassed all of Soviet Asia. In some areas, this expansion has been through essentially original settlement, but in other areas, the Russian culture has been superimposed over indigenous cultures—sometimes spontaneously, sometimes by governmental edict.

Modern Russian, or Soviet, culture is officially atheistic, although strong feeling toward traditional Eastern Orthodox Christianity still remains in some circles; its several languages are all Slavic. Soviet government is strongly socialist and pervades every facet of its citizens' public and private lives; the central government of the Soviet Union is also heavily involved in international affairs on a worldwide scale. The subrealm has a long written history, and its literacy rate has been pushed to very high levels during the last generation. Modern technology is widespread, both in agriculture and in industry, and, though difficult to measure in a Communist system, *per capita* income is now fairly high. The general population's involvement in the arts has also been increased tremendously in the last two generations, and thus a very sizable portion of the working class is exposed to most contemporary arts. Human diet throughout the subrealm is dominated by starchy foods, especially potatoes, and is relatively low in meat and dairy products; wheat and rye are the major bread grains, and roots the major vegetables.

Islamic Culture Realm

The Islamic culture realm is associated primarily with the arid lands of the Old World, for its areas extend from Morocco across northern Africa to Turkey, the Arabian countries, Iran, and Pakistan (Fig. 4–27). Once several outlier regions in central Asia were also included, but the extension of Soviet influence since the 1930s has essentially removed them from the Islamic realm. Thus the realm's present subdivisions are: its Arabian core region; a Berber-European area in northwestern Africa; Negroid areas in western Mali and the Sudan south of the Sahara; Turkey; Iran; and Pakistan.

The *Arabian subrealm* adheres strongly to the Islamic, or Moslem, religion and speaks Arabic, a Semitic language. Political attitudes are relatively naive and simplistic, and the outlook of many is extremely provincial; only in regard to marketing petroleum and resisting an Israeli presence in the Mid-

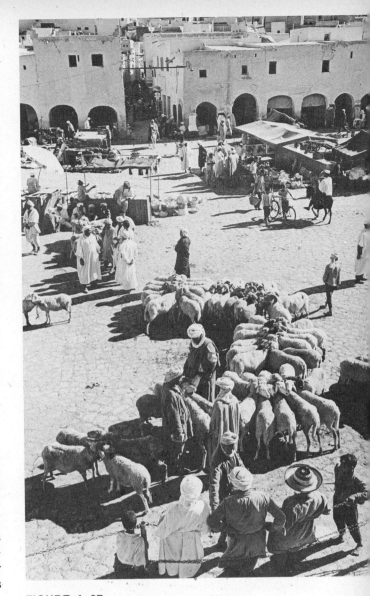

FIGURE 4–27

Ghardaia, an oasis market town in north-central Algeria. (Klaus D. Francke from Peter Arnold)

dle East is there substantial interest in international affairs. These concerns are also the only ones that generate any semblance of unity among the subrealm's otherwise feuding nations and sheikdoms, despite much vocalization in support of Arab unification.

Although it has a very long written history, and in ancient times was a seat of philosophy and literature, the subrealm now possesses a very low literacy rate. Technological research, mechanization, and industrialization are virtually absent, except where introduced by foreigners in pursuit of the area's abundant petroleum. Economic wealth is poorly distributed, and there is no sizable middle class to bridge the gap between the poverty-stricken, illiterate majority and the extremely wealthy aristocracy. Poorly balanced, the subrealm's typical human diet consists mainly of rice, wheat, and dates, with small amounts of milk and milk products and little meat. Alcohol and pork are forbidden by Islamic religion.

FIGURE 4–28

Silver Street, in the heart of Old Delhi, India. (© Screen Traveler from Gendreau)

Indic Culture Realm

The Indic culture realm is roughly coincident with the countries of India, Bangladesh, and Sri Lanka. Its many religions are polytheistic, highly spiritual and mystic, and deeply concerned with the passage of the soul through a series of reincarnations. The use of many languages and dialects in this realm poses great problems in its development of unified nations. The Indian subcontinent long consisted of many separate, and largely autonomous, states. Only since 1947, when it achieved independence from British rule, has India been completely unified under a fairly stable central government. The country's international involvement is still usually minimal, partly because of its many internal problems.

India and the rest of the Indic realm have a very long written history—certainly longer than most European cultures—but are nevertheless beset by widespread illiteracy. The realm has also achieved very little technological development and mechanization and only a relatively minor degree of industrialization; *per capita* income is extremely low, and few people can pursue an interest in the arts or leisure activities (Fig. 4–28). Indic populations are segregated by birth into several socioeconomic strata, or castes, from which there is little escape. The bulk of the people are impoverished and receive inadequate medical attention. Their diet, obtained usually at the minimum subsistence level, consists mainly of starchy foodgrains—rice, pulses, chick peas, lentils, millet, and wheat; and oils—peanut, coconut, sesame, and linseed. It is largely lacking in meats and in dairy products, in part because of religious restrictions. Most Indic dishes are heavily seasoned with a wide range of spices, and their exotic flavors have gained them worldwide acceptance.

East Asian Culture Realm

China, Japan, Mongolia, North and South Korea, and Taiwan comprise the East Asian culture realm, which thus includes about one billion people, or one-quarter of the world's human beings. None of these countries has been under the direct control of a non-Asian power, but the realm has been marked in modern times by turbulent politics and ideological conflict. Warfare and political unrest were hallmarks of the rise and fall of Japan as a major Asian force a generation ago, and since then the ascendance of Communist China has had similar effects within East Asia and beyond. Despite their similarities in race, religion, language, and life styles, the countries in this realm have often been far from harmonious neighbors.

For centuries, while Western societies were experimenting with new ideologies and new technologies, China was the "sleeping dragon" of the East. Since 1949 it has been undergoing a socioeconomic awakening under a Communist government; the country still has undeveloped natural resources that can one day bring it tremendous wealth (Fig. 4–29).

Abundant arable land is not one of them, however; most of the land suitable for food production—10 to 15 percent of China's total and located mainly in the eastern third of the country—is already in use. Thus, many observers question whether China can long feed its growing society, a population expected to include 1.5 billion persons by the end of the century. In both agrarian and industrial pursuits the Chinese are already highly capable, but many substantial technological advancements will have to be made in the near future if so large a population is to continue to experience economic growth.

Japan and Korea have both derived

FIGURE 4–29

A commercial street in Peking, China. (© Georg Gerster, Rapho/Photo Researchers)

much of their cultural heritage from historical China. Traditional Japanese life styles bear distinct imprints of borrowings from China—often carried by means of the Korean land bridge. Examples of this cultural diffusion include Japan's acceptance of both the Buddhist religion, in the sixth century by way of China and Korea, and China's Confucian philosophy of family relationships. And, perhaps even more important, the Japanese borrowed and adapted the basic characters of Chinese in developing a written form of their own language. It should be remembered, however, that these borrowings were made in the distant past and that, long before their first contacts with modern Western cultures, the Japanese had developed a distinctive society of their own—like, yet unlike, the Chinese.

Southeast Asian Culture Realm

Stretching nearly 4,000 miles—from Burma through Indochina and across the vast archipelagos of the Philippines and Indonesia to the shores of New Guinea—and including several extremely diverse peoples, the Southeast Asian culture realm is a truly unified region in name only. Different parts of this realm are almost as different from one another culturally as they are from the surrounding cultural realms. What cultural unity they possess is largely a matter of common indebtedness over the millennia to their mainland neighbors. Most of Southeast Asia's languages, religions, political systems, art, and music had their origins in India and China; and much of the remainder is European or American. Each of the countries in the Southeast Asian realm—excepting Thailand, that is—was for long periods part of one or another of the several European overseas empires of the sixteenth to twentieth

FIGURE 4–30

Stalled traffic in Sumatra, Indonesia. (© Georg Gerster, Rapho/Photo Researchers)

FIGURE 4–31

The village of Torke in Ethiopia. (United Nations)

centuries, and many Americanisms were introduced when the region became a principal Asian battleground of the Second World War. Thus in the Southeast Asian realm East truly meets West, producing much chaos but also infinite richness and variety (Fig. 4–30).

African Culture Realm

The coasts of central Africa became known to Europeans in the fifteenth and sixteenth centuries, but explorations of the interiors did not make much progress until near the close of the eighteenth century. Thus the development of Western social systems in the African cultural realm is fairly recent. For some African peoples the change from tribal isolation to European colonialism to sociopolitical independence occurred within a human lifetime. The vast territory of central Africa was not unknown to foreigners before the European arrivals, however. A considerable Moslem influence preceded the Europeans. The most developed areas of the realm

when intense European colonization began, about 1885, were probably areas of West Africa along the Niger River, areas within the tract of savanna bounded by the Sahara to the north and the forest lands to the south. Today European colonial power has dissipated, and independence prevails over most of the African realm. However the disposition of sociopolitical powers inherent to newly independent states will probably continue to generate serious conflicts and problems throughout the area for some time to come.

The African culture realm constitutes one of the world's major underdeveloped regions; agriculture is not extensively mechanized, and the most successful industrial operations have been those undertaken on a rather small scale (Fig. 4–31). Like virtually all parts of the modern world, the area is also undergoing a major cultural revolution. Its cultural change is characterized by a new acceptance of foreign ways and products. Chief among these is the pursuit of socioeconomic stability through planned agro-industrialization.

REVIEW AND DISCUSSION

1. What is the meaning of the term *race* in cultural geography? What type of features are commonly cited as distinguishing the races? Evaluate the claim that there are probably no "pure" racial groups.
2. A relatively simple racial classification is widely used today in scientific study. Characterize each of its three major divisions, and indicate some of the probable reasons for their major differences.
3. Discuss the origins and present world distributions of the three major races; include references to pertinent geographical patterns, involving, for example, continents, nations, latitudes, or climates. Where would one find "classic" examples of each race in large numbers?
4. Name and characterize the nine major linguistic families. Summarize the global distribution of each family.
5. Discuss the geographic distribution of the Indo-European language family. Trace the diffusion of three or four of its principal languages.
6. Describe several of today's "classic" bilingual societies; include one example for each of the following continents: North America, South America, Europe, Africa, and Asia. What do these examples show about the relationship between biliguality and race or biliguality and culture?
7. Discuss the three major monotheistic religions collectively and singly with respect to their origins, tenets, and regional and national patterns.
8. Discuss the two major polytheistic religions collectively and singly with respect to their origins, tenets, and regional and national patterns.
9. Incorporating as much recent data as possible, discuss the positions of religion within the Soviet Union and China. Do you see any strong relationships between religion and socioeconomic development? Explain.
10. Describe the physical environments of each of the major culture hearths. What features do these environments have in common?
11. Compare and contrast the Old World's four "river-valley" civilizations, with particular attention to development, diffusion, and worldwide influences. How did these river-valley civilizations differ, if they did, from the two non-river-valley civilizations of the Old World?
12. Compare and contrast the two principal New World civilizations with the two non-river-valley civilizations of the Old World, with particular attention to their development, diffusion, and worldwide influences.
13. What is a *culture realm?* How does it differ from a *culture hearth?* In what ways can culture realms be considered extremely dynamic, and of what importance is this dynamism in the use of the culture realm as a research and study tool in cultural geography?
14. What are the distinguishing features of each of the modern world's six major culture realms?
15. The Occidental (European) culture realm is quite extensive. Justify its claim to each of its four European subrealms. Summarize also the characteristics that make each of these four subrealms distinctive.

SELECTED REFERENCES

Benson, P. H. *Religion in Contemporary Culture.* New York: Harper & Row, 1960.
Black, M. *The Labyrinth of Language.* New York: Mentor, 1968.
Chiari, J. *Religion and Modern Society.* London: Jenkins, 1964.
Coon, C. S. *The Origin of Races.* New York: Knopf, 1962.

Coulborn, R. *The Origin of Civilized Societies.* Princeton, N.J.: Princeton University Press, 1959.

Fellows, D. K. *A Mosaic of America's Ethnic Minorities.* New York: Wiley, 1972.

Fisher, C. A. *Southeast Asia: A Social, Economic and Political Geography.* London: Methuen, 1966.

Fisher, W. B. *The Middle East,* 6th ed. London: Methuen, 1971.

Fishman, J. A. *Socio-Linguistics: A Brief Introduction.* Rowley, Mass.: Newbury House, 1971.

Hawkes, J., and L. Woolley. *History of Mankind: Cultural and Scientific Development,* Vol. 1. London: Allen and Unwin, 1963.

Hoebel, E. A. *Anthropology: The Study of Man,* 4th ed. New York: McGraw-Hill, 1972.

Hymes, D. *Language in Culture and Society.* New York: Harper & Row, 1964.

James, P. E. *Latin America,* 4th ed. New York: Odyssey Press, 1969.

Lenski, G. *The Religious Factor: Sociological Study of Religion's Impact on Politics, Economics, Family Life.* New York: Doubleday, 1961.

Lerner, M. *America as a Civilization.* New York: Simon & Schuster, 1957.

MacFadden, C. H., H. M. Kendall, and G. F. Deasy, *Atlas of World Affairs.* New York: Crowell, 1946.

Murdock, G. P. *Africa: Its Peoples and Their Cultural History.* New York: McGraw-Hill, 1959.

Nash, M. *Primitive and Peasant Economic Systems.* San Francisco: Chandler, 1966.

Noss, J. B. *Man's Religions,* 3rd ed. New York: Macmillan, 1963.

Oppenheim, A. L. *Ancient Mesopotamia.* Chicago: University of Chicago Press, 1964.

Pei, M. A. *The Story of Language.* New York: Lippincott, 1965.

Sapir, E., and D. Mandelbaum, eds. *Selected Writings in Language, Culture and Personality.* Berkeley: University of California Press, 1951.

Simoons, F. S. *Eat Not This Flesh.* Madison: University of Wisconsin Press, 1961.

Sopher, D. E. *Geography of Religions.* Englewood Cliffs, N.J.: Prentice-Hall, 1967.

Srinivas, M. N., and A. Beteile. "The Untouchables of India." *Scientific American,* Vol. 213 (December 1965), 13–17.

Welch, G. *Africa Before They Came.* New York: Morrow, 1965.

Willey, G. R. *Prehistoric Settlement Patterns in the New World.* New York: Viking, 1956.

Homage to a chieftain in Uganda. (George Rodger/Magnum Photos)

5

Societies
and Political Order

Political order is basic to cultural development; for without the rule of law and some governmental structure there can be no civilization, only chaos and anarchy.

It is evident that since early in their existence, and long before recorded history, humans have often surrendered much of their individual freedom to the will of society. In fear of numerous animals and environmental hardships, they have usually chosen to live in organized groups, with recognized leaders and rules of behavior. While they do limit the freedom of the individual, such rules have always been regarded as essential to the survival of the group. Their adoption marks the actual beginnings of government, government being no more than the machinery through which the rules of a society are enforced. And, once established, the subjection of the individual to political authority continued to increase in scope and complexity.

Human political groups have taken a variety of forms, of which the *family* is generally believed to be the oldest and most enduring. As families came into contact with one another, they often coalesced to form *clans,* more extensive units that were headed by a chieftain or group of elders. A still broader unit was the *tribe,* also headed by a chieftain or council. In most instances the cohesive element in these early political units was a common ancestry, language, or religion, coupled with geographic proximity and/or an awareness of the advantages to be gained through cooperation and centralized leadership.

It was not until the early nomadic groups settled into more sedentary ways of life that the ownership of definite territory became a strong determinant of human political units. With this new-found attachment to land, small agricultural communities began to appear in those regions of the world having warm climates, adequate water supplies, and fertile soils. Such geographical conditions were found, for example, in the valley areas of the Tigris-Euphrates, Yangtze, Huang, Nile, Ganges, and Indus rivers. The agricultural communities located in these areas and others like them became the earliest examples of the *city-state,* that is, an independent political entity made up of a city and its surrounding tributary region. This kind of central organization allowed some of the area's inhabitants to accumulate wealth and to expand their lands and power through trade and commerce. In short, in such areas control of territory came to equal political and economic power.

The State: Territory and People

The concept that there exists a bond between a group of people and the territory they occupy is a basic one. And, along with the other major cohesive elements of early political units, it is also a basis for contemporary political organization. Today, the entire land surface of the earth is sharply divided into politically organized territorial units referred to as *countries, states,* or *nations.* The people inhabiting each of these land units are also frequently classified in terms of political organization; that is, an American is distinguished from a German, a Frenchman from a Luxembourger, a Thai from a Burmese. The life style followed by each—including clothes, foods, currency, laws, and manner of speech—is generally a reflection of the particular country of which that individual is a citizen.

The State and the Nation

Although considered synonyms, the terms *state* and *nation* should be used with some degree of differentiation. While *state* properly connotes political unity, *nation* properly connotes cultural unity—in effect, then, each word represents a distinct and essentially different type of social bond.

The State. Formally, the modern state is comprised of specific territory and of a body of people who, while often economically and sometimes culturally varied, are bound together politically on many significant levels. Statehood is achieved only after the people occupying a definite territory have been united under a single, *sovereign* government, that is, one officially possessing supreme authority over all of the territory's domestic and foreign affairs. In practice, of course, the degree of authority a government has over the affairs of its territory varies with the relative strength or weakness of the state in the world community.

The Nation. A nation, or nationality, on the other hand, is a body of people who may be only bound together culturally. Several nations may be represented in a single state. Belgium, for example, includes two distinct national groups, the Flemings and the Walloons. Or, a nation may extend beyond the territorial limits of a particular state. For example, the nation of the Kurds is divided politically by several states, including Iran, Iraq, and Turkey (Figs. 5–1 and 5–2). The people of a state owe their allegiance to its sovereign power; the people of a nation can find unity in their sense of "belonging together," even though they may be separated by political boundaries. In short, the modern state is a political community; whereas the nation is a population group characterized by cultural ties, most frequently formed around language, race, religion, place of origin, and/or historical experiences and traditions.

FIGURE 5–1

A Kurdish tribe approaching the mouth of the Prince Ali Gorge in Iraq. The Kurds are a pastoral, tent-dwelling people. (United Nations)

The National State

Ideally, a state should be a reflection of a nation; that is, it should be composed of a single population group, which, for various reasons, regards itself as constituting a unified political community. In this sense, the prime objective of "nation-building" is the achievement of the point at which the membership of the state coincides with that of the nation. The state would then be the political expression of the nation, the instrument through which the nation could protect and assert itself. Such a political unit would properly be called a *nation-state*.

As suggested previously, the nation-state concept is an ideal; it is not demonstrated by the majority of the world's political units. Even a cursory examination of current political organization worldwide shows that most states are multinational.

In most cases, therefore, the state

FIGURE 5–2

The core of the Kurdish homeland, the lower slopes of the Taurus Mountains of eastern Turkey and the Zagros Mountains of northwestern Iran. The Kurds dwell also in the interiors of this area's contiguous states—Iran, Iraq, the Soviet Union, Syria, and Turkey.

101

requires a more exact loyalty than that given the nation. Lucky is the state that has a homogeneous population and no "nationality problems." And even luckier is the one that, usually with the help of a responsive and efficient political system, has been able to unify its people despite their national differences.

When a state develops a nationality of its own, its population is said to have a "concept of nation"; this means that a significant majority of the citizens of the state are aware of their government, prefer it over others, and identify themselves with its policies. The members of such a political unit place loyalty to the group as a whole above any internal political loyalties.

Nationalism. The positive feelings for the modern national state expressed by its citizens are usually described as *nationalism,* a somewhat nebulous term that has been defined as follows:

At its most elementary level, nationalism appears as a conversion and enlargement of the concept of kinship: the individual identifies himself with, and therefore gives willing support to, the political organization and region which he feels belongs to him, and to which he belongs, because the people of all that region and those operating the organization are kin to him. Not that they are kin in the literal sense of common biological origin, but in the sense more meaningful to him that they are like him (Richard Hartshorne, *American Geography Inventory and Prospect* [Syracuse: Association of American Geographers and Syracuse University Press, 1954], p. 193).

Europe Sets the Pace. The rise of the modern national state and of nationalism, which accompanied it, are relatively recent phenomena, first appearing as major political forces in Europe. There, they evolved from the feudal system that developed and flourished in the agricultural life of the Mid-

dle Ages. Characterized by extreme territorial fragmentation as well as a near absence of any contact, even between neighboring communities, feudalism divided land into sections owned and ruled either by members of the nobility or the clergy. These feudal landowners, or lords, allowed others to live on their lands, subject to their control, and for a share in the fruits of their labors. Although they may have sworn allegiance to a king, the lords ruled their estates independently, usually from within the security of fortified castles (Fig. 5–3). The king, a landlord himself, collected taxes from the other lords and led them in battle against foreign adversaries, but he was not the direct authority in the lives of most of his subjects. A tenant's first allegiance was to the landlord, and it was the landlord and the laws of the estate that most influenced a tenant's economic and personal life.

Such a system could not cope with the growth of commerce. The expansion of trade required a single, portable currency and guaranteed rights-of-way. It also produced a commercial class, whose members found it profitable to live close together in towns, and whose landlords were paid only in money, not fidelity. As trade increased within a realm and eventually extended beyond its borders, and as people became less tied to the land, the need for a centralized authority and source of identity became greater.

The national state filled that need. Based on cultural ties, it gave a more mobile population an expanded geographical identity. And since it drew on a much wider base for its financial support and directly controlled its army, the nonfeudal state surpassed feudalism in maintaining internal order and repelling foreign invasion. The basic change, of course, was the centralization of domestic power, which had long been fought by the feudal lords. With this change the state assumed responsibility for a

FIGURE 5–3

A scene from a fifteenth-century French manuscript depicting farm laborers on the grounds of a feudal estate. (Giraudon)

wide range of important human concerns, including the establishment of uniform laws and the administration of justice. Most of the new states were absolute monarchies, but these gradually gave way to parliamentary governments and to the extension of the franchise to more and more members of the society (Fig. 5–4).

Among the first national states to emerge in Europe were those of France, England, Spain, Switzerland, the Netherlands, and the Soviet Union. Among the last were Italy and Germany, both of which remained divided into small principalities and dukedoms until very late in the nineteenth century, at which time they achieved unification under the leadership of centralized monarchies. In present-day Europe there are still some reminders of feudalism existing in the form (if not the administration) of such "ministates" as Andorra, Liechtenstein, Monaco, and San Marino (Fig. 5–5). The political unit that predominates is the national state, which, since its European beginnings hundreds of years ago, has spread to nearly every part of the world.

Threats to National Unity

It is virtually impossible for any modern nation-state, even those in Europe, to remain totally unified at all times. At one time or another internal frictions are bound to develop; some may be resolved peacefully, others may erupt into riot, or even civil war. Whatever the results may be, this is never-

FIGURE 5–4

Magna Carta, the vital document to which King John reluctantly affixed his seal in 1215. Essentially a guaranteed "bill of rights" for England's nobles, it limited the legal powers of the king and is regarded as a landmark in the long development of the British "constitution." The words are Latin. (Bettmann Archive)

theless true for the newest states as well as for the oldest ones.

Communalism. When individual citizens of a country identify themselves with, and give their primary loyalty to, a racial or cultural group rather than to the state, they are said to have a *communal outlook.* This so-called *communalism,* based primarily on religion, was instrumental in 1947 in the division of the Indian subcontinent into Moslem-dominated Pakistan and Hindu-dominated India. In those countries that are comprised of several nationalities, or subnations—such as Switzerland, the United Kingdom, Belgium, Yugoslavia, Canada, India, and Sri Lanka (Ceylon), to mention but a few—communalism is often the most obvious potential threat to national unity.

Tribalism. In general, tribal groups do not strongly identify with the states in which they live. They possess their own sets of laws and customs and are usually located in remote areas of their states, far removed from population centers. As a result, the state that contains tribal groups cannot be totally united until it has penetrated their areas and gained the strong support of, or control over, the powerful, rural tribal chieftains.

In several parts of Africa, tribal participation in the state is unusually strong. Some African governments are dominated by a single, large tribe, with varying participation by one or more smaller tribes. Dissatisfaction on the part of one or another of the less-powerful tribes is occasionally the cause of much internal strife. Such was the case in Nigeria in the 1960s, when a rebellion by the Biafran minority resulted in a major civil war and their own near-annihilation.

Economic Protectionism. Disharmony seemingly based on cultural differences may actually be, more fundamentally, a confron-

FIGURE 5–5

San Marino, the world's oldest and smallest republic. The hilltop castle shown here was built in the thirteenth century, and it served as a defensible retreat during invasions of the agricultural lands below. (Bob and Ira Spring)

tation between different economic groups. Those in lower-income groups may join together on the basis of their cultural ties to seek greater governmental power and improvements in their economic condition. The communal problem in Northern Ireland, for example, resulting from the friction between the Catholic minority and Protestant majority, has definite underlying socioeconomic implications.

Regionalism. When sharp cultural and/ or economic disparities exist between different areas of a state, they may foster serious regional disunity. A region that feels it is unfairly treated by the government may demand greater local autonomy. If that demand is not satisfied, then a movement for total independence from the state may ensue.

Separatist movements of varying magnitudes can be found today throughout the world. Significant ones include those within the French Catholic community of the Province of Quebec, the Basque region of Spain, and remote parts of Western Australia.

The State: Organization and Power

Every state reflects a different approach to the exercise of sovereign power. Each has a different influence on the way its people live and the way its natural and cultural resources are utilized. The power of a state depends, to a large extent, on how well it is able to organize and manage its territory.

Territorial Administration

As discussed earlier, there are forces within the boundaries of all states that are capable of threatening national unity. A state's ability to deal with these forces, especially those that develop regionally, depends largely on its system of territorial administration. With few exceptions, the territory of most national states is divided, for administrative purposes, into smaller units. For example, the states of the United States, India, or Mexico, the provinces of Spain, and the republics of the Soviet Union represent the highest order of civil division within their respective national states. Although all such administrative subdivisions within a single state are totally subordinate to its government, some may be given special status.

In order to maintain as much national unity and power as possible, civil administrative divisions are delegated some degree of local autonomy; the amount depends on the internal conditions of the state and on its type of government. At one extreme, a state can have a *unitary* form of government, that is, a form in which authority is highly centralized; at the other, it can have a *federal* form of government, in which authority is highly decentralized.

Whatever the state's official form of government, adjustments toward greater centralization or greater decentralization of power are frequently made during its lifetime in response to changing problems. In a crisis, such as war or natural disaster, the national government may very quickly take over a far more extensive range of powers; in a national emergency, the central government of India, for example, has the constitutional power to take over complete control of any of its states and put it under presidential rule. On the other hand, during periods of relative stability, the national government may give more power to its subdivisions, thus implying that regionalism, though probably not eliminated, no longer threatens the state with disunity. In most instances the unity and power of a state depend on the achievement of a proper balance of authority between the national government and its civil divisions.

Unitary States. Civil divisions with very little authority are characteristic of states that have a unitary system of government; such a system is best suited to populations that are homogeneous and cohesive. However, even a state that is essentially centralized may allow a significant degree of local autonomy. The government of the United Kingdom, for example, though primarily unitary, grants significant local autonomy to many of its civil divisions, notably Scotland, Wales, and Northern Ireland. China, the largest unitary state in the world, has five major "autonomous regions," including Inner Mongolia, Kwangsi, Sinkiang, Ningsia, and Tibet. None of these once-rebellious areas was granted autonomous status, however, until it was deemed to be securely under Chinese control.

Federal States.   Civil divisions with the greatest degree of authority are normally found in those states with federal systems of government, such as Brazil, Switzerland, Canada, Australia, and the United States. However, just as some unitary states have made adjustments toward greater decentralization, some federally organized states actually function more like centralized, or unitary, ones, as is illustrated by the governments of South Africa, Yugoslavia, and the Soviet Union.

In some states, the administrative subdivisions each represent a different national group. For example, India under Nehru reorganized its administrative divisions to correspond to its major national linguistic groups. Only time will tell whether this will help to unify or divide the Indian people in their attempt to build a national state.

Socioeconomic Organization

Typically, only a small percentage of its total territorial area furnishes most of the important socioeconomic elements that allow a state to function. This vital percentage, the *ecumene*, generally includes the country's densest communication and transportation networks, its chief cities and largest aggregates of people, the major concentrations of natural resources and industry, and the best agricultural land. For example, the vast open spaces of Siberia contribute relatively little to the maintenance of the Soviet Union, which depends more strongly on the well-developed region around Moscow and other parts of Soviet Europe.

The areas that make up the ecumene may vary considerably in their contributions to the nation. Those that are the most effective are commonly referred to as *core areas* (Fig. 5–6). They are usually the nuclei from which the state grew, and, frequently, the national capital is located in or near one of them (Fig. 5–7). As time passes, however, it is not unusual for core areas to develop in other parts of the state. Thus, for example, in addition to the core area around Sydney, Australia also contains core areas near Melbourne and Perth. Each state, within its own territorial confines, has environmental characteristics that differentiate it from other states. Some, due to their location or size, are endowed with an abundance of inherent wealth; others are not as fortunate. However, no matter how potentially rich a state may be, its actual wealth and power depend on how well its territory is organized and managed.

Today, the national government of each state has the chief responsibility in formulating and executing a national development policy and in determining national priorities. In short, the national government can, and usually does, set the stage for progress or decline in its territory. To this extent, the national government and its leaders bear supreme responsibility for the quality of life within the territory.

Whether a state is young or old, it may

be quite skillful, or rather inept, at the fine art of governing and at setting developmental policies. Of course, the choice between the available alternatives depends upon each state and its particular ideology.

Those governments that actually own or control various economic means of production, such as industrial plants, transportation facilities, banks, and postal services (communist governments control all economic activities), tend to have a much more direct influence on the direction and speed of national development. Thus, for example, China has surpassed India in governing and in the setting (and implementation) of developmental policies.

In order to strengthen its power and to ensure the well-being of its people, most states pursue national policies that will strengthen relations with areas beyond their own territorial limits. Such is the stimulant that has led to international trade and, in a bygone era, to the worldwide spread of European colonization.

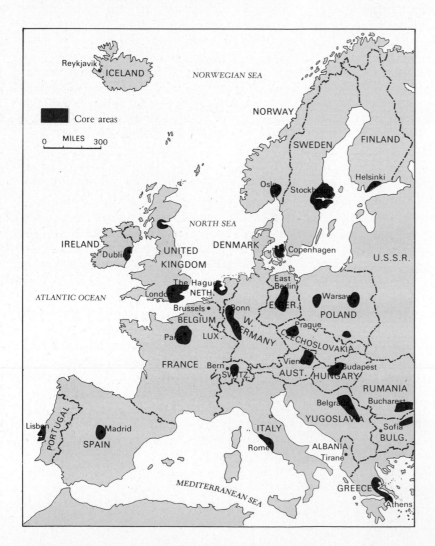

FIGURE 5–6

Core areas of Europe. On this continent, as elsewhere, an economic center is often the political heart of the nation.

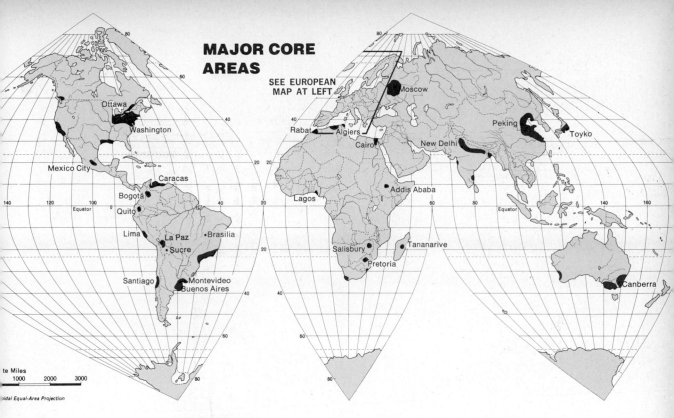

MAJOR CORE AREAS

SEE EUROPEAN MAP AT LEFT

Ottawa
Washington
Mexico City
Caracas
Bogotá
Quito
Lima
La Paz
Sucre
Brasilia
Santiago
Montevideo
Buenos Aires

Moscow
Rabat
Algiers
Cairo
New Delhi
Peking
Toyko
Lagos
Addis Ababa
Salisbury
Tananarive
Pretoria
Canberra

te Miles
1000 2000 3000

oidal Equal-Area Projection

FIGURE 5–7

Few countries of the world have extensive or multiple core areas. In the vast majority of states, the capital city is essentially the only core area.

International Relations

The State System

At present the international community is composed mostly of about 150 independent states or nations, with a small number of other political units of subordinate rank making up the balance (Plate II). The primary goal of each of these is the self-preservation of the unit as a whole along with the attainment of the best possible standard of living for its people. Since, to date, there is an absence of any active or genuine form of world government, each state feels that it must work separately to jealously guard its own national interest. The operation of this territorial methodology is called a *state system*, and it can include relations based on conflict as well as those based on cooperation.

Colonialism

The state, it has been theorized, is like any organism in nature, in that it goes through stages of growth and decline. And, just as the strength of an organism depends on the sustenance it obtains, so the strength of a state depends on territory. A state's strength and ability to grow is thus often in direct proportion to its ability to expand.

FIGURE 5–8
Ruins of the Roman settlement Leptis Magna, on the southern shore of the Mediterranean, in Libya. (Rev. Raymond V. Schoder, S.J.)

Colonialism, an expression of the expansionist tendencies characteristic of many states, involves the control taken by a state of areas and peoples other than its own. Apparently a cyclic phenomenon, it is by no means a new one. Examples of extensive colonization, or "empire-building," occurring long before the most recent wave of European colonialism are numerous. At its zenith, the empire built by the ancient Romans extended far beyond their homeland and subjugated peoples in Europe, Asia, and Africa (Figs. 5–8 and 5–9). In the Americas, the Aztec Empire also grew by colonial acquisition, and its expansion was not halted until the empire was defeated by the Spaniards in the early 1500s (Fig. 5–10). Today, many independent states, some of which were themselves part of colonial empires within the very recent past, can be said to follow colonialist policies. India and the United States are but two of many examples.

European Colonialism

A unique characteristic of the European period of colonialism, which began in the fifteenth century, was its unprecedented scale. This wave of territorial expansion affected every continent of the world and lasted, with significant strength, for over five hundred years.

This growth was prompted, at least initially, by economic interests; and one of the major influences on the newly industrializing European states was their acceptance of the mercantilist philosophy that the prosperity of a state depends on its ability to sell as much as possible and buy as little as possible. Since opportunities elsewhere in Europe were somewhat limited, each major European state was eager to obtain overseas possessions that would serve as exclusive markets for its expanding economy and provide a duty-free supply of raw materials.

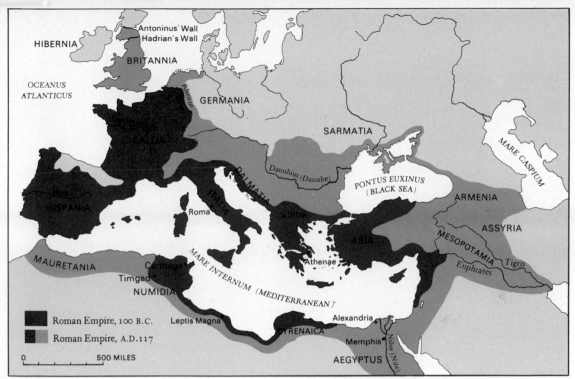

FIGURE 5-9

The Roman Empire. As early as 100 B.C. the authority of Rome extended far beyond Italia; and by A.D. 117, when the empire reached its zenith, Rome controlled the major part of the world then known to Europeans.

FIGURE 5-10

Empires of Middle and South America in the early 1500s. Each of these empires—Aztec, Maya, and Inca—had grown extensively beyond its original territory by the time the Spanish fleets arrived at their respective shores.

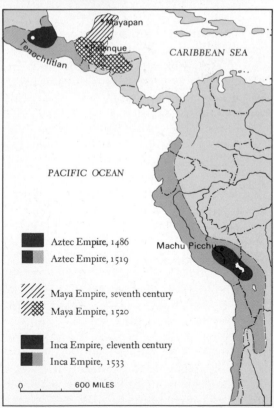

Economic penetration through trade was usually followed by political penetration, and this occurred until almost the entire non-European world was divided among the European powers. The dependencies that resulted represent a wide range of political entities with varying degrees of sovereignty, including such forms as colonies, dominions, condominiums, mandates, trusteeships, protectorates, and spheres of influence.

Usually one thinks of a dependent area

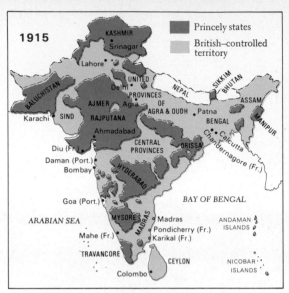

FIGURE 5–11

The nationalization of the Indian subcontinent. Left, throughout the British occupation the subcontinent comprised over 600 princely states. Right, when British rule came to an end in 1947, these princely states were unified into two independent nations, India and Pakistan (West and East). In 1971 East Pakistan became the independent state of Bangladesh, and in 1975 India absorbed Sikkim.

as a noncontiguous territory remote from the *metropole,* or mother country. But many instances of national expansionism have involved not only overseas areas but areas contiguous to the expanding state as well. Several present-day states have dependent areas located even within their national boundaries; such areas—among them the Yukon Territory in Canada, Amapa in Brazil, and the Northern Territory in Australia—often have limited self-governing powers, and they are generally administered directly from the national capital.

Decolonization and New States

Colonialism has been the primary means by which Western European patterns of culture have been diffused throughout the world. The political consequences of this, both good and bad, have been tremendous.

Colonialism, in the traditional sense, is today almost totally nonexistent. Most of the colonial territory acquired by the European powers during the Age of Colonization now comprises independent states; only a handful of colonial dependencies remain. Since 1776, when the United States proclaimed its independence from Great Britain, colonial ties throughout the world have been breaking.

The Spread of Ideologies. In some ways, the mere fact of European colonialism helped set the stage for its decline. For with the Europeans came political unification, including even the joining together of many areas, once noninteracting or at odds, into colonial units. This promoted the development of common interests among some of these previously separate areas, which sometimes led, in turn, to a new and wider sense of political community and purpose (Fig. 5–11). When combined with the spread of such ideas as political equality, democracy, progress, and nationalism—the mainsprings of Western culture—these coalescences made it all but impossible for the colonial powers to refuse demands for self-determination. Still, until

112

about World War I, independence came to European colonies sporadically and slowly.

It was not until World War II that this process was greatly accelerated and intensified. Over 50 percent of the independent states that exist today have come into being since that period; it may be said that the actual beginning of this tremendous increase in the number of sovereign states was Lebanon's declaration of independence, in 1941. Between that year and the present, only a generation after the emergence of the Lebanese nation, over eighty new states have emerged — mostly in Africa, the Middle East, and Asia (Fig. 5–12). In 1960 alone, seventeen new states emerged — all in Africa.

In the meantime, such states as China, Iran, and the United Arab Republic — which, though sovereign in name, were long subject to degrees of control by various foreign powers — strongly asserted their independence; nationalism and the desire for self-determination were finally coming of age in the non-Western world. The process begun such a short time ago continues today, but it does so at a much reduced rate.

Nation-State Building.   All nation-state building, in the modern sense, involves not only the creation of a unified central government with effective administrative control over a precisely defined area but also the development of a truly national and relatively uniform culture; it is not easy and cannot be accomplished overnight. Most states grow as a dominant group, or core area, imposes its control and culture over an even broader, and usually more culturally diverse, area. It was through this process that most of the European states developed.

The Global Pattern of Independence. Today's preponderance of sovereign, independent states, tightly packed worldwide, is historically unprecedented; and it has necessitated a total reordering of world politics.

As in the past, there is little reason to believe that the present pattern of state boundaries will remain constant. New states are constantly being born, and existent ones are frequently altered; as a result, inventories of the world's independent states and international boundaries are constantly in need of revision. In 1965 Singapore seceded from the newly formed Federation of Malaysia, and became a completely independent state; in 1971 Bangladesh, formerly East Pakistan, won its independence; in 1975 a separate Turkish-Cypriot state was proclaimed in the Turkish-occupied northern sector of the island of Cyprus.

In addition to those formed as a result of political division, there are new states that

FIGURE 5–12

A Ghanaian woman celebrating the election of Kwame Nkrumah as the first president of the republic. (Camera Press from Photo Trends)

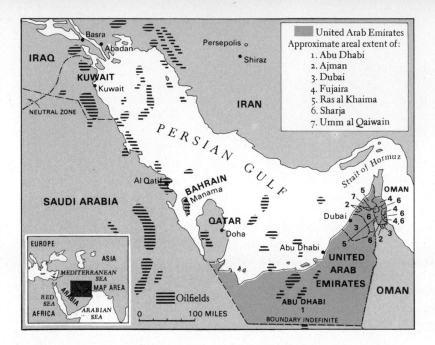

FIGURE 5-13

The United Arab Emirates. By 1972 sheiks of the formerly British-supported Trucial States had agreed to create a federation. As is true of other Arab countries, vast oil reserves give the seven sheikdoms of the UAE extraordinary international importance.

owe their existence to the consolidation of territory into larger units. In 1971, the Persian Gulf ministates of Ajman, Dubai, Fujaira, Sharja, Umm al Qaiwain, and Abu Dhabi (the largest and richest of these) united to form the Federation of Arab Emirates, despite old animosities between many of the rulers; the only former Trucial state remaining, Ras al Khaima, joined early in 1972 (Fig. 5-13). These seven individual shiekdoms, which now comprise the United Arab Emirates, have thus individually gone the way of such defunct countries as Texas, Malacca, Serbia, Montenegro, Sikkim, Latvia, and Estonia.

Nationalism and Irredentism

Areas that have gained independence from European rule have tended to model their political structures on the European state system. And though their indepen-

114

dence was usually accomplished in planned stages supervised by the metropole, numerous problems have invariably resulted. At the root of many is the fact that the boundaries of the new states generally coincide, at least roughly, with their former colonial boundaries; thus, in many parts of the world, the new boundaries divide peoples who are culturally and ethnically alike. In a model state system, boundaries would be drawn in order to unify closely related peoples; but the population of the real world is too heterogeneous and intermixed to permit such exact political groupings by culture. Most states, not only the former colonies, are multinational, in that they contain one or more national *minority groups*. For example, there are French-speaking people in Canada, German-speaking people in France, Moslems in India, Hindus in Pakistan, Asians in East Africa, and Chinese in Southeast Asia. Many states encounter some difficulties assimilating their national minorities.

Assimilation or Separation. All multinational states, especially the newer ones, are eager to generate a new national culture or national consciousness, in order to help stimulate national unity. When two or more different culture groups are brought together in a political-territorial unit, some degree of assimilation will assuredly take place. There will often be times in the course of the acculturation process, however, when a nondominant group may feel that its culture is being threatened with extinction; and it may thus be prompted to initiate a movement to reassert its national identity. The problem this presents for the state is intensified greatly if the group demands independence or reunion with a ''motherland'' beyond the state's borders.

The motherland in such instances is usually a neighboring state, which may demonstrate its support of the dissatisfied group, in various ways. At the very least, it may appeal to the host government to improve the treatment of the group. More drastically, the motherland may claim that, perhaps both on historical and cultural grounds, the territory and people involved are actually a part of its domain. Such a claim between neighboring states can lead to demands for a shift in boundaries, in order to achieve a closer correspondence between state and nation; armed clashes over the disputed territory may ensue. When a state makes such a territorial claim in order to regain territory, it is said to be following an irredentist policy.

The term *irredentism* is derived from Terra Irredenta, an area claimed by Italy in 1878 as an unredeemed part of that nation. The world abounds with examples of such territorial claims, some latent and some more pronounced. Germany's irredentist policy toward the Sudetenland accounts for the repeated attempts to reunite this part of Czechoslovakia with the German ''fatherland.'' The Sino-Soviet border dispute, which has lasted for some time, also has irredentist aspects, as do Pakistan's claims to the Indian state of Kashmir and claims by the Philippines to the Malaysian territory of Sabah (formerly North Borneo). One of the most noted examples in Africa is the irredentist tension between Somalia and its neighbors — Ethiopia, the Territory of Afars and Issas, and Kenya.

Cases involving irredentism may have varied resolutions. Occasionally, instead of risking conflict over a boundary shift, the states involved agree to relocate the people living in the disputed area. This course is usually problematic, for seldom are adequate provisions made for the refugees.

Shatter Belts. Irredentist problems tend to be most pronounced in areas characterized by great physical and cultural diversity. Usually located at a crossroad, a disputed area is often one that has served as a ''corridor'' for many different peoples, each leaving its own mark on the cultural landscape. Such transition zones are commonly referred to as *shatter belts,* a term that implies their political fragmentation. The constant changes in population in a shatter belt area preclude the establishment there of strong national cores around which a dominant and unified state could establish control. Thus, the combining of different areas in the formation of new states and the repeated redivision of other areas are characteristic of all the shatter belts of the world (Fig. 5–14). Continual territorial change has always been accompanied by great social and economic instability. This furthers the problem of political fragmentation, as it makes it easier for stronger outside powers to extend their control and influence in such areas. Today, for example, the Soviet Union's sphere of influence pervades almost all of the Eastern European shatter belt.

FIGURE 5-14

The nationalization of Europe, 1815–1976. The general stability of political boundaries in western Europe contrasts dramatically with the constant boundary changes in eastern Europe, one of the world's shatter belts; this instability reflects both internal friction and external pressure. For example, the state of Poland, which originated nearly one thousand years ago and was at one time a great power in eastern Europe, ceased to exist as a separate state in 1795. Poland reappeared as a state in 1918 but, during the Second World War, suffered partition; restored, it exists today with new boundaries. The states of Estonia, Latvia, and Lithuania have similar histories.

Tension Zones and Buffer States

Although the entire land area of the world (with the possible exception of Antarctica) has been claimed and divided politically into sovereign units, there are still states dissatisfied with the extent of their territories. Since they tend to equate the acquisition of additional territory with an increase in power and prestige, nation-states rarely pass up an opportunity to expand their territorial limits, even when it may jeopardize their national unity.

In past ages, it was relatively easy for states to expand, because there were still many *frontier areas,* that is, unclaimed territories open to penetration and occupation. But with relatively few such areas remaining, no state can expand its territory today without violating, to some extent, the sovereignty of another state. Furthermore, in this age of military alliances, any major claim by one state on the territory of another, regardless of the underlying cause, will usually be met with some degree of resistence. The result of such claims has been the creation of numerous *hot spots,* or areas of international tension. These are most commonly located along boundary lines, but they may also encompass entire districts, states, or island groups.

Especially in the areas of severe dispute, where powerful states are generally involved, various tension-easing devices may have to be employed until the dispute is settled. The presence of a *buffer state,* an independent (and usually small) state between hostile countries, has often been exploited quite effectively to reduce friction in some instances of actual or impending armed conflict. Many states have served as buffers: in Europe, the Benelux countries (Belgium, the Netherlands, and Luxembourg) have served as buffers between the frequently warring governments of France and Germany; Switzerland has helped to keep tensions from developing between these same two powers, while doing the same for Italy and Austria. The states of Eastern Europe—shatter belt countries—once serving as a buffer between the opposing ideologies of the Western European states and the Soviet Union, no longer do so, since most of Eastern Europe has been absorbed into the Soviet Union's sphere of influence. Such things as the Berlin Wall give visual proof of the seriousness of the tensions that can develop when two such opposing and powerful ideological groups are allowed to come into direct contact.

Some of the states in other parts of the world which have served as buffers include: Afghanistan, Mongolia, Nepal, Thailand, Laos, and Uruguay. Although coast-dwelling peoples have always had an interest in the oceans, until recently this large portion of the earth has been utilized only superficially—primarily as an avenue for trade and communications and, insatiably, as a fishing ground. In the past, it also served as a buffer between differing peoples, a function now impaired, as many states are beginning to extend their territorial jurisdictions farther and farther seaward in order to help satisfy the needs of expanding populations ashore.

The Territorial Sea

Ever since the growth of naval power and, with it, the threat of attack from the sea, coastal states have felt the need to extend their sovereignty rights to the zone of water immediately adjacent to their coasts—a zone referred to as the *territorial sea.*

Self-defense is not the only reason that states try to establish a seaward boundary. There are countless marine resources, both foods and minerals, in the sea and under the seabed.

Global Sovereignty

As land dwellers, human groups throughout history have had as a primary concern the establishment of sovereignty over the dry lands of the earth, areas that constitute slightly less than 30 percent of its surface. The modern state, the expression of this desire for territorial sovereignty, is distinguished by boundary lines that, while clearly marked and recognized on maps, are not detectable on the landscape itself, except when they coincide with such natural features as rivers and mountain ranges. Thus, where none of these exist, states establish artificial boundary markers and designate border check points. Of all the dividing lines created for contemporary states, however, none equals the scale of the ancient Great Wall of China (Figs. 5–15 and 5–16) or the walls built centuries ago in Great Britain by Roman occupation forces (see Fig. 3–7).

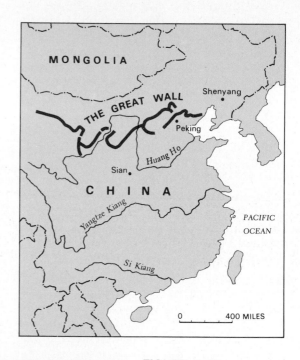

FIGURE 5–15

The situation of the Great Wall, a portion of which is shown in the photograph at left.

FIGURE 5–16

The Great Wall of China. Replacing a wall created in the third century B.C. as a protection against nomadic invaders, the present wall was begun about five hundred years ago, during the Ming dynasty. It is about 20 feet high and 20 feet wide and extends across northern China from Peking to the Kansu Corridor, a distance of approximately 1,500 miles. (Brown Brothers)

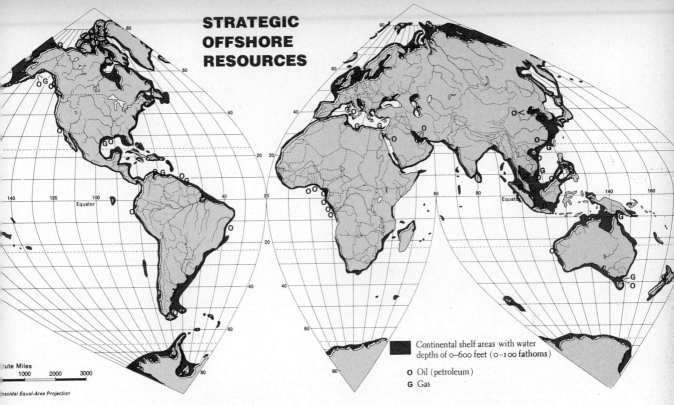

STRATEGIC OFFSHORE RESOURCES

Continental shelf areas with water depths of 0–600 feet (0–100 fathoms)

O Oil (petroleum)

G Gas

FIGURE 5–17

In addition to being an increasingly vital source of oil and gas, the world's continental shelves are becoming more and more important as sources of salt, sulphur, magnesium, and other minerals.

The New Frontier

Now that humans have extended their domain over practically all the early land frontiers, they are taking an ever-greater interest in the only surface frontier that remains — the oceans, especially in the continental shelf areas of the world. Today, the bulk of the world's fish catch continues to come from shelf waters, such as the fishing banks off the coasts of New England and Newfoundland and those in the North Sea. Nearly 20 percent of the world's petroleum and natural gas now comes from the shallow waters of the continental shelves (Fig. 5–17). The current bonanza in the exploitation of these vital submarine resources is taking place in shelf areas, such as those in the North Sea, the Persian Gulf, the United States Gulf Coast, and those off the coasts of California, Alaska, Venezuela, western Africa, Southeast Asia, and China (Fig. 5–18). This activity, along with the increased size and use of seagoing oil tankers, has helped to intensify the desire of coastal states to protect their shorelines against accidental pollution.

While about one-fifth of the countries of the world are landlocked, a vast majority of them have territorial waters; sovereignty over these areas gives them not only greater national security but, equally important, the right to exploit sought-after marine and submarine resources. To this end, the rapid development of oceanic technology is now a high priority of many states.

FIGURE 5–18

An oil rig off the coast of England. Such rigs are a mixed blessing; for while they provide access to sorely needed energy reserves, they also pose the threat of serious environmental pollution through spillage. (Mobil Oil Corp.)

Conflict Over Breadth of the Territorial Sea

Although all states accept, and understand the purpose of, the concept of the territorial sea, they have yet to formulate any international agreement as to a uniform breadth for this space. This situation, combined with the fact that boundary lines are much more difficult to regulate on water than on land, has been the cause of much confusion; it has also greatly increased the possibility of armed conflict between countries over the control and ownership of ocean waters and ocean-bottom areas. Such rivalries over disputed waters reflect, not only

the age-old struggle for commercial and naval control of the high seas, but also the active competition for the mineral resources and fisheries of shelf areas. A case in point is the "Cod War" of the mid-1970s, in which Iceland claimed that British trawlers were illegally using its coastal waters, over which it claims exclusive fishing rights.

It may be observed today that the breadth of the territorial seas of various states ranges from a few claims of over twelve miles (protested but still effective), to several claims of twelve, nine, six, four, and three miles. Most of the major maritime nations, including the United States and Great Britain, claim a three-mile limit.

Three miles has been the extent generally preferred by those states upholding the freedom of the seas, a concept accepted by—or imposed upon—the world in the nineteenth century by the major maritime nations, to whom order on the seas was essential. But this convention has since given way to the current state of chaos. The present impetus for the extension of sovereignty over sea space has developed primarily within the last few decades, especially among developing countries with comparatively few land resources.

In order to appreciate more fully the position of numerous states seeking to maintain traditional limits and the freedom of the seas concept against expanding claims of offshore sovereignty, one must understand some of the consequences of adopting even a twelve-mile territorial limit on a global basis. For example, numerous strategic straits—such as Bab-el-Mandeb (at the mouth of the Red Sea), Gibraltar, Dover, and Malacca—and narrow channels located beside continental margins or between islands in archipelagoes would have to be reclassified from high seas to territorial seas; and, as a result, it is possible that they would no longer be open to all ships. If "high-seas corridors" were strictly maintained through such waterways, then the problems of a new limit could be minimal; but if strategic straits and channels were totally nationalized, many difficult questions would be raised. Would custom give all shipping a right of "free transit," or would only the right of "innocent passage" be honored? Of course, each coastal state would be free to determine what constitutes "innocent passage," since, by international law, it is defined as that which is *not prejudicial to the peace, good order, or security of the coastal state.*

An associated problem concerns archipelagic states, such as Indonesia and the Philippines, that want to extend their dominions to include the waters between even their outermost islands. Allowing all archipelagoes to legally claim such intervening waters would reduce significantly the total area of the high seas and thus further restrict freedom of access to the traffic lanes and treasures of the seas.

Future Expansion of the Territorial Sea

The trend since 1958, when the first Law of the Sea Conference, sponsored by the United Nations, was convened, has been to extend territorial waters. At the 1958 conference in Geneva, most of the participating states were in favor of a three-mile limit. Today over half of the member states have claimed limits of six to twelve miles, and about a dozen have asserted control over more than twelve miles. A few states, including Chile, Ecuador, and Peru, have actually claimed exclusive fishing rights in the waters up to 200 miles off their shores.

The law of the sea, like all international law in a state system, is created by consent, through formal agreements, or through custom. In light of this, it seems rather unlikely that any future international tribunal will decide that twelve-mile claims are illegal, *per se.*

Recent claims to additional territorial waters are, no doubt, harbingers of things to come. As long as there is serious concern over national security and substantial economic advantage to be gained from greater limits, there is little possibility of worldwide agreement on the width of the territorial sea. And, if an international settlement of the matter is not soon reached and enforced, the resultant scope and havoc of "sea-grabbing" may overshadow the colonial "land-grabbing" of past centuries.

FIGURE 5–19

Cities of the Hanseatic League. Although most of its member cities were German, this medieval association, which flourished during the fourteenth century, influenced trade in cities as distant as London and Novgorod and Bergen and Krakow.

International Organizations

The evolution of political society has progressed to the present-day's voluntary grouping of states into multistate organizations. The best-known state groupings of the past are, perhaps, the Greek city-states, the Hanseatic League of northern Europe, and a number of other similar trading leagues of the late Middle Ages (Fig. 5–19). Twentieth-century multistate organizations are distinguished from these mainly by their number and scale.

In the modern world, any sovereign, independent nation can be in great peril if it relies only on itself; but, on the other hand, the creation of global union, or world government, is still a utopian dream. What is plain, however, is that between complete national isolation and total interaction among the earth's peoples, an important middle ground is developing. Sovereign nations are attempting to work together in large groups for some purposes, while maintaining their rights to independent action for others.

Global Organizations

An encouraging sign in the promotion of global cooperation has been the relative success of the United Nations. Since its inception in 1945, this organization has increased its membership from about 50 to over 140 states. Formed to replace the League of Nations, which had been relatively weak and ineffectual from its inception in 1919, the United Nations continues the purpose of the

League in several ways. Like its predecessor, it has as its primary purpose the prevention of war and political conflict and the establishment of international peace and security. In the pursuit of this goal, the United Nations has served as an international forum, where political disputes can be aired and negotiated. Although its record in this regard has not always been successful, the United Nations, most observers agree, has been, perhaps by its mere presence, of inestimable value to the world.

Beyond its role in political conflicts, the United Nations has achieved its importance largely through its cultural and socioeconomic work. Together, the several subsidiary agencies of the United Nations have been, perhaps, the most energetic international advocates of cultural, economic, and social progress among the peoples of the world. On the premise that the development of international as well as regional economic and social cooperation is a major prerequisite for the ultimate solution of political conflicts, these agencies have attempted to improve every aspect of human welfare—among these, health, education, and economic development (Fig. 5–20). Within the realm of cultural

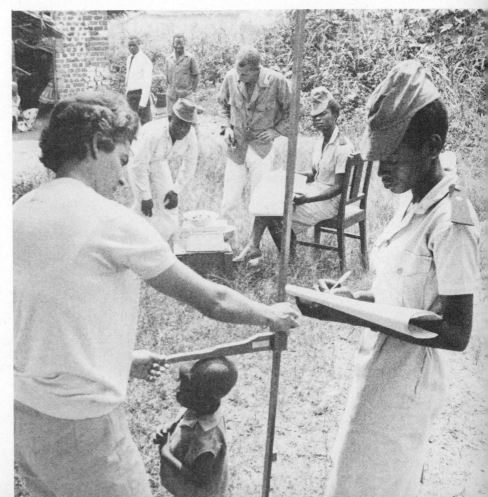

FIGURE 5–20

The measuring of a child's height during a nutrition survey conducted in Gabon by the United Nations Food and Agricultural Organization. (United Nations)

and economic development, four regional Economic Commissions established by the United Nations encompass nearly the entire world: ECAP, for Asia and the Pacific, 1947; ECE, for Europe, 1947; ECLA, for Latin America, 1948; and ECA, for Africa, 1958. Each commission serves as an important instrument for multistate cooperation within its own region.

Regional Organizations

Regional cooperation is a relatively recent phenomenon in international relations. Mainly in Europe and Asia, but in Africa and the Americas as well, the thrust of regional integration has accelerated rapidly since the end of the Second World War. If continued, it may provide a valid substitute for colonialism, which is now socially outmoded and uneconomical, and new paths toward the equalization of human rights and opportunities among all the peoples of the world.

Regional integration is a phenomenon of both the developed and the developing worlds; it can be seen in operation in both the Communist and non-Communist worlds and across all the continents as well. The most sophisticated and successful of the new regional integrations is the European Eco-

FIGURE 5–21

The memberships of two modern trade associations—ASEAN and the Common Market.

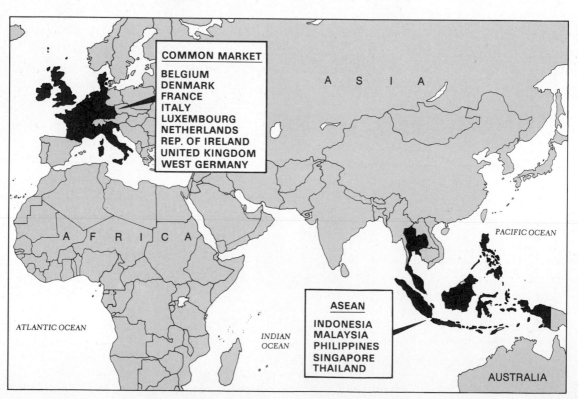

COMMON MARKET
BELGIUM
DENMARK
FRANCE
ITALY
LUXEMBOURG
NETHERLANDS
REP. OF IRELAND
UNITED KINGDOM
WEST GERMANY

ASEAN
INDONESIA
MALAYSIA
PHILIPPINES
SINGAPORE
THAILAND

nomic Community (the Common Market), which helped to raise Europe from the ashes of the last world war to its present socioeconomic heights. Another, quite different in structure and original purpose, is the Organization of Petroleum Exporting Countries (OPEC), which in the mid-1970s proved the theory of "strength in unity" to a dismayed world energy market.

Along with economic organizations, regional integration may also be represented by military, political, or cultural bodies, or by organizations that often serve as a combination of two or more of these. For instance, most collective defense associations — such as NATO, CENTO, SEATO, and the Warsaw Pact — whose *raison d'être* tends to be rather short-lived, usually supplement their central

purpose with projects in various cultural and economic spheres. Undoubtedly, the most promising regional organizations for the future are the cultural-economic groupings; the two best models of these are probably Europe's Common Market (the European Economic Community) and Asia's ASEAN (the Association of Southeast Asian Nations) (Fig. 5–21).

It should be kept in mind though, that all the various groupings, so far organized since World War II, have at one point or another lacked one or more of the essential elements that would mark any one of them as an unqualified success. But several of them have become qualified successes — which is all that one can say for any such grouping, even the European Common Market.

Comparative Regional Cooperation Studies: The Common Market and ASEAN

Western Europe and the Common Market

After World War II, Western Europe lay in ruin, and Europeans realized that in order to rebuild their societal and economic structures, they would have to mount a cooperative effort. Europe's postwar recovery program was very successful, and perhaps the most important aspect of this new cooperative vision was that it helped pave the way for broader economic unification.

There were many cooperative institutions established to help in the economic unification of Western Europe after World War II. Among these was the Organization for European Cooperation (OEC), which was designed to administer the aid received from the United States through the Marshall Plan. The European Payments Union (EPU) also helped to administer foreign aid and was

also instrumental in achieving a tighter economic integration among the European nations. It encouraged the governments of each Western European country to think of its separate financial accounts in relation to the whole of Western Europe rather than as separate and unrelated problems.

The European Coal and Steel Community (ECSC), formed in 1952, served as the first true step toward the eventual economic unification of Western Europe. Its primary goal was to promote the production of coal and steel and the free movement of these between the member countries.

In 1958, encouraged by the success of the European Coal and Steel Community, Belgium, France, Italy, Luxembourg, the Netherlands, and West Germany formed the European Economic Community (EEC), more commonly known as the *Common Market*.

Before the formation of the Common

Market, trade among these six countries was greatly restricted, because of high tariffs, import quotas, exchange controls, and other customs regulations. Thus, to insure strong socioeconomic coordination, the European Economic Community was designed as both a customs union and a common market. Within a customs union, the member countries eliminate tariffs and other restrictions to trade on products exchanged between them, while adopting common tariffs on products exchanged with nonmembers. Relaxing the trade regulations among the six countries increased the market for their respective products and allowed for greater mobility of capital and labor throughout their territories. Only through the creation of close, cultural and economic ties between the six could the final goal of complete political cohesion among them be accomplished.

The formation of the Common Market launched its six member countries on a bold adventure, designed to stimulate socioeconomic growth, ensure governmental maturity, and provide lasting mutual prosperity. The door was left open for other countries to join the organization, as full members and/or as associates. And in 1973, when Denmark, Great Britain, and the Republic of Ireland joined, as full members, the Common Market became a union of nine and a stronger stabilizing force in the economic and political worlds.

Southeast Asia and ASEAN

Southeast Asia is a region of separate and very distinct nations. For hundreds of years, wide cultural and political diversities (and disparate levels of economic development) have, quite naturally, prevented feelings of unity among them, while discouraging the interdependencies that foster regional cooperation.

After the Second World War, the newly independent states of Southeast Asia stood isolated from one another; although, geographically, they were neighbors, few of them were accustomed to sharing their problems or goals. Their lines of communication led outward from Asia to the capitals of Europe, as did, to a very large extent, their thinking and interests. Externally at least, intraregional contacts and communications had remained undeveloped under colonial rule; and intraregional trade and commerce had been largely discouraged.

Although very close ties have not existed among the nations of Southeast Asia for centuries, there are forces at work today helping to bring about a sense of regional involvement and identity. And, there does seem to be a growing feeling of regional consciousness.

Among the most outstanding regionalist forces are: first, a growing awareness, on the part of Southeast Asian leaders, that their countries share many major problems, largely in the area of socioeconomic development; second, the increase in intraregional communications (brought about, in part, by regional airline services, telecommunications systems, and increasing diplomatic exchanges); third, the growing trend toward institutionalized cooperative ventures in the world, including the Asia Pacific region; and fourth, the realization by Asian leaders that in the postcolonial era their nations must provide for their own political and economic security and shield their region from the threat of outside political intervention or internal socioeconomic decay.

The important idea to keep in mind though, is that all four of these very prominent factors have helped to facilitate and encourage the involvement, by Asian leaders, in the affairs of their neighbors. This has led to the development of a sense of regional consciousness which has led further to an interest by Southeast Asian leaders in establishing institutions of regional cooperation for their mutual benefit.

The most important step so far taken toward effective regional cooperation has been the successful formation of the Association of Southeast Asian Nations (ASEAN). In 1967 the ministers of five Southeast Asian nations met in Bangkok to form this new organization, a successor to the then dormant Association of Southeast Asia (ASA). ASEAN's five charter members included Malaysia, the Philippines, and Thailand—the three original ASA members—as well as Indonesia and Singapore.

Officially, ASEAN's chief aims are those of socioeconomic development and regional strengthening; but the organization's activities also seem directed toward independence from all outside influences. The economic and social projects undertaken by ASEAN since 1967 include a host of cooperative ventures in agricultural technology and production, industry, transportation, trade, tourism, and the development of educational facilities and student-faculty exchanges. Because of the present low degrees of economic development in each of the member nations, the goal of ASEAN is not simply to integrate the economies of its member-nations in the manner of the European Common Market

but also to provide a means by which they can assist one another in social, scientific, and administrative matters. ASEAN has also been important as an unofficial forum, where political disputes between member countries (such as the dispute between Malaysia and the Philippines over Sabah) can be arbitrated.

Even in the face of steady progress, it must be recognized that Southeast Asia's economic climb will be a long and frustrating one. The increase in economic development and trade within the region since the conception of ASEAN has been relatively small, in terms of its goals; many of the nations within the region still tend to be dependent upon trade with areas outside of it. (And this outside trade is often mutually competitive and barely economical, as, for the most part, the nations of Southeast Asia sell raw materials on the world market in competition with one another.) Nevertheless, ASEAN must be considered a viable experiment in regional cooperation. Its new Secretariat, built in Jakarta, symbolizes both ASEAN's intention to remain and grow and Indonesia's leadership within the organization. It is possible that by the late 1970s ASEAN may be as unified as the Common Market, perhaps even enjoying some direct association with its European counterpart.

REVIEW AND DISCUSSION

1. Would civilization, as we have come to know it, be possible without law and political order? Discuss your position on this question and support it with examples.
2. Compare and contrast the concepts of the state and the nation in terms of their "bonds of unity." Evaluate your findings in terms of the concept of the nation-state.
3. What is nationalism? Could it exist if there were no national states? Explain.
4. Of what significance is the fact that national states and nationalism first appeared as major political forces in Europe?
5. No national state is totally immune from internal dissension. With the aid of appropriate examples, identify and discuss some of the major threats to national unity.

6. Compare and contrast the unitary state and the federal state; cite examples of each. How does the ecumene contribute to the power of a state?
7. How does a state system function?
8. What distinctions can be made between colonialism and imperialism? In what places has one occurred in the absence of the other?
9. In your opinion, was European colonialism a positive influence or a negative influence on the world in terms of diffusion and acculturation?
10. How has the state system been affected by decolonization and the recent increases in new states? Have world tensions increased in intensity, or have they just assumed new forms? Explain.
11. Do only new states follow irredentist policies? Explain. When a state makes a territorial claim against another state is that claim always based on historical and cultural grounds? Discuss.
12. What is a buffer state, and what is its significance? Cite two examples of such states.
13. The importance of the territorial sea has been increasing in recent decades. Why? What, if any, related changes should be made in international maritime law?
14. In what areas other than politics and military alliances have global and regional state organizations made substantive contributions? Discuss with the aid of specific examples.
15. Compare and contrast the Common Market and ASEAN in terms of their goals, programs, and achievements.

SELECTED REFERENCES

Alexander, L. M. *World Political Patterns*. Chicago: Rand McNally, 1957.

Boggs, S. W. "National Claims in Adjacent Seas." *Geographical Review*, Vol. 41 (April 1951), 185–209.

Bowett, D. W. *The Law of the Sea*. London: Manchester University Press, 1967.

Bruel, E. *International Straits*, Vols. 1 and 2. London: Sweet and Maxwell, 1947.

Burghardt, A. F. "The Bases of Territorial Claims." *Geographical Review*, Vol. 63 (April 1973), 225–45.

Cobban, A. *National Self-Determination*. Chicago: University of Chicago Press, 1944.

De Blij, H. J. *Systematic Political Geography*, 2nd, ed. New York: Wiley, 1973.

East, W. G., and A. Moodie, eds. *The Changing World: Studies in Political Geography*. New York: World Book, 1956.

Emerson, R. *From Empire to Nation*. Boston: Beacon Press, 1960.

Fawcett, J. E. S. "How Free Are the Seas?" *International Affairs*, Vol. 49 (January 1973), 14–22.

_____. "The Development of International Law." *International Affairs*, Special Issue (November 1970), 127–37.

Fisher, C. A. "The Malaysian Federation, Indonesia and the Philippines: A Study in Political Geography." *Geographical Journal*, Vol. 129 (September 1963), 311–28.

Frank, T. *Roman Imperialism*. New York: Macmillan, 1914.

Fried, M. *The Evolution of Political Society*. New York: Random House, 1967.

Ginsburg, N. S. "The Political Dimension: Regionalism and Extra-Regional Relations in Southeast Asia." *Focus*, Vol. 23 (December 1972), 1–8.

Gordon, B. K. *The Dimensions of Conflict in Southeast Asia*. Englewood Cliffs, N.J.: Prentice-Hall, 1966.

Gottmann, J. "Geography and International Relations." *World Politics,* Vol. 3 (January 1951), 153–73.

Hallstein, W. *United Europe: Challenge and Opportunity.* Cambridge, Mass.: Harvard University Press, 1962.

James, P. E., and C. F. Jones, eds. *American Geography: Inventory and Prospect.* Syracuse, N.Y.: Syracuse University Press, 1954. (See esp., Richard Hartshorne, "Political Geography.")

Kohn, H. *The Idea of Nationalism.* New York: Macmillan, 1944.

Kristof, L. K. D. "The Nature of Frontiers and Boundaries." *Annals of the Association of American Geographers,* Vol. 49 (March 1959), 269–82.

Lipset, S. M. *Political Man: The Social Bases of Politics.* New York: Doubleday, 1959.

MacFadden, H. C. "Toward Regional Cooperation Among Asian Nations." Unpublished manuscript, 1974.

———. "Changing Pattern of Sovereignty Over the Straits of Malacca and Singapore." Masters Research Paper (Thesis), University of California Los Angeles, 1973.

Mayfield, R. C. "A Geographic Study of the Kashmir Issue." *Geographical Review,* Vol. 45 (April 1955), 181–96.

Pearcy, G. E. "Geographical Aspects of the Law of the Sea." *Annals of the Association of American Geographers,* Vol. 49 (March 1959), 1–23.

Pollard, V. K. "A.S.A. and A. S. E. A. N. 1961–1967: Southeast Asian Regionalism." *Asian Survey,* Vol. 10 (March 1970), 244–55.

Pye, L. W. *Aspects of Political Development.* Boston: Little, Brown, 1966.

Regional Co-operation in Asia. Annual meeting of Directors of Development Training and Research Institutes, Tokyo, 10–14 March 1969. Development Centre of the Organisation for Economic Co-operation and Development.

Roy, S. J. *The Theory of Sovereignty.* Calcutta, 1923.

Shanks, M., and J. Lambert. *The Common Market Today — And Tomorrow.* New York: Praeger, 1962.

Silvert, K. H. *Expectant Peoples: Nationalism and Development.* New York: Random House, 1964.

Soja, E. W. *The Political Organization of Space.* Washington, D.C.: Commission on College Geography, Resource Paper No. 8, Association of American Geographers, 1971.

Thompson, J. E. *The Rise and Fall of Maya Civilization.* Norman: University of Oklahoma Press, 1956.

United Nations, Sea-Bed Committee. "Archipelagic Principles as Proposed by the Delegations of Fiji, Indonesia, Mauritius and the Philippines." Document No. A/AC.138.SC.11/L.15, 14 March 1973.

Vaillant, G. C. *The Aztecs of Mexico.* New York: Doubleday, 1950.

Whittlesey, D. *The Earth and the State.* New York: Holt, 1939.

Contour-planted pineapple fields in Hawaii. (Dole Pineapple)

6

Mosaic of Agricultural Land-Use

The Preagrarian Scene

Although *Homo sapiens* evolved as a species as long as 50 thousand years ago, the beginning of their agrarian pursuits are believed to be much more recent. Whenever and wherever agrarian life began, however, its inception marks one of the monumental steps in the long rise of civilization: the first conscious reshaping of the environment by human beings to suit their own needs. Recent attempts at dating the first human agrarian activities indicate that they may be much older than previously suspected. Cultivation and pastoralism may have been primary activities of the species for at least the past 10 thousand years.

Equally probable, and even more surprising, is the suggestion of some findings that many advanced agricultural practices and techniques were developed, somewhat simultaneously, on opposite sides of the world—in the Fertile Crescent region of the Middle East and, later, in parts of Middle America (Fig. 6–1). If these distant agrarian centers did develop independently and somewhat concurrently, there is reason to believe that agrarian pursuits are not, as some have believed, chance happenings in the course of cultural history but rather inevitable steps in the slow and painful ascent of intelligent life on the earth.

The Agrarian Revolution

Diffusion

From the early agrarian centers in the Middle East and Middle America, human groups apparently spread their domesticated plants and animals and their agricultural techniques to other regions, where favorable environmental conditions prevailed (Figs. 6–2 and 6–3). Thus the Agrarian Revolution began, and with it came a new and far more

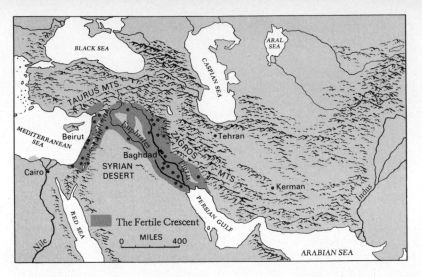

FIGURE 6–1

The Fertile Crescent. Archeological finds indicate that agriculture was probably begun in the forested mountain slopes in the northernmost part of this area and later undertaken in the more fertile lowlands to the south; the dots represent early agricultural sites.

enlightened era for humanity. The world became its home rather than just an uncontrollable wilderness in which to wander.

Agrarian influences probably spread from the Middle Eastern center into Europe, possibly as early as 6000 B.C., and then, within the next two millennia, into central Asia and along the southern Mediterranean shores. Thriving agrarian cultures apparently existed in China's northeastern Huang River

FIGURE 6–2

Agrarian influences spread from the Middle East into Europe as early as 6000 B.C., and north and south from Middle America as early as 4000 B.C. The location and time of most plant domestications cannot be known with certainty; thus many plants are considered to have several places of origin.

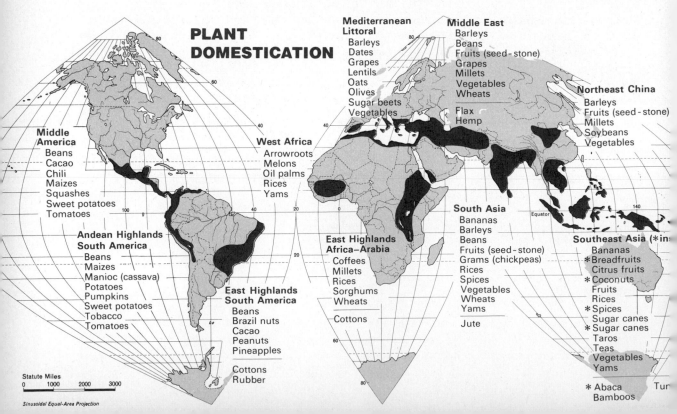

PLANT DOMESTICATION

Mediterranean Littoral
Barleys
Dates
Grapes
Lentils
Oats
Olives
Sugar beets
Vegetables

Middle East
Barleys
Beans
Fruits (seed-stone)
Grapes
Millets
Vegetables
Wheats

Flax
Hemp

Northeast China
Barleys
Fruits (seed-stone)
Millets
Soybeans
Vegetables

Middle America
Beans
Cacao
Chili
Maizes
Squashes
Sweet potatoes
Tomatoes

West Africa
Arrowroots
Melons
Oil palms
Rices
Yams

Andean Highlands South America
Beans
Maizes
Manioc (cassava)
Potatoes
Pumpkins
Sweet potatoes
Tobacco
Tomatoes

East Highlands South America
Beans
Brazil nuts
Cacao
Peanuts
Pineapples

Cottons
Rubber

East Highlands Africa–Arabia
Coffees
Millets
Rices
Sorghums
Wheats

Cottons

South Asia
Bananas
Barleys
Beans
Fruits (seed-stone)
Grams (chickpeas)
Rices
Spices
Vegetables
Wheats
Yams

Jute

Southeast Asia (*in
Bananas
*Breadfruits
Citrus fruits
*Coconuts
Fruits
Rices
*Spices
Sugar canes
*Sugar canes
Taros
Teas
Vegetables
Yams

*Abaca
Bamboos

Tur

Statute Miles
0   1000   2000   3000

Sinusoidal Equal-Area Projection

Valley as early as 3500 B.C., featuring millets, soybeans, and other crops largely or totally of local origin. By about 3000 B.C. agrarian cultures were also to be found in the Indian subcontinent's Indus Valley and in Southeast Asia. In the Western world, agrarian cultures spread from Middle America, beginning as early as 4000 B.C., into the Peruvian region and central interior of South America and, later, northward beyond Mexico.

Many references to agrarian practices in the Eastern world are found in the Old Testament as well as in early chronicles of the oldest known civilizations—the Egyptian, Babylonian, and Chinese (Fig. 6–4). The Romans, somewhat later, provide the first extensive record of efforts in the arts of plant breeding and animal husbandry, arts in which they attained impressive skill. They were familiar with the uses of fertilizers and crop rotation and with several methods of irrigation. As their empire expanded, their knowledge of agrarian techniques was carried across Europe and to northern Africa and western Asia.

Human Significance

Today, agrarian activity is universal. Wherever there are people there is foodstuff and other agricultural resources, and wherever there is agriculture there is the basis for human survival. More than half of the world's total labor force is involved in agrarian pursuits. Some of these are still quite primitive, others reflect highly advanced scientific theory and technology— which sustain human life (Figs. 6–5 and 6–6).

FIGURE 6–3

In general the regions of animal domestication coincide, quite naturally, with the regions of plant domestication. And as with plant domestication, the acceptance of dual centers of origin for many animals reflects the impossibility of dating early domestications with precision.

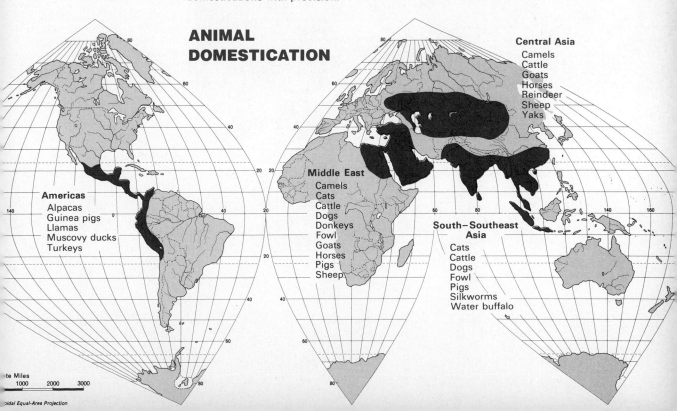

ANIMAL DOMESTICATION

Central Asia
Camels
Cattle
Goats
Horses
Reindeer
Sheep
Yaks

Americas
Alpacas
Guinea pigs
Llamas
Muscovy ducks
Turkeys

Middle East
Camels
Cats
Cattle
Dogs
Donkeys
Fowl
Goats
Horses
Pigs
Sheep

South–Southeast Asia
Cats
Cattle
Dogs
Fowl
Pigs
Silkworms
Water buffalo

te Miles
1000 2000 3000

oidal Equal-Area Projection

FIGURE 6–4

The Harvest, a Theban tomb painting (about 1415 B.C.) that depicts the reaping, measuring, and recording of a wheat crop. The *registers,* or rows, of the painting are read in sequence from bottom left to top right. (Photograph by Egyptian Expedition, The Metropolitan Museum of Art)

Major productive sectors	World labor force (in percentages)
Agriculture	51.0
Grazing	1.0
Forestry	.5
Hunting–fishing	.5
Mining–drilling	1.0
Industry	20.0
Services	26.0
Total	100.0

FIGURE 6–5

The differentiation of the world labor force into major productive sectors.

LABOR FORCE IN PRIMARY ACTIVITIES

Percent
- Over 75
- 51–75
- 25–50
- Under 25
- No data

Miles
1000 2000 3000

dal Equal-Area Projection

FIGURE 6–6

Well over 50 percent of the total world labor force is employed in primary activities. On a country-to-country basis, the percentage usually correlates inversely with socioeconomic advancement.

Foods for Survival

Human Nutritional Needs

Never before has there been so much food for so many, and so many with so little (Fig. 6–7). One of the major questions facing humanity today is whether, and how, the earth can provide food for the human populations of tomorrow. If present population trends continue, today's population of 4 billion will increase to one of 7 billion by the year 2000—nearly doubling in a single generation. This projection is staggering for several reasons, not the least of which is the fact that food supplies, too, will have to double

by the year 2000, in order to just maintain present consumption levels (Fig. 6–8). If allowances are made for the much-needed raising of dietary standards for all peoples to acceptable nutritional levels, the same population projection demands that food output be increased threefold by the year 2000.

To begin to comprehend the problems of feeding today's masses and tomorrow's even greater human numbers, we must understand a little of the basic nutritional needs of all people, needs that ignore ancestry, location, or custom. If their traditional foods are available in sufficient quantity, and with

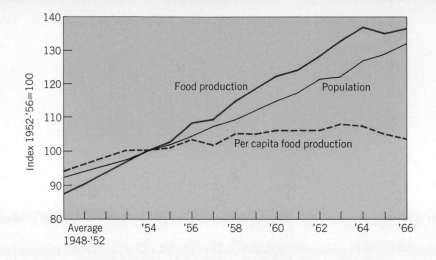

FIGURE 6-7

There have been substantial increases in world food production in recent decades; however, nearly equal rises in world population have kept the *per capita* increases in food production relatively small.

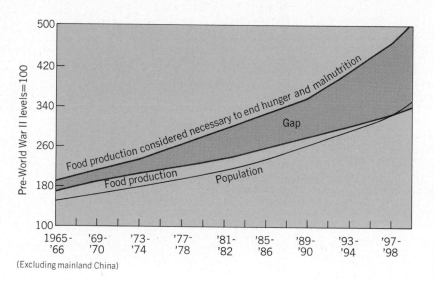

FIGURE 6-8

Projected increases in world population, probable food production, and necessary food production to the year 2000 show a widening gap between foods needed and foods in supply. (© 1966–67 by the New York Times Company. Reprinted by permission.)

reasonable regularity, most people will have a food intake that is fairly adequate. The undernourishment and malnutrition suffered by most peoples of the world stems mainly from the insufficient availability of some, or all, of their traditional foods, a lack of purchasing power, or ignorance in the selection and preparation of the foods available. Even a global abundance of foods equitably distributed, however, would not immediately solve all the world's food problems.

Foods in Supply

Most human nutritional needs can be satisfied by a few simple foods, most of which are produced at relatively little expense in developed and developing countries alike. Those produced worldwide include the true staple foods of humankind: the cereal grains—rice, wheat, and maize (corn)—and fruits and vegetables. The others, considered staples by the affluent and luxuries by the less affluent, are largely such animal-source foods as meats, milk, and dairy products. Cereal grains and produce—mostly carbohydrates—account for most of the food intake of the world's population, particularly among the 80 percent that live in poverty. Most human diets, then, supply largely carbohydrates; they are usually lacking in proteins and fats, as well as in many of the vitamins and minerals most easily obtained from meats and dairy products.

Needed Foods

Estimates of actual world food production and consumption, and of the quantities of food needed to achieve a higher standard of living in this and future generations, are frequently difficult to assess and interpret, because of the many different methodologies available. The most widely accepted index is the United Nations Food and Agricultural Organization's listings of "standard daily *per capita* caloric requirements," which estimate human caloric food needs by age, body size, sex, work activity, and environmental differences. On the basis of these FAO estimates, it is projected that the ideal minimum *per capita* average daily caloric need is 2,300 calories; and that a *per capita* daily food intake of less than 1,700 calories constitutes starvation. The FAO also estimates that, at present market levels, the *per capita* world average daily caloric production is about 2,400 calories. On the surface, these figures appear to suggest that there is a food sufficiency, and even a food surplus, throughout the world. But, when "spoilage" (averaging 10 to 25 percent in most foods) and failures or inequities in distribution to consumers are considered, the reality of the gap between caloric *need* and caloric *availability* becomes all too evident (Fig. 6–9).

Estimates of the *per capita* average in-

FIGURE 6–9

A food dole in India during a local drought. (Henri Cartier Bresson/Magnum)

take of protein are probably better guides to the quality of the human diet than are estimates of caloric consumption. Malnutrition is largely a matter of protein deficiency. Where animal source foods are essentially lacking, a wise and liberal consumption of many kinds of cereal grains and produce (usually requiring a knowledge of nutrition) is necessary if adequate amounts of the nutrient are to be obtained (Fig. 6–10).

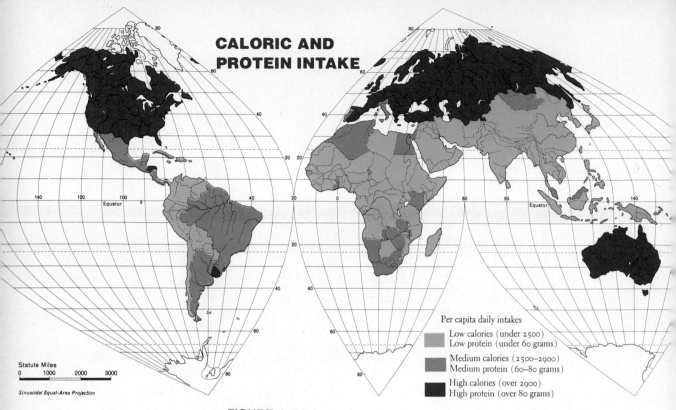

CALORIC AND PROTEIN INTAKE

Per capita daily intakes

Low calories (under 2500)
Low protein (under 60 grams)

Medium calories (2500–2900)
Medium protein (60–80 grams)

High calories (over 2900)
High protein (over 80 grams)

Statute Miles
0   1000   2000   3000

Sinusoidal Equal-Area Projection

FIGURE 6–10

Human nutritional levels vary considerably throughout the world. And since different foods have different values to the body, *per capita* protein intake is a better guide to world nutrition than either caloric consumption or total absorption by weight.

Environmental Potential and Cultural Development

Spatial Fragmentation

The magnitude and variety of agrarian development have always been limited by the environment. The present, somewhat uneven global distribution of agricultural production can thus be explained, at least in part, as being a consequence of the continuing need for adjustment of cultural development to environmental potential (Fig. 6–11). This situation should be considered only a temporary condition of a changing world; for it is all but certain that the distribution of agrarian centers will change in the future as

it has in the past. The more difficult questions are how much it will change, and in what ways; at present, these can be answered only with rough predictions.

The development of a new technology in food production has progressed to levels unimagined even a generation ago. But can this pace continue? Will there be scientific and technological developments to revolutionize agriculture in the future, or has a stasis been reached? Assuming that human inventiveness knows no bounds, as the saying goes, it is reasonable to expect that as new ideas continue to evolve, there will be some capable of affecting humankind's agrarian pursuits directly. Such things as hybrid corn, "miracle," or high-yield, rice and wheat, and *hydroponics* (the growing of plants in solutions and without the mechanical support of soil) may well be only harbingers of an accelerated pace in agrarian technological development, a pace that may be able to keep food supplies in balance with the growth in population. However, with all that can reasonably be expected of future technology, there will probably always be areas of the world where crops cannot be grown profitably and where most, if not all, pastoral pursuits cannot be practiced. The

map in Figure 6–11 gives a generalized view of the present global spatial potential for crop and animal production.

Spatial Controls

The distribution of agricultural activity is determined by a number of controls—some environmental and some cultural—operating interdependently. The predominant environmental controls are climate, landforms, drainage, soils, and vegetation. The most influential cultural controls are cultural inheritance and social attitudes, plant

FIGURE 6–11
Human habitation is strongly influenced by local environmental conditions, especially those that have a direct effect on agricultural production.

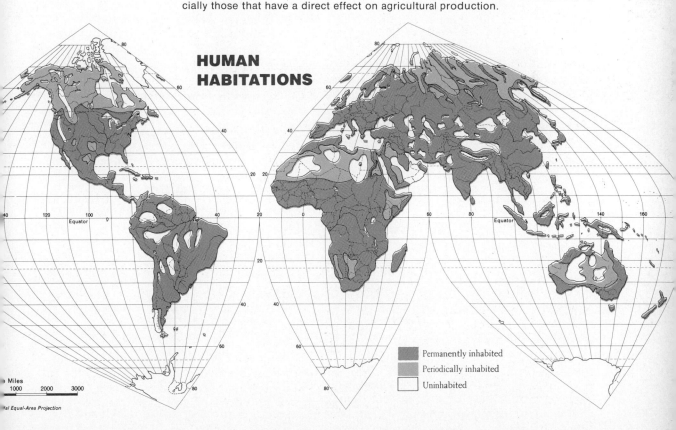

HUMAN HABITATIONS

Permanently inhabited
Periodically inhabited
Uninhabited

Miles
1000   2000   3000

al Equal-Area Projection

and animal selection, capital and labor, socioeconomic status, government, transportation and markets, and competing activities.

In general, the influence of environmental factors, considered both singly and as a group, declines as cultural factors advance in sophistication and complexity. For example, as a rule, environmental factors tend to exert more influence on simple agrarian societies than on more technologically advanced agrarian societies.

Since these environmental and cultural factors do not operate singly, it is somewhat artificial to assess them singly. However, their interactions are so complex, and their effects on agriculture sometimes so indirect, that a multiple-factor assessment tends to be suitable only in specific type studies.

Environmental Controls Over Agriculture

Climatic Controls

Each plant species has specific environmental requirements for and limitations to successful growth. Some plants are very tolerant, that is, capable of adapting to many varied conditions; while others have very restrictive environmental requirements. Notwithstanding the importance of landforms, the most potent environmental control over agrarian production is climate. Every plant, domesticated or wild, thrives best under some specific combination of temperature, moisture, wind, and light; each will tolerate other combinations for only limited periods.

The climatic element most critical in plant growth is that of temperature. Poleward, lower and more varying temperatures as well as shorter growing seasons progressively inhibit the production of crops and the growth of all wild plant life as well; while equatorward, higher and more uniform temperatures coupled with year-round growing seasons impose far fewer restrictions. Some crops, such as maize, can adapt to wide temperature ranges, and so are cultivated at several different latitudes. But other crops have a much smaller tolerance area. Commercial cotton, for example, has a poleward limit that lies approximately along the mean summer isotherm of 77° F., about 35° North latitude in the United States and 40° North latitude in China; and such food crops as sugar cane and bananas do not thrive in areas very far beyond the tropical regions. Temperature factors directly control the range of food crop and nonfood crop production, and thus there is strong competition by nonfood crops, such as cotton and other fibers, for the world's favored agricultural lands.

The situation is more complex than it appears at first glance, however. For, although maize can grow in a wide range of temperatures—thus allowing it to become a staple crop in southern, central, and western Africa, in much of South and Middle America and, of course, in the Corn Belt of the United States—to mature as a grain, it needs a lengthy period of hot summer days and warm summer nights. Hence it does not grow well in cool-summer, west-coast marine climates; and, therefore, it is virtually absent among the crops of Europe growing north of Italy and west of Hungary. In Minnesota, Wisconsin, and Michigan, all north of the Corn Belt, short and cool summers preclude the production of maize as ripened grain; thus, in these states the ears are harvested green, ground, and stored in silos as winter fodder for dairy cattle. In both this western portion of the Dairy Belt and that of the Corn Belt, maize is produced for animal feed, but, in each region, the crop is harvested, processed, and fed to the animals differently.

Within certain limits, humans are able to encourage plant growth by altering natural temperature conditions. The growing areas of several crops highly sensitive to freezing, for example, have been extended by the artificial raising of minimum temperatures in the fields at critical times. In southern Italy, citrus fruits are protected against frost by the building of roofs over entire orchards; each roof is made of boards spaced far enough apart to admit sunlight but close enough to reflect downward a considerable amount of ground radiation, which might otherwise be lost into space at night. In California's lemon and orange groves, cold lower layers of air are dispelled by currents of warm air blown earthward by motor-driven propellers set atop high towers; and, especially at night, air temperatures are raised by ground-level oil-burning heaters.

Moisture availability is another climatic element that serves to set limits on plant growth. Every crop and wild plant has a "dry limit"—some also have a "wet limit"—and an optimum moisture requirement. Crops are almost totally nonexistent in the world's vast desert areas, except where assisted by irrigation, and, in semiarid lands, their growth is seriously restricted (Fig. 6–12). Most major crops are produced universally in a pattern that closely mirrors moisture availability. An exception, wheat is commonly produced in semiarid to moist subtropical and midlatitude regions—but seldom in regions where heavy rainfalls occur during harvest periods, or within the tropics.

Landform Controls

Both major and minor features of the earth's crust exert considerable control over agrarian activities. The influence of land-forms operates both indirectly, through the climatic complex which, in turn, affects vegetation and soil, and directly, through land-use adaptability. Most of the world's agricultural lands are concentrated within broad regions that are comprised mostly of plains and undissected plateaus. Wherever the terrain is rough, as in mountain areas, cultivation is markedly limited, if not altogether precluded. Even in hilly regions and in areas having dissected plains and plateaus, cropping is often seriously restricted by the limited use of machines possible in such areas and the resultant prohibitive costs (Plates II and III).

Agrarian societies forced from flat lands into rougher terrains have survived. But, in general, mountain areas are notably lacking in agrarian development, with small mountain valleys accounting for most of their crop production. Adverse climatic conditions, due largely to higher elevations, and the problems of soil scarcity and short growing seasons all contribute to the lack of extensive agrarian development in the world's mountain regions—and, consequently, to the scarcity of ancillary cultural features, such as roads, housing, market centers, and irrigation systems.

Under some circumstances, however, even the most rugged mountain regions may become agricultural areas. If population densities are high in the flat lands, if the cost of labor is low and the food supply even lower, and if there is no market for labor other than the direct production of food at a subsistence level, great effort may be made to extend arable land to the mountain areas. This often necessitates the construction of *hillside terraces,* sometimes so narrow that only a single row of trees or a few rows of wheat or rice can grow on them. These terraces may form seemingly endless tiers up a mountainside, and individual trees or vines may be planted wherever the landform offers a pocket of soil big enough to support a plant. California and

FIGURE 6–12
The effect of irrigation on Quincy Valley in Washington. Above, an aerial view of the valley as it appeared in 1952—an unproductive, semiarid landscape. Below, the same view in 1957, when five years of irrigation under the Columbia Basin Project had transformed the valley into a rich agricultural region. (Bureau of Reclamation)

Illinois require that a field be big enough and flat enough for a tractor or combine to maneuver on. But in Greece, Crete, and Spain, for example, grape vines and walnut, carob, and olive trees are grown singly on steep, rocky hillsides; they are later harvested manually and the crop is carried away in baskets or sacks on the pickers' heads or backs. Similarly, in Indonesia and the Philippines, rice is grown on terraces located on the steepest of hillsides (Fig. 6–13). Perhaps the most extreme examples of how planters overcome nature in this manner are to be found in Scotland and Ireland; there, to permit the raising of potatoes, hillside terraces hewed in rock have been filled with soils concocted of peat from nearby bogs, sand composed largely of shell fragments from the beaches, and seaweed gathered along the shores. Al-

FIGURE 6–13

Terraced agricultural lands. Above, olive groves in the province of Alicante, Spain. (Heleva Kalda/Monkmeyer) Below, rice paddies in Luzon Island, Philippines. (Ewing Galloway, N.Y.)

though certain landforms act as deterrents to agriculture and other forms of human activity, when the pressure is sufficiently great, human beings can often overcome many terrestrial disadvantages and make use of seemingly unusable areas.

Drainage Controls

In many parts of the world, poor drainage conditions almost completely preclude human attempts to develop agriculture over extensive areas. Such conditions range from low wet spots in river floodplains to extensive coastal marshes too low to drain and reclaim for productive uses. Other regions are too frequently subject to damaging flooding (*natural drainage*) to sustain regular cropping; still, people often gamble on them, and some suffer periodic devastation as a result — roads, crops, dwellings, irrigation systems,

and a host of other cultural developments being destroyed in a few hours.

The decision as to whether or not certain areas in a country should be drained or left unchanged commonly has depended upon both the socioeconomic value of the crops that could be raised on such land and the population pressure present in adjoining dry areas. The Netherlands a heavily populated nation, hard pressed for agricultural land, undertook the draining of its coastal marshes centuries ago; today, much of its most productive land lies well below sea level, protected by dikes against the incursion of the sea. In central California, the chance to extend the area in which to grow such high-value crops as asparagus and rice has made the draining and diking of delta lands at the confluence of the Sacramento and San Joaquin rivers worthwhile. On the other hand, little serious thought has been given to draining and improving such areas as the vast coastal swamps of eastern Borneo,

FIGURE 6–14

A herd of goats in Big Bend National Park, Texas. Sharp-hoofed and voracious, such animals prod and bite the grass cover close to its roots and thus can do great injury to the soil of their grazing area. (National Park Service)

areas where population density is very low and huge areas suitable for agriculture are still unused.

Soil Controls

Agrarian development also depends, of course, on soil, which cannot be divorced from the elements of climate and vegetation in terms of its role as an environmental control. However, soil can be quickly destroyed or gradually improved independently of these other factors. Overpopulation, resulting in overcropping and overgrazing, along with poor cultivation practices can do much to destroy a good soil. And, once started, this destruction is difficult to halt and the soil, difficult to redeem (Fig. 6–14). Generally, the more economically advanced a country is and the more recent its agrarian practices, the more deliberate is the handling and maintenance of its soils.

Almost any soil can be rendered more suitable for the raising of a specific crop, through the use of appropriate fertilizers. And, it may well be that a better understanding of plant fertilizers and their proper application will play a large part as steps toward solving the ever-increasing world food crisis.

Vegetation Controls

Native vegetation also has a share of control over the world's agrarian activities, mostly inasmuch as it serves as an impediment to human efforts. Until the late 1800s, for example, the tough sod cover of the world's vast grasslands largely discouraged their cultivation; only after the availability of machinery like the steel plow were such regions, including the prairies and steppes of the United States, efficiently utilized for crop production. And, even with modern technology, the equally vast forest regions of the world are still forbidding obstacles to such human endeavors as crop tillage and animal husbandry.

Nevertheless, all crops are but domesticated versions of wild plants, bred to human tastes and, in many cases, dispersed widely into new environments and cultures. Thus potatoes, tobacco, maize, cacao, and rubber were domesticated in the New World and spread to the Old World; and, similarly, wheat, sugar cane, cotton, coffee, tea, oranges, and many lesser crops were domesticated in the Old and then introduced into the New World.

Cultural Controls Over Agriculture

The nature and global distribution of agrarian development have always been influenced, in large measure, by a variety of cultural controls, at times in conjunction with environmental ones and at other times in direct opposition to them. For example, cultural factors are at least partly responsible for the fact that there have always been areas of the world in which crops well-suited to the local environment have not been pro-

duced; and, as an even more frequent result of such factors, there have been areas in which ill-suited crops have been produced. These situations have usually developed through the misapplication of cultural controls due to an inadequate understanding of them, or through the misapplication of fully understood controls due to strong pressures from socioeconomic, political, traditional, and/or religious segments of the community.

Cultural Inheritance

Personal life styles and social attitudes passed down from generation to generation exert considerable influence over not only the type of agrarian activities any given human group adopts but, indeed, whether it will adopt one at all. For, in addition to those cultures that exist where no agrarian activities are possible, such as the Eskimo culture of the Arctic fringelands, there are others that, given their environmental conditions, could have developed very satisfactory agrarian life styles, but did not. Among these latter groups are the hunting-and-fishing peoples to be found in parts of tropical and midlatitude coastal lands, for example, the boat people of Hong Kong. The cultural inheritance of these groups includes no knowledge of or experience in cultivation or pastoralism, and the life styles followed by many of them are rather precarious.

However, in the majority of cultures by far, at least traces of agriculture have been present. Even most early cultural groups had knowledge of the rudiments of plant production and animal raising and some understanding of climatic conditions and soils as well. As these early peoples migrated, they took their biotic technologies with them, packing their valuable seeds and tools on the backs of domesticated animals. Thus they extended their agrarian ways to new areas, benefiting both themselves and the people with whom they came in contact. The cereal grains were probably the first foods to be shared with distant peoples in this fashion. Rice production, for example, probably spread from its source area in southeastern Asia until, today, it is practiced throughout Asia, wherever natural conditions are promising. Cultural groups in other parts of the world have also become aware of the food value of rice and adopted its production. Thus, ironically, commercial rice-production

in the southern United States, which is characterized by the use of modern production techniques and by high per acre yields, now serves as a model for the traditional rice-producing peoples of the world to study and emulate.

But, despite their dispersion, most staple crops are still more closely identified with the cultures of their source areas; for instance, the most distinctive "rice cultures" are those in Southeast Asia, and the primary "maize culture" is that in Mexico.

Plant and Animal Selection

Throughout the first millennia of agrarian activity, most successful human attempts to control the development of plants and animals were probably either accidental or the results of trial and error. In today's world, selection and breeding have advanced to new levels, with specialists able to develop plants and animals suited not only to particular environments but to particular cultural needs as well. As an example, scientific efforts have resulted in the creation of new types of wheat that are more resistant to drought conditions, better adapted to shorter growing seasons, less susceptible to the diseases common to humid areas and, perhaps of greatest importance, capable of much higher yields (Fig. 6–15). Such agricultural feats would hardly have been possible even a century ago.

The possibility of selecting and breeding crops with genetic resistances to diseases and pests has attracted plant breeders for half a century or more but, as yet, only limited beginnings have been made. Success in this area would not only release farmers from worry and costly disease and pest controls, but also spare consumers many of the scarcities and price escalations that result from crop failures.

Capital and Labor

To bring land under cultivation and insure its productivity, capital (money) is usually necessary. In some instances, the amount of capital needed is small; in others, it is very large. The establishment of a farm in the southern portion of Canada's northern forest region requires comparatively little capital: land costs there are relatively low; the acreage needed for such a farm is small; many of the materials needed for fences, barns, homes, and fuel can be obtained from the forest by the farmers themselves. In addition, access to hunting-and-fishing in the area can augment the family's food supply, while an abundance of wild hays can be cut to help feed the farm animals.

In contrast to this situation is the large amount of capital needed to set up a wheat ranch in North Dakota: here, the price of land is high; large tracts of land are necessary for successful commercial production; several kinds of expensive machinery are needed; fertilizers must be purchased; and wages must be paid. Also, reserve funds must be available to "ride out," not only possible crop failures resulting from drought, storms, abnormally heavy precipitation, plant diseases, and occasional locust plagues, but also those times when the market price for wheat is low. Even more capital is needed to establish a tropical plantation, especially one in a new area: land must be purchased, or leased; vegetation must be cleared away and continual work must be done to prevent its return; planting and cultivation costs are high; and fertilizers must be purchased. In addition, several years must elapse before there will be any return on the investment. For example, it takes anywhere from seven to nine years to bring a rubber plantation into production, during which time expenditures are heavy and income is nil.

Conditions in some parts of the world are such that land can be made productive only through huge investments of capital; and, often, government assistance as well as private capital may be necessary. This is particularly true in the development of desert and steppe areas, which require the building of such elaborate water-supply systems as reservoirs, main canals, lateral canals, small ditches, and flood-control works; and additional capital is required to meet the water costs that continue after these systems have been completed. If the agricultural use of these lands depends on the extraction of groundwater, then drilling, pumping, and maintenance costs will be involved. Heavy capital outlays are also necessary to develop swamp or marshlands for agricultural use: expensive drainage ditches must be dug and

FIGURE 6–15

Wheat—the staff of life for half the world's people. Left, the traditional wheat of Pakistan; right, MEXIPAK 65, an improved, or "miracle," wheat. (Ford Foundation).

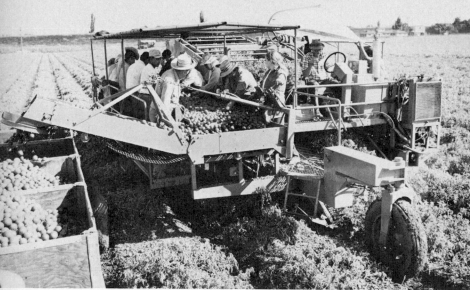

FIGURE 6-16

Different agricultural labor requirements. Above, a family farm in an Amish area of Pennsylvania that is worked by the owner and horse-drawn equipment. (Grant Heilman) Below, a California vegetable farm on which harvesting involves a hired labor force and complex machinery. (Blackwelder Corp.)

maintained; drain pipes must be laid in the fields; and, very often, pumping must be carried on. Thus, in one way or another, the availability of capital plays a vital part in the shaping of the world pattern of agriculture.

Some crops and some systems of agriculture have high labor requirements; others have low ones (Fig. 6–16). In any case,

labor is always involved in agriculture to some degree; and, since labor must be paid for, except where a family can itself furnish all the labor needed, it is closely related to capital. On the Canadian farm mentioned above, the cash outlay for labor is practically nil. But on the Dakota wheat ranch, despite the wide use of machinery, labor costs are appreciable. And on the tropical plantation, they are still higher; for, even if individual wages are low, the great number of laborers required makes the total cost very high.

The problem of labor, of course, cannot always be solved by the availability of capital. In some agricultural regions, there is a severe shortage or a complete deficiency in the supply of labor; and often, the problem is compounded by the inability to find laborers elsewhere or, if found, to get them to go to the areas where they are needed. These conditions present one of the major obstacles to the production of rubber in such remote areas as the Amazon Basin. In contrast, in industrialized nations, particularly the United States, urban life has proved so attractive that a great influx of manpower into the cities has occurred. This has drained farms of much of their labor force, and, since there has been no compensating flow from the cities, it has thus created another, different kind of labor problem.

Socioeconomic Development

Two-thirds of the world's population lives in so-called developing countries, and the other third, in relatively developed ones (Fig. 6–17). The agrarian sector in most of the developing countries dominates the economy, which is based largely on subsistence farming and only sparingly on technology and industrialization. Such lack of development does not denote an absence of industrialization alone, however. In most cases, the agrarian sectors are themselves inefficient, often due, in part, to social institutions that make the adoption of new procedures slow and difficult.

Rapid agrarian advancement within this large segment of the world is obviously greatly handicapped wherever technology cannot be extensively and skillfully em-

ployed. Most of these countries are poor, not in terms of land, climate, or individual abilities, but in terms of organized application of modern techniques. India, Indonesia, and Zaire are only some of the agrarian countries whose populations live at low economic levels on land of considerable unused potential. On the other hand, Japan, New Zealand, and Denmark offer examples of people living at much higher economic levels on land of relatively little natural potential.

Government and Politics

Under any and all forms of government, some physical and cultural controls over agriculture may have less than their usual importance. If agricultural activities take the form and location dictated by the government, wheat may be grown in a region that is better-suited for maize, cotton may occupy land better-suited for soybeans, and these and other food crops may be raised in regions more easily adapted to grazing or forestry. Such misapplications are often the result of a government's attempts to promote self-sufficiency for its people, regardless of cost, or to ensure a harvest large enough to accommodate sales to other nations. Strong governmental control of this sort affects the agriculture of only a few nations, but among these are two of the major powers in world agriculture, the Soviet Union and China.

Control of agriculture within national boundaries is by no means limited to totalitarian states; nontotalitarian countries may also establish direct or indirect agricultural controls. At times of overproduction, a government may pay its independent farmers not to plant particular crops and may deny them certain privileges if they fail to cooperate. In other instances, a collapsing market may be reinforced by government price-setting or by large-scale government buying.

DEVELOPED (ABOVE WORLD AVERAGE GDI)

Africa	Americas	Asia	Europe	Oceania
South Africa	Argentina	Israel	Austria	Australia
	Canada	Japan	Belgium	New Zealand
	Chile	Soviet Union	Czechoslovakia	
	Cuba		Denmark	
	Mexico		Finland	
	Puerto Rico		France	
	United States		Germany, E.	
	Uruguay		Germany, W.	
	Venezuela		Hungary	
			Ireland	
			Italy	
			Netherlands	
			Norway	
			Poland	
			Sweden	
			Switzerland	
			United Kingdom	

DEVELOPING (BELOW WORLD AVERAGE GDI)

Africa	Americas	Asia		Europe
Algeria	Bolivia	Afghanistan	Syria	Albania
Cameroon	Brazil	Bangladesh	Taiwan	Bulgaria
Egypt (U.A.R)	British West Indies	Burma	Thailand	Greece
Ethiopia	Colombia	Cambodia	Turkey	Portugal
Ghana	Costa Rica	China	Vietnam	Rumania
Liberia	Dominican Republic	India	Yemen	Spain
Libya	Ecuador	Indonesia		Yugoslavia
Malagasy	El Salvador	Iran		
Morocco	Guatemala	Iraq		
Mozambique	Haiti	Jordan		
Nigeria	Honduras	Korea		
Rhodesia	Nicaragua	Laos		
Sierra Leone	Paraguay	Lebanon		
Sudan	Peru	Malaysia		
Tanzania		Nepal		
Tunisia		Pakistan		
Uganda		Philippines		
Zaire		Saudi Arabia		
Zambia		Sri Lanka		

FIGURE 6-17

A categorization of developed and developing nations on the basis of *per capita* gross domestic income (GDI).

For example, during the Great Depression, when the world coffee market dropped to a very low level, the Brazilian government bought huge amounts of coffee from its citizens in an attempt at providing price support. Though much of the coffee was stored in warehouses, thousands of pounds of it were wasted, being dumped into the sea or burned. These same agricultural controls have also been used at various times in the United States. Agriculture may face other types of governmental controls as well. In many parts of the world, vast areas are set aside to serve as national forests, parks, and game preserves. Within them, all private uses of land, including agriculture, are stringently regulated or prohibited.

The quality and packaging of those exported agricultural products that cross international boundaries are often subject to strict governmental regulations; and the importation of crops is sometimes prohibited from certain areas but allowed from others. Many of these rules represent attempts to ensure the consumption of high-grade, disease-free products; but, sometimes, such regulations are imposed for purely political reasons.

Tariff laws also affect the movement of farm products. The extremely high prices set by many of these laws are established in order to prevent imports; others are made just high enough to protect domestic farmers from the competition of foreign products that can be sold cheaply due to their low production costs. The United States tariff on foreign sugar, for example, though not high enough to prevent imports, does enable domestic raisers of sugar cane and, especially, sugar beets, to meet foreign competition. This law is very effective because, without it, there probably would be no commercial sugar-cane or sugar-beet production in the continental United States.

Transportation and Markets

The problems of handling, moving, and exchanging agricultural products are extremely varied. If products are consumed by their producers, transporting them is usually fairly simple: in China, most of the rice produced is consumed within sight of the field where it grows; in Ireland, most of the potatoes grown are consumed on the farms that produce them. When commercial production of goods is involved, however, rapid and efficient means of transportation are of paramount importance. If a product such as sugar cane is not moved quickly from the fields to the mills, the juice in the stalks will sour; if bananas are not picked and shipped while green, they will be overripe when they reach distant ports. In short, the problem of transportation is particularly critical when any perishable product is involved. Where the proper type of transportation is not available, certain kinds of agricultural production cannot succeed, no matter how favorable all other physical and cultural factors may be.

Wheat, once harvested, is practically imperishable; yet, even the handling of this durable crop demands special transport equipment and storage facilities. The harvested wheat must be hauled to the railroad, where it is stored and kept dry in large elevators until it can be transferred to railroad cars and then moved to milling centers for processing or to ports for export (Fig. 6–18). Canadian wheat from southern Manitoba, for example, is transported first by rail to Fort William, on Lake Superior, then by lake boat to such ports as Kingston, on Lake Ontario, or Montreal, on the St. Lawrence River, and then across the Atlantic to a large wheat-receiving port, such as Liverpool, from which it may be carried to Asia or Africa.

Obviously, there is no point in producing commodities for the purpose of moving them over long distances unless there is a market for them at their destination. The price, which is extremely variable, which any product can command on the market is the final determinant of much farm production. The southwestern United States could be used as a supplier of huge quantities of natural rubber (from the guayule plant, a desert shrub), if rubber could command a selling price high enough to cover the extraordinary costs. Bananas might be produced in Greenland, under artificial conditions, if they could be sold at the high prices such an operation would require. When prices are high, even distant and marginal areas might be able to get their goods to market and sell them at a profit. When prices are exceptionally low, even regions favored by optimum natural conditions and proximity to markets may have trouble showing a return on their investment. Thus, a region may produce a cer-

FIGURE 6–18

Crop transportation and storage. Left, a newly cut cargo of Philippine sugar cane as it arrives at a refinery from fields nearby. (Philippine Travel and Tourist Association) Right, wheat elevators near a long-haul railway in Colorado. (Grant Heilman)

tain crop in some years but not in others, or farmers may withhold their goods from market in order to save additional, unredeemable costs or in hope of increased prices. Throughout the world, the production and distribution of agricultural goods is more closely determined by market values than by consumer need. Thus local scarcities, even in the area in which a crop is produced, may continue as long as markets elsewhere provide a greater monetary return.

Competing Activities

There are many parts of the world where certain crops are not grown, in spite of their being admirably suited to such production. That these lands are not under cultivation is usually because they have been given over to more valuable uses. In metropolitan Los Angeles, the once-numerous thriving and profitable walnut and orange groves, as well as vegetable and dairy farms, have been displaced by "urban sprawl"—by homes, factories, and freeways. As profitable as it once was on these lands, agriculture could not compete with urbanization. An interesting result has been the encouragement of agriculture in new areas removed from the spreading metropolis. Much the same process has occurred in many other metropolitan areas. As large cities have grown larger, and as nearby towns have become their satellites, land that once held farms has become the site of apartment houses, shopping centers, and factories; and the farms have had to move on (Fig. 6–19).

Some displacements of agriculture are more abrupt: in north-central California, for example, during the late 1800s, huge dredges in search of gold chewed up many farms and left, in their stead, only debris-piled wastelands. Since the early 1900s, ranches in Texas and Oklahoma have given way to "forests" of oil derricks. In this same period, parts of New England and the mid-Atlantic states have seen their farmlands become re-

sort and recreation areas, and other sections of the country have had power shovels and mining scars take the place of barns and planted fields. Though it does not represent an abuse of the environment, many mountain valleys and basins have also been lost to agriculture through their inclusion in national forests and parks. Thus, in one manner or another, competing activities, some regrettable and some commendable, continue to curtail or displace agricultural activities in many areas.

FIGURE 6–19

A recently built shopping center in Lancaster, Pennsylvania, on a site formerly occupied by small farms. (Grant Heilman)

Von Thünen's Location Theory

Because of the multitude of cultural and physical variables, there is no simple way to explain the spatial pattern of agricultural activities in the real world. The job is made easier, however, when approached by means of theoretical models, in which the number of variables can be controlled.

One of the first theoretical models for agricultural land-use was developed by Johann Heinrich von Thünen (1783–1850) and published in 1826 in his work *The Isolated State*. In the formulation and development of this theory, von Thünen drew heavily on his experience as a gentleman farmer on the North German Plain as well as on his knowledge of works by such prominent contemporary economic theorists as Adam Smith and David Ricardo.

The general intent of von Thünen's work, especially from a geographic point of view, was to demonstrate the influence of various cultural and physical factors on the spatial arrangement of different types of agricultural activities. For example, he was especially interested in determining the role of agricultural prices and distance from the marketplace in forming the rural land-use pattern in a free-enterprise system.

In order to do this, he developed a series of models; the first was the simplest, and the others, progressively complex modifications of the original. Each of the models represented an "isolated state," a totally self-contained, self-sufficient country with no outside connections of any sort—in a sense, each was a country in a test tube, to which he could add various elements as desired. His first model, or isolated state, for example, included the smallest number of elements: a single marketplace with a rural tributary area, or *hinterland*, surrounding it. In order to more closely approximate reality, this arrangement was complicated in subsequent models by the addition of multiple markets, a navigable river, tariffs, and so on.

About his initial model, von Thünen made these assumptions:

(1) There is a single urban market centrally located on a flat plain with uniform environmental characteristics (topography, climate, soils, fertility, and so on), and this market and its hinterland, solely dependent on each other, freely exchange all goods and services.

(2) The state's economic system is free and competitive, and it encourages the entrepreneur to maximize profits as permitted by the process of supply and demand.

(3) For any given product, all land is equal in terms of on-site production costs and productivity per unit.

(4) Finally, there is one mode of transportation (the horse-drawn wagon) throughout the plain, providing equal accessibility to the marketplace from all parts of the hinterland.

The first major variable in the model is the cost the farmers incur in getting their products to market. These transport costs are directly proportional not only to their distance from the marketplace but also to the weight, bulk, and perishability of the products involved. The second major variable is the price of each agricultural product, which is determined in the marketplace by the law of supply and demand.

Thus, the spatial pattern of agriculture in this von Thünen model depends primarily on the interaction between transport costs and market price. It is through the mechanism of *economic rent* that these variables exert their influence. The term *economic rent* refers to payments required for the use of scarce, nonreproducible resources. In the context of von Thünen's model, it is the amount paid by a farmer for a unit of land, a resource that is scarce and in fixed supply. Since the allocation of land around the marketplace is based on competitive bidding, the cost of this nonreproducible resource is determined solely by the existing demand for it.

The more profit a farmer can expect to make per unit of land, the higher his bidding power (or manageable economic rent) and, thus, his chance of occupying land close to the central market. Note that a farmer's profit is measured not in terms of return per unit of weight (pound, kilogram, and so on), but rather in terms of return per unit of land (acre, hectare, and so on). Since, due to the farmer's transportation costs, the margin of profit per acre for a particular product decreases with increasing distance from the market, there is a distance from the market beyond which a product would bring no profit at all. Thus, to be profitable, all products must be produced on the market side of their critical distance. However, since only the most valuable product can provide the amounts commanded by the most desirable areas in competitive bidding, this product will be the only one adequate in the near-market areas. Farms in adjacent areas, with higher transportation costs, will be at a disadvantage if they produce the same product; their chances of showing a profit are better if they avoid competing with near-market areas and produce the next most profitable product. Farms even farther from the market will find it advisable to avoid both the most profitable product and the runner-up or any product produced in an area that is closer to the market than they are.

The result is the formation of a series of distinct circular zones around the market, each with its own agricultural products (Fig.

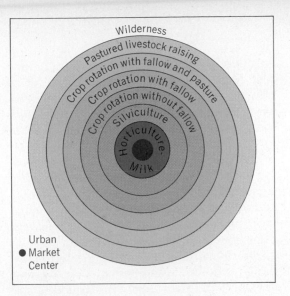

FIGURE 6–20

The agricultural zones that develop around von Thünen's urban market center.

6–20). The farmers whose products yield the higher per acre profits are found on the more expensive land closer to the market, and those whose per acre profits are lower occupy the less expensive land farther from the market.

On the basis of von Thünen's assumptions about transportation costs, the maximum distance from the market at which a given product can be produced profitably tends to vary inversely with the difficulty involved in transporting it. In von Thünen's time the restrictions of heavy, bulky, and perishable products were particularly acute.

On the land closest to the market center, farmers maximized their profits by selling milk and such horticultural items as fruits and vegetables. The market demand for these highly perishable products (due, mainly, to poor techniques of food preservation and slow means of transport) determined the extent of this first zone. Inhabitants of zone two specialized in silviculture. This seemingly odd use of such expensive land actually made good sense during von Thünen's time, because forest products were the main source of both fuel and building materials.

Furthermore, the rapid decrease in economic rent (profit) due to the increasing cost of transportation meant that these bulky commodities could not be produced too far from the market. Zones three, four, and five all featured commercial crop and livestock farming, with the intensity of cultivation decreasing outward from the market. Zone three had a one-field system of intensive crop rotation, and its marketable items were grains, potatoes, and any surplus livestock products. Zone four had a two-field system that allowed it to alternate sowing and fallow periods without halting production; its most profitable products were rye, livestock, and butter and cheese. Zone five had a less intensive, three-field rotation system wherein each farm was equally divided between cropland, fallowland, and pasture; this zone offered the same marketable products as zone four, but in smaller quantities. Zone six was devoted to pastured livestock-raising — an *extensive*, or low-labor, form of land-use; its commercial products included livestock, which could be walked to market, and such processed dairy foods as butter and cheese, which, less bulky and perishable than the products of zone one, could also be transported economically. Beyond the last zone was a wilderness area, considered unprofitable for any commercial agriculture.

Following this basic and very simplistic model, von Thünen extended his theoretical analysis through models with variables more complex than those attending a single centrally located market. Although none of his models corresponded to any real-life situation exactly, the basic locational principles he developed have been the foundation for many subsequent land-use theories and are still of value today in the spatial analysis of various cultural activities.

REVIEW AND DISCUSSION

1. What is the significance, in terms of cultural change, of findings suggesting that the early development of many advanced agricultural practices and techniques occurred somewhat simultaneously on opposite sides of the earth?
2. One of the world's major problems today is supplying the food needs of its growing population. Discuss and evaluate this problem, in light of the projected population increases by the year 2000. What are some of the major causes of undernourishment and malnutrition in different parts of the world?
3. FAO estimates place the world *per capita* daily caloric production at about 2,400 calories and the minimum *per capita* daily caloric need at about 2,300 calories. On the basis of these figures, there would appear to be a world *per capita* caloric sufficiency, but in fact there is a deficiency. Discuss.
4. Which probably serves as a better guide to the "quality" of the human diet, estimates of protein consumption or estimates of caloric consumption? Explain.
5. "In general, the influence of environmental factors, considered both singly and as a group, declines as cultural factors advance in sophistication and complexity." Discuss and evaluate this contention. In what ways is it valid and/or invalid with respect to the Dust Bowl area of the United States?
6. Of all the environmental controls over agrarian production, which exerts the most influence? Why? Provide two examples that illustrate how human beings have begun to overcome this environmental control as well as others.
7. Of all the cultural controls over agrarian production, which is the most potent? Does this cultural control exert equal influence in all parts of the world where it is operative? Explain with appropriate examples.

8. What was von Thünen attempting to demonstrate by means of his theoretical models?
9. What cultural controls are operative in von Thünen's location-theory model?
10. Explain the pattern of agricultural land-use in the area around von Thünen's central marketplace. Why does this pattern develop? To what extent would it be likely to occur in the real world?

SELECTED REFERENCES

Braidwood, R. J. "The Agricultural Revolution." *Scientific American,* Vol. 203 (September 1960), 131–48.

Chisholm, M. *Rural Settlement and Land Use: An Essay in Location.* London: Hutchinson University Library, 1962.

Clark, C. *Population Growth and Land Use.* London: Macmillan, 1968.

Clark, C., and M. Haswell. *The Economics of Subsistence Agriculture.* London: St. Martin's, 1964.

Cutler, H. "Food Sources in the New World." *Agricultural History,* Vol. 28 (April 1954), 43–49.

Ehrlich, P. R., and A. H. Ehrlich. *Population, Resources, Environment.* San Francisco: Freeman, 1970.

Flannery, K. F. "Ecology of Early Food Production in Mesopotamia." *Science,* Vol. 147 (12 March 1965), 1247–55.

Grotewold, A. "Von Thünen in Retrospect." *Economic Geography,* Vol. 35 (October 1959), 346–55.

Hall, P., ed. *Von Thünen's Isolated State.* Oxford: Pergamon Press, 1966.

Harris, D. R. "New Light on Plant Domestication and the Origins of Agriculture." *Geographical Review,* Vol. 57 (January 1967), 90–107.

Higbee, E. *American Agriculture.* New York: Wiley, 1958.

———. *Farms and Farmers in an Urban Age.* New York: Twentieth Century Fund, 1963.

Holden, C. "Food and Nutrition." *Science,* Vol. 184 (3 May 1974), 548–50.

Isaac, E. *Geography of Domestication.* Englewood Cliffs, N.J.: Prentice-Hall, 1970.

Kramer, S. N., and the editors of Time-Life Books. *Cradle of Civilization.* New York: Time, Inc., 1967.

MacFadden, C. H. "Food and Man in Ceylon." *Papers of the Michigan Academy of Science, Arts, and Letters,* Vol. 38 (1953), 323–29.

Malthus, T. R. "An Essay on Population," Vol. 1. New York: Dutton, Everyman's Library, 1933.

Peet, J. R. "The Present Pertinence of von Thünen Theory." *Annals of the Association of American Geographers,* Vol. 57 (December 1967), 810–11.

Sauer, C. O. *Agricultural Origins and Dispersals.* New York: American Geographical Society, 1952.

———. "Sedentary and Mobile Bents in Early Societies." *Social Life of Early Man.* Publications in Anthropology No. 31. Viking Fund, 1961.

Spencer, J. E. *Shifting Cultivation in Southeast Asia.* University of California Publications in Geography No. 19 (1966).

Staley, E. *Future of Underdeveloped Countries.* New York: Praeger, 1961.

Von Thünen, J. H. *Der Isolierte Staat in Beziehung auf Land-wirth-schaft und Nationalökonomie,* 3 vols. Hamburg, Germany: Friedrich Perthers, 1826.

"The World Food Problem." *Report of the Panel on the World Food Supply.* Vols. 1, 2, and 3. Washington, D.C.: U.S. Government Printing Office, 1967.

Al Qatif, a Saudi Arabian coastal town surrounded by irrigated date gardens.
(Standard Oil Co., N.J.)

7

Agrarian Societies:
Changes and Diffusions

For perhaps three million years human beings lived by hunting and gathering; only about ten thousand years ago did there develop on this planet more complex forms of agrarian living. The types of agricultural societies now in existence thus represent the latest stage in a relatively short period of human responses to natural and cultural agrarian controls. Their functional diversity is, with certainty, even more recent, developing, for the most part, within the last two hundred years and owing its extent mainly to spatial variations in the incorporation of technology and scientific knowledge. For the purposes of this text, therefore, contemporary agricultural peoples are divided into *preindustrial agrarian societies* and *industrial agrarian societies* (Fig. 7–1).

Preindustrial agrarian societies:
  Subsistence
    Nomadic hunting and gathering
    Nomadic herding
    Shifting cultivation
    Sedentary subsistence farming
      Rice-dominant, or sawah, regions
      Non-rice-dominant regions

Industrial agrarian societies:
  Commercial
    Crop and livestock farming
    Dry-grain ranching
    Tropical plantations

FIGURE 7–1

The major types of agrarian societies in existence throughout the world.

Preindustrial Agrarian Societies: Subsistence

Nomadic Hunting and Gathering

Nomadic hunting-and-gathering people still exist over some sparsely populated but extensive regions of the world (Fig. 7–2).

Like most nomads before them, they occupy some of the earth's least favorable lands, those rejected by the inhabitants of permanent settlements because of extreme weather conditions or rugged terrain (Fig. 7–3).

Theirs are largely the fringe areas of the inhabited world, seemingly barren lands with little apparent potential: the poleward margins of the Americas and Eurasia; scattered interior areas of Middle America, South America, and Africa; and the highland portions of Southeast Asia. Anthropologists have long since learned that geographic isolation is an important safeguard to the continuing existence and life style of these hunting-and-gathering societies. Most of these groups have dwindled drastically in the last hundred years, and today they comprise no more than a quarter of a million people, the majority of whom are found in Africa. Notable among them are the Bushmen of the Kalahari Desert, in southern Africa, the Negritos of the Philippines, and a number of Indian tribes of South America.

Nomadic Herding

With the earliest domestication of animals (which may even predate the first plant domestications), many nomadic peoples turned from hunting as their principal livelihood to herding. Hours once spent stalking and attacking game were now devoted to tending groups of relatively pacific animals —to moving them between areas of pasture

FIGURE 7–2

The regional development of predominant livelihoods has been influenced not only by local environmental conditions but by technological levels, cultural practices, and political policies as well.

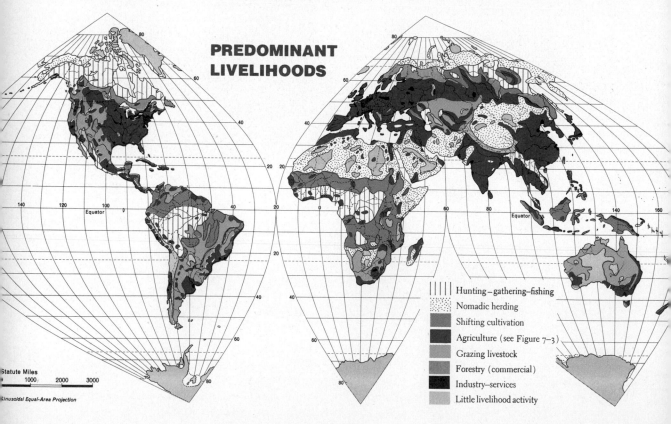

PREDOMINANT LIVELIHOODS

Hunting–gathering–fishing
Nomadic herding
Shifting cultivation
Agriculture (see Figure 7–3)
Grazing livestock
Forestry (commercial)
Industry–services
Little livelihood activity

and water and protecting them from predators and the elements. By their labors, the herders gained fairly dependable supplies of milk and, with selective slaughtering, blood, meat, clothing, and building materials.

The contemporary herder can generally support more people than the hunter-gatherer, but faces, almost equally, the disadvantages of forced group transience. Although not daily at the mercy of their surroundings for food, nomadic-herding societies, like hunting-gathering peoples, can be quickly devastated by almost any natural disaster. Without adequate shelters and artificial support systems, their herds can be wiped out by even a mild drought or flood. And, since they reckon wealth in terms of animals owned, and seldom receive cash, nomadic herding societies rarely have any accumulated purchasing power with which to replace a flock or herd (Fig. 7–4).

Present-day nomadic herders are located largely in the arid and semiarid regions of the Eastern world, where their areas form a broad belt across North Africa, the Middle East, and much of central Asia, an east-west distance of well over eight thousand miles. The domestic animals characteristic of the nomadic-herding societies in these regions are cattle, sheep, goats, camels, and horses.

FIGURE 7–3

Only about 10 percent of the world's land area is used for crop production—a very low percentage given the average yield per acre and the number of people to be fed. Moreover, some of the lowest yields occur in the most densely populated areas.

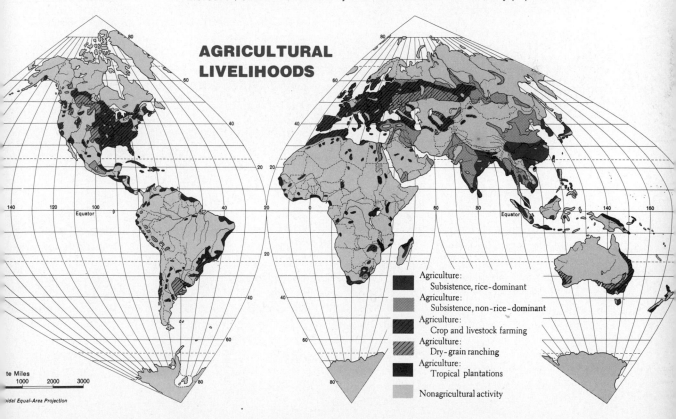

AGRICULTURAL LIVELIHOODS

Agriculture:
    Subsistence, rice-dominant
Agriculture:
    Subsistence, non-rice-dominant
Agriculture:
    Crop and livestock farming
Agriculture:
    Dry-grain ranching
Agriculture:
    Tropical plantations

Nonagricultural activity

te Miles
1000   2000   3000

idal Equal-Area Projection

FIGURE 7–4
Malian nomads in Upper Volta's Christina Wells. These nomads migrated from Mali in search of water, but found only more drought and starvation, hardships widespread in northwestern Africa in the late 1960s and early '70s. The woman pounds scarce bits of grain for her family, but the trees and a steer have already succumbed to the drought. (United Nations)

Shifting Cultivation

After perhaps three million years as hunters and gatherers, and a brief time as nomadic herders, human beings advanced to their first involvement in rudimentary cultivation, by tending a few plants in a succession of small forest clearings. The trees in these clearings were usually either felled or girdled and left standing for firing, the ashes of the small trees being mixed with forest litter and spread over the dark soils as natural fertilizer. The ground was then dug with sticks or hoes, and plants or seeds — usually a variety of beans, yams, taro, cassava, melons, and other hardy horticultural plants — were

inserted. When the fertility of a clearing declined and weeds overpowered the crops, a new area was cleared (Fig. 7–5).

With this shifting cultivation there developed, for the first time in human history, the possibility of semipermanent settlement and attachment to the land. And the need to traverse vast areas in pursuit of game, or to move continuously in search of pasture for herds and flocks, was thus greatly reduced.

Shifting cultivation became widespread over many parts of the world, particularly within tropical-humid regions of Africa, the Middle East, Middle America, northeastern China, and southern and southeastern Asia. It is still the prevailing form of agriculture in many parts of the world and is known, variously, as *milpa,* in Latin America; *fang,* in Africa; *ladang, taung-ya,* and *chena* in parts of southern and southeastern Asia; and the Old English term *swidden* is sometimes used by Western research scholars to mean a "burned clearing." Today, there are probably fifty million people practicing shifting cultivation; more than half of them are located in central Africa and Indonesia (Fig. 7–6).

Sedentary Subsistence Farming

Humanity's first major step into agriculture, through the practice of shifting cultivation, was followed, in the Middle Stone Age, by the development of *sedentary subsistence farming,* the working of a specific piece of land on a long-term basis to satisfy personal food needs. This prehistoric form of agriculture persists in many contemporary societies and affects about half the people of the world; it is still the major livelihood in the tropical and midlatitude lands of southern and eastern Asia. This way of life produces all or most of the available foods and other essential materials used by almost two billion people; but seldom does it provide

FIGURE 7–5

The practice of slash-and-burn agriculture in the Amazon Basin, Brazil. (Loren McIntyre, Woodfin Camp)

FIGURE 7–6

Much of the world's land area is ill-suited to human occupance based upon agriculture. Many societies thus eke out an existence within environments that are too cold, too dry, too hot and wet, and/or too high and steep for easy cultivation.

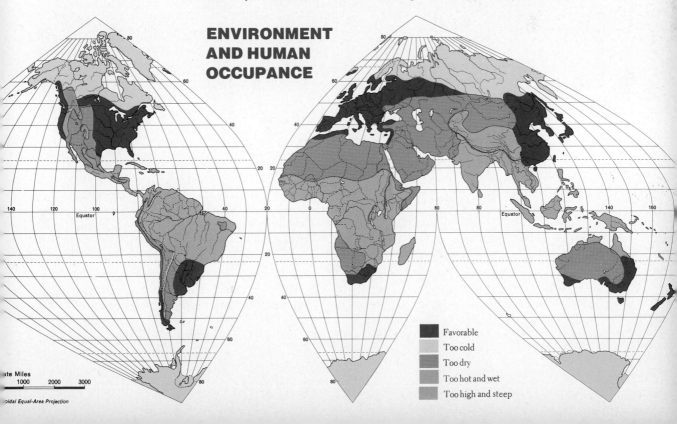

ENVIRONMENT AND HUMAN OCCUPANCE

Favorable
Too cold
Too dry
Too hot and wet
Too high and steep

surpluses to be stored or sold. Subsistence agriculture is also *intensive,* that is, it uses high amounts of human labor per acre.

The sedentary subsistence-agriculture societies of today differ very little from those of ancient times. Typically, their farm plots are only one or two acres in extent and are often fragmented into several widely separated miniplots; these are usually devoted to the growing of different crops, in order to provide the family with some semblance of dietary balance, and intensively worked by family members, with the help of few tools,

few or no draft animals, and practically no mechanical power (Fig. 7–7).

The dominant crops of most sedentary subsistence-agriculture societies—rice, in wet areas, and wheat, millet, and leguminous plants, in drier areas—are all foods high in starch and low in proteins and fats. In some areas these starchy foods are accompanied, in the human diet, by leafy vegetables, usually in fair variety but small quantity, by bananas and other fruits, and by small and infrequent additions of meats, poultry, and diluted dairy products.

FIGURE 7–7
Near New Delhi, India, a small subsistence farm tended by family members with the aid of a pair of bullocks and some simple tools. (Marc and Evelyne Bernheim, Woodfin Camp)

Rice-Dominant, or Sawah, Regions.
Rice, the staple food of much of southern and eastern Asia, so strongly dominates life and fortune from India to Japan that this entire area is sometimes called the "rice crescent," or the *sawah,* or wet-field rice, culture (Fig. 7–8). A major crop in world agriculture for several thousand years, rice today feeds more than one-third of the world's people. Its dominance throughout southern and eastern Asia is due primarily to the region's terrain and climate (Plates III and IV; Fig. 6–13). Because they generally thrive under irrigation, rice fields are largely free from cyclical harvest failures and produce continuously high yields over long periods; their crop is relatively simple to produce and store and makes a highly adaptable and easily prepared basic food.

The vast Asian rice crescent includes the countries of Pakistan, India, Sri Lanka, and Bangladesh—in South Asia; Burma, Thailand, Cambodia, Malaysia, Singapore, Vietnam, Laos, the Philippines, and Indonesia—in Southeast Asia; and Taiwan, China, North Korea, South Korea, and Japan—in East Asia (Plates II and III). Most rice production in this region is confined to the flatter coastal lands and flat-bottomed river valleys. In some areas, however, spectacular yields have been developed from hillside terraces, the oldest and most spectacular of which are those on Luzon Island, in the Philippines; others can be found in Sri Lanka, Japan, southern China, and Java.

In only a few regions—among them, Burma's Irrawaddy Delta and Thailand's peninsula—is rainfall usually sufficient for

FIGURE 7–8

Most of the world's rice production occurs in eastern and southern Asia, with China and India accounting for over 55 percent of the annual total. Most of the world's rice trade takes place within the same areas.

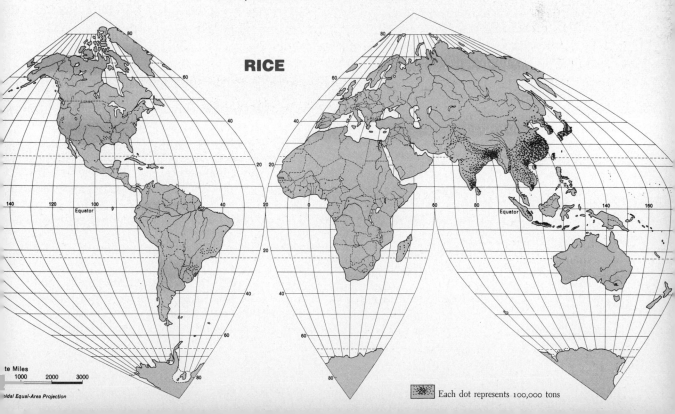

RICE

Each dot represents 100,000 tons

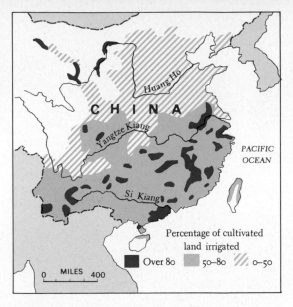

FIGURE 7–9

The extent of irrigation in China, the most intensively irrigated portion of the vast rice crescent. (Adapted from R. R. C. de Crespigny. *China: The Land and Its People*, St. Martin's Press, New York, 1971.)

rice production; in most rice-producing areas, some type of irrigation system has had to be developed and must be used every planting season. In the most intensively irrigated portion of the rice crescent, central and southern China, over 50 percent of all cultivated land is irrigated, with the percentage surpassing 80 in some sections (Fig. 7–9). Many other countries have developed irrigation as intensively as China, though over smaller areas relatively. Throughout most of the rice crescent, two rice harvests are commonly achieved in any one year; but where irrigation is particularly well regulated, three crops a year are not unusual. Illustrative of the complex irrigation systems necessary for rice production in much of Asia is the Mekong River Development Project. Like the Tennessee Valley Authority, in the United States, and most of the other great water-control projects completed or under construction in southern and eastern Asia, the Mekong project is multipurpose, combining irrigation, flood control, and power production.

The production of rice in Asia is an arduous task, one in which human labor is used almost exclusively. Following the first monsoons the soils are turned, by hand with a mattock or by bullock-drawn plows, and then flooded and worked into a thin sludge. Then, young rice plants are transplanted from nursery beds to the newly prepared fields (in Asia, a job done almost exclusively by women); finally, the plants are tended, weeded, and harvested (undertakings involving mixed labor). Most harvesting is done by hand with a sickle or knife, each head of rice being cut from its stalk separately to ensure minimum loss of the precious grains.

The breeding and raising of animals for human consumption is relatively minimal throughout most of the sawah system; however, many animals are used in the fields for draft purposes (but even they are provided little feed or pasture and thus must forage on the roadsides and irrigation embankments). As long as the traditional underemployment in sawah areas prevails—and few other occupational outlets seem in the offing—there will be no real incentive to further mechanize any major phase of Asian rice production. Humans will continue to carry the brunt of the workload (Fig. 7–10).

Where extensive mechanization has been applied to rice production—in areas of southern Europe and the southern and southwestern United States—much higher yields per acre have resulted. Rice harvests in California, for example, average about 4,500 pounds per acre; while those in Asian countries average 1,600 pounds per acre, with China at 2,100 pounds and Japan leading at 3,800 pounds. Japan's high yields per acre result largely from advanced techniques in seed selection, the use of quality commercial fertilizer, plentiful irrigation, and widespread use of mechanical equipment designed especially for sawah production.

China's relatively high productivity is due largely to extensive use of organic fertilizers, including much "night soil" (human waste), and fairly advanced techniques of seed selection and irrigation; some successful harvests have also been attributed to the extended use of deep plowing and close planting. India's generally low efficiency levels in rice production, lower than either Japan's or China's, are attributable, in part, to less favorable climatic conditions, less well developed irrigation, and rather decided deficiencies in seed selection, fertilization, and pest control. However, the introduction of some Japanese agricultural methods into India has already shown some beneficial results.

IR-8, the so-called miracle rice — a high-yielding hybrid-grain plant developed in recent years at the International Rice Research Institute in the Philippines — has been cultivated experimentally in several Asian countries with good to mediocre results — varying usually with environment, expertise of farmers, informed use of commercial fertilizers, proper irrigation, and proper weed and pest controls. If most of these variables can be controlled, IR-8 seems to promise yields of two to six times those of traditional rice strains. Thus it may be the key to sustained increases in Asian rice production and thereby a stimulus to the region's socioeconomic progress (Fig. 7–11).

Non-Rice-Dominant Regions. Although adjacent to the sawah lands, most of the dry interior areas of India, Pakistan, and China north of the Yangtze River, as well as inland portions of Southeast Asia, differ from them considerably in terms of agriculture. This disparity reflects marked differences in moisture availability and a perhaps related regional contrast in individual wealth. Since their rainfall is deficient and their people cannot afford the high costs of irrigation, these interior areas of Asia must produce

FIGURE 7–10

Women planting rice in Vietnam. (Air France)

FIGURE 7–11

The threshing of IR-8, or "miracle" rice, at Manila's International Rice Research Institute. (The Rockefeller Foundation)

FIGURE 7-12

Terraced loessal fields in the highlands of northern interior China. (Marc Riboud from Magnum Photos)

food grains other than rice; their fields are planted with wheat, kaoliang, millets, and sorghum and, secondarily, with such crops as grams (chickpeas), peanuts, cotton, and sugar cane.

In the interior areas of India and Pakistan, *per capita* productivity is among the lowest in the world; there are too many people, on too little land, with too little irrigation and agricultural technology. In addition, in some places an antiquated land-tenure system severely hampers both the incentive and the efficiency of the people. Recently, land-reform movements, some meaningful governmental extension services and financial support, and improved seed grains and fertilizer supplies have helped to increase *per capita* production in some of these areas for the first time in generations. Much more is

needed, however, to cope with the minimal needs of the burgeoning population and with the often extreme weather. Many of Asia's hot and dry interior lands, especially those in India, are heavily dependent on the rains of the monsoons; when the monsoons fluctuate, in either arrival time or amount of rainfall, crops in these areas suffer and frequently fail. With little or no food in reserve, the subsequent food shortages are often severe.

In China, where the landscape grades rather suddenly from the rice fields south of the Yangtze River to the winter wheat and kaoliang fields north of that river, agriculture is not quite as precarious as it is in Pakistan or India. The northern interior areas of China are mainly flat expanses of fertile and less fertile soils, with rainfall less frequent and certain than that in the area to the south, and many periods of alternating drought and devastating flood. However, in spite of its dryness and poor irrigation systems, northern China is a highly productive region, providing much of the country's major domestic food grains, wheat and kaoliang, and a wide range of secondary crops, including barley, peas, soybeans, peanuts, maize, fruits, vegetables, sweet potatoes, and tobacco. Particularly in the highlands to the northwest, this productivity is helped by broad deposits of rich eolian silt, or loess. Several hundreds of feet thick in places, these deposits can support good agricultural production despite marginal rainfall and little irrigation. Many parts of these loessal highlands have been terraced in order to check the erosion of their valuable soils (Fig. 7–12). The lands of China north of the Yangtze could, of course, produce even more food and fiber if sufficient irrigation were available. Thus, building an adequate irrigation system is a task the Chinese have undertaken with great vigor in the past two decades; and the millions of laborers at work in this cause, though equipped with hand tools and few machines, have apparently made surprising progress (Fig. 7–13). If widespread famines are to be avoided, this kind of development must soon be undertaken on a large scale throughout Asia.

FIGURE 7–13

Dam building on the Huang Ho. To improve irrigation and flood control near the river, the Chinese have completed many such arduous construction projects in the past two decades. (© Henri Cartier-Bresson and Magnum Photos)

Industrial Agrarian Societies: Commercial

Many of the world's agrarian societies have been transformed, through the application of modern industrial technology, from various stages of crop- and livestock-raising, into industrial agrarian societies. These changed societies have learned how to utilize industrial planning, organization, and marketing techniques in the production and distribution of raw materials. In contrast to the subsistence farming described earlier, the average farm in an industrial agrarian society produces goods primarily for sale rather than solely to meet the nutritional needs of its occupants.

Crop and Livestock Farming

Typical of the industrial agrarian society is the practice of combining large-scale crop production and livestock raising, or *mixed farming*. Although different farms may raise different sorts of crops and livestock, most commercial mixed-farming operations follow similar practices of crop rotation (Fig. 7–14). Such practices are essential to high-productivity farming, for they maintain and build natural soil fertility by varying, with each crop, the net chemical output of the land.

Alternating fields so that there are always some left fallow, in order for their soil to regain its strength, is probably the oldest form of crop rotation, but it is usually considered too wasteful to be used in commercial farming. More viable is the practice of rebuilding exhausted soils by following a soil-depleting crop with the planting of soil-enriching legumes. Leguminous crops allow a soil to replenish its chemical supply, mainly by providing it with nitrogen. They also serve as fodder for livestock and allow a

farm to raise more animals with little increase in its feed costs. These animals, in turn, supply manure (which can be used in soil maintenance), food, and, if they are marketable, cash income. Such coordination of crop and livestock production is essential to maximum utilization of agricultural land.

The crops generally included in crop-rotation systems in Europe, the United States, and the Soviet Union comprise three groups: row-tilled plants, such as maize, potatoes, beans, and sugar beets; close-drilled grains, such as wheat, oats, barley, and rye; and deep-sod-rooted hays, such as alfalfa, clover, and lespedeza. Typically, a rotation cycle can successfully include the raising of these crops in three, four, or even five stages. For example, a four-stage rotation cycle might begin with the planting of wheat or barley, as the cash crop; followed by alfalfa, for hay and pasture and as the means of adding nitrogen to the soil; followed by sugar beets or potatoes, to clean and cultivate the soil; and, lastly, by maize, for livestock feed and further soil cultivation (Fig. 7–15). Whatever the number of stages or the specific crops, a sound rotation system is one in which crops are mixed so as to provide not the highest possible immediate profits but the most profitable and most serviceable yields consistent with long-term, high soil-fertility.

In Europe, the average commercial crop and livestock farm consists of about 50 to 100 acres; the typical farm in the United States is a little larger, about 80 to 240 acres; and, in the Soviet Union, collective farms in the Ukraine, each housing hundreds of families, extend over several thousand acres (Fig. 7–16). The working of rented land, or *tenant farming*, is quite common in present-day commercial agriculture; and, among farmers

FIGURE 7–14

A large mixed crop and livestock farm in Pennsylvania. (Grant Heilman)

FIGURE 7–15

Maize production is heavy in North and South America, Europe, Asia, and Africa, with the United States accounting for half the world total. The world trade in maize is meager in comparison to the world trade in rice or wheat.

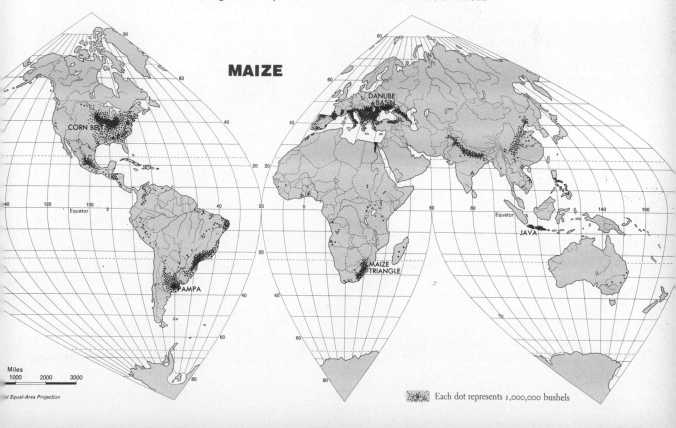

Each dot represents 1,000,000 bushels

in Europe, it is even preferred. Not as widely practiced in North America, tenant farming in the United States today usually serves as a hopeful step toward ultimate ownership of the land. Europe, because of its smaller farms and the general strain on its economy following two world wars, trails considerably behind the United States and the Soviet Union in terms of agricultural mechanization but not much in type and variety.

Commercial crop and livestock farming dominates a broad region of Europe, from the Mediterranean to the North and Baltic seas, and extends across the Soviet Union, in a narrowing wedge, to beyond the Ural Mountains. In the United States, it is most evident in the eastern half of the country, from the Gulf and Atlantic plains northward to the Great Lakes and westward to beyond the Mississippi River.

The Corn Belt (the small middle region of the United States stretching from central Ohio to central Nebraska) comprises the world's most highly concentrated examples of large-scale commercial crop and livestock farming (Fig. 7–17). Much of the huge quantities of feed grains this region produces is converted into meat and fats by its large populations of commercial beef cattle and swine (Fig. 7–18).

Commercial agriculture in midlatitude regions of the southern continents is similar in form to that in Europe and North America, but it is much smaller in scale and less developed. Agricultural regions of South America, Africa, and Australia have relatively low per-

FIGURE 7–16

A collective farm in the Ukraine. In addition to tending the commune's fields, the member families raise fruits and vegetables in small private plots behind their homes. (Sovfoto)

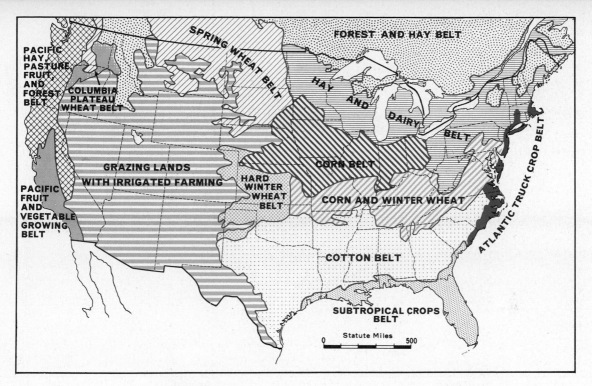

FIGURE 7–17

Agricultural regions of the coterminous United States and southern Canada. The array of physical conditions in this vast area allows it to produce a wide variety of products throughout the year. Even in the winter months, fruits and vegetables are being harvested in southern California and along the Gulf Coast.

FIGURE 7–18

Livestock production in the coterminous United States. A. Beef cattle, which, though raised in most sections of the country, are most numerous in the western part of the Corn Belt and elsewhere in the Great Plains. B. Swine, which are also major animal products of the Corn Belt.

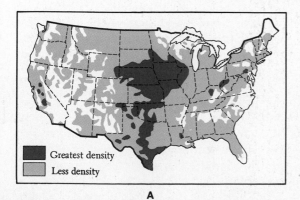

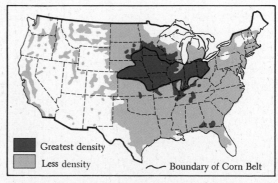

173

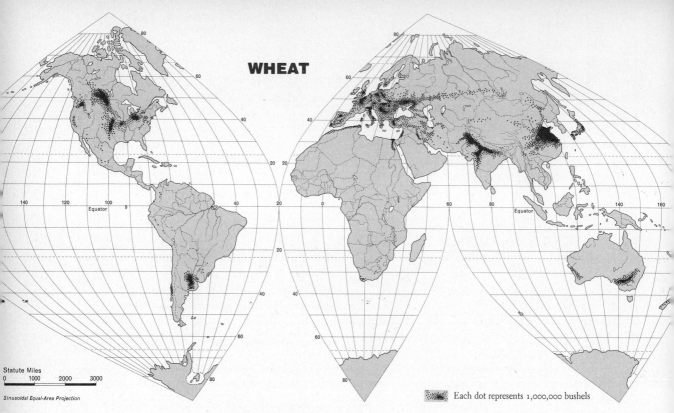

WHEAT

Statute Miles
0   1000   2000   3000

Sinusoidal Equal-Area Projection

Each dot represents 1,000,000 bushels

FIGURE 7–19

Wheat production takes place in all the continents, particularly in the midlatitudes of the Northern Hemisphere. Trade in wheat is also nearly worldwide.

centages of their total land devoted to the growing of crops, as much more of it is given over to use as semipermanent pastureland. This illustrates the fact that large-scale crop and livestock farming has not yet become widespread beyond Europe, North America, and the Soviet Union, where it has been a necessary way of meeting the expanding needs of these heavily industrialized societies.

Dry-Grain Ranching

The large-scale agricultural system developed most recently is *dry-grain ranching*, in which a farm produces a single dry grain to the virtual exclusion of other crops. As a provider of human foods, wheat-dominated monocultures of this sort constitute a system

that is second only to that of sawah agriculture (Fig. 7–19). For, today, the dry grains are as essential to the diet of one half of the world as rice is to the other half.

With dry-grain ranching, many of yesterday's frontier grassland-prairies—grazing lands at best, vast wastelands if the sparse summer rains failed—are today among the world's most specialized commercial food-producing regions, spilling their bounty of wheat and lesser crops into practically every country of the world. Commercial dry-grain ranches usually comprise more acreage than is typical of any other agricultural system. Many of these ranches in North America and the Soviet Union are a thousand acres in extent, and, in these areas, one comprising several thousand acres is not considered unusual; per-acre yields on a dry-grain ranch,

174

however, are low, with returns of under a dozen bushels (720 pounds) per acre occurring frequently; harvests are uncertain; labor is minimal; mechanization is high; tenancy is negligible; and population is probably less dense than in any other major agricultural system (Fig. 7–20).

Wheat, the chief product of most dry-grain ranches, is raised in many countries, but is consumed at so high a rate that few of them can produce as much as they need. To meet their resultant deficiencies, then, most countries must buy wheat from the few wheat-surplus countries that exist. Among these few are the United States and Canada, which devote large portions of the lands astride their common border to commercial wheat production; thus, a highly productive wheat region extends across the plains of the United States, from Texas to the Dakotas, and far into those of Canada, in the provinces of Saskatchewan and Alberta.

The Soviet Union's large commercial wheat region extends 2,000 miles in length, from the southern plains of European Russia into Asia, beyond the Ural Mountains. The European part of this region, that which lies west of the Volga River, includes the soil-rich Ukraine, the "breadbasket of Russia," and is thus the most productive agricultural area of the Soviet Union.

In the Southern Hemisphere, the most productive commercial wheat areas are the *pampa* of Argentina and the southern part of Australia (Fig. 7–21). Although these regions account for relatively little of the world's total production (3 percent each), both Argentina and Australia are important for their large wheat exports, which often total as much as half their annual production. The world's largest exporter of wheat is the United States, providing 40 percent of the total wheat export, and Canada, whose exports total about half that amount, is second; France and the Soviet Union are the third and fourth largest, and Australia and Argentina follow. Australia exports its wheat principally to southern Asia, largely to India, but some goes to its Commonwealth partner, the United Kingdom, a country that over many decades has had only about a 30 percent self-sufficiency in staple foodstuffs.

FIGURE 7–20

The harvesting of wheat, by automatic combines, on a Soviet State Farm near the Black Sea. (Sovfoto)

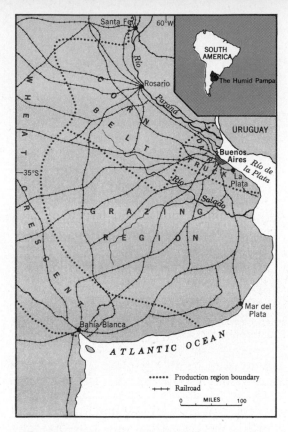

FIGURE 7–21

The humid *pampa* (grassland) of Argentina. Its fertile, level lands and mild-humid climates allow it to be the country's major food-producing area. Particularly productive is the semiarid western wheat crescent.

Tropical Plantations

In the eighteenth and nineteenth centuries, European colonialism led to the development of new agricultural societies across much of the world's humid tropical forest lands. Highly specialized, extremely commercial, and technologically advanced, these settlements, or *plantations,* still have an economic importance to the world beyond that normally attending the limited amount of land they occupy, as well as a substantial political importance to their host countries.

The islands in the Gulf of Guinea were probably the first sites of such plantations, but it was the sugar plantations of tropical northeastern Brazil and, later, those of the Caribbean Islands that firmly established this new type of agricultural society. Beginning in the late eighteenth century, colonialism brought the plantation system into Asia as well (Fig. 7–22). India and Ceylon (now Sri Lanka), Southeast Asia, and the East Indies were all introduced to the "great experiment" (Fig. 7–23). Unlike most agricultural societies, whose development has been gradual and evolutionary, the commercial tropical plantation was conceived and planned and

FIGURE 7–22

Tropical plantations. Left, cacao groves in the Caribbean. (Hershey Foods Corporation) Right, a tea plantation in Sri Lanka's central highlands. (United Nations)

then imposed, rather suddenly, for the satisfaction of personal or national coffers and international markets.

The original tropical plantations ranged in size from corporate estates of thousands of acres to small units of a few acres; most were owned and managed by foreigners, and some employed a foreign work force as well. Today, many of the small holdings are locally owned and operated, and a considerable number of the estates have been taken over by local corporate groups or local governments. There has always been a high degree of specialization on commercial tropical plantations, and, usually, each produces one crop exclusively; this is most commonly sugar cane, pineapples, citrus fruits, cacao, bananas, coffee, tea, coconuts, spices, or rubber. Often the specialization is so complete that the plantation does not produce even basic foodstuffs for its labor force and must acquire these at high cost from distant markets.

It is not surprising that, in the course of its development, the commercial tropical plantation, unique and in some respects unnatural, has had to face innumerable natural and cultural obstacles, not all of which have been negotiated to the satisfaction of its host countries. Yet, despite the great difficulties that remain, the disappearance, or even decline, of this type of agricultural society in the near future seems very unlikely. This is because socioeconomically, it is much too important to all concerned, especially to those host countries attempting to establish a sound economy under a newly independent government.

FIGURE 7–23

Aspects of agriculture in Sri Lanka. About two-thirds of the nation's agricultural lands are in tea, rubber, and coconuts; the relatively small acreage devoted to vegetables and livestock gives the country only about a 60-percent self-sufficiency in foods.

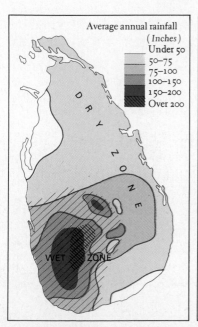
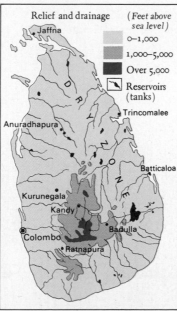
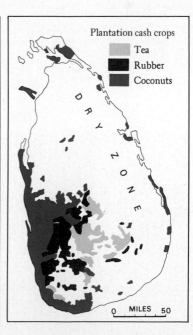

Trends in the Agrarian Infrastructure

Agrarian Reform and Productivity

Changes in rural agrarian institutions and concepts, usually considered together as *agrarian reform*, are certain to take place in the near future, in both the developed and developing countries of the world (Fig. 7–24). In many areas of Asia, Africa, and Latin America, outdated systems of land tenure still slow down the adoption of new and improved production methods, making it next to impossible for farmers to achieve relatively decent living standards. Often without the security of proprietorship over

their land, some farmers have little incentive to improve their holdings through the use of expensive irrigation or drainage systems, fertilizers, or storage facilities. Excessive fragmentation of land holdings, through antiquated inheritance practices, also frequently prohibits efficient agriculture. A dozen miniplots scattered over a several-mile area are too distant to be profitably fertilized and cultivated; underuse and misuse of land and labor are the obvious results.

However, large tracts of land can also be a handicap to greater agricultural efficiency, for the successful utilization of such holdings requires an expertise beyond that developed

FIGURE 7–24

The pitch for a cooperative rice mill at Abakaliki, in eastern Nigeria. Agrarian reform has been underway in Nigeria for several decades; and agricultural cooperatives, in existence there since the 1930s, are today important factors in the country's socioeconomic development. (United Nations)

on the small farm, as well as huge investments of capital. They are also particularly subject to absentee landlordism, which, by dividing ownership and management, has exacted a heavy toll on effective land utilization. And, in some of the more densely populated countries, especially in Asia and Africa, the ownership of large tracts of land has also led to *rack-renting,* an ancient system in which tenant farmers are charged rents equal, or nearly equal, to the full annual returns from the land. To save their families from the squalor of overcrowded cities, where they will find high costs and little chance for employment, farmers working under this system live year after year in debt and make it a burdensome legacy to their children.

If properly undertaken, the redistribution of the world's agricultural lands, in terms of both ownership and use, could not only directly cause the living standards of many farmers to be improved but could also indirectly effect the advancement of whole countries toward a condition of food sufficiency and, thereby, proper nutrition for their populations. Such agrarian reform will be slow and painful and, of course, prone to the evils of self-interest; but, being a key to the further spread of agricultural technology and greater motivation on the part of the farmer, it seems a prerequisite to solving the world food crisis and to maximizing the earth's agricultural productivity.

The Agricultural Labor Force

Authoritative estimates place the size of the world's labor force at approximately 40 percent of the total world population, or an estimated 1.5 billion people. Included in this number, supposedly, are all the men, women, and children engaged in productive employment, whether full- or part-time, salaried or unpaid. In considering such estimates, it should be remembered that interpretations of "productive employment" as well as demographic reporting systems vary dramatically from country to country. While, in such countries as the United States and Canada, much detailed information on population characteristics is both collected and published, there are some others that do not even conduct a regular general census.

To increase the accuracy of international employment studies, the United Nations Statistical Commission has devised a system that combines dozens of diverse occupations into several general groupings, which in turn are divided into three broad sectors (designated as *primary, secondary,* and *tertiary*) of societal activity (Fig. 7–25). Based on estimates made by the United Nations International Labor Organization, primary activities (mainly agriculture) generally employ about 54 percent of the total world labor force; secondary activities (mainly industry) account for nearly 20 percent of the total; and tertiary activities (varying with each particular country), represent the remaining 26 percent of the labor force.

Certainly among the most revealing facts to emerge from the United Nations' data on world employment is the absolute

FIGURE 7–25
The general tripart division of basic types of labor.

Primary societal activities:
agriculture, grazing, forestry,
hunting–fishing–gathering,
mining and drilling
Secondary societal activities:
industry, construction,
energy production, etc.
Tertiary societal activities:
services, transportation,
commerce, communications,
banking, education, etc.

predominance of the agricultural labor force, which comprises 51 percent of the world total (see Fig. 6–5). And even when modern agricultural techniques offer an alternative, throughout much of the world heavy expenditures of human labor are still required to raise food. In many countries of Asia and Africa the percentage of the labor force in agriculture rises well above the average, reaching as high as 70 percent in India and 85 percent in Thailand, for example. These percentages are particularly startling when compared with the 6 percent of the labor force engaged in agriculture in the United States.

Generally, the percentage of its people engaged in such primary activities as agriculture declines as a country develops economically; one reason for this is the simple fact that labor from agriculture will be siphoned off to fill jobs in new areas of the economy. Since national economic development can be arduous, especially where illiteracy or opposed customs are entrenched, it will probably take decades for some countries to experience a substantial decline in their high levels of agricultural employment.

REVIEW AND DISCUSSION

1. Enumerate some of the extensive regions in which nomadic hunting-and-gathering peoples live. What physical or situational characteristics do these regions have in common that explain their use by such groups? What cultural or political characteristics do these regions share that explain their type of occupance?

2. Sedentary subsistence farming, which began some ten thousand years ago, persists in many contemporary societies. Assess this major form of agriculture with respect to geographical distribution and population patterns.

3. Discuss the basic characteristics of the rice-dominant, or sawah, agricultural society that dominates the lives of most Asians. How would the adoption of modern technologies reduce the weaknesses and enhance the strengths of this system? What role do animals play in this form of agriculture? Can their role be increased, and how would such an increase affect the whole society? What role can "miracle" grains play in Asia's future?

4. In matters important in cultural geography, compare and contrast the non-rice-dominant societies of southern and eastern Asia with their neighboring rice-dominant, or sawah, societies.

5. What factors have influenced the transformation of many agrarian societies into industrial agrarian societies? What are the sociocultural advantages of such a change? How would the transformation of all agrarian societies into industrial agrarian societies affect the welfare of humankind?

6. Commercial crop and livestock farming dominates a broad region of Europe and much of the Soviet Union and the United States. Is it a natural consequence of the physical environments and cultures involved, or does it seem to be an imported and ill-suited system in one or all of these areas?

7. In what regions and in what ways did European colonialism promote the development of plantations? What were some of the major cultural impacts of this "imposed" agricultural economy in Asia and Africa? Why have many of the Asian and African countries that became independent in this century retained and even expanded their plantation economies under their new governments?

8. What type or types of agriculture are practiced in the region in which you live? What are the main physical and cultural factors that have influenced their development?

9. How do you think the world pattern of agrarian societies might change if there were heavy restrictions on the movement of agricultural products in international trade?

10. In light of its many surplus agricultural productions in recent decades, why is the United States concerned with increasing its agricultural productions? How does its agricultural labor force compare with those of other countries?

SELECTED REFERENCES

Anderson, E. *Plants, Man, and Life.* Boston: Little, Brown, 1952.

Brown, J. R., and S. Lin. *Land Reform in Developing Countries.* International Seminar, 1967. Phoenix, Ariz.: The Lincoln Foundation, 1967.

Cantor, L. M. *A World Geography of Irrigation.* New York: Praeger, 1970.

Chang, Jen-hu. "The Agricultural Potential of the Humid Tropics." *Geographical Review,* Vol. 58 (July 1968), 333–61.

Chao, Kang. *Agricultural Production in Communist China.* Madison: University of Wisconsin Press, 1970.

Chen, Cheng-siang. *Taiwan: Economic and Social Geography.* Taipei: Fu-min Geographical Institute, 1963.

Gregor, H. F. *Geography of Agriculture.* Englewood Cliffs, N.J.: Prentice-Hall, 1970.

Griffin, P., R. Chatham, A. Singh, and W. White. *Culture, Resource and Economic Activity.* Boston: Allyn & Bacon, 1971.

Hayama, Y., and V. Rutlan. *Agricultural Development: An International Perspective.* Baltimore: Johns Hopkins Press, 1971.

Highsmith, R. M. "Irrigated Lands of the World." *Geographical Review,* Vol. 55 (July 1965), 382–89.

MacFadden, C. H. "Mechanized Rice Production in California." *Il Riso* (Milan, Italy), Vol. 14 (December 1965), 325–29.

Nath, V. "The Growth of Indian Agriculture." *Geographical Review,* Vol. 59 (July 1969), 348–72.

Nulty, L. *The Green Revolution in Pakistan.* New York: Praeger, 1972.

Schultz, T. W. *Transforming Traditional Agriculture.* New Haven, Conn.: Yale University Press, 1964.

Staley, E. *Future of Underdeveloped Countries.* New York: Praeger, 1961.

Ucko, P. J., et al. "Swidden Systems and Settlement." *Man, Settlement and Urbanism.* London: Gerald Duckworth, 1972.

Udo, R. K. "Sixty Years of Plantation Agriculture in Nigeria: 1902–1962." *Economic Geography,* Vol. 41 (October 1965), 356–68.

Sunlit transmission towers along the road from Karangi to Karachi, in Pakistan.
(United Nations)

8

Societal Pacemakers: Energy

The Nature of Energy

The constant increase in human dependency on environmental energy sources has made them important pacemakers in societal advancement. These energy sources and their innovative uses have been the key to some of humanity's highest attainments to date, as well as to its dreams of creating a better world in which to live. Gradually, humans have learned to control and utilize many energy forms far greater than their own limited muscular capability. Ever since early cave dwellers first experimented with fire, humanity's quest for ways to survive, and to improve its physical well-being, has been tied, in both concept and action, to the effective harnessing of one, or several, of nature's many energy forms.

But, one might ask, what *is* energy? For, though human beings are always surrounded by it, some may have great difficulty in defining energy; it is easier to explain what energy *does*. To most of the world's people, energy is that which gives them the added strength and extra hands with which to fulfill their needs and wants. In a very direct way, energy controls not only all the world's societal systems but also all the activities that take place within them—from such large-scale activities as agriculture, industry, mining, transportation, communications, and national defense down to such smaller-scale activities as the provision of food supplies, automobiles, and home appliances for the satisfaction of individual daily needs.

The only significant source of the huge and constant flow of energy on the earth is the sun, which, as it speeds through space, emits tremendous amounts of energy, a small fraction of which is intercepted by the earth as *solar radiation*. Of the minute fraction of solar radiation obtained by the earth, an even smaller fraction is synthesized and stored by the earth's vegetation. It is this stored chemical energy that serves as the major energy source for the earth's animal life, including humans. When plants and animals die, much of this energy is buried with their remains under other earth materials. Thus subjected to long burial amid the earth's internal heat and pressure, the remains of ancient plants and animals have been transformed into *fossil fuels,* that is, coal, petroleum, and natural gas. These forms are the principal sources of stored energy upon which modern humanity depends.

Energy Thresholds and Cultural Evolution

The Use of Fire

The ability to produce and control fire was certainly the greatest triumph won by early humans in their struggle toward achieving mastery of the earth's major energy sources. The use of fire enabled these primitive peoples to expand their hunting-and-gathering activities, both in variety and extent. For example, many more kinds and parts of plants and animals, some indigestible by humans when raw, could now be made edible by cooking; and, perhaps, most important, human settlements could now be extended into cool, and even cold, climates. In these and other ways, this single cultural achievement allowed human beings to gradually increase their numbers and to establish their dominance over lesser primate forms.

The First Agricultural Revolution

About ten thousand years ago, as discussed earlier, more effective utilization of human energy, through the domestication of plants and animals, led to the first *agricultural revolution.* No longer forced to rely solely on hunting and gathering, human beings progressed beyond such practices and began to develop an entirely new behavioral pattern, one that was based on the raising of plants and animals. With this major step into agriculture, they crossed their first important energy-use threshold. However, for many millennia, human life remained a monotony of labor, as all work was still done by the muscle power of humans and beasts. Only gradually were the new and improved tools developed that made it possible for agriculture to require less human labor.

The Use of Water Power

After the first agricultural revolution, nearly eight millennia passed before human beings, approaching their second major energy-use threshold, learned that some of their tasks could be performed by simple mechanisms operated by the natural forces of water. The first of these was the *water wheel,* a huge wheel turned by the weight of falling water or by the momentum of flowing streams. This primitive device supplied the energy necessary to do such things as raise water from wells and cisterns or grind grain into flour. In order to take advantage of the water wheel's help in these and other essential tasks, people began to establish their settlements on the banks of streams (at waterfall sites) from which substantial water power could be obtained (Fig. 8–1).

But, for reasons one can only postulate, it took another millennium—or more than thirty generations—for humans to advance to a point at which they could make any more complicated applications of the water wheel. Moving water, whose energy was harnessed essentially by means of the water wheel, continued to serve as humanity's dominant source of energy until the time of the Industrial Revolution; it was widely available, easy to control and utilize, and essentially inexhaustible.

Energy Diversification

The peoples of Europe reached a third energy-use threshold by about the tenth century, when they began to use the energy supplied by water wheels for a greater range of purposes. The mechanisms themselves had been improved, and they were now harnessed to new or more effective hoisting and pumping equipment and to various new specialized devices. In these combinations, they became effective in a multitude of basic tasks performed previously only through muscle power; these included the sawing of wood, the hammering of metals, the pressing of fruits, and the processing of textiles.

Two other important mechanical developments also occurred in this era. The first of these was the successful adaptation of the *cam,* a conveyor of motion that soon came to be a feature both of machines used to perform rather precise operations, and of heavy-duty machines used in such operations as stone crushing (Fig. 8–2). The second development was the adaptation of the *crank,* a mechanism that converts circular motion to linear motion, as in the operation of a pump cylinder or a piston.

The Use of Wind Power

By the fifteenth century, some European societies had attained a fourth energy-use threshold by improving on the concept of the *windmill,* which they borrowed from

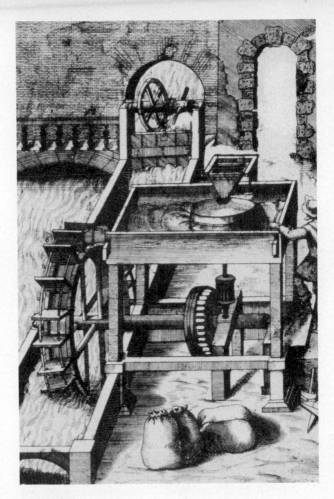

FIGURE 8–1

An early water wheel being used in the grinding of grain into flour.

older Eastern civilizations. This enabled them to make wind another major source of energy, a development that was of particular importance in areas remote from dependable sources of flowing water. This ability to exploit several energy resources allowed medieval Europe to achieve more rapid and more extensive economic advances than were made during the same period in other parts of the world. European countries began to surge economically at home and to reach out to other continents with the first hints of overseas colonialism in modern times. In a few other relatively advanced regions of the

FIGURE 8-2

An early cammed axle in combination with a water wheel (beyond the wall). As the wheel turned the axle, the axle's *cams*, or knobs, raised the hammers (at left), thus converting the wheel's rotary motion into vertical motion.

world, much of the same advanced technology was introduced and accepted—but without much interest or vision for development. Nowhere else was the developmental equipment as complete, or the urge to master the forces and gifts of nature so great, as they were within European societies. The results were that Europe advanced socioculturally and socioeconomically relatively rapidly, while other societies with less cultural drive remained as they had been for ages, some even being content to retrograde through

inaction. But today those same "other societies" are rapidly reversing their views and their actions.

Coal: The Industrial Revolution

In the sixteenth and seventeenth centuries many new machines were invented for use in Europe's rapidly expanding textile and engineering industries, but the capacity of all such machinery remained subject to the availability of harnessible wind and water power. More convenient and more controllable energy sources were urgently needed. The many operable but highly complex and inefficient steam engines developed during these two centuries represent the long-time European attempt to make coal one of these new, more practical sources of industrial energy. Success did not come until 1769, when James Watt (1736–1819), a Scottish engineer and inventor, patented a radical redesign of a coal-burning steam engine (or "fire engine") invented in England by Thomas Newcomen half a century earlier. Far more efficient and economical than any of its predecessors, Watt's steam engine was put on the market in 1776 and immediately became industry's most effective energy-converting machine (Fig. 8–3).

This new "fire engine" and the improved versions that followed brought about tremendous increases in the industrial output and wealth of all the European societies that adopted them. In England, they were major factors in the developing industrial revolution, which eventually affected not only the country's economic structure but many of its social systems as well. Yet, although European colonialism was already spreading around the world, the new coal-based technology and its resultant industrial development did not always follow the colonial flags.

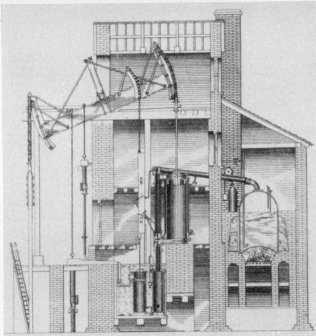

FIGURE 8–3

Eighteenth-century steam engines. Left, Newcomen's engine, which used steam to move a vertical piston that in turn activated a horizontal "rocker-beam." (Smithsonian Institution) Right, Watt's more efficient steam engine; it used steam both to move the piston upward and to return it to its original position and required only one-fourth the coal used by Newcomen's engine in comparable tasks. (Brown Brothers)

Petroleum: The Transport Revolution

Although they were used in raw forms in the Eastern world over three thousand years ago and in the Western world at least a thousand years ago, it was not until very late in the nineteenth century that petroleum and natural gas became of major significance to human beings as energy sources. The widespread use of *petroleum*, a flammable liquid found in portions of the upper layer of the earth, followed the production of the first internal-combustion engines, most of which operated on the refined petroleum product known as *gasoline*. Together, the internal-combustion engine and its portable fuel made possible the first commercial means of motorized transportation, and thus they

played a vital part in one of the most noticeable and far-reaching changes in human living patterns.

Electrical Power

Without the use of electricity, the worldwide, and even regionwide, distribution of the vast energy available from coal, petroleum, and natural gas would seem an insurmountable undertaking. It is fortunate for modern humankind that the basics of electrical technology have been largely understood since the late nineteenth century and that their implementation has progressed rapidly. Today the conversion of fossil fuels, wind, water, and nuclear fuels into *electrical energy*, which can be transmitted readily in great quantities by means of high-voltage grids, has become a common practice throughout much of the world, in most of the underdeveloped countries as well as in the highly industrialized ones. Among humanity's energy-use achievements to date, the mastery of electrical-energy creation and long-distance transmission undoubtedly represents one of the major thresholds.

The Use of Nuclear Energy

Since the mid-twentieth century, when human beings discovered the basic principles of *nuclear fission* and *nuclear fusion,* a tremendous new source of energy has been available to the world. Like so much of the other technologies born of war, the ability to penetrate the nucleus of an atom has proven to be highly adaptable to peaceful purposes. For example, there are thermoelectric plants in which the intense heat produced during nuclear fission is converted into electricity. Such applications of nuclear energy are still relatively few in number, but they give promise of being at least a partial answer to the world's expanding energy requirements.

Modern Energy Bases and Imbalances

The Changing World Energy Bases

During the last few decades, much of the world has been rapidly converting from the use of coal to the use of petroleum and natural gas, both of which have been inexpensive and convenient sources for everything from gasoline and other fuel oils to neon signs and plastics. And, due in part to the ease and versatility of these two energy sources, human beings have consumed more of the earth's energy resources in this brief period than they did in all their previous history; moreover, this sort of acceleration is expected to continue, with total energy consumption doubling at least every generation. And the result? All known petroleum deposits are being depleted much more rapidly than most of the world's other energy resources. Oil and gas supplies are shrinking rapidly, costs are rising alarmingly, and availabilities are being seriously threatened.

Although most people give little thought to their daily use of the earth's energy resources, much of humanity now depends, directly or indirectly, upon energy consumption for its survival. In many societies of the world, the supplies of human food, clothing, and shelter evolve largely through the utilization of energy and the other natural resources in increasingly complex systems. Uses of energy resources, in particular, are so interwoven into the fabric of the modern industrial society that its socioeconomic foundations suffer markedly when denied their accustomed flow of energy. And if this denial were prolonged, many people in such a society would find it difficult to feed themselves at even subsistence levels. Nuclear science and necessity may soon provide the world with more consistent flows of energy, but, at present, high-energy-consumption societies remain almost totally dependent on unevenly distributed fossil fuels, water, and nuclear fuels. Indeed, *per capita* consumption of these basic energies is perhaps the truest index of the socioeconomic level of a contemporary society.

World Energy Imbalances

Wood, dung, peat, charcoal, and other biotic materials were used by human beings as domestic and commercial fuels for thousands of years; but during the period of the Industrial Revolution, coal became the "energy king," and for half a dozen generations, its use continued to exceed that of all other energy sources combined. Until well into the present century, when petroleum and gas became the new "miracle" fuels, coal supplied much more than one-half of the total energy consumption of most countries of the world; it powered the factories, drove the ships, and largely supplanted firewood in the heating of homes and public buildings. Thus, coal became one of the principal prerequisites of national economic development; countries with little or no coal could not, and did not, become industrialized.

But the world's energy preferences have changed dramatically in recent decades, with coal now accounting for only a little more than 35 percent of total energy consumption and petroleum and gas consumption rising to about 40 percent and 20 percent respectively. (Waterpower accounts for another 2 percent, as hydroelectricity, and other sources supply the balance.) In the United States, the energy shift has been even more pronounced than elsewhere. Between 1940—when coal supplied 45 percent of the energy consumed in the nation—and the mid-1970s, the United States shifted to an energy-consumption pattern in which both oil and gas played larger roles than did coal, which then represented only 20 percent of national energy consumption (Fig. 8–4).

Currently, two nations produce and consume about one-half of all the energy resources used by human beings; the United States consumes about 30 percent and the Soviet Union, about 20 percent (Fig. 8–5). The more than 140 other nations of the world, representing nearly 90 percent of its popula-

	United States		Europe	
	1940	1975	1940	1975
Coal	45*	20	80	45
Petroleum	35	40	10	40
Natural Gas	15	35	1	6
Hydroelectric	3	4	8	8
Other energy sources	2	1	1	1

* In percentages.

FIGURE 8–4

The major energy sources in the United States and Europe in 1940 and 1975. Between these years, both these high-energy-consuming regions underwent decided shifts in their energy bases, relying less and less on coal and more and more on petroleum and gas.

tion, divide the other half among them, with 20 percent consumed by western Europe. This means that only a relatively small percentage of the world's energy production and consumption takes place in all of Asia, for example, where more than half the world's people live. These facts serve to illustrate the obvious and great energy imbalance that presently exists among the world's human societies.

Energy Crisis—or Evolution?

With the energy consumptions of new and old industrial countries alike continuing to spiral upward at almost unbelievable rates, reserves of petroleum and other fossil fuels are already in jeopardy (Fig. 8–6). Although this situation had been predicted by some observers for decades, most political representatives did not even begin to sound warnings of overuse until the mid-1970s. These belated indications of the rapid dwindling of energy supplies have finally awakened world concern to the possibility of a severe energy shortage. Some of the present sense of crisis has, no doubt, been created to foster particular political or monetary concerns, but most of the alarm reflects the hard fact of decreasing energy supplies and rising energy demands.

FIGURE 8–5

Electric lighting in use over the eastern United States, as photographed by a meteorological satellite 450 miles above the earth. The largest and brightest spots coincide with the locations of major metropolitan areas. (Westinghouse Electric Corp.)

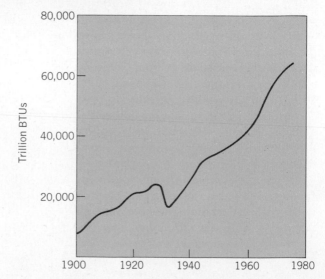

FIGURE 8–6

Energy production in the United States since 1900—by means of both fossil fuels and hydroelectric sources.

190

Future Energy Alternatives

Traditional energy resources are rapidly declining, creating an international energy crisis — as exploding populations and skyrocketing consumption rates overtax finite supplies. Energy consumptions have doubled in recent decades and are expected to double again within the next twenty-five years. In response to the decline in traditional energy sources, new *energy alternatives* are needed for the future — entirely different sources to sustain rapidly expanding populations and their complex technological societies. Some of the most promising energy developments for the future are solar energy, geothermal energy, tidal power, and nuclear energy. But what are the likely benefits and problems of such new energy sources for future societies?

Solar Energy

Among the energy alternatives inhabitants of the earth may pursue in the future, certainly the most abundant and most readily available is *solar energy,* or solar radiation, which each day provides the planet with energy equal to one-half of *all* its remaining fossil-fuel reserves. A great hope of human beings, through all eras, has been to harness the vast energies of the sun. Historical records reveal many notable attempts at this and some successes — although one suspects that fact has sometimes been mixed with fiction. For example, using a line of shields as reflectors, the Greek mathematican and inventor Archimedes is supposed to have concentrated enough solar energy, or heat, to set afire the sails of a Roman fleet as it besieged the Sicilian city of Syracuse, in 212 B.C.; Antoine Lavoisier, a French chemist, is said to have used concentrated solar energy, or heat,

to melt iron in 1774; and Swedish-American engineer and inventor John Ericsson is credited with creating, in the late 1860s, the first steam engine powered by direct solar energy. Modern research on the uses of solar energy began in the 1930s, when American solar scientist Charles Greeley Abbot invented a steam engine that operated on solar energy concentrated by means of parabolic, or bowl-shaped, mirrors.

Many such *solar steam engines* have since been used in small-scale electric generation and water pumping, particularly within the developing countries of the tropics; but no engine with a solar boiler has yet been able to compete with the relatively cheap combustion engine. *Solar cookers,* or stoves with parabolic reflectors, have been used in everyday food preparation for the past century, again most successfully within tropical countries, where, however, high cost prevents their widespread adoption (Fig. 8–7). *Solar distillation,* which uses flat rather than parabolic collectors, has been employed worldwide for many centuries in salt production; but its first large-scale commercial application probably occurred during the nineteenth century in the desalting of water for Chilean nitrate mines. Today, solar distillation is still widely used in commercial projects, such as the operation of salt pans that precipitate considerable salt annually from sea water. With the growing recognition of the energy crisis, *solar heating* for industry and homes has also attracted considerable attention in recent years and, within this generation, may become the first widespread application of solar energy (Fig. 8–8).

Solar furnaces are designed for the high-temperature-heating needs of many industries and, utilizing a huge parabolic mirror and several flat mirrors, can usually achieve

FIGURE 8-7

The testing of a *solar cooker* at the National Physics Laboratory, New Delhi, India. In the pressure cooker shown here the boiling time of water by means of this solar device is about 10 minutes; in a saucepan, about 30 minutes. (United Nations)

temperatures well above 1,000°F. Felix Trombe, a French scientist who has built a number of solar furnaces at Mont Louis in the French Pyrenees, in 1970 completed the world's largest solar furnace (near Odeillo); it develops more than 1,000 kilowatts of power, reaches temperatures over 6,000°F., and can melt through a steel plate three-eighths of an inch thick in less than 60 seconds (Fig. 8-9). Trombe's huge furnace has a central parabolic mirror that extends 148 feet high, and this awesome centerpiece receives and concentrates solar rays directed to it by sixty-three flat mirrors set higher up the mountainside. Each panel mirror is itself about 18 feet square, and turns slowly with the moving sun.

Solar batteries are fairly recent devices that can convert rays from the sun directly into electricity. They represent an application of the photovoltaic method announced by Bell Telephone Laboratories in 1954. By 1958, solar batteries had become a feature of space exploration equipment.

FIGURE 8-8

An industrial-scale, flat-mirror solar energy system, at Valley Forge, Pennsylvania. (Time-Life Picture Agency)

Solar energy research has been greatly accelerated in the United States since the general recognition of the energy crisis. For example, through a special program of the National Science Foundation, the monies available to support the work of solar researchers were increased from practically zero in the 1960s to $13 million in 1974.

Geothermal Energy

In response to the energy crisis, increasing attention has been focused in the last decade on the potential of geothermal resources in the generation of electric power. As the term implies, *geothermal energy* is the "natural heat" of the earth. The source of this heat is the earth's highly plastic interior.

As a result of the decay of radioactive materials and such forces as pressure and friction, the temperature at the molten center of the earth reaches 1,000°C. (1,832°F.). This core heat migrates outward to the earth's crust in a constant flow that becomes less intense as it approaches the surface. Thus, the heat of the earth's crust normally increases 30°C. (54°F.) with each additional kilometer toward the center, or 48°C. (89°F.) with each radial mile. Existing as exceptions to this rule are countless "heat pockets," or *geothermal reservoirs*, places at which unusual geologic conditions have created pressures and heat much more intense than is typical at such depths. These pockets are frequently associated with areas of past volcanic activity and tend to occur at fairly shallow depths— that is, within a few thousand feet of the surface (Fig. 8–10). Where subsurface waters, or groundwaters, accumulate and come into contact with the interior's superheated rock materials, geothermal hot water and steam are formed. These forms of geothermal energy are most apparent on the earth's surface when they are vented as geysers and active volcanoes. In the absence of such natural venting, subsurface steam, superheated

FIGURE 8–9

The huge parabolic mirror of the solar furnace at Odeillo, France. (© Sipa-Press, Liaison Agency)

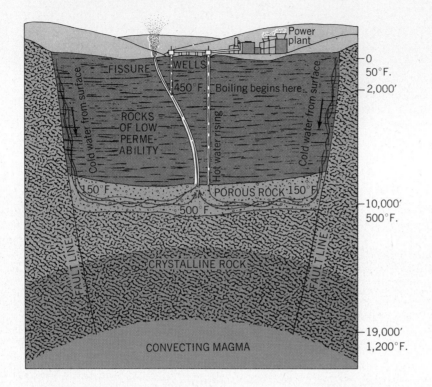

Power plant

FISSURE WELLS

450°F. Boiling begins here

Cold water from surface

Cold water from surface

ROCKS OF LOW PERMEABILITY

Hot water rising

150°F. POROUS ROCK 150°F.

500°F.

FAULT LINE

CRYSTALLINE ROCK

FAULT LINE

CONVECTING MAGMA

0
50°F.

2,000'

10,000'
500°F.

19,000'
1,200°F.

FIGURE 8–10

A diagrammatic cross-section of a natural hot springs and geyser area. Surface water seeps down through the faults to deep layers of porous rock, which are heated, through convection, by the still deeper magma. Wells driven into the geyser, or fissure, or into the deep porous rock can tap their hot water and steam for utilization by electric power plants on the surface.

water, and dry heat can be tapped by means of artificial wells. Geothermal energy thus tapped may be used for many purposes, including the operation of conventional thermoelectric power plants and space heating.

Studies by the United Nations suggest that the total energy contained in subsurface dry-steam, wet-steam-and-water, and dry-hot-rock materials is practically unlimited; or, in other words, that the geothermal energy constantly "stored" in the upper 25,000 feet of the earth's crust is more energy than all the probable human populations of the earth could ever use. The question is no longer *whether* geothermal energy is present and available in sufficient quantities to be utilized on a large scale in many parts of the world, but in what manner it can be utilized most efficiently and with the least environmental disturbance.

The commercial use of geothermal energy is already a long-established practice in some countries of the world. The first facility using geothermal steam to generate electric power went into operation at Larderello, in the Italian province of Tuscany, in 1904 (Fig. 8–11). New Zealand has had a system of geothermal wet-steam electric power plants since the early 1950s, and Iceland, the Soviet Union, and Hungary use geothermal wet-steam-and-water for home heating and for some industrial purposes; most of the homes and buildings of the town of Hveragerdi, Iceland—and 45,000 homes throughout the country—are heated from these sources. Two cities of the United States, Boise, Idaho, and Klamath Falls, Oregon, have used geothermal energy for heating buildings since 1890 and 1930 respectively. Japan has successfully used geothermal steam for generating electric power for several years, and the Mexican government has recently completed a 75,000 kilowatt geothermal electric power plant at

FIGURE 8–11

The geothermal electric power plant at Larderello, Italy. The pipes in the foreground carry steam from nearby wells to the plant, where it is used to turn turbines. The large spool-shaped condensers cool the volcanic steam after it has been used. (Jack Birns, Time-Life Picture Agency, © Time, Inc.)

Cerro Prieto, which is located near the Mexico–California border.

By the mid-1970s, the countries of Italy, Iceland, New Zealand, the United States, the Soviet Union, Japan, and Mexico were collectively generating some 1,000 megawatts of geothermal steam electric power—at costs averaging one-third to one-half less than those of other energy alternatives.

Commercial geothermal interests in the United States have been centered in the Geysers area, north of San Francisco. Private companies interested in using geothermal dry steam for electric power generation have been drilling there since 1960 (Fig. 8–12). The present total capacity of the Geysers field is about 200 megawatts, but by 1980 the area's geothermal steam should be generating several thousand megawatts of electric power — at costs less than those of comparable fossil or nuclear operations. A second geothermal area, one rapidly gaining attention since the early 1970s, is the Imperial Valley in southern California; its wet steam and water are of interest to almost all of the country's major oil companies. The total estimated power-generating capacity of the Imperial Valley's geothermal energy is 30,000 megawatts. The Mono Lake area of California's eastern Sierra Nevada is also commonly thought to have geothermal power potential; and, while less frequently mentioned in this context, an area near the Gulf of Mexico covering 150,000 square miles of Texas and Louisiana may offer even greater promise. Several other promising areas of geothermal energy exist in the western United States, but many of them — included in federal lands, which were

not available for development until 1970 — have not yet been leased.

Of the three distinct types of geothermal energy — dry steam, wet steam and water, and dry hot rocks — dry steam is the type preferred for power generation, because it is environmentally clean and easy to use; however, it is the least-available type worldwide. Dry-steam fields are restricted mainly to northern California (the Geysers fields), Japan, and Italy. Wet-steam-and-water fields are found in New Zealand, Mexico, Hungary, Iceland, the Soviet Union, and southern California. Geothermal energy in the form of wet steam and water is twenty times more abundant than dry steam, and its high temperatures allow it to be used directly to heat buildings or to generate electric power. However, only the third type of geothermal energy, dry hot rocks, seems to be nearly lim-

FIGURE 8–12

Geysers north of San Francisco, California. (Dow Chemical Co.)

itless and universal. The temperatures of this type of geothermal energy are usually lower than those of the two other types, for dry hot rocks reflect the normal temperature levels of the earth itself, rather than some irregularity of nature. Yet, since the heat of the earth increases at the rate of 30°C. (54°F.) per kilometer of depth below the surface, rocks even 5 kilometers deep would suffice in a home-heating system, and those 9 kilometers deep would be sufficient in the operation of an electric power plant.

The most logical and feasible way of tapping the hot-rock heat of the earth's crust is by "drilling and hydrofracturing," a technique somewhat similar to oil drilling and recovery in pressureless fields. One well is drilled, perhaps to a depth of 15,000 to 20,000 feet. Cool water is then pumped to the bottom of the well under very high pressure; there, as it heats, the water fractures the surrounding rock. After this stage of fracturing is completed, a second well is drilled to "tap" the top levels of the fractured zone—and thus create a circulation system, or "hydro-loop." Water is then continuously pumped into the first well, heated within the fractured zone, and then forced to rise to the surface through the second "tap" well. This entire procedure involves only relatively inexpensive present-day technologies.

The environmental impacts of geothermal-energy recovery vary considerably. Iceland's geothermal waters are "fresh" enough to drink; but California's geothermal steam and water is high in salts and minerals. However, most geothermal steam and water impurities can be desalted, demineralized, and degassed quite economically. But, at the same time, all geothermal-energy-recovery technology should be carefully monitored for possible earthquake effects. Geothermal energy, particularly in the form of dry hot rocks, has great potential and, if handled with reasonable care, will count importantly among future energy alternatives.

Tidal Power

The harnessing of *tidal power* has been a human practice for centuries. While some early European settlers in the New World dammed streams and rivers and built traditional water wheels, others found an energy source in the rhythmic ebb and flow of the tides. In 1734, a complex tidal water wheel that generated some 50 horsepower was put into operation at Slades Mill in Chelsea, Massachusetts, where it was used in the grinding of spices. Another eighteenth-century tidal mill was located in Rhode Island and was equipped with water wheels that weighed 20 tons and measured 26 feet wide. Numerous other tidal mills were constructed in the eighteenth and nineteenth centuries, especially on Passamaquoddy Bay, between Maine and Canada on the Bay of Fundy—the only area of North America that is today considered a suitable site for the large-scale generation of electric power by means of tidal energy.

The ultimate demise of these and other eighteenth- and nineteenth-century tidal power experiments must be attributed to the competition provided in electric power production by cheaper energy sources, such as fossil fuels and water power. Early tidal plants were small and could not meet the needs of the new large industries for high volume and low costs. This situation remains essentially true today, having been accentuated by the competition of nuclear fuels.

Few of the world's coastal areas offer the tidal extremes and locational conditions necessary for large-scale electric power generation. The Bay of Fundy, the only one of these areas located within North America, includes nine commercially exploitable tidal power sites (Fig. 8–13). Two other areas considered highly suitable for electric power development are the Severn River estuary in southwestern England and the Rance River estuary in northwestern France. Other possi-

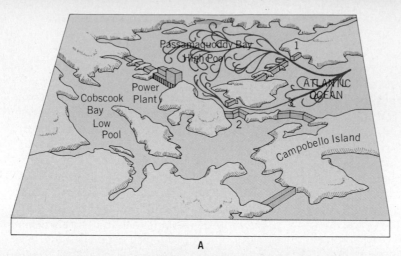

A

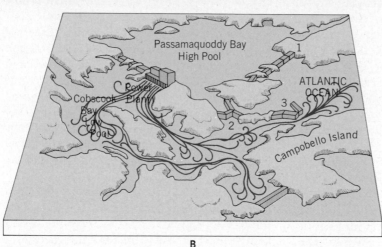

B

FIGURE 8–13

The expected effect of a tidal power project proposed for Passamaquoddy Bay. A. Water is trapped in Passamaquoddy Bay, the high pool, by the opening of gates at points 1 and 2 to the rising tide; the gates are closed just before the outgoing tide begins. B. Water in Cobscook Bay, the low pool, flows through the gate at point 3 during low tide, creating a maximum difference between the water levels of the two pools. Water from the high pool can then flow downward into the low pool, in the process passing through generators in the power plant.

ble areas, all of which require further study to determine their suitability, are in France, the Soviet Union, and the Cook Inlet area of Alaska.

France pioneered in the development of tidal electric power on an industrial scale by completing, in 1965, a unique dam and 240,000-kilowatt generating plant that arcs across the tidal estuary of the Rance River in Brittany. The Soviet Union later built an experimental 400-kilowatt tidal electric power plant near the White Sea in the northwestern part of the country. Soviet engineers say that the project's objectives were reached and that further study into the uses of tidal energy is now warranted.

There are definite environmental disadvantages inherent in building such gigantic dams across any river estuary or inlet. The marine population is disrupted and sometimes permanently damaged, and the landscape is often marred by the facility and its related activities. But these same effects occur around a fossil-fuel or nuclear plant, and perhaps to a greater degree. Therefore, as high-consumption rates deplete traditional energy supplies, tidal power will no doubt be developed wherever practicable—including Passamaquoddy Bay in Canada, which made a "false start" in this direction in the 1930s, and comparable sites in England, France, and the Soviet Union. However, since it is restricted in its occurrences and, for practical purposes, unportable, tidal power cannot be regarded as one of the future's principal energy alternatives.

Nuclear Energy

Humanity is now on the threshold of the nuclear age, which offers much more promise of cheap and abundant power than any other period in history. Within a generation or two, nuclear energy will be the lifeblood of all human societies.

Nuclear Fission and Fusion. There are two ways of producing nuclear energy, by fission and by fusion. All conventional nuclear reactors burn "cores" of natural uranium fuels, whose atoms split, or *fission*, and release vast amounts of energy, or heat. Today's nuclear electric power plants and nuclear submarines are all powered by energy produced by the fission process. In natural uranium the isotope uranium 235 is fissionable—when the nucleus of a uranium 235 isotope is struck by a neutron (one of the particles of an atom), the atom splits into two, releasing still more neutrons; these in turn strike other nuclei and prompt a *chain reaction* in which quantities of heat are emitted. This heat can be transferred to a liquid coolant (usually water) surrounding the fissionable "core" and, through a system of mechanical heat exchangers, used to raise the steam necessary to turn the turbine generators often found in electric power plants and submarines (Figs. 8–14 and 8–15).

Nuclear *fusion* takes place when two lightweight atoms unite, or fuse, to form a heavier nucleus. This occurs only under tremendous heat and pressure and releases immense quantities of energy. The sun is itself a gigantic nuclear fusion device, for it constantly fuses ions (atoms) of light hydrogen to create the heavier atoms of helium. During this process, mass is "lost" and changed into energy—the energy released becomes heat. When science understands how to control this fusion, which it has already employed in an "uncontrolled" form in the hydrogen bomb, humanity will have virtually unlimited power at its command.

Major Uses of Nuclear Energy. Controlled nuclear energy (fission) is already playing a constructive role in the generation of electricity. Nuclear energy is now the fastest-growing means of electric power production in the United States and Canada, as well as in most of Europe and the Soviet Union; and many other countries of the world have already constructed experimental and commercial nuclear electric power plants. Within another decade, most countries, including many developing ones, will have soundly established industrial complexes that can use nuclear energy to achieve major health and welfare benefits for their people.

But the nuclear revolution will by no means involve only the productions of vast quantities of electric power. Other uses of nuclear energy, including the production of fresh water from sea water and other brackish waters, will be extremely important worldwide. Developed and developing countries alike have an increasing need for cheaper and more plentiful water supplies. By 1990, nuclear energy should be sufficiently cheap—and available—to be used in most agro-industrial and municipal desalinization operations, which are particularly necessary in the semiarid and drought-prone regions of the world. In some areas this and other uses of radioactive substances in agriculture, industry, and medicine will contribute as much to future living standards as will nuclear electric power production.

Some Nuclear Problems. Although it offers great benefits in many areas of society,

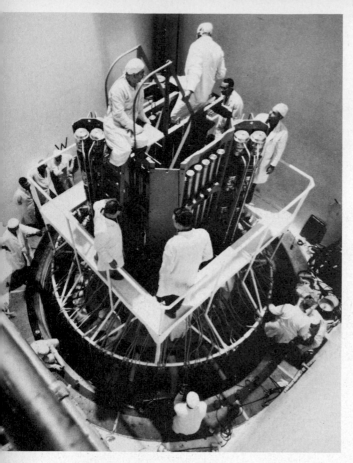

the use of nuclear energy is also fraught with more potentially dangerous problems than is the use of traditional fossil fuels. If they are to live safely with the benefits of nuclear energy, human beings must first solve the problems it presents; its damage cannot be undone. Foremost among these problems is the need to control nuclear weapons production, excessive radiation, and nuclear wastes.

The awesome and lethal power of *nuclear weapons* is attested to by the mass destruction wrought in the Japanese cities of Hiroshima and Nagasaki, by the detonation of two relatively low intensity nuclear bombs in August 1945. Some 78,000 people in Hiroshima and 27,000 in Nagasaki did not survive the blast, and thousands more were harmed by radiation. Many of today's nuclear weapons are fifty times more powerful than the bombs dropped on Japan, with destructive powers equivalent to one million tons of TNT (Fig. 8–16).

FIGURE 8–14

The construction of the reactor core at the Shipping-port nuclear electric power plant, near Pittsburgh, Pennsylvania. Completed, the core is now shielded by thick layers of stainless steel, water, and concrete. (Fritz Goro, Time-Life Picture Agency, © Time, Inc.)

FIGURE 8–15

Electricity through atomic energy. The radioactive *reactor core* heats water, which then transfers its heat to a second water system in a *heat exchanger;* the steam that is thus formed within the exchanger is used to drive a turbine, which operates a generator that feeds electricity to the power lines.

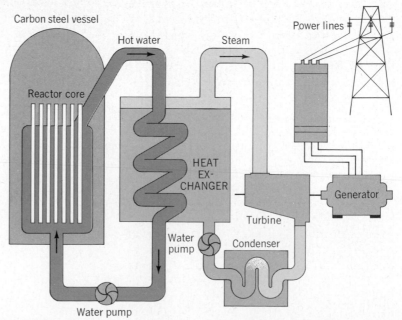

FIGURE 8-16

The mushroom cloud that arose over Nagasaki, Japan, following the August 1945 nuclear bombing. The death and devastation at ground level were much more enduring and horrific. (USAF)

Excessive radiation may occur from both wartime and peaceful uses of nuclear energy. Even in peacetime the accidental escape, or release by a saboteur, of radioactive particles from nuclear power plants or nuclear bomb stockpiles is an ever-present possibility. Although to a much reduced degree, the dangers of radioactivity extend as well to more common occurrences, such as the operation of x-ray machines, micro-wave ovens, and color television sets.

Nuclear, or *radioactive, waste* must be disposed of in a safe manner so its radioactivity will not contaminate any part of the environment. Disposal by burying in the

FIGURE 8–17

A mechanical arm manipulating a capsule in the encapsulation and underground storage of radioactive wastes at a government facility built for their disposal, in Hanford, Washington. The operator of the remote controls is protected from radioactive contamination by the glass panel, which is 3 feet in thickness. (Atlantic Richfield Co.)

ground or dumping in sealed containers into the open ocean have both been tried with fair success and as yet with no major adverse consequences (Fig. 8–17). But such waste-disposal problems will become more difficult as more nuclear electric power plants are put into operation in the decades ahead. As yet there is no fail-safe solution.

Today's Nuclear Countries. Since the early 1950s, more than twenty-five countries of varying sizes and socioeconomic levels have conducted nuclear research and built nuclear electric power plants for their expanding energy needs. This group includes the world's leading agro-industrial nations, the United States, the Soviet Union, Japan,

West Germany, the United Kingdom, France, Italy, and Canada; several smaller industrial and industrializing European countries, including Belgium, the Netherlands, Luxembourg, East Germany, Denmark, Norway, Sweden, Switzerland, Spain, and Ireland; the several industrializing countries of India, Pakistan, China, South Korea, and Israel in Asia; Brazil and Argentina in Latin America; and Australia (Fig. 8–18).

The United States achieved its first production of electric power from nuclear energy at Arco, Idaho, in 1951; and its first small-scale use of nuclear energy for commercial power production occurred four years later. The nation's first full-scale nuclear electric power plant, the second in the

FIGURE 8–18

Some of the world's proliferating nuclear power plants. Top left, the experimental superheat reactor at Pleasanton, California. (General Electric) Top right, Sweden's first commercial nuclear power plant, in Oskarshamn, Sweden. (Swedish Information Service) Center right, Wylfa, Britain's most powerful nuclear power plant, at Anglesey, North Wales. (Wide World) Opposite, the Peach Bottom nuclear electric power plant, in San Jose, California. (General Electric)

world, did not begin full operations until December 1957, at Shippingport, near Pittsburgh. Ushering in a new era of nuclear transportation, the United States Navy launched the first nuclear-powered submarine, the *Nautilus,* in 1954, and a nuclear-powered merchant ship, the *Savannah,* in 1959. Today, there are several nuclear submarines, and dozens of nuclear electric power plants dot the United States from coast to coast (Fig. 8–19). The government's Energy Research and Development Administration (formerly the Atomic Energy Commission) predicts that nuclear electric power plants will be generating about 30 percent of the na-

tion's electricity by 1980 and about 60 percent by the year 2000.

The United Kingdom established the world's first full-scale nuclear electric power plant, at Calder Hall, on the west coast of England, in October 1956. The production of nuclear electric power has progressed rapidly within the United Kingdom in the last two decades, the country's need for cheap power being greater than that of comparable nations. (Electrical production from coal costs twice as much per unit in Britain as it does in the United States.) Today, many nuclear electric power plants have been constructed in Britain, mainly along the western coast-

FIGURE 8–19

United States nuclear electric power plants: 22 operable, with 9,131,800 total kilowatt capacity; 55 being built, with 46,605,000 total kilowatt capacity; and 49 planned, with about 48,524,000 total kilowatt capacity. (After: U.S. Atomic Energy Commission, September 1971)

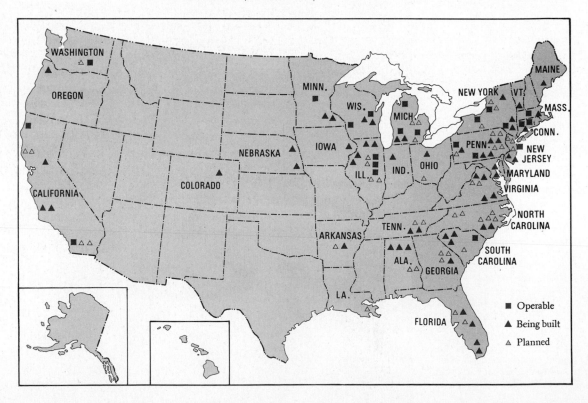

line; they include a large new experimental "breeder" reactor (which produces power and converts natural poor-grade uranium into additional fissionable fuel), at Dounreay in northern Scotland.

The Soviet Union undertook intensive research into nuclear energy shortly after World War II and, in the same period, built some of the world's largest hydroelectric plants to take care of its short-term energy demands. The vast area of the country makes nuclear plants very attractive, for they do not require long hauls of such relatively bulky materials as coal and oil. The Soviet Union built its first small-scale nuclear electric power plant in the 1950s, at Obninsk, and several large-scale plants in the 1960s; one of its most modern large-scale plants, an installation capable of generating 1,000 megawatts of electricity, is located on the Don River, at Novovoronezhskiy.

In Canada, basic nuclear research and power production are both featured in the national energy program. Canada's first nuclear electric power plant was completed in 1962, near Chalk River, Ontario, on the Ottawa River. And the first 2,000-megawatt unit of a new nuclear electric power complex has been completed recently at Pickering–Port Hope, near Toronto. Canada's reactors use natural (low-grade) uranium as fuel, and *heavy water* as a cooling agent.

In Europe, many aspects of nuclear-energy use are being approached regionally. Several countries of western Europe—France, West Germany, Italy, Belgium, the Netherlands, and Luxembourg—joined together in 1957 to form the European Atomic Energy Community (Euratom); in 1973 the group was extended to include the United Kingdom, Denmark, and Ireland. Together, Euratom members are planning an electric power base that will insure economic prosperity and promote regional self-sufficiency; thus nuclear energy figures prominently in their plans. Six European countries—France, Italy, Norway, Sweden, Denmark, and Switzerland—each have established their own independent nuclear research programs as well.

REVIEW AND DISCUSSION

1. Discuss the several energy thresholds humankind has reached since its first controlled use of fire. Include references to specific energy sources and their impact on human activities.
2. If world population continues its present trend and doubles by the year 2000, massive increases in energy consumption will soon occur. What do you think the next decade holds in store with regard to energy types, consumption controls, regional availabilities, and technologies?
3. Can the current excesses in energy utilization be reduced effectively on a purely local basis, or must any correction be attempted worldwide in order to be effective? Why? How would a change in the energy base help to correct the problem? What have been some of the reasons for and the consequences of such changes in the past?
4. Compare and contrast the major forms of energy available today in terms of their convenience and control by humans.
5. Although several future *energy alternatives* are evident, the expectation is that for some time to come humans will remain largely dependent on the traditional and rapidly dwindling fossil fuels—coal, petroleum, and natural gas. Discuss the reasons for this continuance, especially as it relates to *culture lag*.

6. One of the many drawbacks to solar energy's becoming a major source of large-scale power in the immediate future is the fact that the arrival of sunlight on the earth is interrupted in many locales by thick cloud cover. Discuss some of the implications of this problem, including some possible solutions.
7. What is geothermal energy? Name and describe the three major types. In what areas of the world does each type predominate? Which type has the greatest potential for human use in environmental, technological, and economic terms?
8. What are some of the major disadvantages of tidal power as a means of solving the present energy crisis?
9. Explain, in nontechnical terms, the difference between nuclear fission and nuclear fusion.
10. Nuclear power has been described as humanity's best hope for plentiful "clean" energy. Present several arguments that support or oppose this point of view.

SELECTED REFERENCES

Baldwin, C., and E. McNair. "California's Geothermal Resources." *Report to the 1967 California Legislature.* Sacramento: Joint Legislative Committee on Tidelands, 1967.

Barnaby, F. *Man and the Atom: The Uses of Nuclear Energy.* New York: Funk & Wagnalls, 1971.

Brinkworth, B. J. *Solar Energy for Man.* New York: Wiley, 1972.

Clark, W. *Energy for Survival: The Alternative to Extinction.* Garden City, N.Y.: Doubleday Anchor, 1975.

Daniels, F. *Direct Use of the Sun's Energy.* New Haven, Conn.: Yale University Press, 1964.

Ehrlich, P. R., and A. H. Ehrlich. *Population, Resources, Environment.* San Francisco: Freeman, 1970.

Engler, R. *The Politics of Oil.* Chicago: University of Chicago Press, 1969.

Garvey, G. *Energy, Ecology, Economy.* New York: Norton, 1972.

Glaser, P. E. "Power from the Sun: Its Future." *Science,* Vol. 162 (November 1968), 857–61.

Gregory, D. "The Hydrogen Economy." *Scientific American,* Vol. 228 (January 1973), 13–21.

Hammond, A. "Geothermal Energy: An Emerging Major Resource." *Science,* Vol. 177 (September 1972), 978–80.

Hammond A., W. Metz, and T. Maugh. *Energy and the Future.* Washington, D.C.: American Association for the Advancement of Science, 1973.

Hull, O. *A Geography of Production.* London: Macmillan, 1968.

Inglis, D. R. *Nuclear Energy: Its Physics and Its Social Challenge.* Reading, Mass.: Addison-Wesley, 1973.

Ion, D. C. *The Significance of World Petroleum Reserves.* Proc. 1B: 25–36. Seventh World Petroleum Congress, Mexico City, April 1967.

Landsberg, H., L. Fischman, and J. Fisher. *Resources in America's Future.* Baltimore: Johns Hopkins Press, 1963.

Lincoln, G. A. "Energy Conservation." *Science,* Vol. 180 (13 April 1973), 155–62.

Manners, G. *The Geography of Energy.* Chicago: Aldine, 1967.

Mischke, G. "The Search for Fusion Power." *Naval Research Reviews,* Vol. 24 (April 1971), 1–16.

National Academy of Sciences—National Research Council. *Resources and Man.* San Francisco: Freeman, 1969.

Odum, H. T. *Environment, Power, and Society.* New York: Wiley—Interscience Press, 1971.

Oort, A. "The Energy Cycle of the Earth." *Scientific American,* Vol. 223 (September 1970), 54–63.

Rocks, L., and R. Runyun. *The Energy Crisis.* New York: Crown, 1972.

Schurr, S., and B. Netschert. *Energy in the American Economy: 1850–1975.* Baltimore: Johns Hopkins Press, 1960.

Seaborg, G. T., and W. R. Corliss. *Man and Atom.* New York: Dutton, 1971.

Skinner, B. J. *Earth Resources (Energy).* Englewood Cliffs, N.J.: Prentice-Hall, 1969.

Thirring, H. *Energy for Man: Windmills to Nuclear Energy.* Bloomington: Indiana University Press, 1958.

Twentieth Century Fund. *Europe's Needs and Resources.* London: Macmillan, 1961.

United Nations. "Natural Resources." *Science and Technology for Development,* Vol. 2, 1963.

Vennard, E. *The Electric Power Business.* New York: McGraw-Hill, 1962.

A fertilizer plant on Mindanao Island, Philippines. (United Nations)

9

Modern Societies and Agro-Industry

The Evolution of Modern Societies

The modern factory system, characterized by expensive machinery and wage labor, originated in England during the last decades of the eighteenth century. It had an immediate impact upon the culture of that country and has since given rise to revolutionary cultural changes throughout much of the world. The introduction of this system into a given society is thus aptly referred to as the beginning of its own industrial revolution. In most instances, this revolution has meant more jobs, better food supplies, more consumer goods, better housing, and more leisure time. Unfortunately, however, it has also given rise to unsightly factory districts, pollution, alienation, and a sharp decline in craftsmanship (Fig. 9–1).

Today, even after several generations of intense technological development, the industrialization of the world is still incomplete. For, while England's Industrial Revolution has spread to many societies throughout the world and brought remarkable rises in their standards of living, even during periods of population growth, many other societies have remained virtually untouched, in any direct way, by the industrial process and must therefore endure without its benefits.

Early Industrialization

The first instances of industrialization were an array of machines, some old and some new, and the development of new sources of energy to run them. Most of the early advances were related to the production of such goods as textiles, ironwork, and pottery, all goods for which there was already an established and expanding demand.

The production of cotton textiles first gained prominence in England in about 1600, but, at that time, such products provided no serious challenge to the popularity of domestic woolens and cotton prints imported from India. Textile production pro-

FIGURE 9–1

A massive and less than picturesque industrial complex in the upper Ruhr Valley, near Dortmund, West Germany. (United Nations)

gressed rapidly during the early 1700s, when a ban was placed on the importation of India's cottons, which had become a threat to the English wool industry. The first of the major inventions in cotton manufacturing was not long in coming. The "flying shuttle," as it was called, appeared in 1733, and, replacing the hand-thrown shuttle, it soon increased the capacity and speed of English looms considerably. This created an immediate need for improvement in the traditional spinning process, and many tried their hand at finding a suitable solution to the problem (Fig. 9–2).

In the 1760s and 1770s, several of these attempts produced inventions that soon revolutionized the spinning process; chief

among these was Hargreaves' spinning jenny, Arkwright's spinning water frame, and Crompton's spinning mule (Fig. 9–3). By 1785, Cartwright's power loom had also appeared, but its widespread use was delayed somewhat by violent opposition from hand-loom weavers, who intimidated fellow workers and committed acts of sabotage, including the burning of several textile mills.

In iron production, as in textiles, a series of technological developments carried England and the other early industrial countries through several rapid stages of advancement, each stage bringing both higher production levels and greater social problems. Perhaps the most significant of these developments occurred in 1709, when one Abra-

FIGURE 9–2

The simple sort of spinning wheel in use in the early 1700s. (Bettmann Archive)

FIGURE 9–3

Improved mechanical spinners. Above, James Hargreaves' spinning jenny, invented in 1770. The model shown here was built by the U.S. Patent Office for the Chicago Exposition of 1893. (Smithsonian Institution) Below, Samuel Crompton's spinning mule, which combined drawing rollers and Hargreaves' stretching device. (Bettmann Archive)

ham Darby succeeded in processing coal into coked cinders that could perform as well in smelting and was without the toxic sulfur content of unprocessed coal. The many other technological advances in the iron industry included air pumps, steam hammers, and lathes for making heavy tools.

As has been mentioned in early chapters, the major medieval sources of mechanical power, the windmill and the water wheel, could not meet the new demand for power in the dawn of the industrial age. And throughout the seventeenth century and most of the eighteenth, attempts to perfect a steam engine also failed to provide an adequate response. A successful version of the steam engine, though patented by James Watt in

1769, was not marketed until 1776. But once available, Watt's steam engine was soon being used widely in cotton mills, steel mills, and pottery works throughout Europe. The perfection of the steam engine had removed a stubborn impediment to the expanded use of heavy equipment in factories of all sorts and in many mining operations as well (see

FIGURE 9–4

Pen and ink sketch (1870) of the weaving room of an early mechanized textile mill in Northampton, Massachusetts. (Bettmann Archive)

Chapter 8). The dramatic technological change wrought in the early stages of western Europe's industrial revolution enriched the lives of many Europeans, but it also brought many others new types of hardship. With the mechanization of most textile and iron production, the factory system quickly became institutionalized (Fig. 9–4).

Social modernization did not start as soon or as easily. The new system fostered many abuses and inequities, among them long hours, low wages, and unsafe working conditions. Nevertheless, the concentration of jobs created a steady influx of workers from rural areas into new industrial towns, which were sometimes run by the local manufacturing interest and were usually beset by poor and insufficient housing and inadequate sanitation. And as the number of industrial workers grew, comprising more and more women and children, so did the abuses to labor (Fig. 9–5). Around 1790, in response to the needs of the burgeoning industrial working class, trade unions began to be formed in England. But they seldom developed without strong opposition from factory owners, who

often combined to lobby for their own interests. Thus the people immediately involved in the growth of industrialization became formally divided into opposing camps, each of which was also beginning a struggle with the prevailing social structure.

Continuing Industrial Diffusion

After 1800 the industrial revolution continued its rapid growth and diffusion from England across Europe. As continental Europe's large and progressive societies both absorbed and nourished the incipient industrial revolution, they reached out to new places through trade, and their industries thrived on the widening markets and new supplies of raw materials. Initially, these continental neighbors learned from England, drawing on its industrial technology and organization and attracting some of its engineers and workers. But by the mid-nineteenth century these countries were taking their own directions in the building of machines and the generating of power to run them, and they were producing goods of variety and quality.

By 1870, the countries of Europe had formed an industrial inner zone and an agrarian outer zone. The inner zone included England, Germany, France, Belgium—the most industrialized societies of northwestern Europe—and the adjoining fringes of Italy and the Austro-Hungarian Empire. This zone had not only most of the heavy industry in Europe but most of its skilled labor and management, technology, and transportation and commerce as well. The outer zone was still basically agrarian, with some incidence of handicrafts and light industry; and each of its societies was dominated, for the most part, by wealthy landowning classes, whose lands were worked by a poor and illiterate peasantry.

In the final decades of the nineteenth century the main thrusts of industrialization were firmly established in the United States and fairly well rooted in Russia and Japan; these countries have since become the three leading industrial societies of the world, with the United States and the Soviet Union accounting for one-half of the world's industrial output in the 1970s. Japan, West Germany, the United Kingdom, and France pro-

FIGURE 9–5

For centuries in many early industrial countries young children were among those who worked long and hard in mines and factories. Here, a young nineteenth-century textile worker makes adjustments to her spinning frame. (Bettmann Archive)

vide an additional one fourth, and much of the remaining one-fourth is produced by Canada, Italy, China, India, Poland, and Czechoslovakia. The industrial output of all the other countries of the world, which number well over one hundred and represent quite a sizable majority of the world's population, constitutes the very small fraction outstanding.

The Twentieth Century

As the twentieth century began, the world's seven major powers—the United States, the United Kingdom, Germany, France, Italy, Russia, and Japan—could well be recognized as internationally viable and established nations. During the next decades some of these nations would also develop rudimentary industries within some of their overseas colonies and spheres of influence.

In the aftermath of the two world wars European colonialism declined, and the newly independent nations in Asia and Africa immediately forged their own industrialization programs. Varying degrees of success mark these programs to date, but all the nations involved have gained more industrial experience and added new dimensions to their cultural foundations. Although continued progress will be slow and laborious, even where their initial success has been greatest, industry will eventually become a major socioeconomic component in all these former colonies.

No twentieth-century society can be modernized through a simple transfer of technological devices, however. Developing a nation's ability to feed and clothe its people is not simply a matter of planting more acres, building more factories, and installing more

FIGURE 9–6

A power station and passers-by in Balpahari, India. Social change in this area northwest of Calcutta lags well behind its halting advance into industrialization. (United Nations)

machines. Rather, it often involves a slow and orderly reconstruction of a great many socioeconomic factors (Fig. 9–6). But at least, with selective technological assistance from older industrial societies, today's developing nations need not always tread the slow and frustrating path of mechanical trial and error; history offers them solutions to many of their problems.

In this respect, if no other, the late arrival of such a nation among the world's independent states may actually be one of its assets. For a new nation can leap across the century of experimentation that was required of its industrial predecessors and implement the latest industrial technology almost at once; it can learn and benefit from the mistakes, as well as the successes, of the older industrial countries. The United States learned and borrowed from Europe in this fashion, and later, in the twentieth century, both the Soviet Union and Japan borrowed from Europe and the United States in their industrial rises.

Modern Societal Infrastructures

Agro-Industrial Societies

The people of preindustrial nations make their livelihoods largely through primary activities, such as agriculture, herding, forestry, hunting and fishing, and mining. The beginnings of modern societies have usually been accompanied by population shifts away from agrarian areas toward new urban centers and industry.

In preindustrial agrarian societies most labor is involved with food production in an essentially rural environment. In industrial societies, improvements in agricultural efficiency decrease the number of farmers needed to effect preindustrial levels of farm production; more food producers work off the farm—in machinery factories, fertilizer and pesticide plants, water supply facilities, processing plants, and trading complexes— at activities that are part agricultural and part industrial (Fig. 9–7). All of which, quite obviously, reduces the proportion of the total working population engaged in agriculture. In brief, it is increasingly apparent that agricultural production becomes more efficient when associated with the industrialization process in any society: total output increases, and worker output increases.

Many of the world's developed societies achieved their present high levels of industrial production largely through unplanned, socially chaotic, and often environmentally costly processes. Most of today's developing nations cannot afford such socioeconomic chaos, and none of the world could long bear prolonged disregard of the environment. There are those who argue that the quickest road to economic self-sufficiency for the developing nations is the establishment of crash programs of heavy capitalization for industry, at *any* cost; there are many more who maintain that economic stability can best be achieved by such nations through a planned balance of primary and secondary activities—that is, modern *agro-industrial* societies with balanced and integrated agricultural-industrial economies.

Such planned and balanced activities create chain reactions of ideas, associations, and actions. Balance creates interdependency attitudes and interacting relations, which will help prevent the creation of the weak

FIGURE 9–7

The mechanization of agriculture. Left, a pineapple cannery in Honolulu, Hawaii. (Dole Photo) Below, an egg "factory" in California. (Goodyear)

agrarian versus the powerful industrial societies, or dominant urban-industrial structures and subordinate rural-agricultural structures.

Advantages of Secondary Economic Activities

Achieving a balance between agriculture and industry, rather than continuing to rely on primary economic activities, is an economic advantage to any nation. Perhaps one of the most obvious ways in which industry is more attractive than agriculture is in flexibility of techniques, methods, competition, and output. Decreasing returns, for example, may be postponed in industry more effectively than in agriculture—by improving techniques, raw materials, machinery, energy supplies, and even quality control. Significant change, which may be accomplished by high-level policy decisions and "overnight" reorganization in industry, may well take years in agriculture. Industry also has greater control over production, which it can usually slow, accelerate, or even terminate at will; agriculture, on the other hand, has its pace dictated largely by nature and is characterized by a plant-and-wait pattern. And, further, the quality of almost any industrial operation can be increased if there is sufficient desire and financial means; workers can be educated, and better raw materials can usually be obtained. The physical elements of agriculture—soil and water—on the other hand, cannot be controlled with the same ease and success.

Trends in Agro-Industrial Societies

Labor-Intensive or Capital-Intensive?

Once a nation in the contemporary world decides to industrialize, it must often face the problem of whether to develop labor-intensive or capital-intensive industries. This question has been debated a great deal in recent years; but, particularly among the people of the developing nations themselves, there seems to be a growing preference for labor-intensive industries. Capital-intensive industries—iron and steel plants and petroleum refineries, for example—require immense investments of capital but employ only a relatively small permanent labor force (Fig. 9–8). Thus, emphasis by a developing nation on capital-intensive industry will do little to alleviate the underemployment and unemployment problems of its citizens; and unless a large portion of the citizenry is involved in the new modes of employment, cultural adjustment to industrial life styles will be slow.

But all too frequently, in more recent times, developing countries have opted for large, capital-intensive industrial operations, which they felt were necessary to confirm their status as independent nations. There has been serious neglect of labor-intensive industries—that is, food processing and the manufacturing of light consumer goods—which require relatively large numbers of workers and, usually, smaller expenditures for machinery and power. While helping to distribute national income and wealth, the greater employment provided by labor-intensive industries would make it possible for much more of the population to gain the experience necessary to handle complex industrial operations, which in many developing countries are staffed largely by foreigners.

FIGURE 9–8

Capital- or labor-intensive industry. Above, an oil refinery near Philadelphia, Pennsylvania, that represents a vast capital investment but supplies few jobs for local residents. (Sun Oil Company) Below, a large jute mill in Dacca, Bangladesh, that requires only a relatively small expenditure for machinery and power but gives steady employment to approximately 20,000 people. (United Nations)

Cultural Impacts on Labor

The world's labor force, which includes about a billion and a half people, is distributed unevenly among the three major types of productive activities: primary activities, basically agriculture, comprise 54 percent of all labor; secondary activities, or jobs in industry, account for 20 percent; and tertiary activities, or services, amount to 26 percent (see Fig. 7–25). Two culturally important phenomena can be seen in the data represented by this distribution. One is the persistence of a predominant and widespread agricultural labor force in the social structure. The other is the effectiveness of the much smaller segment of the labor force in industry, for it produces more than double the earnings of agriculture (Fig. 9–9). The reasons for this contrast in labor efficiency are fairly evident. Industry is simply better suited than agriculture to labor organization, training, and in-

LABOR FORCE IN SECONDARY ACTIVITIES

Population percentage
- Over 35
- 26–35
- 15–25
- Under 15
- No data

ute Miles
1000 2000 3000

oidal Equal-Area Projection

FIGURE 9–9

At least 20 percent of the world's total labor force is employed in secondary activities, or industry. On a national level the percentage of the labor force in such activities is usually indicative of general socioeconomic development.

centives, and, worldwide, industry makes greater use of planning, mechanization, and technology.

Competent management is an important segment of the labor force required in any industrial operation—whether in a highly industrial country or a developing nation; decisionmaking in long-range planning and development, a vital part of management, can determine success or failure in any industry in any country. But it is particularly critical in the early stages of industrialization, when it is more difficult to absorb the costs of scarce materials and energy. A wrong planning decision can delay a developing nation's industrial success for several years—a postponement that few young governments can afford.

New Roles for Government

In order to pursue a viable plan of industrial development, the government of an agricultural society may, at the same time, have to carry out a program of general socioeconomic development. The thrust of such a program involves the expansion of the industrial base, utilizing both domestic and foreign capital and materials; and the program usually provides for balanced allocations of the country's resources to the various sectors of the national infrastructure. Guidelines for the use of these allocations within each sector must be carefully established and maintained to avoid "status influences" and obsessions. In total, such socioeconomic developments involve such basic domestic concerns as agriculture, food and industrial resources, transportation, communications, energy resources, financial and insurance services, and of course the functioning industrial structure itself.

The governments of many developing nations also try to ensure that the recovery of their countries' raw materials serves the regional or national pursuit of economic diversity; some make certain that any enterprise involving the extraction of domestic minerals is controlled by nationals, and that profits from such an operation are kept within the country and plowed back into its economy. Quite frequently, high tariffs are levied on imported goods that can be produced domestically; but tariffs are usually kept low on heavy machinery, most energy materials, and manufactured articles imported for finishing. Government management of the shift from agriculture to industry is also beginning to rely on more direct appeals to the profit motive, although many of these new concepts are more difficult to implement. Those that seem to have the best chances for success include selective subsidies, especially to industries seeking foreign markets; industrial loans at low interest rates; and tax incentives operative for limited time periods.

Factors in Industrial Location

Modern industry, like modern agriculture, is, at its best, an efficient partnership between human beings and the environment. A great many environmental factors had a decisive influence on the spatial pattern of the world's first major industrial centers, and many of these factors continue to play a role in determining the rate at which a new nation proceeds with industrialization. However, in most instances today, it is the cultural factors affecting industrialization that eventually prevail. This diminution of the control exerted by environmental factors owes most of its extent to fairly recent technological developments, especially in the provision of energy and transportation.

Industry today enjoys far greater locational freedom than it did even a generation ago. Thus, either in considering the present scope of industrialization or in contemplating industries of the future, one must remember that most of today's major industrial centers were established *before* the recent advances of technology in transportation and energy use. And, owing to a sort of "industrial inertia," most of these centers have undergone few substantial changes; once established, industrial sites—like agricultural areas, or individual people—tend to continue their accustomed pattern, even though it may have become at least marginally uneconomical.

In the early stages of a country's industrialization, most factories and plants tend to locate near a natural resource vital to their operation—for example, a coal or cotton field, a waterfall, a forest, or the confluence of two rivers; their locations are not usually influenced so much by the accessibility of cultural phenomena, such as labor, capital, markets, and road and rail transport. Most of the factories in industrializing countries are largely self-contained, their raw materials, fuels, and markets being supplied locally. Such provincialism in industry prevailed throughout much of the United States even less than a century ago, and it still exists on a small scale in all of the heavily industrialized nations.

Labor

Modern industry, despite all the work done by machines and automation, still requires abundant supplies of human labor —from the administrative to the unskilled. Every developed industrial society utilizes all the different kinds of labor simultaneously; and an employment range nearly as broad is a prerequisite for any society seeking industrial progress. Unfortunately, in most industries, and especially internationally, competent executives are more difficult commodities to acquire than energy sources, machinery, or even capital.

Within a given country or international economic community, the labor force is generally highly mobile. Since the beginning of the industrial revolution in the United States, there have been constant migrations of labor from rural areas to the country's industrial towns, where the migrants hoped to find better employment opportunities. During the Depression era, such migrations flowed eastward and westward; and, in the early 1940s, the frantic industrial expansions of a nation at war drew thousands of Americans into new industrial towns in the South and Far West. In Europe in the postwar years, the establishment of the Common Market has led to large migrations of industrial workers from the southern member nations into Germany, France, Belgium, the Netherlands, and Luxembourg.

Markets

As a locational factor in industry, markets are rapidly increasing in importance. All of today's most developed industrial nations have large and stable domestic markets as well as more or less extended international markets. In recent years it has become more widely recognized that each industrialized or industrializing country is its own best customer; and the essence of this realization can be applied to most regions and cities as well. Northwestern Europe, for example, consumes much of its own industrial production, leaving only limited quantities of some products for export, mainly to markets in underindustrialized areas of Asia, Africa, and Latin America. The northeastern United States and the Moscow region of the Soviet Union are also largely self-sustaining; and, at another level, the same is true of the industrial cities of Tokyo, New York, and London. Yet by and large the distribution of industrial goods is no longer primarily within local markets. More and more industries are equipping themselves to serve distant national and international markets.

Transportation

The operation of a successful modern industrial enterprise requires that the necessary fuel and raw materials move dependably from their source regions into the factory and that the finished products reach their local, national, or international market in good condition and in good time. Transportation and communication systems have thus become vital to any industrial undertaking, whether it is a bottling works whose only markets are within a 50-mile radius or a giant petroleum-refining company with worldwide resource locations and markets.

The transportation of heavy materials before the advent of the railroad, in 1825, was limited largely to waterborne traffic, and it was usually slow and unscheduled. Wondrous developments in the technology of transport were to take place: the spread of the railroad, almost worldwide, between 1825 and 1900; the addition of the now ubiquitous truck, after 1900; the one-day-to-anywhere airfreighter, after 1950; the ocean-going supertanker, in the 1960s; the mechanized container ships, after 1970 (Fig. 9–10).

However, the nuclei of today's major industrial regions and many of the lesser ones were already established by the early nineteenth century, and all were associated with tidewater or navigable lakes or rivers. During the last century and a half, railroads and highways have filled these regions with a network of ancillary land routes, but they have not shifted the major industrial regions to any noticeable degree.

Capital

Capital availability has traditionally been rated as an important factor in the location of industry. For even if sufficient finan-

cial resources are available for initial installations, expanding production and marketing costs can soon outstrip original plant investments. Tremendous amounts of capital are usually needed to buy large inventories of raw materials and fuel, finance new machinery and technology, pay wages and salaries, maintain plant and transportation systems, develop and expand markets, and pursue research and planning. Countries or regions in which financial institutions offer industry abundant capital, or credit, attract both new and relocating enterprises. Societies that do not provide liberal financial assistance stand little chance of developing strong industrial centers. Both Spain and India, very different in many other aspects of industrialization, are among the nations that face this problem; the United States and Switzerland are two of those that do not. A complete classification of the world's nations on the basis of capital availability reinforces the implication of these examples: that a country's industrial success does not depend on land area, as does most of its success in agriculture.

FIGURE 9–10

Controversial but efficient, the containerization equipment shown here can move a large cargo from ship to truck far more swiftly than is possible through manual operations. Containerization can thus help to decrease per-unit shipping costs and secure the transportation of high-value goods. (Seatrain)

Industrial Location Theory

It is obvious from the preceding discussion that the problem of where to locate a factory is a complex and difficult one. Thus, it is often helpful to represent locational principles in terms of theoretical models. In studies of industrial location, the model very often used is one developed early in this century by Alfred Weber. Despite some criticism over the years, this theory has served as the basis for many subsequent locational and industrial theories and still provides a valuable simplification of an often complex topic.

The Weber Theory

Alfred Weber, a German economist, was the first to publish a general theory on the location of industrial activities. Published as the *Theory of the Location of Industries,* in 1909, it was intended to be applicable to all types of industry under all types of economic, political, and social systems. Even though his major area of concern was the distribution of secondary activities, the basic principles Weber developed are applicable to other economic locational problems as well. The major criterion Weber considers operative in the selection of a site is *least cost*. He makes clear that his method of analysis is not intended to predict or explain actual industrial locations but merely to provide a basis for evaluating the numerous variables that influence them.

Weber begins his theory with a number of assumptions:

(1) There is a single isolated political state with a homogeneous culture (including technological development) and uniform physical characteristics.

(2) The products from each producing unit in the country are sold at a single market.

(3) The number and combination of natural resources (raw materials and fuels) as well as their distribution varies from case to case.

(4) The country has a uniform mode of transportation (the railway), with transportation costs increasing in direct proportion to distance and weight. Natural resources and finished products have equal transportation costs.

(5) The distribution of the labor force and wage rates is restricted to certain locations. Whereas at each of these locations the labor supply is unlimited, the prevailing wage rate is fixed and differs from place to place.

Within the context of these assumptions, industrial site selection in Weber's analysis is based on two major variables. The first and more important is transportation costs.

Transportation Costs. In Weber's analysis, the problem is simply to determine the point at which a factory will incur the least transport cost in (1) procuring its necessary raw materials/fuels and (2) delivering its finished product to market. In order to solve this problem it is necessary to know (1) the relative weights (weight loss) of the raw materials/fuels and the finished product involved and (2) the distance over which they have to be transported. (Since it is assumed that the natural resources and the finished product incur equal transportation costs, it would not be necessary to calculate the weight loss of the finished product.) The next step, then, is to establish weight and distance criteria for the natural resources.

In regard to weight, the natural resources can be categorized as either *pure* (that is, they lose no weight in processing) or *gross* (that is, they lose some or all of their weight in processing); all fuels, for example, suffer a loss of almost all their weight in processing. In regard to distance, the natural resources can be either *ubiquitous* (that is, they are available nearly everywhere) or *localized* (that is, they are available only at specific locations).

To demonstrate the influence of least transport cost on the location of industry, Weber uses a number of cases as examples.

Let us begin with the simplest case, which involves only one natural resource and the market. (1) If the raw material is ubiquitous and either pure or gross, then the factory would tend to be located close to or at the market in order to avoid paying any transportation costs. (2) If the raw material is localized and pure, then the factory can be located either at the market, at the raw material source, or anywhere in between these two points; the transportation costs in each instance would be the same. (3) If the raw material is localized and gross, then the factory would tend to be located at the source of the raw material, for there would be no sense in paying to transport waste material closer to the market.

This case helps to demonstrate that, as a general rule, localized rather than ubiquitous natural resources tend to force the location of factories away from the market. In addition, the same basic principles used for determining industrial location under simple conditions can also be used in cases where more than one natural resource is involved.

In cases involving more than one raw material, no two of which lie on the same direct line to the market, Weber makes use of various locational figures. For example, in a situation with two natural resources and one market, he uses a locational *triangle,* each corner of which represents one of the three factors involved. If, in such a situation, both of the localized resources are pure, then chances are high that the factory will be located at the market. If, on the other hand, either one or both of the resources are gross, then the location of the plant will be at the point in the locational triangle that achieves a balance, or equalization, in the transportation costs of the two resources; such a site would not necessarily be at the market.

In a situation involving three raw materials and a market, Weber uses a locational *polygon.* For still more complicated cases, where four or more resources are involved, he employs a mechanical device known as *Varigon's frame.* In this device the relative influence of the various factors—resources and the market—is represented by appropriately scaled weights that are suspended off the edge of the frame's circular top by wires over pulleys. The point at which the connected wires are in balance on the top of the circular disk is the theoretical point of least transport cost and therefore of the factory location.

Labor Costs. Whereas in the first part of Weber's analysis the ideal location for a factory is based solely on least transport cost, in the second part the ideal location is the point at which the combination of transport and labor costs is the lowest.

In order to illustrate the method Weber uses to determine this point, let us use a simple example involving one localized gross raw material and a market. In the diagramming of such a situation, shown in Figure 9–11, each concentric circle, or *isotim,* that is drawn around the individual market and raw material areas represents one unit of transport cost per ton of product. In this particular instance the least-transport-cost location for a factory would probably be at the raw mate-

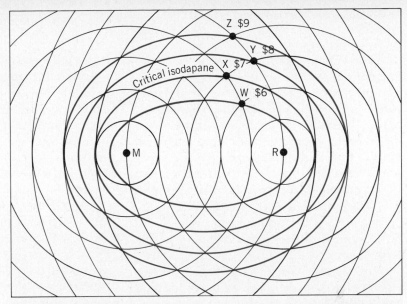

	R	W	X	Y	Z
Transportation cost	$ 5	$ 6	$ 7	$ 8	$ 9
Labor cost	$ 8	$ 6	$ 6	$ 6	$ 6
Total cost	$13	$12	$13	$14	$15

FIGURE 9–11

A diagrammatic representation of Weber's industrial location theory.

rial source (R), in which case each ton of product sent to market would incur 5 units of transport cost.

If, however, the factory were located at point W, the total transport cost to market, based on the total number of isotims involved, would be 6 units per ton of product (two concentric circles from the raw material source plus four concentric circles from the market). The solid red line, which point W is located on, is called an *isodapane* and is used by Weber to connect points of equal transportation cost—in this case, all points of 6 units. In similar fashion, all points along the isodapanes on which points X, Y, and Z are located would incur total transport costs of 7, 8, and 9 units respectively.

The isodapane is of most value when other variables—such as labor costs, taxes, rent, and subsidies—are combined with the basic variable of transport costs in determin

ing the optimum least-cost location for industry. When such variables are involved it is possible that some point other than R would have the greatest advantage. In all cases involving multiple variables, an isodapane can be used to determine how great an advantage must exist at an alternate location in terms of labor costs in order to offset the location's disadvantage in terms of transport costs.

For example, if we know that at point W the cost of labor per ton of product is $2 less than at point R, we first find the isodapane (point X) along which transportation costs are $2 greater than at the point where they are the lowest (point R). Weber calls this the *critical isodapane* because its higher transport cost would exactly equal the relatively lower labor cost at point W, thereby establishing a balance between total costs at points X and R. Since point W lies inside this critical isoda

225

pane, it is advantageous for the factory to be transferred to this point from the least-transport-cost location, because the lower labor cost outweighs the additional transport cost. However, it would not be advantageous for the factory to be transferred to any point outside this critical isodapane (Y or Z), because the additional transportation cost would outweigh the savings in labor cost.

To summarize, if the sole factor is transport cost, then the least-cost location would be at point R; if the cost of labor is the sole factor, then the least-cost location would be at points W, X, Y, or Z; and when these two factors are combined, the least-cost location is at point W.

Other Locational Principles

In the real world, where there are no perfect conditions, decisions regarding industrial location are based on a complex interaction of dynamic variables, not on theories. But as a guide in making these decisions, planners often employ various locational principles that are derived, in part, from theory. The following is a sampling of such principles: (1) industries should be located at the point of least production cost; (2) industries should be dispersed inter-regionally in order to encourage regional self-sufficiency; (3) industries should be located so as to reduce the socioeconomic differences between town and country; (4) industrial location should be based to some extent on defense needs; (5) industries should be located so as to improve the quality of the environment.

At present, the distribution of most industry does not reflect such principles. If they can be more effectively applied in the future, not only the industrial regions but all the world should benefit.

REVIEW AND DISCUSSION

1. Compare the industrial developments in western Europe during the eighteenth century with the present-day industrial development of most societies in the Third World.
2. How did the dramatic technological changes wrought in the early stages of western Europe's industrial revolution enrich the lives of many Europeans? What hardships did they bring?
3. Which seven countries could correctly be called "industrial societies" at the turn of the twentieth century? What national features account for their early industrialization?
4. With respect to socioindustrial development, what are some of the disadvantages faced by nations that have only recently become independent?
5. The beginnings of modern societies have usually been marked by population shifts away from agrarian activities and toward urban commerce and industry. Discuss and evaluate some basic social consequences of these population shifts, both to groups and to individuals.
6. Most modern societies recognize that socioeconomic stability can best be achieved through the planned balance of primary and secondary livelihoods. Evaluate this view in terms of your own culture and locale, and then in terms of some culture and locale not your own.
7. Enumerate and explain some major advantages offered by secondary economic activities (especially industry) but not by primary activities (especially agriculture).

8. With respect to efficiency and productivity, compare and contrast the labor and technology used in agriculture with the labor and technology of industry. How could a better balance be established between them throughout the world, and what would be the socioeconomic gains?
9. Why and how and to what degree are markets increasing in importance as locational factors in world industry?
10. Identify and evaluate the advantages and the disadvantages in using the Weber theory for the purpose of analyzing industrial location.

SELECTED REFERENCES

Alexandersson, G. *A Geography of Manufacturing.* Englewood Cliffs, N.J.: Prentice-Hall, 1967.

Ashton, T. S. *The Industrial Revolution, 1760–1830.* London: Oxford University Press, 1968.

Birnie, A. *An Economic History of Europe.* London: Methuen, 1966.

Burton, I., and R. W. Kates. *Readings in Resource Management and Conservation.* Chicago: University of Chicago Press, 1965.

Froehlich, W., ed. *Land Tenure, Industrialization, and Social Stability . . . in Asia.* Milwaukee: Marquette University Press, 1961.

Greenhut, M. L. *Plant Location in Theory and in Practice.* Chapel Hill: University of North Carolina Press, 1956.

Hammond, J., and B. Hammond. *The Rise of Modern History.* London: Methuen, 1966.

Hull, O. *A Geography of Production.* London: Macmillan, 1968.

Isard, W. *Location and Space Economy.* Cambridge: Massachusetts Institute of Technology Press, 1956.

Lösch, A. *The Economics of Location,* trans. by W. H. Woglom and W. F. Stolper. New Haven: Yale University Press, 1954.

Mantoux, P. *The Industrial Revolution in the Eighteenth Century.* London: Methuen, 1966.

Miller, E. W. *Geography of Industrial Location.* Dubuque, Iowa: Brown, 1970.

Mountjoy, A. B. *Industrialization and Underdeveloped Countries.* Chicago: Aldine, 1967.

Mumford, L. *Technics and Human Development.* The Myth of the Machine, Vol. I. New York: Harcourt, Brace and World, 1967.

O'Brien, R., and the editors of *Life. Machines.* New York: Time, Inc., 1964.

Rosovsky, H., ed. *Industrialization in Two Systems.* New York: Wiley, 1966.

Smith, D. M. "A Theoretical Framework for Geographical Studies of Industrial Location." *Economic Geography,* Vol. 42 (April 1966), 95–113.

Staley, E. *The Future of Underdeveloped Countries.* New York: Praeger, 1961.

Trewartha, G. T. *A Geography of Population.* New York: Wiley, 1969.

United Nations. "Industry." *Science and Technology for Development,* Vol. 4, 1963.

_____. "National Resources." *Science and Technology for Development,* Vol. 2, 1963.

Weber, A. *Theory of the Location of Industries,* trans. by C. J. Friedrich. Chicago: University of Chicago Press, 1929.

A conveyor laden with a newly made sheet of aluminum. (Reynolds Metal)

10

Industrial Societies: Diffusion and Regionalism

In recent decades in the world's industrially developed societies, and in many of its developing societies as well, traditional life styles and values have been overturned with marked rapidity and varying degrees of social dislocation. Within an average human lifetime, such nations as the United States and its industrial peers in Europe and Asia have changed from rural, horse-and-buggy societies into urban societies of the jet age. Today this sort of dynamic societal change continues to spread around the world unabated — perhaps even with mounting vigor and promise. People nearly everywhere on earth are now gaining greater understanding of themselves and their potentials and demanding better life styles through fuller employment and fuller utilization of their own natural resources. For centuries, industrialization and its higher standards of living inched their way around the globe; but, in the last fifty years, as cultural and political self-determination has asserted itself, the pace of industrialization has accelerated.

Industrial Societies of Northwestern Europe

The major industrial societies have traditionally been found within the Western world, and Northwestern Europe is the oldest and among the most significant of all the world's industrial regions (Fig. 10–1). The many industrial societies within the European region extend from the North Atlantic coast of the United Kingdom east to Poland and south to the shores of the Mediterranean; they reach their highest density in an area that includes portions of northern France, the Benelux countries (Belgium, the Netherlands, and Luxembourg), and West Germany. This multinational complex is the

INDUSTRIALIZATION

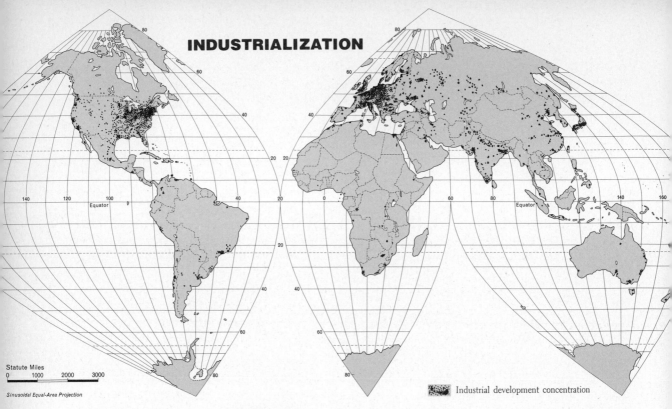

Statute Miles
0 1000 2000 3000

Sinusoidal Equal-Area Projection

Industrial development concentration

FIGURE 10–1

Industry is concentrated in western Europe, the northeastern United States, the European portion of the Soviet Union, and Japan, but is spreading rapidly into less-developed areas of the world.

greatest concentration of skilled labor, technology, and industrial facilities the world has ever known—the fountainhead of today's global industrial scramble (Fig. 10–2).

United Kingdom

Most of the modern industrial developments in the United Kingdom, or Great Britain, lie on the flanks of its central mountains, the Pennines; however, the remaining new industry in the region is widely dispersed, mainly because of the changing nature of industry and the progress of national programs of industrial relocation (Fig. 10–3). Still, despite even the most recent developments, it is the original industrial centers of the

United Kingdom, particularly those flanking southern sections of England's Pennine Chain, that predominate in the region, both in terms of productivity and of quality.

The English Midlands, or Birmingham area, at the southern end of the Pennines, contains the greatest concentration of heavy industry in the United Kingdom—iron and steel, machinery, transportation equipment, and automobiles. Northward lies the Lancashire area, long the cotton-manufacturing heart of Great Britain. The city of Manchester and its satellites are still associated with cotton textiles, but diversification has reduced the importance of their products. Eastward, across the Pennines, is the Yorkshire area, where woolens, textile machinery, and cutlery have been paramount for centuries. To the south, the London area, like most capitals of the world, has a great concentration of light industries that produce a variety of consumer goods, both for domestic consumption and for export. The Newcastle area, in northern England, produces steel, ships, and machinery. Scotland's industries stretch from the Firth of Clyde to the Firth of Forth, with two major ones, shipbuilding and metalworking, centered largely at Glasgow. The industry of Wales is concentrated in the south and includes numerous metal works.

If the London area is excepted, there is a very close relationship between the presence of coal and the location of industry in the United Kingdom. Coal fields were the foundation of Europe's industrial revolution and of most of the world's subsequent regional industrialization; and institutional inertia has allowed little change in the distribution of industrial regions, despite the development of more portable fuels.

Industry has probably become more vital to the United Kingdom than to any other major region. England turned so largely to the factory for a living during its long colonizing period that it has ever since neglected its full agricultural potential; today, as a result, two-thirds of its basic foods must be imported. Closely studded with the hallmarks of mechanized industry, this area depends for survival upon a continuous industrial-commercial process—import, manufacture, and export.

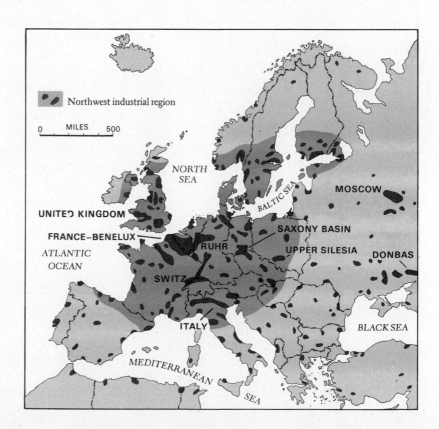

FIGURE 10-2

Industrialization in western Europe, the world's largest contiguous industrial region.

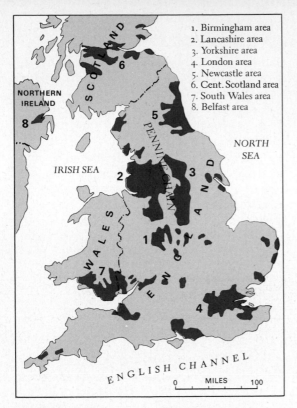

1. Birmingham area
2. Lancashire area
3. Yorkshire area
4. London area
5. Newcastle area
6. Cent. Scotland area
7. South Wales area
8. Belfast area

FIGURE 10–3

Industrial centers of the United Kingdom. Except for the London and Belfast areas, all are closely associated with major coal fields.

Northern France–Belgium

The multinational western half of Europe's industrial core—mainly northern France and Belgium, but also Luxembourg and the Netherlands—must be considered a vital industrial region. Underlying much of it are rich coal fields in Belgium and France, and the abundant Lorraine iron ores of France can be reached by the area's navigable waterways. The French sector, including Strasbourg, Nancy, and Metz, is especially important for its heavy industry, while the Lille area is dominated by textiles. Belgium's industrial cities are widespread, with Brussels, Antwerp, Ghent, and Liège all involved

in the production of such heavy materials as iron and steel, machinery, and railway equipment. Although part of Europe's central industrial core, northern France and Belgium still present a quiet rural scene little marred by smokestacks and congestion.

West Germany

The lower Rhine–Ruhr valleys of West Germany comprise the most highly developed industrial region in Europe. This is the famous Ruhr Valley, and like its American counterpart, the Pittsburgh region, its name is synonymous with modern heavy industry; in fact, the two regions are the most productive heavy-industry concentrations in the world. Fed by its own coal fields and by the nearby Lorraine iron ores, the Ruhr has long been the heart of European heavy industry. Dortmund, Duisburg, and several of its other cities produce large amounts of iron and steel, which in turn have spawned a wide range of manufactures, including heavy machinery, locomotives, and armaments. The Ruhr was practically destroyed by Allied bombing during the Second World War, but it has since been totally rebuilt; it now far surpasses its prewar magnitude and is probably more modernized than the Pittsburgh region.

South of the Ruhr is a slightly less developed area, the middle Rhine–Saar region, which stretches along the middle Rhine Valley to include such well-known cities as Mainz, Frankfurt, and Mannheim. The iron, steel, and chemical industries are predominant in this region (Fig. 10–4).

Northern Switzerland

The Swiss have made the northern part of their country into an important industrial region, even though such resources as coal,

232

FIGURE 10–4

West German industry, extremely varied and highly developed, is represented here by the Eberfeld plant of Farbenfabriken Bayer, manufacturers of pharmaceuticals, chemicals, and photographic materials. (German Information Center)

iron ore, petroleum, natural gas, strategic minerals, and even agricultural raw materials for industry are practically nonexistent within the country. With highly skilled labor and imported source materials they produce many high-profit, light industrial goods, ranging from diesel engines and machine tools to fine clocks and watches and optical equipment. The Swiss have also managed to complement their industrial sector with a

truly balanced agrarian sector, which makes their country an excellent example of an agro-industrial society.

Northern Italy

Although lacking practically every basic raw material for industry—including coal, petroleum, natural gas, iron ore, and even strategic minerals—Italy has developed an important industrial society in its northern sector, one that incorporates both heavy and light industry; and at the same time the country has continued to develop its specialized Mediterranean agriculture. Italy's industrial structure, unique in the West, is based largely on hydroelectric power, imported source materials, and relatively cheap labor. Both the Alps and the Apennines supply the hydroelectric power that has made possible the industrialization of such cities as Milan, Turin, and Padua in the Po Valley region, and such other industrial centers as Genoa and Florence. Italy well exemplifies that even a nation nearly devoid of natural resources and traditional fossil fuels for energy can industrialize on a major scale.

Secondary European Centers

In addition to the major industrial regions of western Europe, there are many scattered centers that are especially important to the countries in which they are located. Significant among them are such industrial regions as the Saxony Basin of East Germany and the Upper Silesia area in southern Poland, as well as a host of industrial nodal cities, such as Stockholm, Hamburg, Munich, Warsaw, Prague, Budapest, Belgrade, and Barcelona.

Industrial Regions of the United States

As a consequence of many factors, such as abundant natural resources, highly developed transportation networks, mass production technologies, availability and mobility of large amounts of capital, and freedom from physical devastation by war, the United States is now the world's leading industrial society. Its first major step toward this state began in the aftermath of the First World War, and the country's industrial growth has surged to unprecedented heights since midcentury.

Northeastern Region

From very small beginnings in New England during the early colonial days, industry in the New World spread westward with the steady march of settlement and transportation, growing in intensity and diversity decade by decade (Fig. 10–5). The great northeastern industrial region, that part of the United States in which industry is most highly concentrated, extends from New England westward beyond the Mississippi, and from the Great Lakes–St. Lawrence Valley to beyond the Ohio Valley (Fig. 10–6). If superimposed upon western Europe, this portion of the United States would extend from the United Kingdom to Poland and from southern Sweden to the Mediterranean.

Within this region are most of the coal mines and electric power plants, and half of the petroleum refining plants, of the United States. Close by are major source areas for petroleum, natural gas, iron ore, and a wide variety of other essential raw materials. The region contains most of the coke ovens, blast furnaces, and steel mills of the United States. Within its limits are manufactured most of the nation's automobiles, locomotives, and railroad cars, as well as most of the machine tools, machinery, textiles, and clothing. Just as the region possesses great wealth in source materials, transportation facilities,

FIGURE 10-5

A steel plant of the early 1900s, in Bethlehem, Pennsylvania. The large circular machine in the foreground was used in pig casting. (Bethlehem Steel Company)

FIGURE 10-6

Industrialization in the coterminous United States and southern Canada. These areas have developed industrial centers from coast to coast, but industry remains most heavily concentrated in the northeastern United States, which is also the leading industrial region of the world.

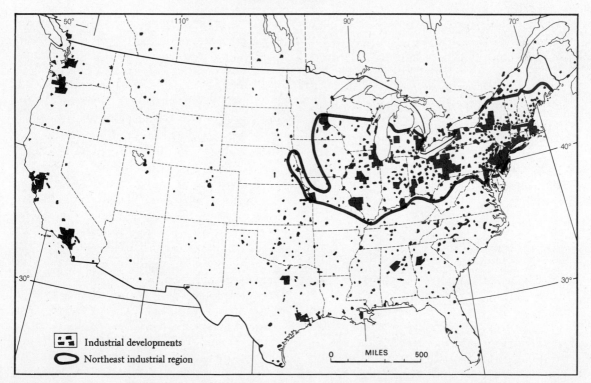

Industrial developments
Northeast industrial region

MILES
0   500

and machines, it also has the highest population density and largest total population of any comparable part of the Americas. People are present in sufficient numbers not only to make, operate, and repair the machinery of industry but to transport and buy much of the manufactured products that they produce; at the same time, the population maintains and constantly expands the world's most highly effective large agricultural complex. Thus the region is truly a large-scale agro-industrial society.

Iron and Steel. The United States has led the world in iron and steel production for the last half century. The long-established producing area centered in the cities of Pittsburgh, Youngstown, and Cleveland normally provides a bit over one-third of the country's total iron and steel, serving primarily the large industrial markets in Pennsylvania, Ohio, Michigan, and New York (Fig. 10–7). Within this area are brought together the Lake Superior iron ores and the Pennsylvania and West Virginia coals.

The country's second oldest iron-and-steel producing center is the Chicago–Gary area, which normally produces a little under a third of the national total. Developed in the early decades of this century to supply the

FIGURE 10–7

A modern steel plant at Lackawanna, New York, on Lake Erie. The 4,000-foot canal shown here handles ore boats that travel the Great Lakes, and its mechanical unloaders take the cargoes directly to the plant. (Bethlehem Steel Company)

needs of the new West, this area brings together iron ores from Lake Superior and coal from both the nearby Illinois Basin and the distant Appalachian fields.

A still more recently developed center, one that accounts for approximately one-sixth of the nation's iron and steel, surrounds the east coast cities of Baltimore, Philadelphia, and Trenton. These nodal tidewaters receive much of their iron ore from foreign sources, such as Venezuela, eastern Canada, Chile, and Sweden. Long ocean hauls from these foreign sources are less costly than would be the short rail hauls necessary to move Lake Superior ores from southern Lake Erie ports to the Atlantic seaboard.

Machinery and Transportation Equipment. Machinery and transportation equipment are manufactures closely associated with the iron and steel industry within the northeastern industrial region. Combined, they have the highest value of any major group of manufactured products in the United States.

Machine tools—forges, presses, drills, lathes, and the like—are the machines that help fashion other machinery and such finished products as automobiles, airplanes, tractors, typewriters, and locomotives. Machine tools are manufactured throughout the Northeast, to serve a region-wide market. Textile machinery still is manufactured primarily near the original textile centers of New England and Pennsylvania, although much textile manufacturing has spread into the southern Appalachian region in recent decades. Electrical machinery is made rather widely throughout the Northeast, to serve expanding regional markets. But agricultural machinery production, located near the largest market, is much restricted to the Ohio to Iowa sector, with over half of it concentrated in Illinois.

Most of the nation's automobile and truck production is concentrated in southern Michigan and adjoining parts of Ohio, Indiana, Illinois, and Wisconsin (Fig. 10–8). Especially noted centers are Detroit, Pontiac, and Flint in southeastern Michigan, and Toledo, Ohio. Automobiles require such a great variety of source materials and specially fabricated parts that many satellite industries have sprung up in and near the major automobile centers. The close relationship between the automobile industry and many other industries in the United States is illustrated by the fact that in recent years the automotive industry has consumed about 20 percent of the nation's steel output, 20 percent of its copper, 30 percent of its nickel, 25 percent of its lead, 75 percent of its plate glass, and 80 percent of its rubber products— as well as a large amount of the national production of gasoline, oils, and greases. Thus, it is easy to appreciate the close relationship between Detroit automobile production and Arizona copper, Chicago–Gary steel, Ohio plate glass and rubber tires, and many other production regions and their products. Many automobiles are assembled in the East, the South, and the West; but the major component parts, such as bodies, engines, and power drives, are manufactured in the Michigan region and shipped to the numerous assembly plants.

Foods. The northeastern region of the United States produces and processes great quantities of foods. Flour milling is done both on the western fringe of the region, near the chief wheat-growing regions, and on the Great Lakes waterway. Important flour-milling centers include St. Paul, Minneapolis, Kansas City, and Buffalo. In meat packing, Chicago once was the principal center, but there are many other cities of equal or greater importance today, such as Omaha, St. Paul, Detroit, and New York; this decentralization makes for better marketing. Spe-

FIGURE 10–8

Automobile assembly plants. Left, early Chevrolets receiving a final check on an assembly line in Flint, Michigan, in 1918. Right, modern cars undergoing the installation of carpeting and seats. (General Motors Corp.)

cial breakfast foods are made from a variety of cereal grains, and the distribution of the principal processing centers reflects the general population pattern. Canned, frozen, and dried fruits and vegetables are prepared throughout the northeastern region, from the western Great Lakes to the Atlantic coast.

Textiles. Nearly a third of all United States cotton textiles are produced in the southern New England–eastern New York–Pennsylvania section of the northeastern industrial region, as are over three-fourths of the nation's woolen goods and half its rayon fabrics. Production of synthetic fibers in the northeastern industrial region is highly localized in eastern Pennsylvania and adjacent New Jersey, with New York and southern New England accounting for most of the remainder. The raw cotton and raw wool necessary for the textile industry must be obtained from outside sources, but the finished textiles are sold primarily within the region, to the many clothing industries concentrated largely in New York and Chicago.

Other Industries. In addition to the major manufactures already mentioned,

238

there are many others in the northeastern industrial region that are only relatively less significant. Chemicals are produced and consumed within the region mainly in the area from the Atlantic seaboard to Chicago. Other industrial activities include petroleum refining and ore smelting, which are scattered throughout the region, the greatest concentrations being in New York, Philadelphia, Detroit, Chicago, and St. Louis.

Southern Appalachian–Gulf Coast Region

Of considerably less importance than the mighty northeastern industrial region is the southern Appalachian–Gulf Coast region, which encompasses a dozen states from Virginia to Texas. This is not a homogeneous region. Agriculture still dominates its economy, but industry is growing rapidly, changing the face of the South and causing deep-seated economic and cultural changes that are being felt throughout the nation. Many of the states of the southern Appalachian–Gulf Coast region lead the nation in the manufacture of important industrial products—Virginia in synthetic fibers, the Carolinas in tobacco products and cotton textiles, and Texas in petroleum, petrochemicals, and synthetic rubber. Since the beginning of industrialization in the South, textiles, concentrated in the southern Appalachians, have constituted the area's most important group of products, and they will probably continue to do so for some time. No other part of the United States, with the exception of southern California, is attracting industry in greater volume, or gaining more rapidly in wealth, purchasing power, and general well-being than is the southern Appalachian–Gulf Coast region.

West Coast Region

Far removed from the great industrial concentrations of the eastern United States are the relatively recent industrial developments scattered along the Pacific coast. These have come into being primarily in response to local market demands in a rapidly growing part of the nation. The west coast industrial region is quite fragmented spatially, and will not be as densely occupied as its eastern counterparts for many years. A few major metropolitan areas contain most of the developments. In the Pacific Northwest, Seattle and Portland dominate; while in the Pacific Southwest, San Francisco, Los Angeles, and San Diego are the major centers of industrial concentration.

Important contributing factors in the location and development of the varied industries in this region are such source materials as iron ore, cotton, foodstuffs, and timber; markets that are rapidly expanding and remote from eastern suppliers; such power and fuel supplies as petroleum and hydroelectricity; and a climate that is highly attractive to many people. Today the west coast industrial region is important nationally for its aircraft, aerospace, petrochemical, and motion picture industries, and locally for automobile assembly, meat packing, iron and steel, aluminum, tin containers, beet sugar, clothing, and timber products (Fig. 10–9).

FIGURE 10–9

Lumbering in Humboldt County, California. While the western United States provides great quantities of timber for markets worldwide, vast areas of its giant redwoods are preserved from commercial use in state and national parks. (Redwood Empire Association)

Industrial Regions of the Soviet Union

Industrial developments in czarist Russia were comparatively minor, but the Soviet Union, built from the remains of the old Russian Empire following the 1917 revolution, has made rapid industrial progress. It now stands second only to the United States in total industrial production. Complete government control of agriculture, mineral and energy resources, transportation, and labor has had one main objective—to strengthen Soviet industry, whatever the cost.

Most Soviet industrial developments are concentrated in four major regions, widely separated by vast agricultural expanses. Three regions are in Europe: the Moscow region, the oldest; the Donbas region, the largest; and the Ural region, the most nearly self-sufficient. The Kuzbas region, the newest, is in Asia (Fig. 10–10). Important factors that have contributed to the concentration and development of industry in these regions are the local availability of such source materials as minerals, textiles, and foodstuffs; such energy supplies as coal, petroleum, natural gas, and hydroelectricity; markets that are rapidly expanding and locally oriented by virtue of limited Soviet transportation; and a communist economy dedicated to the pursuit of regional and national self-sufficiency.

FIGURE 10–10

Industrialization in the Soviet Union. The four major industrial regions of the nation —Moscow, Donbas, Urals, and Kuzbas—are located in its European and west-central Siberian areas, in close association with rich mineral and energy concentrations.

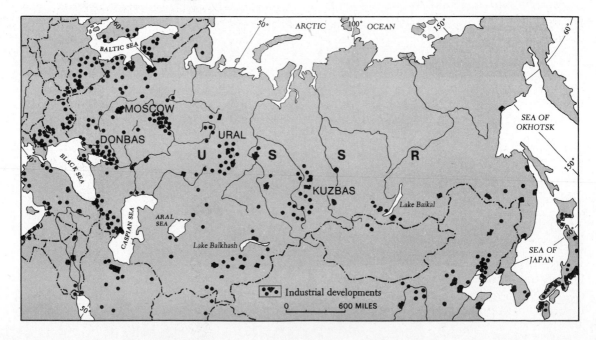

Moscow Region

The Moscow region was the oldest and largest in czarist Russia and had developed, like many others in the world, during the late nineteenth century, primarily because Moscow was the original nucleus of the old Empire. Industry was, and still is, varied, but the emphasis is on light industry and consumer goods to supply the traditionally large capital-city market with such products as textiles, clothing, and foods, and in recent years with various luxury items (Fig. 10–11). The region is not well favored with minerals and energy resources, but the surrounding plains are well developed agriculturally.

Donbas Region

The Donbas region is the principal heavy-industry region of the Soviet Union. It stretches across the eastern Ukraine, near the famous coal fields of the Donets Basin. The rich iron ore deposits near Krivoi Rog to the west are easily available, as is manganese in the same general region. In addition to its very large iron and steel production, the Donbas region supplies other important heavy-industry products, such as locomotives, tractors, industrial chemicals, cement, and armaments. There is a railroad shuttle system between the Krivoi Rog iron ore fields and the Donets coal fields that allows a heavy exchange of coal and iron and thus the development of iron and steel production in both areas. The Donbas industrial region is surrounded by the broad expanse of the Ukrainian Plain—the Soviet breadbasket—where the nation's agriculture still is most heavily concentrated; together the Donbas and the Plain represent an excellent agro-industrial development.

Ural Region

During czarist days the Ural region produced about one-fifth of the Russian Empire's iron and steel, as against two-thirds produced in the Donbas region. But the strategic interior location of the Urals has prompted recent Soviet planners to push the country's industrial development there, as well as even farther eastward into the central Asian regions. These two regions, the Urals and central Asia, now combine to produce half the Soviet Union's iron and steel, representing a significant planned eastward shift in major heavy industry.

The Ural region stretches 500 miles along the southern half of the Ural Mountain range and includes such heavily industri-

FIGURE 10–11

Fur processing near Lake Baikal, for the Moscow region. The wearing of animal furs and skins remains one of the few primitive clothing customs widely pursued in modern societies. (Harbrace by Jacques Jangoux)

alized cities as Magnitogorsk in the south and Sverdlovsk farther northward. Today the Ural region is probably as nearly self-sufficient as any industrial region in the world, for its recognized mineral and energy resources are sizable and in great variety. Before the 1960s, however, little coal was known in the Urals; supplies of coal were hauled by rail from the Kuznetsk Basin 1000 miles eastward and from the Karaganda coal fields 600 miles southeastward. With such an economic handicap, this region would probably not have become a significant industrial region had the Soviet Union been operating under a "free economy" rather than a "controlled economy."

Kuzbas Region

The first large blast furnaces in the Soviet Union were installed in Kuznetsk, in Siberia, in 1932. This operation started the large-scale industrial development of the Kuzbas region in central Asia, 1000 miles east of the Urals, midway to Lake Baikal. Coal from the huge deposits of the Kuznetsk Basin and local iron ore and manganese deposits combine to form the base of this new industrial region. The Kuzbas industrial region lies on and just south of the Trans-Siberian Railway and includes such new industrial cities as Novosibirsk, Krasnoyarsk, and Novokuznetsk.

Industrial Societies of Asia

Japan

"Britain of the East."   During the past half century Japan has made astonishing industrial progress; it now stands third in world industrial production, exceeded only by the two industrial giants, the United States and the Soviet Union. Stimulated by new ideas and technologies from the West following its defeat in World War II, Japan has changed from a feudal, underdeveloped, agricultural nation into a highly organized, progressive, agro-industrial state within a single generation. Over 20 percent of Japan's labor force is employed in some industrial capacity. This is the highest proportion in all of Asia and is comparable to the somewhat less than 30 percent employed in industry in the United States (Fig. 10–12).

In natural resources needed for modern industry Japan entered the twentieth century a poor nation. It is still a very poor nation in most of the basic minerals and in petroleum

and natural gas. But in the past few decades, by a combination of peaceful and aggressive actions, Japan has obtained more and more natural resources from other countries, mainly in eastern and southeastern Asia and throughout the Pacific. Peaceful measures have netted raw cotton, petroleum, and scrap iron from the United States; iron ore from Australia and India; and petroleum from Indonesia. Aggressive measures, which began in 1932, for a time netted iron ore and coal from Manchuria, rubber from Malaya, and petroleum and tin from Indonesia. All these imports, combined with the nation's own meager resources, have provided an industrial base that has enabled Japan to become the "Britain of the East," competing with the United States and the industrial nations of western Europe for a sizable share of the world's markets. Decisive defeat during World War II frustrated Japan's attempts to dominate the Asiatic world and drive out established Western interests; but in the years

FIGURE 10–12

Indicative of the technological sophistication of Japanese industry, an array of combing machines at a spinning mill in Hamamatsu. (Consulate General of Japan)

since military defeat, the nation has completely rebuilt its industrial machine by peaceful means, including financial aid from the United States, and has exceeded its prewar levels of production and world trade.

Southern Honshu Region. For all practical purposes Japan has only one major industrial region (Fig. 10–13). This is the southern rim of the main island of Honshu and the adjoining tip of the southern island of Kyushu. The northern anchor of this region is the Tokyo–Yokohama center. Nagoya forms a second focal point 200 miles southwestward, and Osaka–Kobe, facing the Inland Sea 100 miles beyond, a third. Okayama, Kure, and Hiroshima are strung

farther along the Inland Sea coast. The southern anchor of the region lies in a group of small industrial cities lying across the Shimonoseki Strait on the southern island of Kyushu.

India

Before the beginning of European colonialism in Asia, India enjoyed a relatively advanced system of cottage industries, one that produced basic items for domestic consumption and luxury goods for foreign trade; it was such goods, in fact, that first attracted European trader-colonizers to Asian shores. The 150 years of British control brought

243

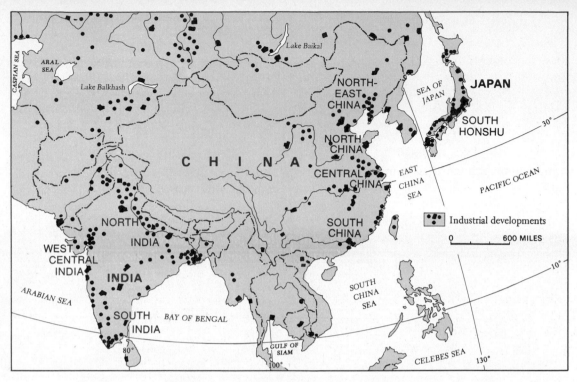

FIGURE 10–13

Industrialization in East and South Asia. Modern industry is now spreading across the densely populated lands of China and India, as it did across Japan earlier in this century.

many changes in India's socioeconomic structure, and prominent among them was the stagnation of cottage industries. Raw cotton and other raw materials went west to the home country, and manufactures returned east to the colonial markets; this was true not only in British India, but in all the colonial areas of Asia and Africa. Only after the beginning of the twentieth century was India allowed major progress in basic light industry and some limited developments in heavy industry. Predictably, for a long while Indian industrial production continued to fall seriously short of the country's needs, and even cotton textiles had to be imported from England's Lancashire County to clothe India's millions.

With independence in 1947, British India was divided into India and Pakistan.

India's first efforts after independence were devoted to expanding foodstuff production and bolstering consumer-goods industries. The most important industries were cotton textiles, jute, cement, iron and steel, paper, sugar, chemicals, and machinery, all of which had been established on a small scale under the British. During India's first five years of independence her industrial output increased by over 50 percent in many of these commodities, and nearly doubled in some. India's industrial resource base is fairly good, for it includes large supplies of raw cotton and wool, half the world's jute production, and the world's largest iron ore reserves, as well as considerable coal and sources of hydroelectricity. The nation's great economic weakness is its subsistence agriculture, which cannot produce enough to feed both the farmers and industrialism's nonfood producers. Total food productions in India are large, but they fall far short of the massive quantities needed by the country's 600 million people.

Northern India Region. The Northern India region stretches 1000 miles along the Ganges Valley, from Calcutta nearly to the Pakistan border (see Fig. 10–13). Within the Ganges Valley are a host of industrial cities, such as Calcutta and Burdwan, with jute and cotton textile manufacturing; Asansol and Durgapur, with iron and steel; Varanasi (Banaras), with silk goods; Lucknow and Agra, with woolen and cotton textiles; Delhi, with various light industries; and Ambala and Amritsar, with cotton and woolen textiles (Fig. 10–14). West of Calcutta are the cities of Jamshedpur, Rourkela, and Bhilai,

with iron and steel; Ranchi, with machine tools; and Nagpur, with cotton textiles. The small extension of this region onto the plateau contains the bulk of India's iron ore, coal, and manganese resources; while the eastern, middle, and western sections of the Ganges Valley provide large amounts of jute, wool, and cotton, and such foods as rice, wheat, sugar, and vegetables.

West-Central India Region. The West-Central India region is small in area, and also small in production and variety, compared with the Northern India region. It stretches along the western coast of India for 400 miles, from Ahmadabad through Bombay to Kolhapur, and lies close to India's largest cotton-growing area. Consequently, this is the area in which a large concentration of India's large cotton textile production is found, so

FIGURE 10–14

The developmental range of India's industry. Left, a modern textile mill in New Delhi. Right, a village training center in which part-time agricultural workers learn to operate the handloom, which is still heavily used throughout the countryside. (Ford Foundation)

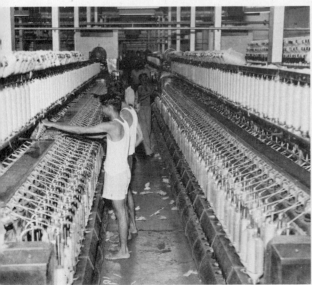

important in clothing the nation's millions. Here also, particularly in the Ahmadabad area, has developed one of India's largest concentrations of cane-sugar refining.

Southern India Region. The Southern India region includes the tip of the subcontinent northward to a line from Madras to Mangalore. Here are concentrated major resources of iron ore, very large amounts of hydroelectric power, and large supplies of raw cotton, wool, and coir (coconut fiber). Upon these resources are based major productions of iron and steel, textiles, machinery, airplanes, electronic equipment, railway equipment, and technical instruments, scattered among such industrial cities as Madras, Bangalore, Mysore, and Madura. Variety rather than specialization is the keynote of industrial development in southern India.

China

China is the most recent of the major societies to undertake industrialization. Few industries developed in China during the nineteenth century, when industry was taking hold in western Europe, the United States, Russia, and Japan, or even after the turn of the present century, when modern industry came to India. China's long delay was due to many factors; the most significant of these were the country's age-old, weak, and chaotic political structure; foreign influences; internal strife; recurring famines; poor transportation facilities; and general socio-economic weaknesses. All these factors combined in fervent resistance to foreign ideas and innovations of any kind, whether from the West or the East. But, since 1949, when it came under the totalitarian control of communism, China has been attempting to industrialize "quickly."

China's traditional industrial resources

are adequate but not abundant and not always conveniently located for efficient development and utilization. However, such handicaps are often manipulated politically when a totalitarian government is set on promoting a particular sector of its economy; industrial efficiency can be bought, to a degree, at the price of human freedom. China has substantial coal supplies, located largely in the northern provinces of Shansi and Shensi and in Manchuria, but also scattered in nearly every province of the country. The country's moderate supplies of iron ore are found in the central Wuhan region and in Manchuria, and during the early 1970s, relatively large reserves of petroleum and natural gas were found to exist in coastal northern China. The distribution of these resources leaves southern China relatively poorly endowed for modern heavy industrialization, but China's considerable hydroelectric potential has been long established over many regions, especially the Huang Ho Valley in the north, eastern Manchuria, and the yet undeveloped fringes of the Tibetan plateau.

During the last two decades, modern industry has made significant inroads into China's age-old cottage industries; today China's production of most manufactures depends almost entirely upon a "modern" factory system. Cotton textiles have become almost totally factory-oriented; hand-weaving has almost disappeared in China. Iron and steel, machinery, cement, railway equipment, foods, ceramics, rubber goods, electronic equipment, sugar, and ships are the country's major industrial items—all of which are emphasized in national production quotas.

Northeastern China Region. Central Manchuria and the Liaotung peninsula in northeastern China encompass the country's largest heavy-industry region (see Fig. 10–13). The greatest industrial concentration is

FIGURE 10–15

The modern steel complex at Anshan, in northeastern China. Like most other working people in China, the labor force in this center commutes by means of bicycles and buses. (Eastfoto)

in the southern area, where appreciable resources of coal and much of the country's iron ore occur in close proximity. Iron and steel plants have been developed at Anshan (built by the Japanese during their occupation of Manchuria) and at Penki; there are shale-oil reduction plants at Fushun, and auto-truck plants at Changchun; and the largest railroad shops, shipyards, and cement plants in China are located in this region (Fig. 10–15).

Northern China Region. The plains of northern China and the Huang Ho Valley contain a considerable amount of the country's industrial development. Here is found the bulk of China's coal reserves; within the general area of Peking, Tientsin, and Tangshan are China's second-largest coal mines and various associated industries. This region also includes cement plants and cotton textile and flour mills. Eastward, in the Shantung peninsula, the important industries are iron and steel, cotton textile and flour milling, and foodstuff production.

Central China Region. The Yangtze Valley, extending from the great port city of

247

Shanghai 1000 miles inland to Chungking, constitutes China's most extensive and most diversified industrial region. The lower Yangtze, with such cities as Shanghai, Soochow, and Nanking, is heavily industrialized. Shanghai, one of the world's largest cities, is also China's largest industrial city, with virtually every type of light industry. The middle Yangtze Valley includes the Central Lakes district, which is well supplied with coal and iron and accounts for much iron and steel production and much ancillary heavy industry near Wuhan. The upper Yangtze Valley, with Chungking at its center, accounts for a varied industrial production that ranges from steel and chemicals to cotton and silk textiles.

Southern China Region. On the delta of the Si River, with Canton as the hub, is concentrated considerable light industrial production, including textiles, cement, rubber goods, and electronic equipment, and serving the large markets of southern China and recently some foreign markets. Because of their large and diversified light industry, Hong Kong, though still British territory, and Macao, still Portuguese territory, can both be included in this southern China industrial region.

Industrial Societies of the Southern Continents

South America

South American industry is conspicuously underdeveloped. One of South America's principal industrial developments is the Río de la Plata region. Important centers there are Buenos Aires, La Plata, and Rosario, all in Argentina, and Montevideo, Uruguay. The Río de la Plata region produces a variety of staple foods, textiles, light machinery, cement, meat, and meat products. In Chile, small industrial areas are found in the central Santiago–Valparaiso region, the southern Concepción–Valdivia region, and

FIGURE 10–16

A tractor-assembling plant in Córdoba, Argentina. This and many other large plants in South America were established by foreign interests, mainly European or American, and produce products of foreign design. (United Nations)

the northern Antofagasta region. These centers produce a wide variety of commodities, including foods, clothing, wines, and some metals products. The only other industrial region of comparable significance is that centering on Rio de Janeiro and São Paulo in Brazil, with productions of some iron and steel, textiles, clothing, machinery, cement, chemicals, and processed foods, as well as the assembling of automobiles (Fig. 10–16).

Africa

Africa is primarily a seller of source materials and a buyer of industrial products; foreign rather than local factories supply most of Africa's industrial needs. Small industrial centers are found around Cape Town and Johannesburg in South Africa, and there are other scattered centers such as those at Port Elizabeth, East London, and Durban, along the southeastern coast of the country. Manufactures consist of clothing, processed foods, wines, household goods, some iron and steel, and automobile assembly. Compared to Africa as a whole, South Africa has made fair industrial progress in recent years.

Egypt has also surpassed most other African nations industrially. When it became a republic in 1953, most of its large-scale industry was of recent development. Even in the 1960s the country's industrial achievements exceeded expectations—production doubled, or nearly doubled, in many basic industries, including textiles, cement, iron and steel, fertilizers, foods, and oil refining. Today Egyptian industry also produces tires, refrigerators, radios, automobiles, and trucks and buses. Most industrial development is concentrated in the Delta, near Alexandria and Cairo, with some of the more recent works strung along the Nile Valley to the Aswan Dam.

Together, South Africa and Egypt account for one-half of Africa's industry. Most of the remainder is provided by Ghana, Morocco, Zaire, and Algeria.

Australia

Many of the industrial products used by the people of Australia are not produced within the country and must be purchased from the United Kingdom, continental Europe, the United States, and Japan. Australia has plentiful supplies of coal and fairly large iron ore deposits, with its largest reserves in the centers near Sydney, and smaller ones near Melbourne and Brisbane. However, it is not well endowed with most of the other necessities of industry. Even so, locally important industrial centers based upon the limited source materials available have developed in southeastern Australia around Sydney, Melbourne, and Brisbane.

Australian industry is diversified, but it is mainly light industry. Of chief importance to other parts of the world is Australia's processing of butter, cheese, and condensed milk, as well as meat packing and the processing of raw wool. Products for local consumption include textiles, clothing, flour, sugar, brewery products, metal articles, and some iron and steel.

Southern Continents in Perspective

The industrial regions of the southern continents are small in number and extent compared with those of the northern continents, but it should be recognized that even a limited industrial region may be extremely important to the country directly concerned. Australia is an excellent example. The country's total industrial productions are very small parts of the world total, but they are vital to the national welfare. The importance of industry in Australia can be measured, for example, by the fact that a higher proportion of the labor force in Australia is employed in industry than is true of the labor force in the United States. Furthermore, most of Australia's people live in large modern cities and, as in so many countries, large cities and industry go together.

REVIEW AND DISCUSSION

1. Why is it that, until relatively recently, the major industrial societies have been found within the Western world? Why and to what degree has the distribution of industrial societies changed in the last three decades?
2. Why is industrial production probably more vital to the United Kingdom than to any other major industrial society today?
3. Identify, as precisely as you can, the environmental and socioeconomic factors involved in the creation and perpetuation of the industrial regions of the United States.
4. Compare and contrast the four major industrial regions of the Soviet Union.
5. What are some of the major reasons for the great success of Japan's rather recent efforts to industrialize?
6. What accounts for the fact that several important industrial societies have emerged in regions that by nature lack practically every basic raw material needed for industry? Cite appropriate examples.
7. Both India and China have tremendous population problems and each is struggling to achieve an agro-industrial balance. Compare and contrast these two countries in terms of industrial development. Which one seems to have the greater industrial potential? Why?
8. Identify and characterize the major industrial societies of the southern continents. In terms of international trade, how do they differ from more highly developed societies of the northern continents?
9. Compare and contrast the industrial development of such diverse countries as the United States, the Soviet Union, Japan, China, Egypt, Ghana, and Australia; mention such factors as areal distribution, degree of self-sufficiency, diversification, and growth rate.
10. Using specific examples, discuss the differing effects of culture—that is, negative or positive—on the development of industry in different regions or nations of the world.

SELECTED REFERENCES

Alexandersson, G. *A Geography of Manufacturing.* Englewood Cliffs, N.J.: Prentice-Hall, 1967.

———. *Industrial Structure of American Cities.* Lincoln: University of Nebraska Press, 1956.

Chen, Cheng-siang. *Taiwan.* Taipei: Fu-min Geographical Institute, 1963.

Estall, R. C. *New England: A Study in Industrial Adjustment.* New York: Praeger, 1966.

Fleming, D. K. "Coastal Steelworks in the Common Market Countries." *Geographical Review,* Vol. 57 (January 1967), 48–72.

Li, Choh-ming, ed. *Industrial Development in Communist China.* New York: Praeger, 1964.

Mayer, H. M. "Centrex Industrial Park: An Organized Industrial District." *Focus on Geographic Activity.* New York: McGraw-Hill, 1964.

Miller, E. W. *A Geography of Industrial Location.* Dubuque, Iowa: Brown, 1970.

Nakayama, Ichiro. *Industrialization of Japan.* Tokyo: Center for East Asian Cultural Studies, 1963.

Pounds, N. J. G. *Geography of Iron and Steel.* London: Hutchinson University Library, 1959.

Pryde, P. R. "The Areal Deconcentration of the Soviet Cotton-Textile Industry." *Geographical Review,* Vol. 58 (October 1968), 575–92.

Rodgers, H. B. "The Changing Geography of the Lancashire Cotton Industry." *Economic Geography,* Vol. 38 (October 1962), 299–314.

Rogers, E. M. *Diffusion and Innovations.* New York: Free Press of Glencoe, 1962.

Sharer, C. J. "The Philadelphia Iron and Steel District: Relations to Seaways." *Economic Geography,* Vol. 39 (October 1963), 363–67.

United Nations. "World of Opportunity." *Science and Technology for Development,* Vol. 1, 1963.

An Indonesian village on the island of Bali. (Pan American)

11

Settlement Types and Contrasts

Major Contrasts in Settlement

Mobile Versus Sedentary

Among the human population in some parts of the world, there are still large kinship groups that move from one place to another without permanent abode.

These people are nomads, and, in most instances, their way of life is dependent on herds of grazing animals (usually horses, sheep, or goats) whose keep means a constant search for areas of plentiful grass (Fig. 11–1). Though a nomadic group may attach itself to a specific location long enough to build a complex of semipermanent shelters, the time soon comes when local sources of grass for the animals are exhausted and it is necessary to move to a new area.

Nomads who rely heavily on pasturage are found in such diverse areas as the desert fringes (see Chapter 3) and the Arctic tundra.

In other areas, particularly the tropical forests, there are several groups that live entirely upon what they can secure through hunting and fishing, or through the collecting of edible plant products (Fig. 11–2). Such groups are usually not as mobile as nomadic groups that maintain herds and must search for pasturage. Among the least mobile of them are the Eskimos of the Arctic fringelands, who, anticipating the seasonal migrations of their prey, usually move their settlements to locations known to them and to which they have frequently returned.

Unlike such groups, however, most of the world's peoples are tied to specific places on the surface of the earth. These *sedentary*, or fixed, populations provide relatively long-lasting patterns and forms of settlement that can be observed and compared as essential elements in a thorough understanding of the cultural phase of the human habitat.

FIGURE 11–1

Settlements of nomadic peoples, such as this Mongolian yurt, are usually easy to construct and move. (American Museum of Natural History)

FIGURE 11–2
A temporary home constructed of giant palms in the forests of Venezuela. (© Jacques Jangoux)

Dispersed Versus Agglomerated

The types of settlements devised by sedentary populations vary widely. At one extreme is the isolated dwelling that houses a single individual or family; at the other, a group of dwellings that stand side-by-side and house hundreds of people. In some of the world's large cities, where skyscrapers pile one occupant's space on top of another's, the total vertical distance of housing can be greater than the city's horizontal extent.

When individual dwellings are scattered over the land, the settlement pattern is said to be *dispersed.* When dwellings are packed close together, the settlement pattern is described as *agglomerated.* Complete dispersion is understood to mean an arrangement of single dwellings (and their associated buildings) that suggests no grouping or clustering. Complete agglomeration, on the other hand, implies a close massing of dwellings and other buildings with no isolated dwellings between clusters. Possible, too, is the mix, or combination, in which agglomerated settlements are spotted throughout a general background of dispersed settlement.

Being highly gregarious, humans tend to live in groups rather than alone, but not necessarily in a fixed place. There is ample evidence to show that humankind existed first as wandering tribes and that it established permanent settlements only after it had achieved some mastery of agriculture. Reflecting the isolation and internal cohesiveness of these tribes, the first sedentary populations assumed an agglomerated settlement pattern. And in many parts of the world, this pattern has persisted. Dispersion, which came relatively late in the history of human settlement, characterizes relatively few political regions of the world; however, those regions are extensive.

Rural Versus Urban

Any distinction between rural and urban is a relative one. There is no sharp line that divides rural folk from urbanites. But one of the most reliable differentiations is that a *rural* population is one predominantly engaged in securing life's basic necessities directly from the land, while an *urban* population is one that has little or no involvement in the initial production of foods or materials used for shelters and clothing; rather, most urban dwellers are engaged in secondary and tertiary activities, such as transporting, manufacturing, buying or selling raw or manufactured materials, educating, and managing affairs of state. The other criteria commonly used to distinguish between urban and rural communities are much more problematic.

Distinctions between rural settlements and urban ones are often made on a statistical basis, through the use of population figures. However, this method can become somewhat confusing, especially when applied in comparisons of different countries. One finds that there is very little agreement in the international community as to what constitutes the minimum population of an urban community. For example, in Denmark any settlement with a population over 250 is considered urban; but in Canada and Chile the minimum figure is 1,000, and Panama classifies as urban only those places with no less than 1,500 inhabitants. A number of countries—Argentina, Austria, Czechoslovakia, West Germany, and Portugal, for example—require at least 2,000 inhabitants, while, in general, the United States, Mexico, and Venezuela list as urban only settlements of 2,500 persons or more. Still more restrictive are Belgium, India, and Japan, which classify as urban only those settlements with a population above 5,000. Switzerland and Spain exceed even this requirement, however, by making 10,000 their demarcation between rural and urban. Last in this escalating scale is the United Nations, which sets a minimum population requirement of 20,000 when it lists urban communities.

Some classifications of populations as urban or rural are also based on their spatial arrangement. Obviously, rural populations are more often arranged in dispersed patterns than are urban populations. Yet, rural folk need not necessarily be scattered over the land; in fact, there are more agglomerated rural populations throughout the world than there are dispersed ones. And with urban population almost entirely agglomerated, it is estimated that fully three-quarters of the world's population lives in agglomerations of one type or another.

With today's huge populations in such centers as London, New York, and Tokyo, the world's total urban population is about equal to its total rural population. And most of the urban settlements that do exist are found in the Western world, specifically Europe and areas colonized by European peoples. The populations of the Eastern world, where over half of the earth's inhabitants live, are almost entirely rural agglomerations.

Micro Versus Macro

Various terms are currently used throughout the world to suggest a general categorization of settlements, based primarily on their size and on the number and complexity of functions performed. Although useful here and in similar discussions of fundamentals, this classification is not suitable for all settlement analysis.

Within this classification, one of the simplest types of settlement is the individual *farmstead,* which is usually composed of a single dwelling for humans and a barn or shed where domesticated animals are kept and equipment is stored. Another very sim-

FIGURE 11–3

Examples of settlement types usually considered rural. Top left, an isolated farmstead in the wheatlands of South Dakota. (Rotkin, PFI) Top right, a roadside near Glendale, California. (Harry W. Rinehart) Center, a hamlet in Pennsylvania. (Pennsylvania Dept. of Highways) Bottom, a village in Monroe County, Wisconsin. (U.S. Dept. of Agriculture)

ple type of settlement is the *roadside,* usually a lone commercial establishment — such as a gasoline station, drive-in eating place, small general store, motel or inn — located beside a highway (Fig. 11–3). Larger than a roadside is the *hamlet,* a settlement made up of several buildings that serve residential, commercial, and social purposes. Typically somewhat larger and more diversified is the *village,* which generally includes schools and churches and other public facilities. In general, all these settlements — farmstead, roadside, hamlet, and village — are considered rural.

Next in this settlement classification is the *town,* which offers more services than the village but fewer than can be found in the average *city;* the essential distinction between a town and a city is a matter of structural complexity, the city being the more complex settlement. *Metropolis,* a term loosely used to refer to any very large city, implies the presence of *satellite cities,* settlements that have become tied to, or nearly engulfed by, a huge urban nucleus; London, Paris, and Los Angeles are among the examples. The term *conurbation* is used to describe a large area of unbroken urban development created by the growth and coalescence of several neighboring cities; although still separate settlements by statute, these cities function so interdependently that they seem to be a single urban unit. Next in the progression of settlements is the *megalopolis,* or giant conurbation, examples of which include the stretch of metropolises that extends from Boston to Washington, D.C., along the northeastern seaboard of the United States, and a comparable urban belt from Tokyo to Osaka in Japan.

Rural Settlement

Even today, in this machine age, dependence upon primary production from the land is fundamental to human existence. Direct use of the land is still the way of life for the majority of human beings; in other words, most of the world's populations are rural. Their spatial arrangement on the land is the matrix in which urban populations are set.

Agglomerated Rural Settlement

A rural agglomeration is a group of relatively closely built structures surrounded by fields, pastures, or woodland areas. Human dwellings constitute much of the cluster, but there are also storehouses for agricultural produce and tools, and shelters for livestock.

There may also be, in more advanced societies, a church, a school, and a town hall. Practically the entire population is concerned with cultivating the surrounding land or with raising animals — in living directly from the land. To augment their living, some of the inhabitants may engage in selling surplus commodities. For example, someone in the settlement may offer various foods for sale and possibly add to that small tools or other farm supplies. Professional people — such as doctors, ministers, and teachers — may reside in the agglomeration. But most of the life of the settlement is tied to the land, and, except as the settlement contributes its agricultural surpluses to the outside world, it is essentially self-contained. The rural settlement is first and foremost the dwelling place of an agricultural society.

Rural settlements in different parts of the world vary widely in appearance and structure; they often share no common characteristic except function (Fig. 11–4). A rural agglomeration is always the dwelling-place of a group engaged in direct use of the land. Beyond that, the number, size, appearance, and arrangement of buildings correspond to the traditions and habits of the particular group of people and to the nature of the land from which they derive their living.

For example, the average village in many parts of Japan consists of a cluster of bamboo-and-thatch dwellings and sheds, so tightly pressed together as to allow only narrow passageways between adjacent buildings. The whole settlement occupies a bit of ground only slightly above the level of the surrounding irrigated rice paddies. Seldom are there roads leading to and from the village. Narrow pathways along the tops of low dikes separating the rice paddies are usually the only ground routes between one village and the next (Fig. 11–5).

The inhabitants of a village leave it early in the day to work their paddies and return again at night. A farmer's land is seldom in one continuous piece, but rather it is in several fragments in scattered locations around the settlement. The daily life of the inhabitants, often members of only a couple of large family groups, is a pulsing out onto the land and back into the village. Both the scattered nature of the landholdings and the intensity of the agriculture demand constant attention. The village is the focal point from

FIGURE 11–4

La Calera, 40 miles north of Bogotá, Colombia. It is typical of South American villages in that it features a church and a public square. (Standard Oil Co., N.J.)

FIGURE 11–5

A settlement on Japan's Izu Peninsula that is representative of most Oriental rural agglomerations. Its bamboo-and-thatch dwellings and their garden plots are surrounded by diked rice paddies. (Bob and Ira Spring)

which a small portion of the human habitat functions.

The hamlets or villages in many parts of Europe are in considerable contrast to those of the Orient. In southern France, for example, villages like Turenne are common. Turenne crowns the top of a low hill with fields spreading down the slopes and away from the settlement. The village is roughly rectangular in shape, with a chateau at one end and a church at the other. Forming the sides of the rectangle are houses built side-by-side. There is thus enclosed a public *plaza,* or "square," with exits on either side of the church and chateau. Immediately back of the houses on the hill slopes are small kitchen gardens. Farther down the slopes are larger fields and, beyond them, pastures and patches of woodland (Fig. 11–6).

There is the same daily movement out from the village to the fields and back, but it does not have the regularity of that of the Oriental village: agriculture in France is less intensive and demands less attention. In addition, the village is not so completely a family settlement. Finally, the European village is linked by roads to the transportation net of the larger area; it is not nearly as self-contained as the Oriental village.

In certain other parts of Europe—in Hungary, for example—rural agglomerations of several thousand people are not uncommon. These villages cover considerable land areas, with each dwelling and its farm buildings set on a small plot. The farm buildings are distinctly clustered, arranged along streets to form collected settlements set in open cultivated or pastured land.

FIGURE 11-6

The hilltop village of Eze, in southern France. In the manner of many European settlements, its houses and terraced fields surround a medieval castle built on the village's highest ground. (American Museum of Natural History)

In the eastern seaboard regions of the United States, particularly in New England and the South, agglomerated rural settlement was the early mode. In colonial New England, farmhouses were built close together, usually fronting on a *common*. The common was originally a pasture area collectively owned and used by all the inhabitants of the village. Where it still remains today, it has become a park. In the South, the establishment of plantations that required large labor forces led to the importation of slaves and to another kind of rural agglomeration, the compact slave quarters.

These few examples suggest that there is great variety in the detail of rural agglomerated settlement throughout the world and within small portions of it as well. The unifying characteristic is the tie of the people to the land.

Dispersed Rural Settlement

Smaller than the hamlet or village is the isolated farmstead, a settlement unit usually composed of a family dwelling and a few

barns and sheds. Fields, pastures, and other land from which the family draws its living stretch out from the central unit, uninterrupted by other buildings. The distance between farmsteads may be slight, perhaps a quarter of a mile, or great, as much as several miles (Fig. 11-7). There is none of the compactness of the agglomeration, nor is there the daily flow of large numbers of people to surrounding fields. Land used intensively generally lies close to the farmstead itself. Extensively cultivated lands, pastures, and wooded areas are farther away. Each farm serves as a unit in itself, not as a fragment of a larger integrated hamlet or village.

World Distribution

The farm village characterizes the greater part of the Orient. Except in a few relatively small areas (such as Hokkaido, the northern island of the Japanese group), isolated farmsteads are rare. Throughout the southern islands of Japan, the densely peopled plains of China, Southeast Asia, and India, closely set, compact hamlets and villages are sprinkled thickly through the intensively cultivated flatter lands.

In parts of the Middle East and Africa—the lowland of the Tigris and Euphrates rivers and the valley of the Nile, for example—rural agglomeration persists almost exclusively. In other parts of Africa—such as the Guinea lands, the Congo Basin, or parts of the East African Plateau—the agglomerated pattern of rural settlement is repeated.

The hamlet or village is the characteristic settlement unit throughout most of southern and eastern Europe. Even into the western part of that continent, it continues as a prominent form, but with the dispersed pattern becoming more and more prevalent farther northwestward. Yet even in northwestern Europe, the incidence of dispersed rural population fails to mask the continent's basic agglomerated pattern.

As indicated, colonial settlements in the New World were of the agglomerated sort.

Throughout parts of South and Middle America, agglomeration in rural areas is still the rule; but in the United States and Canada it is now virtually absent, having been replaced in most areas by dispersion. In the United States, especially, the farm village is essentially a relict form; in only a few cases, as in some of the Mormon settlements of Utah, does it represent a functioning unit.

It is in the lands settled or colonized in this millennium by peoples of northwestern Europe that the dispersed pattern of rural settlement is most characteristic. Thus, Canada, like the United States, is an area of scattered rather than clustered rural population; so too are the greater parts of Australia, New Zealand, and areas of European colonization in Latin America and south and east Africa. The habit of agglomeration has been lost in these areas.

FIGURE 11–7

A dispersed rural settlement pattern composed of farmsteads, near Madison, Wisconsin. (Rotkin, PFI)

Urban Settlement: Origin and Diffusion

Urban settlements are as old as civilization itself; the word *civilization* is, in fact, derived from the Latin word *civilis,* meaning a citizen of a politically organized society, such as a city-state. Indeed, one of the major features of a civilized society is thought to be the ability to support an urban way of life. And many of the characteristics commonly attributed to a civilized people are similar to those considered typical of urbanites; in fact, they are practically synonymous.

In most analyses, civilized society is described as a group of people who have developed some form of organized religion, a system of writing, and the fundamentals of science. Furthermore, their social structure is advanced enough to allow a rather extensive division of labor. This means that certain specialized groups, such as farmers, herders, and fishers, are responsible for providing the food, while miners, craftspeople, merchants, clerks, soldiers, and others provide services and manufactured goods. Such institutions as government and religion are managed by kings, princes, priests, and other officials.

In order to support such a highly developed division of labor, a society would have to possess a number of attributes more complex than those that characterize a so-called primitive culture. Thus, complexity is an essential distinction between a civilized society and a primitive society.

Similarly the establishment and growth of an urban settlement requires not only technological advances and a favorable physical environment but a workable societal organization as well. An urban society is characteristically organized into classes of specialists, one of which is a ruling elite. In the simplest urban settlements it is the responsibility of this group to see to it that the food needed by the settlement's inhabitants is obtained from source areas and properly distributed or stored. In more complex settlements the ruling group is also concerned with the planning, construction, and maintenance of large-scale public projects, including municipal buildings, travel routes, and water supply systems.

Early Settlements

Mesopotamia. Diverse evidence indicates that human beings spent several millennia in sedentary communities before the development of the first truly urban settlements. These are believed to have appeared around 3500 B.C., mainly in an area comprising the fertile valleys of the Tigris and Euphrates rivers. Throughout ancient times this southernmost part of Mesopotamia (then known as Sumer), and the area to the north (then Akkad), spawned many urban communities, some of the most prominent of which were Babylon, Eridu, Lagash, Ur, and Kish (Fig. 11–8). The birth of these first urban centers marked the beginnings of the *urban revolution,* a development that is as important to the cultural growth of humankind as the agricultural revolution some 5,000 years before it and even the industrial-scientific revolution some 5,000 years after it.

Certain functional characteristics were common to all these early urban settlements. In each settlement, for example, the power of the ruler was based heavily on religious dogma, and the socioeconomic base reflected a limited number of specialized services. Most ancient urban dwellers were either government and military officials, clergy, craftspeople, merchants, or farmers; and each of these groups tended to be found in a different section of the settlement. The average total population of these early urban centers, though difficult to estimate, undoubtedly exceeded that of the typical Neolithic village.

One of the most important developments associated with the early spread of urbanism was the invention of writing, which enabled cities to keep records, chronicle historical events, and codify laws. Only with the help of the written word could a social organization on a large and rather complex scale be developed and maintained.

The Nile Valley and Other Areas.   Mesopotamia was not the only ancient culture hearth to generate urban settlements. Several Egyptian villages in the valley of the Nile developed into urban communities by about 3000 B.C., and, within five hundred years, urban centers could also be found in the Indus Valley of present-day Pakistan. Among

these were the highly organized and wealthy cities of Mohenjo-Daro and Harappa, which were in their day among the leading metropolises of the world. By about 1500 B.C. urbanization had begun as well in China, principally along the Huang Ho River. In the Western Hemisphere, villages with urban characteristics did not develop until about 500 B.C.; the first examples were located in Middle America.

There is some question as to whether the idea of the city spread around the world or was arrived at independently in each area of early urban development. Since the evidence thus far uncovered shows a considerable time lag in the occurrence of urban centers in different places, it would seem that diffusion, rather than invention, exerted the stronger influence in the growth of urbanization. The earliest known urban centers of the New World may represent exceptions to this

FIGURE 11-8

Mesopotamia's ancient sites and cities. Many of these early urban centers were small agricultural villages long before they developed into cities.

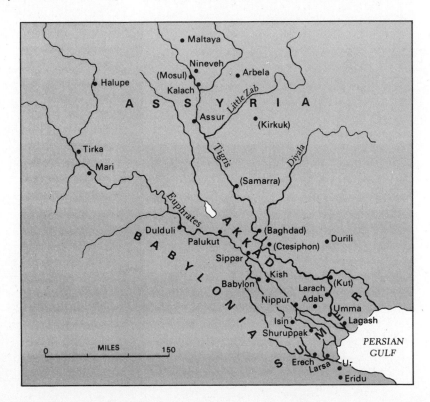

rule, however; for it is very likely that such Middle American urban settlements as the Mayans' Tikal and the Aztec capital Tenochtitlán (now Mexico City) evolved independently of almost any Old World influences.

The Influence of Empire. As the early centers of urbanization grew and became more powerful they became less immediately involved in agriculture and more dependent on the surrounding lands for nutritional support. Control of these lands — and, sometimes, more distant ones as well — was thus essential, and often prompted military invasion and conquest. By conscripting many of their former enemies and taxing or confiscating their holdings, some of the independent urban centers, or city-states, became powerful enough to establish empires and, by blending many of the cultural traits of their colonial territories, even generated new civilizations.

The spread of urbanization around the Mediterranean and into Europe, for example, was closely associated with the development and spread of the Greek, Phoenician, and Roman empires. In order to secure their colonies, the seats of power found it necessary to establish numerous outposts that could serve as administrative, military, and trading centers. And, not surprisingly in the light of their extreme dependency, there seems to be a close correlation between the rise and fall of an empire and the life span of the urban settlements it established or reinforced. The Roman Empire provides a particularly good example of this relationship between imperialism and urbanization. Areas around the Mediterranean that were once part of the Roman Empire are today filled with "dead" cities, settlements that prospered while the empire was strong, withered when it fell, and never recovered their imperial vitality; among these ruined cities are Stobi in southern Yugoslavia and Timgad in Algeria. On

the other hand, most cities of the Roman Empire did not die, but many — including Rome, the capital — did experience temporary declines in population.

Medieval European Settlements

Urbanization in Europe reached another important stage during the Middle Ages, the thousand years following the fall of the Roman Empire. European city life, which had flourished at the height of the empire, ebbed sharply after the fall of Rome, in 476. Intercity travel was greatly restricted by the ensuing fragmentation of power, and trade between cities nearly ceased. As their economic base dwindled, the existing cities lost many of their inhabitants to the countryside; and the development of new cities stalled. Dependent on surrounding communities for most of their provisions, cities were particularly vulnerable in the general state of confusion and disorder that gripped much of Europe in the centuries after the imperial collapse: the Vikings were attacking from the north and by the mid-800s were raiding the Mediterranean; various nomadic groups, including the Huns, were invading from the east; and the Arabs were penetrating from the south; moreover, the Europeans were at war with one another.

Thus began what is commonly referred to as the Dark Ages — a period that lasted roughly from A.D. 400 to 1000. During this period European civilization suffered severe setbacks; it was not until the end of the Crusades, in the thirteenth century, that the continent began to emerge from its decline. While Europe was submerged in the Dark Ages, however, most other parts of the world were not; indeed, during this era many non-European urban communities, such as Constantinople (Istanbul), Cairo, Mecca, Baghdad, Canton, Peking, the Mayan city of Tikal in Guatemala, and other Middle American urban centers, were growing and, in some cases, flourishing.

But in spite of the disorder that prevailed during the Dark Ages, most European cities survived, some resorting to massive walls and moats as protection against attack (Fig. 11–9). The population of these urban centers was thus often limited to the number of people who could be accommodated within the confines of the city walls and fed by the agricultural lands within the immediate vicinity. If a city was not walled, then, when under attack, its inhabitants usually took refuge in the area's most fortified and strategically placed castle. Thus, for defense

and, generally, for economic reasons as well, the castle of the local noble served as the nucleus of many medieval settlements; and from the ninth to the fifteenth centuries feudalism reigned.

Not until the end of the Dark Ages, with the rudimentary beginnings of modern industry and commerce, did Europe resume the development of an urban way of life. An increase in trade brought about a gradual return of the peasant to the city in search of jobs and, eventually, led to the development of craft guilds. These were the predecessors of the modern trade union, and, in several areas of Europe, they became the means by which the newly created middle class gained

FIGURE 11–9

Dubrovnik, Yugoslavia, a medieval (probably sixth century) walled city located on the Dalmation coast. Although under Venetian control for more than a century (1205–1358) as a result of the crusades, Dubrovnik has, for the most part, enjoyed full autonomy as a city-state, reaching its height as a trading center in the fifteenth and sixteenth centuries. It has also been a model of urban development and planning. Even in medieval times, zoning laws controlled its building construction, sanitary facilities, and water supplies. A public medical service existed in Dubrovnik as early as 1301; its first pharmacy was opened in 1317; and by 1432 the city had its own orphanage. (Harvey Stein)

political power. Cities became strongholds of the traders, whose power was eventually used to end the control of the feudal nobility.

The gradual revival of trade during the twelfth and thirteenth centuries also prompted great trade fairs, which in turn encouraged the growth of both the host cities and the contributing urban settlements. With this rebirth of intercity cooperation, such cities as Genoa and Milan, in northern Italy, were revived as trading centers, and Cologne, London, Danzig, Amsterdam, and Paris also grew in size and stature. Their close ties allowed the cities to maintain political independence from the declining feudal principalities and dukedoms that surrounded them. However, this autonomy was rather short-lived, as the emergence of the nation-state brought centralized power and authority.

Industrial Cities

The industrial revolution had a profound and lasting influence on the nature of urban settlements. Throughout the medieval and early colonial periods, European cities grew and changed at a relatively slow pace; but in the late decades of the eighteenth century the beginnings of large-scale manufacturing generated a completely new and revolutionary type of urban settlement, the industrial city.

Since the industrial revolution had its origins in England, it is not surprising that England was also the home of the first industrial cities. Among these were Manchester, Sheffield, and Stoke-on-Trent, important early manufacturing centers for cotton textiles, iron and steel, and pottery, respectively. The growth of industrial cities in other parts of the world during the eighteenth and early nineteenth centuries quite naturally coincided with the slow and somewhat limited spread of industrialization in this period. And although the industrial revolution was responsible for creating a number of new cities, many of those that came to be industrial centers by the mid-nineteenth century had been major commercial centers in ancient or medieval times. In Europe, these transformed commercial cities included the capitals London, Berlin, and Moscow as well as such secondary cities as Milan, Hamburg, and Poznan.

The advent of the industrial city was largely a consequence of the widespread application of new sources of energy, particularly coal-generated steam power. Up to this time the primary source of power, other than wind and water, had been animate rather than inanimate—specifically, human and animal muscle. The growing importance of coal in such areas as the Ruhr Valley, Appalachia, and the Donets, for instance, was in turn responsible for the development of such cities as Essen, Wheeling, and Donetsk, respectively.

The industrial revolution altered the established social patterns of these cities. Less-than-attractive factories were now often located in or near the heart of town, and within walking distances of them stood the cheaply built and cramped row houses and tenements in which many of the factory workers lived. Frequently the wealthy classes moved from the center of the city to outlying sections in order to avoid the crowding and unpleasant conditions associated with inner-city life. This tendency represented a reversal of the preindustrial residential pattern. But although people of different socioeconomic backgrounds usually congregated in different neighborhoods, as indeed they had done in preindustrial cities, industrialization brought urban populations increased opportunities for social contact and exchange, especially with the development of factory centers and transportation systems. The re-

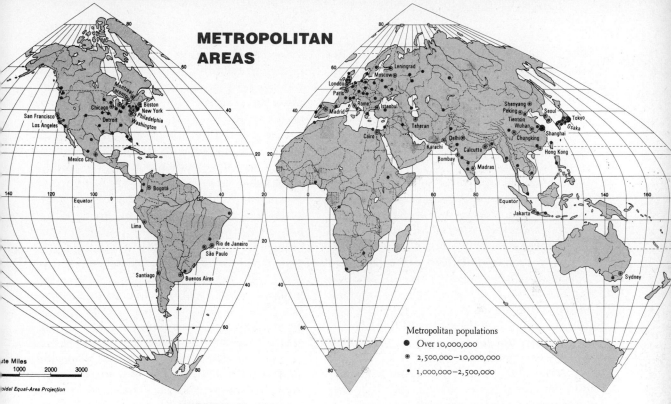

METROPOLITAN AREAS

Metropolitan populations
- ● Over 10,000,000
- ◉ 2,500,000–10,000,000
- • 1,000,000–2,500,000

te Miles
1000 2000 3000

pidal Equal-Area Projection

FIGURE 11–10

In this distribution of selected metropolitan areas exceeding one million persons, only those urban centers with more than 2.5 million inhabitants have been named.

sult was a considerably more fluid social structure within most industrial centers than had existed previously.

Industrialization also brought with it marked increases in urban populations; the factories needed workers, and improvements in farming technologies, such as the mechanical reaper and the cotton gin, had reduced the number of jobs available in agriculture. Further, improved methods of food preservation, water supply, and local transportation allowed for the comfortable maintenance of a greater concentration of people. The result was an ever-increasing migration of people from rural to urban centers.

But as early industrial cities grew in size, there was a corresponding growth in the number and complexity of urban problems. Urban dwellers, especially those in the inner city, were constantly troubled by overcrowding, poor sanitation, crime, and pollution—thus, they suffered widespread disease and high death rates.

World Distribution

Despite the long and constant growth of urban settlements, they remain relatively limited in their distribution over the world (Fig. 11–10). The large city is not a feature of areas with low population densities. There are, however, exceptions to this generalization. Madrid, for example, with a population of over three million, stands conspicuously on Spain's thinly populated Meseta (central plateau), and Tehran rises abruptly out of almost empty surrounding lands. But,

267

overall, the thinly populated areas of the world are nearly devoid of great cities.

The large urban center is also not a feature of the great lowland areas of the low latitudes. The relatively few exceptions include such cities as Bombay, Calcutta, Singapore, Djakarta, Canton, Hong Kong, and Manila in the Asiatic sphere, and Rio de Janeiro, São Paulo, and Mexico City in Latin America. And elsewhere in the low latitudes, some of the regions' (and the world's) highest population densities exist in areas without cities. Thus, since cities can exist amid low populations and high populations can exist where there are no cities, it is apparent that urbanization is not a necessary concommitant of high population density (Plate VII).

Examination of the distribution of cities reveals no strict tie to climate. And though mountains usually preclude the growth of large cities, landforms are seldom major determinants in the distribution of urban settlements; nor can native vegetation or soil be demonstrated to be the outstanding control. Of all the physical elements of the environment, minerals and water appear to have had the greatest influence on the growth of new cities. However, while "mining towns" do exist, not all mineral areas contain or lie close to an urban settlement. One is forced to conclude, therefore, that the world distribution of cities cannot be accounted for primarily in terms of physical setting.

Considering the history of urbanization, one comes to realize that the world distribution of cities more sharply reflects the spread of a particular culture than it does the occurrence of any physical element. In modern times, urban living has become more and more an earmark of what we call Western civilization. As the culture of the West spread over the various continents, urban settlement spread with it. Indeed, much of the urban development since the Middle Ages has been the result of foreign enterprise or domination. Certainly, most of the large-scale urban developments in Asia, Africa, and the Americas took place after these lands were colonized or brought within the European sphere of influence; the coastal areas of these continents, in particular, are peppered with such important colonial cities as Quebec, Boston, Rio de Janeiro, Dakar, Cape Town, Calcutta, Singapore, and Manila. Instead of developing slowly from rural settlements, as did the cities of early history in lands near the Mediterranean, urban settlements in these colonized areas were often created almost "ready-made," by adventuresome or fleeing European city dwellers.

In those colonized areas where Western, or, more specifically, European, culture has become dominant—in the United States and Australia, for example—urban settlements now involve more of the population than they do in the regions of their origin. Where Western culture has come only in the form of government or commercial activity, as in India or China, Westernized urban settlements have likewise appeared, but they rest as unassimilated forms on a base of rural settlement types.

Characteristics of Modern Urban Settlements

Site and Situation

Site.   The exact position of an agglomeration on the land is considered to be its *site.* For example, the original site of the city of Singapore (established in 1819) included an area of only about 3 square miles (now the most congested central city area) on the southern tip of the island of Singapore, which itself has a total land area of only about 227 square miles (Fig. 11–11). The present site of urban Singapore includes about 50 square miles. However, some people wish to do away with the old distinction between "Singapore City" and "Singapore country" and consider the whole island an urban complex.

Situation. To understand any agglomeration, it is necessary to appreciate its relationship to the area in which it is located, its regional position or *situation.* This does not mean the precise location or site, which is indicated by latitude and longitude, but rather the relationship of the agglomeration to the region it serves. Fortunately, Singapore has geography on its side: it stands less than a mile off the southernmost tip of the Malay Peninsula at the funnel point of the Straits of Singapore and Malacca. Thus, strategically located at the major crossroads of the Eastern world, Singapore could hardly have helped but become a great center of commerce and

the strategic hub of power during the long span of European colonialism in Asia. A product of the mercantilist era, Singapore was transformed under British rule from a bit of desolate swamp into a great commercial and strategic center. Today, Singapore is the rubber market for the Eastern world and the *entrepôt* (distribution center) and trading crossroads for all Southeast Asia. And with the growing importance of this region, Singapore may soon become the world's third major port.

Change Through Time. Both site and situation change with the passage of time. Increase in population in any agglomeration brings with it the expansion of its site over a larger area, as has been suggested in the example of Singapore. Loss of population may cause contraction of the site.

With respect to situation, change is perhaps less obvious, but it is nevertheless real. For example, if a new highway is built

FIGURE 11–11

The site and situation of Singapore, one of the major port cities in Asia. Left, the site of Singapore, on the southern coast of Singapore Island. Right, the situation of Singapore, within Southeast Asia.

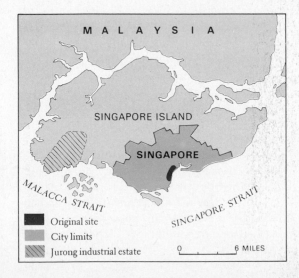

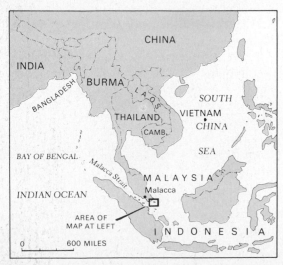

that bypasses an old agricultural market town, the flow of goods to and from the town is thereby diverted, and it may lose its significance as a regional commercial center; the town's situation has been changed.

The situation of an area may also be altered by a regional shift from agriculture to manufacturing; or, new urban centers may arise to replace or compete with an older one. Such was the fate of the port city of Malacca, which lies 100 miles north of Singapore on the Malay side of the Malacca Strait (see Fig. 11–11). With the decline of the sea-based empire of Sri Vijaya and its capital city near Palembang, in the thirteenth century, the way was open for the rise of a new Asian entrepôt. Initially a small fishing village, Malacca began to grow as more and more ships stopped there for provisions on their way through the Straits of Malacca and Singapore; and it gradually evolved into a port of call. Before long, trade became the mainstay of the city. And within a hundred years, Malacca had grown from a trading port to the center of an expanding empire—the strongest state in Southeast Asia. In the fifteenth century it controlled the commerce of the Straits; by the sixteenth century its archipelagic empire encompassed most of the Malay Peninsula and the island of Sumatra, including portions of both sides of the Malacca Straits. Not for several centuries was it to be replaced, by Singapore, as the principal entrepôt in Southeast Asia. The shift to another city occurred in part because Malacca's harbor was not deep enough to accommodate the very large ships of the nineteenth century.

Major Urban Functions

The basic consideration in classifying an agglomeration as urban should be the function, or functions, that it performs; for it

is from this factor, not size, that the essential difference between rural and urban agglomeration derives. But what are the distinctive functions of an urban settlement?

When the names of certain cities are mentioned, specific functions immediately come to mind. For example, Washington, D.C., and New Delhi, being the capital cities of the United States and India, respectively, are readily associated with governing; Detroit, with the production of automobiles; Hong Kong, with shipping and commerce; and Jerusalem, Mecca, and Varanasi (Banaras), with religion. But while each of these cities has been largely associated with one particular function, the existence of nearly all large cities—including those mentioned above—is based on a multitude of functions.

Several different classifications of urban functions have been devised. In general, however, the activities that urban settlements perform may be divided into seven major functions.

The first of these functions is *manufacturing*, which, ordinarily, involves the making or altering of goods for human use and may be performed on a variety of scales, ranging from the complexity of heavy industry to the relative simplicity of handicraft. The next most common function is probably *commerce*, which involves the exchange, either through sale or purchase, of goods and services. Third is *transportation*, the physical movement or transfer of people, goods, and services. This function has two major facets. One is the collection, or the bringing together, of large amounts of goods (or services)—for example, the ores used in a particular manufacturing process may be necessary in such large quantities that the yields of several sources must be sought and combined; the other is the distribution of materials received at a focal point—a port or railhead, for instance—in bulk to subsequent destinations in smaller lots. The fourth urban function is *administration*, or government, a necessary feature of social life that, as discussed in Chapter 5, occurs at several broad levels of complexity—the local, state, national, and international. Also necessary is the function of *defense*, which is most graphically illustrated in fortress towns or military garrisons. The *cultural* function, so-called, is a rather expedient grouping of activities in religion, art, and education. Lastly, the function of *recreation* is growing in importance throughout the world. Health and tourist centers perform the function of recreation.

Broadly defined, then, the major urban functions are manufacturing, commerce, transportation, administration, defense, culture, and recreation. They stand in marked contrast to rural functions. When the population of any agglomeration, regardless of actual numbers, is primarily engaged in cultivating the land or in raising animals, the agglomeration can be described as rural; when the population is in greater part engaged in one or more of the urban functions, the agglomeration is generally described as urban.

Internal Form and Structure

Size. Urban agglomerations cannot be reliably distinguished from rural agglomerations in terms of size, whether it is measured in numbers of people or areal extent. To be sure, rural agglomerations are usually smaller than urban ones, and large centers are usually of more importance than small ones. Yet the small number of buildings and residents in a grain-collecting center in the wheatlands of the midwestern United States may have a regional significance far beyond that of a settlement twice as large in, say, the more heavily populated Northeast.

Nevertheless, for convenience, size is often used to distinguish between rural and urban agglomerations, as in the official census of the United States. But such an arbitrary criterion may lead to a misunderstanding of the significance, or even the nature, of any area's settlements. Only broadly, and then only as a contributing element, should size be a consideration in the differentiation of urban and rural settlements.

Street Patterns. The skeleton of any urban agglomeration is the arrangement of its streets, which may involve some geometrical plan or be completely irregular. Often the natural features of a site conspire to favor certain lines of movement between buildings over certain others and thus to determine the settlement's configuration. But if nature imposes no control, the pedestrian pattern of a settlement develops entirely in accord with the desires or needs of its inhabitants.

In urban agglomerations that are old and had their origins in simple groupings of rural people, the patterns of streets may be quite *irregular*. In many instances the alignment of houses and other buildings was not a matter of great importance to early inhabitants. When such settlements grew larger and found it necessary to have formally designated streets, many irregular routes were recognized officially and allowed to remain. Thus, for example, much of the arrangement of streets in lower Manhattan or in the heart of Paris reflects routes that developed spontaneously, before the city's configuration was subjected to planning.

Sometimes the arrangement of city streets has been determined, directly or indirectly, by government, as when, for the most part, the urban settlements of Spanish America were laid out with a central plaza and streets parallel to its sides. This *rectangular*, or checkerboard, pattern, with streets crossing one another at right angles, is one of the simplest city designs and also one of the oldest; it was the layout of cities founded in ancient times, including Kahun in Egypt and Harrapa in Pakistan. In the central and western United States—areas settled mainly after 1850 and under government control—an attempt to have main roads cross one another at right angles is apparent, and, as is generally true in agglomerations that originated at a crossroads, most additional streets are laid out parallel to main roads—and thus, in this case, at right angles to one another.

Increases in the importance and size of an agglomeration create greater need for speed and ease of access to its center from the periphery. Rectangular arrangements are surpassed in this regard by the *radial* pattern, whereby streets lead from points on the periphery directly to a common center, much as the spokes of a wheel connect the rim to the hub. Cross streets then tend to assume a weblike arrangement. The skeleton of streets in Washington, D.C., for example, is a complex combination of radial and rectangular patterns.

Beyond these three basic patterns—irregular, rectangular, and radial—there are many others that have grown out of the vagaries of individual choice or of real estate

FIGURE 11–12

A westward aerial view of mid-Manhattan showing the uniform rectangular pattern of the area's eastern half. The Empire State Building, on Thirty-fourth Street, is just left of the center. (New York Department of Commerce)

development. These are irregular in a sense, but usually symmetrically so. Circular drives, curving and recurving lines, figure-8's, cul-de-sacs, and dead-end inner courts reached from the four sides of a large rectangular block are some of the familiar forms to be encountered in today's developing urban agglomerations.

All the patterns may occur in combination as well as individually, especially in larger urban areas. As one proceeds uptown, the irregular streets of lower Manhattan give way to streets that form a well-crystallized, rectangular pattern, with only one notable exception, Broadway (Fig. 11–12). The repeating radial patterns of Washington, D.C., are imposed upon a rectangular base. The radial pattern about the Place de l'Etoile in Paris links tenuously to the irregular framework farther into the old city, to the circular boulevards that belt the city, and to the great cross avenues of modern construction that tear across the old irregular pattern (Fig. 11–13). Similarly, where peculiarities of site restrict full development of any one pattern, local modifications are introduced. For example, the city of Syracuse, New York, has a street pattern that is basically rectangular;

FIGURE 11–13

The Place de l'Étoile (Star), in Paris, where the Arc de Triomphe stands in a circle at which twelve radial avenues meet, including (upper left) the broad, tree-lined Champs Élysées (Rotkin, PFI)

FIGURE 11–14

San Francisco, California, a seaport city whose profile is both typical and unique among those of large urban centers. (Transamerica Corp.)

however, much of the city's site is characterized by low but steep hills that prevent an unrestricted rectangular pattern.

Whatever the pattern or combination of patterns formed by the streets of a city, the character of the agglomeration is deeply affected by it. The alignment of houses and other buildings is determined by the position of the streets, and thus the agglomeration acquires a fixed quality. Any planned additions to or detractions from the established pattern, both measures of growth, must in some way be articulated with the existing pattern. Despite changes of detail, the agglomeration as a whole retains a distinctive appearance, determined largely by its pattern of streets.

Profile, or Skyline. Something of the nature of any agglomeration is told by its *profile,* or skyline. In small rural settlements, the buildings are usually low in height and often widely spaced. Individual houses rise above low sheds, and relatively large barns may overshadow all. Thus, although the thin spire of a church may rise near the center and the crowns of trees may soften the roof line, the profile of a small rural settlement is usually rather low-lying, irregular, and jagged.

A very different profile characterizes large urban agglomerations, especially in the more highly developed parts of the world. The outer edges of it may look like the profile typical of rural settlements; but as the center is approached, the buildings rise higher and more massively, suggesting the cross-section of a low, wide pyramid. The roof lines tend to be straight or, in some instances, symmetrically rounded, and constructed forms dominate rather than natural ones (Fig. 11–14).

The skyscraper is responsible for this pyramidlike urban profile, and it has come to be a measure of status as well: the higher the skyscraper, the greater its contribution to the prestige of its city. At present the tallest skyscraper in the world is Chicago's 110-story Sears Tower; it is 104 feet higher than its leading competition—the twin towers of New York's World Trade Center—and 204 feet higher than the Empire State Building.

Only recently has some of the technology used in the construction of such multistoried buildings been made available. Not until the late 1800s, for example, did the electric elevator come into widespread commercial use; and it was even later that the cagelike steel frame used in skyscraper construction became practical and safe. The first skyscraper, the 10-story Home Life Insurance Building in Chicago, was built by William Le Baron Jenney in 1884. Up to that time the maximum height of buildings was severely limited, to about 5 or 6 stories—that being the maximum number the average human could climb several times a day and the maximum number that could be built soundly and attractively without a steel frame.

The high cost of the little ground space available has been the main incentive for building vertically rather than horizontally in congested urban centers. This vertical utilization of space, or the "piling up at the center," is rapidly becoming a characteristic of urban profiles around the world. In Hong Kong, for example, the 52-story Connaught Center represents only one of the many highrises recently completed in Asia. It seems, in fact, that the time is rapidly approaching when the larger urban centers of the world— New York, San Francisco, Chicago, Paris, Berlin, Moscow, Tokyo, São Paulo, Hong Kong, and Cairo—will no longer be distinguishable from one another simply by a glance at their profiles.

Functional Areas.   As described earlier, urban agglomerations perform various func-

tions for the groups living in them and for the area that surrounds them. Each of these functions involves certain distinct types of buildings as well as certain rather well-defined quarters, or districts. On the other hand, there is usually no great difference between one section of a rural agglomeration and another; the form and structure of a rural settlement is comparatively simple.

In contrast to this, an urban center located on a coast and serving as a port will have a definite docking and warehousing district that is quite distinct from, say, the residential district or the college campus. Similarly, a district of retail stores, carrying on the commercial function within the urban agglomeration, contrasts sharply with the scene created by a grouping of factories carrying on the function of manufacturing. Each one of these more or less localized districts performing a distinct function is known as a *functional area.*

Taken together, the functional areas of an urban agglomeration tend to form a discernible pattern. In larger urban agglomerations this pattern can usually be broken down into three distinct sections: the *central business district* (CBD), the *inner city*, and the *suburban fringe* (Fig. 11–15). Each of these broadly defined sections has its own distinct character and its own assortment of functional areas.

It is common, in the United States at least, to refer to the central business district, or "downtown" section, as the heart of the city and, in many instances, the very reason for its existence. Traditionally, this section of the urban settlement has been the one given over both to the high concentration of such special services as large department stores, hotels, specialty shops, and public buildings and to the employment of large numbers of people—most of whom commute to the area from the suburbs. It is usually a part of the settlement that is all but devoid of single-

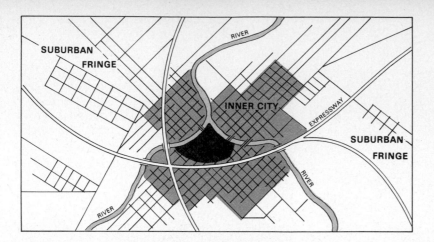

FIGURE 11–15

A hypothetical metropolitan area, or urban center. Its three main sections are interdependent: the *central business district* (CBD), at the core of the area, is also located near the intersection of its major through roads; the *inner city* surrounds the CBD and forms a buffer between it and the third and outermost section, the *suburban fringe*. In reality, each type of section varies in size; the suburbs also tend to be more discontinuous or fragmented.

family residences, although large apartment buildings are often found here in appropriately zoned areas. Similarly, there is generally a manufacturing zone close by. In most urban centers around the world, the central business district is the most accessible section of the metropolitan area, for transportation and communication networks focus on it. In New York City, for example, the CBD is primarily the Wall Street area and the area between 34th and 59th streets; in Chicago, it is based on the Loop at the intersection of State and Madison streets and includes an area five blocks wide and seven blocks long; in London, it includes the area from Saint Paul's Cathedral to the Strand.

Within older settled parts of the Western world, distinctions between the specialized areas of any agglomeration are less clearly marked than in newer settlements. The history of the growth of an urban agglomeration often reveals why its various functions are performed in scattered rather than in collected zones. In European settlements, for example, residence is often maintained close to or in the same building as retail stores; such "shophouses" are very common in Asian settlements as well. The function of commerce may thus be so scattered as to leave no impression of a "downtown" section. Moreover, in Oriental settlements the same building may contain a workshop, serve as the residence of the workers, and, also, house persons engaged in intensive agriculture on a small plot of land nearby.

The arrangement of the functional areas of a city is the result of the interplay of several forces. At an early stage, the intersection of two highways, which may have given rise to the settlement in the first place, may be an attractive site for a store. Here people from the vicinity come to purchase needed supplies or to dispose of surplus agricultural items. In time, a second store may be established because there is a good commercial opportunity. A third enterprise, to be followed by many others, may come next. An inn may be built near the crossroads. Gradually, there appears a nucleus within which all the buildings are used for commerce; they are occupied during the day by the people engaged in the performance of that function but who live elsewhere. A distinct functional area develops—a *commercial core*, or central business district in this instance.

Sometimes, factories are attracted to a commercial core by the presence of a large number of people, the family members of those active in commerce representing a potentially large and readily available labor supply. Wealth accumulated in commercial activity might be available for investment in industry.

Sometimes, however, factories have to be built on the outskirts of a settlement. If past growth of the commercial core has made land values too high and the presence of residences about the commercial core makes adjacent land unavailable, factories are forced to the outskirts. Gradually, under such conditions, there may develop an industrial belt encircling the commercial and residential centers.

The growth of any agglomeration brings with it continual, far-reaching adjustments of its functional areas. If a settlement has developed a commercial core surrounded by residences and that, in turn, is encircled by an industrial ring, further growth in population requires expansion of the residential area. Often the only possibility lies in jumping beyond the industrial ring; soon new residential areas appear on the fringe, sometimes — usually for the workers — close to the factories, and sometimes well away from the factory belt — most often for those who can afford to choose their own site. Here and there, small neighborhood communities may develop, perhaps separated physically from the original nucleus but economically still very much a part of it.

As these newer residential areas spring up, there is usually a decline in the old residential belt located near the center, or commercial core, of the settlement. To such a middle section, or zone, the name *inner zone* or *inner city* is frequently given. Its decline may be accompanied by an outward spread of the commercial core and an inward growth of the industrial belt. Some of its old residences, relics of a more youthful period in the settlement's history, may become rooming houses, gradually deteriorating and eventually being removed to make way for other buildings.

The spread of an urban agglomeration is the result of many factors. Modern transportation, for example, has made it possible for more and more urban folk to live at far greater distances from their work than did most workers in the past. Intangible incentives, such as the desire for space, and tangible incentives, such as lower tax rates, have contributed to the continued migration of urban people away from the urban nucleus. Where this movement has occurred, a zone of interpenetration of urban and rural settlement, the *rural-urban*, or *suburban*, fringe, has come into being.

As its growth and spread continue, distances within the agglomeration, especially between the residential districts and the commercial core, become so great that new scattered nuclei of commerce begin to appear in the outer residential districts. These are the occasional "corner stores," and the "neighborhood shopping centers," so characteristic of growing metropolitan areas in the United States and many other countries. Their appearance begins a trend toward the decentralization of the agglomeration's retail trade, which will tend to adversely affect merchants in the inner city and central business district; they will feel, with increasing intensity, the pinch of competition from the more modern, multipurpose suburban shopping centers.

Similarly, as the agglomeration spreads, details of site, such as steepness of slope or the alignment of a lake shore or a river, may limit the growth of one or another of its functional areas. Chronic traffic congestion may necessitate cutting new streets or widening old ones. This in turn may bring about the rearrangement of functional areas, thus altering the character of the entire urban unit. As its physical and cultural elements continue to interact, the city continues to grow and change.

Centers of Influence and Change

From their first appearance, human agglomerations have been the nuclei of cultural ferment and change. Indeed, they have been both the cause and effect of the innovations in human culture. Usually the larger the agglomeration and the stronger its organizational bonds and purposes, the greater the scope and intensity of its influence. A single well-knit family can strongly influence change in a small settlement; and, allied with its neighbors, it can affect far broader regions.

Thus, throughout history, the heavily populated cities of the world have been the fountainheads of humanity's important social, cultural, and political innovations. Modern-day Paris, for example, exerts a far greater cultural influence, both locally and internationally, than do all the smaller settlements of France combined.

Without such population agglomerations of varying magnitudes, there would be no nations as we know them, nor any large-scale transportation and communication systems, except perhaps on a local, extremely fragmented basis. There would be no international cooperation and competition, and therefore little opportunity for cultural, polit-ical, or scientific exchange; indeed, the prime mechanism for the creation and diffusion of cultural, political, and educational institutions would be almost totally lacking. Without urban settlement, people would be living pretty much as they did fifty thousand years ago.

Urban agglomerations have been the places where scientists, philosophers, poets, and traders have met, argued, and often merged their divergent talents and views. The resulting changes have not always been praiseworthy, but there have apparently been more good ones than bad, because civilizations have, on the whole, tended to more than balance their cyclic declines. Certain cities, in fact, have come to be associated with specific societal changes. Moscow and Leningrad established communism as a modern political reality, and Peking adapted that economic system to the particular needs and way of life of China. London may well lay claim to the creation and diffusion, beginning in the late 1500s, of worldwide colonialism. And, during the late Middle Ages, several northern European cities—among them Cologne, Lübeck, Danzig, and Riga—organized the first large-scale commercial-trading structure, the Hanseatic League (see Fig. 5–19).

Christaller's Central Place Theory

In 1933 the German geographer Walter Christaller published a theoretical work titled *Central Places in Southern Germany,* in which he attempts to explain the distribution, size, and number of settlements that might develop in a given region. Although based on the conditions existing in southern Germany several decades ago, many of the principles set forth in this work are of great value in understanding the spatial relationships of settlements in any region or period. Since the study rests on the proposition that a settlement is centrally located in the region it serves and that, on a group basis, smaller settlements will arrange themselves around a larger central place, it is commonly referred to as Christaller's *central place theory.*

The Model Region

In presenting his theory Christaller provides a model based on the following assumptions:

1. There is an evenly distributed number of rural consumers residing on a flat, uniform, and limitless plain.
2. Each of these rural consumers has the same wealth, income, and desires; and thus purchasing power, or propensity to consume (demand), is distributed evenly over the plain.
3. A transportation system serves all the plain uniformly, providing equal accessibility to all central places of the same type.
4. The single function of each settlement is to provide the rural population with goods and services. There are no mining towns or industrial centers, for example.
5. Producers of goods and services cannot be located adjacent to each customer.
6. Producers should receive a profit from the sale of their goods or services.
7. Each good or service has the same market range regardless of where it is produced.
8. A maximum number of consumer demands should be satisfied from a minimum number of central places.

Assuming these circumstances, Christaller proposed that an even distribution of settlements would develop on the plain, supplying the rural consumers with goods and services they could not provide for themselves—such as processed food, clothing, entertainment, formal education, legal aid, and medical services. The area served by each settlement is referred to as its *tributary area,* or *complementary region.*

Theoretically, since the price of goods and services increases with the consumer's distance from the point of production, the ideal tributary area is circular, with the settlement as its focus—in the manner of von Thünen's model (see Chapter 6); this configuration allows consumers in a maximum number of directions to be supplied at a minimum cost. Each centrally located settlement, or central place, is assumed to have a complete monopoly over its tributary area.

But what size tributary area is required in order to support a particular good or service? Obviously each good or service has a specific *threshold,* or minimum level, of demand, at which it can be sold at a profit. Since propensity to consume is evenly distributed, this threshold can be calculated in terms of numbers of customers. If the number of actual customers is below this minimum level, then the product will not be commercially viable. The territory encompassing a commodity's necessary number of customers is known as its *market range.* In order for a good or service to remain commercially viable, its market range must at least equal its demand threshold. So, when competition for customers exists between central places, the size of their tributary areas is determined by both the market range and the threshold level.

While some goods have a *low* demand threshold and can tolerate a short market range (low-order goods), others have a much *higher* minimum level of demand and, consequently, require a much greater market range (high-order goods). Bread, for example, is a low-order good, whereas the services provided by a specialized lawyer are high-order.

If only goods or services of the same order are produced, and if the entire population cannot be served from a single center, then the central places that develop will be evenly spaced over the entire plain, each one

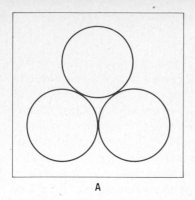
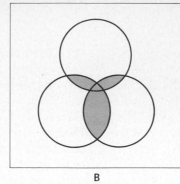
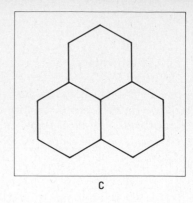

A B C

FIGURE 11–16

Some possible configurations of tributary areas. A. Tangent circles, which leave some areas unserved. B. Overlapping circles, which create competition. C. Hexagons, which leave no area unserved and create no competition.

serving a tributary area of identical size with an equal number of customers. However, circular tributary areas cannot exist in such a situation, because—if the circles just touch—there would be areas where people are residing (by assumption) but not being served, or—if the circles overlap—there would be areas of competition. Christaller's solution was to have each tributary area assume the shape of a hexagon—the geometric form that permits the most efficient coverage of the entire plain (Fig. 11–16).

When goods and services of various orders are involved, the high-order goods, those that require the largest tributary areas, are supplied from only a few of the central places. The low-order goods are supplied from a greater number of central places, each serving a relatively small tributary area. All production centers, however, regardless of their size, remain evenly spaced over the plain.

The Hierarchy of Central Places

On the basis of this differentiation of goods and services, Christaller formulated a

hierarchy of central places that may range in size from as small a unit as the hamlet through the village, town, city, and up to the large metropolis, and even higher if so desired (Fig. 11–17). In his arrangement the production centers that provide commodities of the lowest order are the smallest in size and the most numerous; these centers are rather closely spaced hamlets. The next largest centers are the villages, providing items demanded so infrequently that the tributary area of no single hamlet can support them. Each village will be located on the site of a former hamlet and include among its goods and services all those provided by a hamlet. Its tributary area will be bounded by six surrounding hamlets and will be larger than the tributary area of any one of them. Consequently, there will be fewer villages on the plain than there are hamlets. Following the same procedure, the third-order center, the town, will have its tributary area delimited by six villages; and the fourth-order center, the city, will be bounded by six towns. This progression, which can be used to establish a hierarchy of any number of orders, assumes that *each center at a given hierarchical level produces its own distinct goods and services as well as those of any center at a lower level.*

One of the main principles illustrated by Christaller's central place model is that an item's cost to the consumer—in time and energy as well as money—is usually determined in large part by distance. Consumers are willing to incur the cost of traveling long distances in order to obtain infrequently needed, expensive items; but they will not make the same sacrifice for frequently needed, cheaper items: consumers expect to find a grocery store in their local area but not the services of a stockbroker. In response to this variation in consumer travel, Christaller suggests, there will evolve in any given region a hierarchy of service centers in which size and availability of goods and services are directly related.

And indeed, in most regions of the world there does seem to exist an approximation of Christaller's hierarchy of different-sized settlements. However, it is rare that a settlement provides all the commodities available in centers at lower levels. And further, the number and distributional pattern of modern settlements never more than roughly coincide with Christaller's model.

The ideal symmetrical distribution of central places is prevented by many factors.

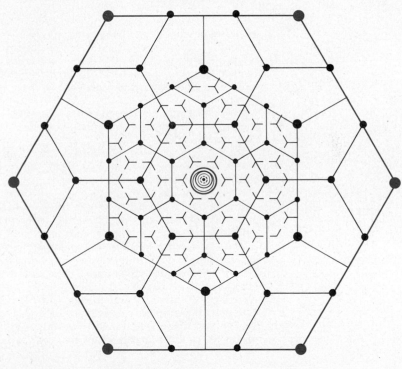

FIGURE 11–17

A diagrammatic representation of Christaller's hierarchy of central places. (It should be understood that hamlets and villages exist over the entire tributary area of the metropolis.)

Settlement		Limit of tributary area
•	Hamlet	– – –
•	Village	——
●	Town	——
⬤	City	——
◎	Metropolis	——

One of these is the clustering of settlements around some natural feature, such as a water body or mineral deposit. Another is the tendency for settlements to develop along transport routes, which are unevenly distributed over the land because of local relief features and the uneven distribution of demand; in many areas the result has been a linear settlement pattern. Moreover, within the last few decades, vastly improved modes of transportation have increased the mobility of people and cargo to such an extent that a settlement no longer has a monopolistic hold over its surrounding area. Today's tributary areas are often international, and changes in the network of central places in one country can promote a considerable reorientation of trade areas within another country. In the real world, central places are dynamic entities; it is not uncommon to see the prosperous settlement of an earlier technological age die or decline as new ones emerge. Thus, although certain elements of Christaller's central place theory are demonstrated in the real world, variation from the ideal centrality of settlements appears to be the rule.

REVIEW AND DISCUSSION

1. Why and in what ways do the types of settlements created by a mobile population differ from those created by a sedentary population? Explain the differences between the various settlement types of sedentary populations.
2. Is there any precise means of distinguishing between a dispersed settlement and an agglomerated one? between a rural settlement and an urban one? Explain.
3. List several examples of each of the following: hamlet, village, town, city, and metropolis. Be prepared to explain your classifications. Are their distinctions clear-cut?
4. Trace the early development and diffusion of urban centers throughout the world. Does there appear to be a strong correlation between imperialism and urbanization? Explain.
5. Discuss and evaluate the impact of the industrializing period on the growth and development of urban centers after the Middle Ages.
6. Differentiate between and explain the geographic importance of *site* and *situation*. Give specific examples of each term.
7. Discuss and evaluate the seven major urban functions. Name several urban agglomerations that perform functions other than these.
8. Describe and evaluate the internal form and structure (size, street patterns, and functional areas) of the population agglomeration you know best.
9. As centers of influence and change, in what fields have cities been pioneers? Cite several examples, preferably from both historical and modern times.
10. To what extent is the hierarchy of central places in Christaller's model region a mirror of reality? Support your evaluation with specific examples.

SELECTED REFERENCES

Ahmad, N. "The Pattern of Rural Settlement in East Pakistan." *Geographical Review*, Vol. 46 (July 1956), 388–98.

Boal, F. W. "Technology and Urban Form." *The Journal of Geography*, Vol. 67 (April 1968), 229–36.

Briggs, A. *Victorian Cities*. New York: Harper Colophon, 1965.

Brush, J. E. "The Hierarchy of Central Places in Southwestern Wisconsin." *Geographical Review*, Vol. 43 (July 1953), 380–402.

Brush, J. E., and H. E. Bracey. "Rural Service Centers in Southwestern Wisconsin and Southern England." *Geographical Review*, Vol. 45 (October 1955), 559–69.

Chinitz, B. "Contrasts in Agglomeration: New York and Pittsburgh." *American Economic Review*, Vol. 51 (May 1961), 279–89.

Christaller, W. *Central Places in Southern Germany*, trans. by Carlisle W. Baskin. Englewood Cliffs, N.J.: Prentice-Hall, 1966.

Demangeon, A. "The Origins and Causes of Settlement Types." in P. L. Wagner and M. W. Mikesell, eds., *Readings in Cultural Geography*. Chicago, 1962, 506–16.

Dwyer, D. J., ed. *The City as the Centre of Change in Asia*. Hong Kong: University of Hong Kong Press, 1971.

Getis, A., and J. Getis. "Christaller's Central Place Theory." *Journal of Geography*, Vol. 65 (May 1966), 220–26.

Gottmann, J. "Why the Skyscraper?" *Geographical Review*, Vol. 56 (April 1966), 190–212.

Green, F. H. W. "Community of Interest Areas: Notes on the Hierarchy of Central Places and Their Hinterlands." *Economic Geography*, Vol. 34 (July 1958), 210–26.

Johnson, J. H. *Urban Geography: An Introductory Analysis*. Oxford and New York: Pergamon Press, 1967.

Lampe, F. A., and O. C. Schaefer, Jr. "Land Use Patterns in the City." *The Journal of Geography*, Vol. 68 (May 1969), 301–06.

Lapidus, I. M. *Middle Eastern Cities: A Symposium on Ancient, Islamic, and Contemporary Middle Eastern Urbanism*. Berkeley and Los Angeles: University of California Press, 1969.

Lewis, O. *Village Life in Northern India*. Urbana: University of Illinois Press, 1958.

Mumford, L. *The City in History: Its Origins, Its Transformations, and Its Prospects*. New York: Harcourt, Brace and World, 1961.

Murphey, R. "New Capitals of Asia." *Economic Development and Cultural Change*, Vol. 5 (April 1957), 216–43.

Pirenne, H. *Medieval Cities*. New York: Doubleday, 1925.

Robson, B. T. *Urban Analysis: A Study in City Structure*. Cambridge, England, 1969.

Sjoberg, G. "The Origin and Evolution of Cities." *Scientific American*, Vol. 213 (September 1965), 54–63.

———. *The Preindustrial City*. New York: Free Press, 1960.

Thomas, E. N. "Toward an Expanded Central-Place Model." *Geographical Review*, Vol. 51 (July 1961), 400–11.

Ullman, E. L. "A Theory of Location for Cities." *American Journal of Sociology*, Vol. 46 (May 1941), 853–64.

Disorder at the base of New York's World Trade Center during its construction.
(© Arthur Tress, Magnum)

12

Challenge
of Urban Growth

Urbanization

The twentieth century, more than any other period in human history, may truly be called the urban age. Though cities as such are not new, the existence of innumerable societies in which more people can be classified as urban than as rural is a unique feature of modern times, a new and revolutionary stage in the long development of cultural institutions. As discussed earlier, cities have been a part of the cultural scene for more than 5,000 years; however, throughout most of that span, they have been relatively small and few in number, their combined populations at any given time accounting for only a small portion of the human total.

In recent centuries, by contrast, not only has the number of urban agglomerations been increasing markedly but, often massive and highly complex, they have been claiming an ever-higher proportion of the world's total population. Until 1800, less than two centuries ago, no more than 2 percent of the world's population lived in urban settlements of 20,000 persons or more. By 1900, this figure had increased nearly fivefold, to 9 percent. And projections indicate that, by the year 2000, urban dwellers will account for well over 50 percent of the total world population, as compared with about 40 percent today. (Of course, such percentages are even higher when based on a definition of urban that takes in settlements of less than 20,000 persons; 20,000 is an arbitrary United Nations standard and, in view of much world practice, a rather high one.)

According to recent studies by the Bureau of the Census, for example, about 75 percent of the people now inhabiting the United States live within the country's urbanized areas (Fig. 12–1). And, also as measured by the bureau, nearly every state in the nation has a population that is at least 50 percent urban, California being the leader with a population that is 90.9 percent urban (Fig. 12–2). Moreover, much the same can be said

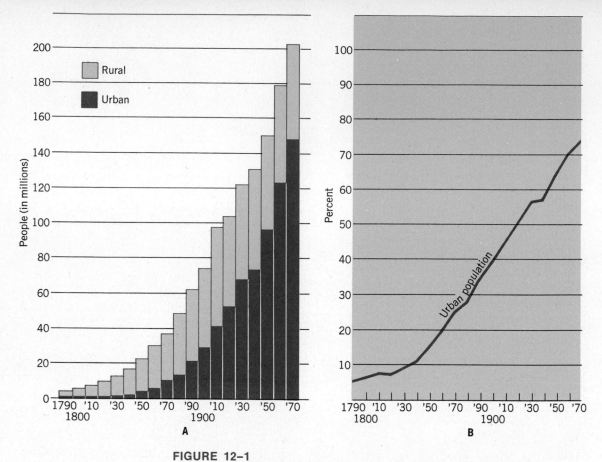

FIGURE 12–1

United States population from 1790 to 1970. A. The rural–urban division. B. The urban population percentage. The country's urbanization has been swift; between 1790 and 1970 the total population grew by almost 200 million, and the urban population rose nearly 70 percent.

of other parts of the world; many societies of western and northern Europe, for example— including Great Britain, the Netherlands, Denmark, and Sweden—as well as several Asian and Southern Hemisphere nations equal, or even exceed, the urban population percentage of the United States.

The trend toward urbanization involves much more, however, than a mere regrouping of people or an expression of the increasing importance of nonagricultural occupations. The high degree of physical and psychological contact related to modern city living has prompted entirely new life styles

and philosophies and a general re-evaluation of many concepts traditionally associated with agrarian societies.

World Patterns

As Figure 12–3 shows, a wide belt of countries characterized by a *low* degree of urbanization stretches across Africa, southern Europe, the Middle East, and on across southern and eastern Asia (excluding Japan); there is also a small outlier of low urbanization in Central America. In contrast, the countries characterized by a *high* degree of urbanization comprise most of North America and South America, and most of northern Europe, as well as the Soviet Union, Japan, Australia, and New Zealand. Within this latter category, the most highly urbanized regions include the northeastern and western coasts of the United States, southern South America, northwestern Europe, Japan, and southeastern Australia. The small, anomalous countries of San Marino and Macao have over 90 percent of their population living in urban settlements; Sweden, Israel, and Australia are over 80 percent urbanized; Canada, the United States, Venezuela, the Netherlands, Chile, Bahrain, and Japan are in the over-70-percent group; and Mexico, Colombia, Greece, Lebanon, and the Soviet Union are among those in the 50-to-70 percent category (Fig. 12–4).

Some of the highly urbanized countries of the world have one city in their urban hierarchy that greatly overshadows all others in terms of population size. But, in general, such *primate* cities tend to be found mainly in the developing countries, especially those with a very recent history of political control by a foreign nation. Most highly urbanized countries include several major urban centers.

FIGURE 12–2

United States urban population percentages. Approximately three out of every four Americans (73.5 percent) live in urban areas, which the government defines as settlements with over 2,500 inhabitants. (United States Department of Commerce, Bureau of the Census, 1970)

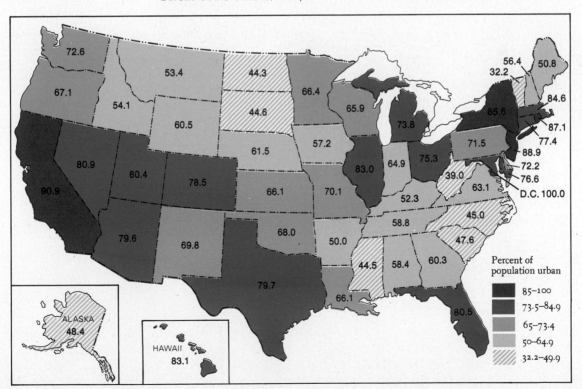

FIGURE 12-3

The average degree of urbanization among the world's nations was approximately 35 percent in the early 1960s; it increased to about 40 percent in the early 1970s, and will probably be well over 50 percent by the year 2000.

FIGURE 12-4

The urban–rural population percentages of selected countries, representing a wide population range.

Country	Total population (in millions)	Urban percentage	Rural percentage
San Marino	0.02	92	8
Australia	13	86	14
Israel	3	84	16
Great Britain	54	76	24
Canada	22	76	24
Venezuela	10	76	24
United States	203	74	26
Japan	104	72	28
Mexico	53	60	40
Soviet Union	247	58	42
South Africa	23	48	52
Yugoslavia	21	39	61
India	563	20	80
China	800(?)	13	87
Nepal	12	4	96

The Socioeconomic Transformation

Close examination of the world pattern of urbanization reveals that degree of urbanization often correlates directly with level of socioeconomic development. Generally the more developed countries have large portions of their populations residing in urban centers, and the less-developed ones have small urban population percentages. In light of this, urbanization may be seen as a collateral process experienced by a country as it undergoes socioeconomic development, especially from an agrarian economy to an industrial economy.

Accordingly, Great Britain, home of the Industrial Revolution, is usually considered as having created one of the first modern urban societies; likewise, intensive urbanization in most of the rest of today's developed societies has occurred only since the mid-nineteenth century and in almost no society of eastern Asia or Latin America until after World War II. Indeed, only a few countries in any region have progressed to the economic level typical of a highly urbanized society. A wide gulf exists between these few and the rest of the world. In Great Britain, for instance, a highly developed country, almost everyone is familiar with cities and the urban way of life, for about 76 percent of the country's population either resides or works in an urban center; but in Laos, a comparatively undeveloped country, not only is the urban population percentage much smaller but the distinctive features of city living are all but unknown to most of the country's rural population. The range of familiarity with cities is wide, and most populations of the world fall between these two extremes.

A Finite Process

The idea that *urbanization* and the *growth of cities* are synonymous is a common misconception. Though the processes they represent have been complementary factors in the creation of urban societies, a distinction should be made between the two terms. In this discussion of cities, *urbanization* is used solely to suggest the percentage of urban dwellers in a given total population. This percentage usually increases with time but may decrease if, for instance, the rural population grows faster than the urban population, either because of a higher birth rate or urban to rural migration. Urbanization, then, should be thought of as a finite process, with a definite beginning and end. Once a population is 100 percent urban, its urbanization process has reached its limit; it cannot go beyond this point.

In contrast, *urban growth,* the establishment of cities and their increases in population, has no fixed upper limit; on the contrary, it can and probably will continue throughout human existence. Even in a country that had become totally urbanized, as none yet has, the growth of its cities could still continue indefinitely if the support of foreign agriculture could be maintained.

The Growth of Cities

In almost every part of the contemporary world, urban centers are on the increase, embracing more and more of the earth's population and areal extent. Most of this increase has involved the expansion of existing urban areas rather than the creation of totally new ones, and the rate of growth has, of course, varied from country to country as well as from one city to another within the same country.

Population

Precise data on many urban populations around the world are somewhat limited; much of the statistical material is outdated or poorly compiled, and data on some areas do not exist at all. In general, however, it may be estimated that a little under two billion of the world's total four billion people now live in urban centers of over 20,000 persons. The United Nations World Health Organization estimates that the proportion of urban dwellers will jump to about 60 percent by the year 2000, when the total world population is expected to be close to seven billion. Thus urban population growth will continue to occur on a scale unknown in the previous evolution of human culture, and what it will mean to the future of the planet is one of the great uncertainties of our times. Among the few predictable aspects of this surge is its dependence on the traditional urban population sources, mainly foreign immigration, domestic rural migration, and natural urban population increase.

Foreign Immigration.   Some of history's greatest increases in urban populations occurred during the nineteenth century, when the steamship and other innovations in long-distance transportation improved the economics of passenger travel and made it possible for great numbers of people to seek a new life in a foreign land. When foreign immigrants came to a new country they tended to settle in the most accessible urban centers, where they were more likely to find employment and speakers of their native language. As a result, many United States cities, especially such ports as New York and San Francisco, became the destination of thousands of newly arriving immigrants, most of whom were natives of Europe and Asia. In this same period, immigrants from Europe, specifically from Great Britain, were also in large

part responsible for the development of many of the then fledgling colonial port cities, such as Sydney, Melbourne, and Cape Town. The cities of Singapore and Hong Kong, colonial products as well, are composed almost entirely of foreign immigrants, primarily southern Chinese.

In modern times, foreign immigration continues to influence urban growth. For instance, in recent years it has had a strong impact on the urban centers of Canada. Statistics show that about half the people who enter Canada each year under its liberal immigration laws settle in the country's three major urban centers—Montreal, Toronto, and Vancouver. These cities, as well as many others located in countries with liberal immigration policies, are finding the influx increasingly difficult to absorb. Some governments are responding by severely limiting the number of new immigrants allowed to enter their country each year.

Rural to Urban Migration.   A factor that has been even more important in urban growth than the immigration of foreign nationals is the intranational migration of people from rural areas to cities. This redistribution of population has been the greatest single cause of the rapid urbanization around the world during the last 100 years or more. The tremendous rush to the cities begun in the late eighteenth century has resulted in the concentration of huge numbers of people in centers not properly prepared to meet their problems. But the migration from rural areas continues, even to cities where there are shortages of such necessities as jobs, housing, and health facilities. This trend reflects the dissatisfaction of rural dwellers with the stagnant economic and cultural life of the village and the lure of vast opportunities, whether real or imagined, to be had in the city. As long as such opportunities exist for some, there seems to be little that can be done to keep thousands of rural dwellers from moving to urban centers in search of better working and living conditions.

There is, on the other hand, little or no evidence that great numbers of urban dwellers are moving to rural areas, except in those few instances where people have been forced back to the countryside by government decree. Even those migrants who come to the city in search of temporary employment are tending to stay for longer periods of time, and more are bringing their families. Furthermore, whereas rural to urban migration once tended to progress in stages—from farm to small town and then to city—adherence to this "law of intervening opportunity" appears to be declining, for more and more migrants are coming directly to the city.

Natural Increase from Within. Urban growth the world over, but most particularly in the developed countries, is becoming increasingly attributable to natural population increase within urban areas themselves. In the expansion of many cities around the world, this population source is now fully as important as domestic migration. Its new prominence results not only from improved health techniques that prolong the human life span but from the relatively high birth rates that exist among many urban populations.

Spatiality and Social Complexity

The spread of urban living since 1900, coupled with unprecedented population increases, has given the world many huge urban centers, more than a few of which are much larger and more complex than the largest city a century ago. London, New York, Tokyo, and Shanghai are only some of the many cities that now have larger populations than many countries. Because of their rising populations, such large cities have "exploded" into the countryside, spreading themselves over greater and greater areas (Fig. 12–5). The degree to which they have grown is somewhat difficult to comprehend in its totality, for increase in size has been attended by even greater increases in complexity. Size increases arithmetically; complexity increases geometrically. Large cities of the modern world represent marked qualitative changes over the past and thus are not merely enlarged versions of traditional cities but entirely new and different forms of human settlement. The comparatively simple way of life typical of urbanites in the past has been replaced by a much more complex way of life that is metropolitan in scope.

Standard Metropolitan Statistical Areas

A metropolitan area can be defined in a variety of ways, but the definition that has become rather widely accepted and used is the one established by the United States Bureau of the Census in its inventories of large urban agglomerations. A basic unit of such studies is one the bureau calls its *Standard Metropolitan Statistical Area* (SMSA) and defines as

a county or group of contiguous counties which contains at least one city of 50,000 inhabitants or more, or twin cities with a combined population of at least 50,000. In addition to the county or counties containing such a city or cities, contiguous counties are included in an SMSA if, according to certain criteria, they are socially and economically integrated with the central county.

The population living in SMSAs is designated as the metropolitan population. The population is subdivided as "inside central city or cities" and "outside central city or cities." The population living outside SMSAs constitutes the nonmetropolitan population (U.S. Bureau of the Census, 1970. For a complete listing of the criteria used to define such SMSAs, refer to Bureau of the Budget Publication, Standard Metropolitan Statistical Areas, 1967, U.S. Government Printing Office, Washington, D.C. 20402).

There are a total of 243 SMSAs in the United States, ranging in size from New York, with 11,571,899 inhabitants, to Meri-

den, Connecticut, with 55,959 inhabitants (Fig. 12–6). And, as depicted in Figure 12–7 on a state-by-state basis, about 68.6 percent of the country's total population resides in SMSAs. Most SMSAs have larger populations living outside their central cities than within them; New York is an outstanding exception. The contiguous counties commonly known as the New York City metro-

FIGURE 12–5

A view of Houston, Texas, which has recently mushroomed into one of the largest urban centers of the United States. (Houston Chamber of Commerce)

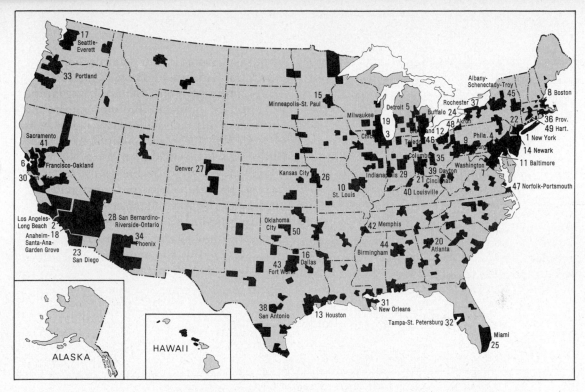

FIGURE 12–6

The Standard Metropolitan Statistical Areas (SMSAs) of the United States. There are 243 in total; the top 50, as ranked by population, are named on the map (space allowing) and listed, with their 1970 populations, in the table below.

1 New York, N.Y.	11,571,899	26 Kansas City, Mo.–Kans.	1,253,916
2 Los Angeles–Long Beach, Calif.	7,032,075	27 Denver, Colo.	1,227,529
3 Chicago, Ill.	6,978,947	28 San Bernardino–Riverside–Ontario, Calif.	1,143,146
4 Philadelphia, Pa.–N.J.	4,817,914	29 Indianapolis, Ind.	1,109,882
5 Detroit, Mich.	4,199,931	30 San Jose, Calif.	1,064,714
6 San Francisco–Oakland, Calif.	3,109,519	31 New Orleans, La.	1,045,809
7 Washington, D.C.–Md.–Va.	2,861,123	32 Tampa–St. Petersburg, Fla.	1,012,594
8 Boston, Mass.	2,753,700	33 Portland, Oreg.–Wash.	1,009,129
9 Pittsburgh, Pa.	2,401,245	34 Phoenix, Ariz.	967,522
10 St. Louis, Mo.–Ill.	2,363,017	35 Columbus, Ohio	916,228
11 Baltimore, Md.	2,070,670	36 Providence–Pawtucket–Warwick, R.I.–Mass.	910,781
12 Cleveland, Ohio	2,064,194	37 Rochester, N.Y.	882,667
13 Houston, Tex.	1,985,031	38 San Antonio, Tex.	864,014
14 Newark, N.J.	1,856,556	39 Dayton, Ohio	850,266
15 Minneapolis–St. Paul, Minn.	1,813,647	40 Louisville, Ky.–Ind.	826,553
16 Dallas, Tex.	1,555,950	41 Sacramento, Calif.	800,592
17 Seattle–Everett, Wash.	1,421,869	42 Memphis, Tenn.–Ark.	770,120
18 Anaheim–Santa Ana–Garden Grove, Calif.	1,420,386	43 Fort Worth, Tex.	762,086
19 Milwaukee, Wis.	1,403,688	44 Birmingham, Ala.	739,274
20 Atlanta, Ga.	1,390,164	45 Albany–Schenectady–Troy, N.Y.	721,910
21 Cincinnati, Ohio–Ky.–Ind.	1,384,851	46 Toledo, Ohio–Mich.	692,571
22 Paterson–Clifton–Passaic, N.J.	1,358,794	47 Norfolk–Portsmouth, Va.	680,600
23 San Diego, Calif.	1,357,854	48 Akron, Ohio	679,239
24 Buffalo, N.Y.	1,349,211	49 Hartford, Conn.	663,891
25 Miami, Fla.	1,267,792	50 Oklahoma City, Okla.	640,889

politan area represent so large a "population pack" that they are no longer considered a single SMSA within the criteria of the Bureau of the Census. The Newark and Paterson–Clifton–Passaic areas, though contiguous to the New York SMSA, do not maintain an economic integration with New York City sufficient to warrant their inclusion in that SMSA. In 1970 the high-population belt, or megalopolis, extending from Boston to Washington, D.C., included one-fifth of the country's total population (or 37.8 million people) and 43 contiguous SMSAs—all within 450 miles north to south and 150 miles east to west. Seven of these 43 SMSAs have a

population in excess of 1 million: New York, Philadelphia, Washington, Boston, Baltimore, Newark, and the Paterson–Clifton–Passaic area of New Jersey (see Fig. 8–5).

A system of SMSAs based on counties —in all areas, that is, except New England, where town and city lines are used—is somewhat arbitrary, to be sure, but in many instances it offers definite statistical convenience. Most important, since more and more urban areas include more than one city, it reflects the real distribution and concentration of urban populations more accurately than would a relatively restricted system based on municipal boundaries.

FIGURE 12–7

State populations in Standard Metropolitan Statistical Areas. Approximately seven out of every ten Americans (68.6 percent) live in SMSAs.

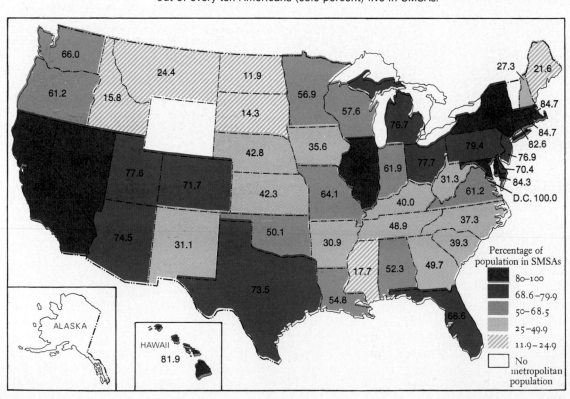

FIGURE 12–8

Commuting by subway in New York City during rush hour. (Sam Falk from Monkmeyer)

Emerging Patterns of Metropolitan Life

The Transportation Tangle

Commuting. That which determines a settlement's form and cohesion is almost exclusively the product of its spatial linkage systems, and the constant movement of people within such systems has become a predominant characteristic of life in contemporary metropolitan areas. In a bygone age most people lived within a short walking distance of their places of employment, but today a very high percentage of urban dwellers have to commute to their places of work (Fig. 12–8).

Among this high number of commuters the majority travel each workday from residences in outlying areas to a central business district; some journey to businesses or factories located in more remote areas; and a few actually go from one metropolitan area to another. In many cases the distances involved are as much as 100 miles each way—although, since expressways and high-speed trains and planes are often employed by commuters, daily commuting distances have come to be measured more in terms of travel time than miles. Commuting has become a necessary evil imposed upon hundreds of thousands of urbanites, and those who must spend an hour or more traveling to work can amass years of unproductive effort before they reach retirement age.

In certain metropolitan centers, among them New York, Paris, and Moscow, commuter trains, subways, and other means of public transit figure prominently in helping people get to and from work; in Los Angeles, and other sprawling cities, and especially in the developing areas of the world where the automobile is just becoming commonly

295

FIGURE 12–9

A phalanx of automobiles surrounding a suburban shopping center in Maryland. (The National Observer)

available, the private car is the primary means of local transportation (Fig. 12–9). In still other centers, such as New Delhi and Saigon, a significant number of commuters rely on motorscooters and bicycles.

So much movement by so many people and vehicles has created huge transportation problems for metropolitan areas. The mere task of getting people from one place to another has become a herculean undertaking. The number one culprit, especially in regard to commuting, seems to be the automobile. It is not only expensive to operate and often inefficiently used but also constitutes one of the primary sources of urban air pollution.

During almost any period of the day— but especially within the morning and evening rush hours—automobile traffic in metropolitan areas can become so congested that

it slows to bullock-cart speed, if not to a standstill; what vehicular movement occurs is often no faster than walking (Fig. 12–10). Airplane traffic around many large cities is also problematic, for, even in good weather, planes must frequently circle a major airport for an hour or more before landing space becomes available. The result is delay and aggravation, and the surfeit of cars, trucks, buses, trains, and airplanes in such relatively small areas imposes a severe strain not only on the nerves but the pocketbook as well. Obviously there is an urgent need for the development of more rapid and more efficient means of transporting people and goods between and within metropolitan areas.

Some Traffic Solutions. The solution to the problem of traffic congestion most frequently put forth is the building of more and bigger expressways. And such construction has been employed successfully in some instances; however, with the constant increase in the number of vehicles in use, the improved conditions it brings never seem to last—particularly in regard to intracity traffic. Furthermore, the proponents of such solutions rarely take into consideration their effects on other aspects of the urban system. Inevitably such construction involves the destruction of historic landmarks and other distinctive buildings, the displacing of people and businesses, and the waste of valuable acreage (Fig. 12–11). The cost in money and human comfort can be enormous, and there is rarely an opportunity for adequate repay-

ment. Increasingly expensive to construct and maintain, expressways and parking facilities often deplete public funds still further by causing at least a temporary decrease in the tax revenues from the land they occupy.

And, of course, if remedial construction is undertaken, it should be based on an accurate analysis of the reasons for the traffic congestion. A major portion of intracity traffic—sometimes as much as one-fourth—consists of vehicles that are only passing through the central business district on their way to other places. To combat this element of the traffic problem, bypasses and loops have been built around some cities, thereby allowing vehicles to skirt the central business district if it

FIGURE 12–10

A traffic jam in Paris. (M. H. Kellicutt, EPA)

FIGURE 12–11

The striated pattern of vehicular facilities—expressways, roads, and parking lots—in a section of Los Angeles. Single-purpose and often vacant, such highway and parking areas represent a relatively unproductive use of urban land. (California Division of Highways)

is not their destination. However, even after circular expressways, or "inner loops," as they are commonly called, have been built and much of this transient traffic is diverted from the city, the problem of controlling the central city's remaining vehicular traffic still requires a solution.

As a step toward this solution, many people argue for more extensive and more efficient means of public transportation. Their contention is that car owners might be persuaded to use trains, subways, and buses on trips to the city if these facilities offered faster and less expensive travel than the automobile can provide. Acting on this principle and following the lead of several other cities, Washington, D.C., has built a rapid transit system based on the "park-and-ride" concept: motorists from the suburbs are encouraged to leave their cars at parking lots just outside the city and continue their trip to the central business district on public transportation. Various other cities around the world are attempting to create or modernize rapid transit systems of their own. Such schemes, however, are usually shortchanged, and greater emphasis is still being placed on the automobile. For example, Hong Kong has recently completed a four-lane submarine tunnel for automobile traffic between Hong Kong Island and Kowloon. Even though this expensive project was intended, in part, to relieve the pressure on the cross-harbor ferries, it is not having the success imagined, because overall traffic increases already tax its capacity.

Future technology may offer more comprehensive solutions to the traffic problem. Many promising new rapid transit systems are already on the drawing board. However, total solutions are not likely to be achieved through the use of new machinery alone. Much depends on proper planning and the coordination of transportation systems with all other aspects of life in metropolitan areas.

Urban Renewal

As urban centers age, their structures and facilities tend to become run-down or outdated and as a result need to be renewed. Most *urban renewal* projects, to date, have focused on the inner portions of their respective metropolitan areas. Even though these sections usually occupy less than 5 percent of the total land area of the agglomeration, they frequently contain as much as 30 percent of its total population. They are also usually the areas with the greatest needs, having been neglected during the years in which rapid growth and modernization were occurring in the suburbs.

Generally speaking, it is in the older parts of the inner city that one finds substandard housing and schools and other structures in a state of disrepair; the number of slums increases; public utilities are insufficient; narrow streets cannot handle the dense traffic; and there are few open spaces or recreational facilities. With rural people continuing to pour into cities, the pressures on urban housing are intensifying; this is especially true in the developing countries. Here millions of people, recently rural but now knocking on the door of urbanization, live in shanty towns consisting of crude shacks and other dwellings that barely provide shelter (Fig. 12–12). In the more advanced nations, most people are somewhat better housed. But even in these countries, too high a percentage of the housing is poorly constructed, run-down, or unsanitary; the poor and disadvantaged end up living in these dehumanizing environments.

FIGURE 12–12

A hillside slum, or *favela*, in Rio de Janeiro, Brazil—one that overlooks portions of the city's fashionable Copacabana beachfront section. (Paul Conklin from Monkmeyer)

Long overdue, effective work on many urban problems has at last been started worldwide. The job involves both the private and public sectors, and governments all over the world have initiated a variety of programs to rid their countries of substandard housing, replace unsatisfactory streets, and update commercial areas and industrial facilities—all in an attempt to create more modern and livable communities (Fig. 12–13). In the United States, for example, it was not until the Federal Housing Act of 1949 was passed that urban renewal was conducted on a firm financial base. Only then were large sums of federal money available for the renewing of old urban areas, and only with such sums can the job be approached on the scale necessary for success. In the last three decades, the degree of government involvement in urban renewal has varied from total responsibility, as in Cuba and the Soviet Union, to the complicated inducements to the private sector by federal, state, and local government in the United States. But whether communist, socialist, or capitalist, countries are making a growing commitment to meet the need.

In some cases the areas in need of renewal are totally chaotic in design and obsolete in construction, necessitating a complete overhaul. In other instances the problems are much less severe and thus require less extreme measures. The different types of urban renewal can be divided into three broad cat-

FIGURE 12–13

In the distance, the construction of a union members' housing project on the Lower West Side of Manhattan. (Magnum)

egories: conservation, redevelopment, and rehabilitation.

Conservation. Conservation projects generally necessitate no major changes in land use. The areas involved are usually not yet blighted, and the work required may involve nothing more than local clean-up campaigns and stricter enforcement of zoning laws and building and health codes. The objective is to encourage people to take pride in their communities through the proper upkeep and maintenance of their houses, stores, and other buildings and facilities. By putting the emphasis on slum prevention, this type of urban renewal project generally requires relatively little expenditure of public funds, and it can go a long way in strengthening community spirit.

Redevelopment. Redevelopment is a much more extensive type of urban renewal. It involves already blighted areas and usually necessitates, therefore, the total redesign of very large tracts of land and even whole neighborhoods. Some parts of a metropolitan area may be completely torn down and then redesigned and rebuilt to accommodate new land-use patterns.

When entire slum areas are cleared away, they are frequently replaced by more profitable office buildings, cultural facilities, condominiums, or apartment complexes. Many of the high-rise apartment complexes are designed to be self-sufficient and include a variety of stores, restaurants, and facilities for entertainment and recreation—all intended to reduce the dehumanizing qualities frequently associated with this kind of residence. Main Place in the business district of Dallas, Lake Meadows in Chicago, and the Civic Center in downtown Los Angeles are all examples of redevelopment projects designed to redevelop blighted areas and bring them into the twentieth century (Fig. 12–14).

Although urban renewal in this form is a step in the right direction, some people question whether its benefits outweigh its disadvantages. Redevelopment all too frequently involves the elimination of historic landmarks, the dislocation of a great many people and shops, and very high costs. When a slum is to be torn down and its residents relocated, there is frequently not enough low-income housing available nearby to accommodate them; even promises that they will be accepted into public housing are usually very slowly fulfilled. Furthermore, the simple fact of being forced to move and live in a different and unfamiliar environment tends to put a severe physical and psychological strain on people, especially the elderly. Inevitably, too, along with poor housing, redevelopment eliminates the jobs of many area residents.

Social critics of urban redevelopment thus claim that it has done relatively little to help the poor and even less to correct patterns of segregation and discrimination. Further, they argue that those who have benefited the most have been the big land developers.

Rehabilitation. Another approach to urban renewal is the rehabilitation of aging buildings—a procedure that precludes the permanent relocation of their tenants. In slum areas earmarked for rehabilitation rather than redevelopment, the basic structure of most of the buildings is solid enough to remain and can absorb the installation of such improvements as new electrical wiring, fast elevators, modern plumbing, and the like. Only occasionally is there the need to tear down a structure, and then an attempt is made to replace it with a new structure that serves the same purpose; for example, a small corner grocery store is replaced by a modern supermarket. Such attempts at renovation have been carried out in various parts of the

FIGURE 12–14

Urban renewal in downtown Los Angeles. Scores of delapidated buildings in this area have been demolished in recent years in order to make way for new constructions (mainly additional public facilities on the scale of the music center, which includes the flattop in the center of the photograph) and for improved roads and highways. (PFI, © Charles Rotkin)

United States: Wooster Square in New Haven and Society Hill in Philadelphia are but two of many examples. Although such rehabilitation projects tend to cause only minimal disruption to a neighborhood and sometimes greatly improve community spirit, their overall rate of success has been lower than expected.

Whichever of these three broad types of urban renewal is used the overriding goal is to increase the comfort and efficiency of the environment for its residents as well as others. Many municipal governments hope that by reversing the decline of the central city areas, they will attract affluent people and businesses back to these areas from the suburbs. Already a significant number of suburbanites, encouraged in part by the rising cost of suburban living, are resettling in the central city. This flight to the city is particularly popular among young business and professional people; many buy town houses in such areas as Washington's Georgetown or Cincinnati's Mount Adams area and then make improvements to suit their own tastes and pocketbook. Some come so they can live close to their work; others want to be able to draw readily upon the city's cultural resources; and others simply enjoy the stimulation of the urban environment. Thus, the appeal of the city persists; after all, it is the cradle of civilization—however uncivilized it may seem.

Most urban renewal programs have been qualified successes. Many people feel that the returns would be much greater if the approach were more comprehensive—for example, metropolitan rather than local. Focusing haphazardly on different sections of a city, rather than planning the revitalization of the whole metropolitan area at once, has frequently meant a lack of coordination in execution and a less than efficient product. Part of the reason for the continuance of the piecemeal approach is, of course, the sheer size of most metropolitan areas; but a more fundamental problem is the fact that most city governments have fragmented jurisdictional authority and as a result there is an urgent need for a comprehensive metropolitan government structure. It is to this need that people must address themselves in the future.

Metropolitan Management

In every country of the world, the task of urban management is becoming more and more complex. City governments are finding it increasingly difficult to operate adequate

urban renewal programs; police, fire, and sanitation services; educational institutions; health and welfare programs; public recreational facilities; and the host of other basic necessities they are expected to provide. Rising numbers of people, inadequate funds, fragmentation and lack of authority, and conflicting areas of jurisdiction are among the major causes of the current crises in urban administration.

The ever-increasing growth of urban populations means that local governments must provide more and more services—and usually at higher and higher costs per unit. The problem is intensified by the fact that, although they lose tax income as affluent residents move to the suburbs, municipal governments must still provide such services as roads and parking facilities for a growing number of commuters and visitors, as well as increased welfare benefits for the low-income people who continue to settle in the cities. To aggravate the problem even further, many of the cities with the greatest needs are also the ones that have the highest proportions of tax-exempt property.

Local governments attempt to increase their tax base in various ways but to little avail. In desperation they have been turning with increasing frequency to federal and state governments for financial support. But, despite federal and state aid, local governments continue to face a serious financial crisis.

Hierarchical Delegation of Authority. The political authority of local governments is delegated from a higher level of government, and the degree of authority granted varies from country to country. Most cities in continental Europe, though subject to the regulations of regional governments, exercise considerable freedom in local matters. In the Orient, state and national governments have tended to retain more control over local governmental units. And in communist countries the centralization of authority is almost total.

In the United States, the federal system predominates. City governments, as is sometimes forgotten, are legally created by the states. Since no reference to local government is made in the United States Constitution, the states have assumed the right to establish and empower whatever forms of local administration suit them. The city's right to adopt its own *charter,* or constitution, and its degree of *home rule,* or autonomy, are defined by the state legislature. Until recently, most states retained fairly tight control over their cities. Until 1962, for instance, state law gave the governor of Massachusetts the right to appoint the police chief of the city of Boston. More recent revisions of the law in such states as Connecticut, Florida, Illinois, and Michigan have all increased significantly the powers of local government. Yet, most state executives and legislatures still retain broad authority over city policy matters, including the nature and rate of local taxation. Undoubtedly, such supervision has its advantages; but it also tends to put local officials, especially mayors, in a kind of legal straitjacket—they have tremendous responsibility but little power.

Fragmented Jurisdiction. Most metropolitan areas are managed by a multitude of local governmental units. In Chicago's Cook County alone, for instance, there are over 1,000 separate and independent governing units. This multiplicity of authority appears to be a characteristic of metropolitan growth. The various units within a metropolitan area may include city, county, and township governments, and, in certain instances, school districts and other special districts and agencies as well. Each one of these local governmental units tends to be concerned only with its own problems and attempts to solve

them, without regard for the welfare of the general area. Moreover, neighboring localities are usually in fierce competition for such assets as recreational space, industry, and residents able to pay taxes.

None of these administrative units has authority over the entire metropolitan area. Consequently, in most cases there is no single governmental body to deal comprehensively with areawide problems, such as control of water supplies, zoning regulations, pollution, sanitation, transportation, or civil defense. This lack of coordination puts a severe handicap on the orderly development of metropolitan regions as a whole.

Of course, some attempts have been made at coordinated metropolitan planning and administration, but generally on a very restricted basis. There are special administrative districts that provide for fire protection, garbage collection, sewage disposal, soil conservation, and park management. In addition, special intergovernmental "authorities" control the construction and operation of such facilities as harbors and airports; notable among them is the New York Port Authority, a tristate agency that oversees the New York metropolitan area's bridges, tunnels, and transportation terminals.

Metropolitan Government. Many argue that a far more promising way to handle the problems of large urban areas is to institute metropolitan governments. Crossing present political boundaries where necessary, each of these governments would be responsible for an entire metropolitan area's police protection, water supply, transportation system, civil defense, pollution control, and other services that seem to be most efficiently administered by an areawide authority. A few metropolitan governments have already been established—in Toronto; Nashville; and Dade County (Miami), Florida. So far, reaction to most of these experiments has been mixed. While some form of centralization is no doubt desirable, the metropolitan government is hardly a panacea. No single administrative unit can hope to deal effectively with the diverse problems of the hundreds of local communities that comprise the largest metropolitan areas, such as New York, Los Angeles, London, Tokyo, Shanghai, and Buenos Aires. In some ways it could even help to further intensify and aggravate existing problems. In many of these centers, indeed, the proposals most often heard are for decentralization of the already cumbersome and impersonal municipal bureaucracies. The ideal, probably, would be a balance between the two.

Planned Urban Land Use

The use of land in an urban environment does not have to proceed haphazardly, with little thought to the needs of the people living and working there. Instead, urban growth and development can be accomplished in a sane, orderly, and humane manner through proper planning and supervision.

Although only recently recognized as a distinct discipline, *urban planning,* in at least a rudimentary form, is believed to be as old as the urban revolution itself (Fig. 12–15). For the most part, however, the history of urbanism and urban growth has been devoid

FIGURE 12–15

Among the excavated ruins of Mohenjo-Daro, the Great Bath, a centrally located, brick construction that was served by the 4,500-year-old city's elaborate drainage system, one not equalled until Roman times. (© Frances Mortimer from Rapho/Photo Researchers)

of planning in the modern sense of the word. Until quite recently, the majority of urban planning was limited to such matters as the design of street patterns and housing blocks.

Most urban growth has thus occurred on a hit-or-miss basis. With this unplanned development have come increasingly polluted, crowded, and, in the opinions of some, ugly and difficult environments in which people must live and work.

Planning for Today's Needs. In response to this situation there has been a major rebirth in urban planning within the last several decades. Concern for the quality of urban life is finally coming of age. People are now beginning to realize that, if civilization is to survive, conservation principles must be applied not only to the natural environment but to the artificial environment as well. Nearly all the world's major cities have some kind of urban planning program, and in some of the larger centers—such as Paris, Tokyo, Rio de Janeiro, and Toronto—there are permanent and well-staffed urban planning departments.

In the United States the job is normally done by a city planning commission, which, in most cases, functions as an advisor to the local governing body. The membership of such a commission usually includes municipal officials and concerned citizens appointed by the mayor or the city manager. The product of the commission's deliberations is frequently a master plan, or a series of maps, graphs, and reports, suggesting procedures for the orderly development of the community. Since planning on this scale involves countless variables, such plans are constantly undergoing revision.

Planning Procedure. Before a master plan can be judged adequate to meet the needs of a community, certain well-defined objectives must be established. These objectives should be arrived at only after a thorough inventory has been made of the community's existing structures, other assets, and socioeconomic patterns. Realistic planning for the effective use of any area should also be based upon a complete inventory of regional assets and possibilities.

Furthermore, planning must be an ongoing process; the various environmental factors, both physical and cultural, are continually changing. Thus the effective master plan for land use is flexible and allows for needed alterations without substantial loss. Indeed, many of the current difficulties associated with various areas have resulted from perpetuation of outdated master plans.

Methods of Implementation. Once a plan that suits its objectives has been devised and accepted, a city government must decide which of the many legal methods at its disposal will best effect the changes the plan recommends. One of the government's chief tools in this regard is its right to establish zoning regulations, statutes that limit the ways in which land can be used and the type, height, and size of the structures built in a given area (Fig. 12–16). Zoning has its limitations, but it has been reasonably successful in helping to avoid undesirable mixes of such facilities as factories, stores, junkyards, and residences.

Local governments also have the right of *eminent domain,* or the authority to purchase at a "fair" price private property they wish to devote to such public facilities as roads, schools, municipal administration buildings, parks, and public housing. An *easement,* or the right to develop a piece of land without actually having to own it, may also be used by local authorities.

Urban Space. There are a great many ways in which to add beauty, recreational opportunities, and a sense of open

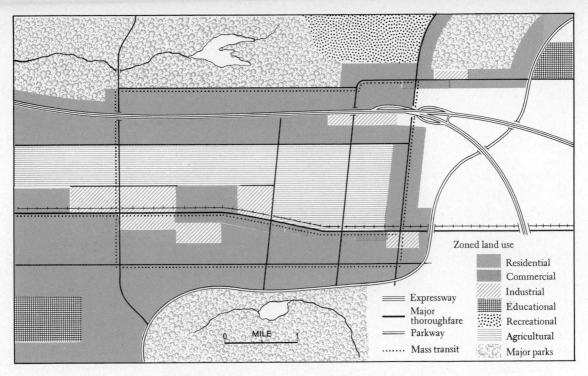

FIGURE 12–16

A simplified zoning map depicting a portion of a hypothetical urban community.

space to densely crowded sections of metropolitan areas. Several cities have successfully retained relatively large areas of land and used them for parks: New York's Central and Prospect parks, Los Angeles's Griffith Park, London's Hyde and Regent parks, and Moscow's Gorki Park of Culture and Rest are examples. However, parks need not be large to be effective. Many small and confined areas have recently been transformed into attractive meeting and resting places known as vest-pocket parks.

In the last few decades, large cities have also encouraged the proliferation of malls and plazas furnished with water fountains, pools, greenery, and sculpture (Fig. 12–17). Since open space at ground level is often in short supply, many cities have also promoted the development of rooftops as gardens and recreation, dining, or shopping facilities.

Still another approach to improving the aesthetics of a city is the designation of greenbelts—that is, wide tracts of land zoned for limited development. Devoid of factories and residences, a series of greenbelts can provide a metropolitan area with a refreshing contrast to its otherwise gray and drab landscape. London and Vienna are among the cities that make use of greenbelts quite successfully.

The construction of public buildings in clusters known as civic centers has been a popular trend among urban planners within recent decades; however, the basic idea is centuries old. It represents an attempt to make public offices and auditoriums aesthetically pleasing and convenient to a maximum number of people, as well as cheaper to construct and maintain. Washington, D.C., Cleveland, Denver, and San Francisco have

FIGURE 12-17

Some planned urban open places. Top left, a vest-pocket park in midtown Manhattan. (Helen Faye) Top right, an outdoor shopping mall in Kalamazoo, Michigan. (*Kalamazoo Gazette*) Bottom left, an enclosed shopping mall in Columbia, Maryland. (© Jerry Watcher, Baltimore) Bottom right, Crystal Court, an interior shopping center in the Investors Diversified Service Tower, Minneapolis, Minnesota. (Hedrich-Blessing, Chicago)

all helped to pioneer the way in this respect.

Many urban planners also endorse a greater utilization of the space below street level. Subterranean malls and arcades, they contend, can house a vast array of facilities, including shops, restaurants, offices, and theaters, as well as walkways that allow pedestrians to avoid the hazards of moving through heavy street-level traffic. Several European cities, especially Stockholm, have for some time been involved in this sort of subterranean planning and thus have served as models for similar efforts in other parts of the world.

Nature areas, civic centers, and subterranean malls are just some of the important types of "in-city" projects suggested by contemporary planners interested in humanizing metropolitan areas (Fig. 12–18). The type

of "out-of-city" project most often promoted by like-minded people is the creation of New Towns.

Planned New Towns

In an effort to solve some of the problems created by established urban centers, particularly the large metropolises, recognized regional planners and others have been encouraging the acceptance of the *new town* concept, which assumes that many urban problems can be avoided if a settlement is properly and thoroughly planned before it is constructed. Ideally, the planned new town is neither totally urban nor totally rural but blends the socioeconomic advantages of metropolitan life with the spaciousness and beauty of the countryside.

FIGURE 12–18

A subterranean shopping arcade in Stockholm, Sweden. (Swedish Information Service)

FIGURE 12–19

Columbia, Maryland, a new town planned with thought to harmonizing cultural elements and the natural environment. (Monkmeyer)

The new town has become a significant phenomenon in the United States only recently. Some of the new towns in existence in the eastern part of the United States include Reston, Virginia, and Columbia and Germantown, Maryland—all three located within 25 miles of Washington, D.C. (Fig. 12–19). In the Midwest are the new towns of Jonathan, Minnesota, situated about 20 miles south of Minneapolis, and Park Forest South, Illinois, which lies just outside of Chicago.

The number of such communities in the United States is still quite small, but, with growing support for the new-town concept, it is expected to increase significantly in the near future. A recent report by the National Committee on Urban Growth Policy recommends that federal funds be used to support the creation, by the year 2000, of 100 new towns with populations of about 100,000 persons and another 10 new towns with populations under 1 million.

Interest in these new urban forms is growing not only in the United States but in many other countries around the world, where new towns have often been a part of the post–World War II rebuilding. Examples include the new town of Evry, France, which is located just outside of Paris; Kortedala, Sweden, near the city of Göteborg; Sha Tin, Hong Kong, near Kowloon; and El Rosario, Mexico, north of Mexico City. The communities of Brasilia, Canberra, and Chandigarh are all fairly recently designed capitals, in the countries of Brazil, Australia, and the Indian state of Punjab, respectively (Fig. 12–20). Some of the most imaginative and successful new towns can be found in Great Britain,

FIGURE 12-20

Brasilia, the new modern capital of Brazil. (Pictorial Parade)

among them Cumbernauld, Livingston, Harlow, Stevenage, Crawley, and Letchworth (Fig. 12–21). This is only natural, though, since it was here in Great Britain that the idea of new towns originated.

More specifically, the concept of the new town was born in England in the early years of this century, when town planner Ebenezer Howard proposed his "Garden City." Howard's city became a reality with the construction of Letchworth (1903) and was later the basis for Welwyn (1920), both towns located about 30 miles north of London (Fig. 12–22). This new type of settlement

(in which each house has a garden) was intended to combine the differing advantages of urban life and rural life and thereby provide a more balanced and wholesome environment than either the established city or the country.

Howard and other early promoters of his idea recognized that there is a population range beyond which such optimum communities become impossible, and thus they chose to set a maximum limit of about 30,000 inhabitants for each of their new communities; this figure is still generally accepted as a demarcation between urban coordination and urban unmanageability. Further, each new community was to be surrounded by a greenbelt, a permanent reserve of open country used only for agricultural or recreational purposes. It was hoped that, by limiting the area in which construction was permitted, the indiscriminate use of valuable crop land would be avoided and the natural beauty of the countryside would be preserved.

It was from these early English models that the modern version of the new town evolved. Usually part of a comprehensive regional plan, the typical post–World War II new town is located some distance outside an established urban center; however, there are some instances in which new towns are located within metropolitan areas and function as satellite towns or suburbs. By providing needed housing and jobs, modern new towns have been able to handle some of the problems associated with the overflow of population from major urban centers. Many new towns have been quite successful in at-

FIGURE 12–21

Stevenage, England, one of the many new towns in Great Britain. (*The Times*, London, from Pictorial Parade)

tracting industry, business, and commerce—thereby further increasing job opportunities and strengthening the position of the towns as growth points for the surrounding region.

New Town Design. Goals other than decentralization and land conservation have also been given high priority in the design of new towns. For, to be lastingly successful, a new town should be able to accommodate growth and change without undue disruption. Thus, at least in the planning of these settlements, care is taken to balance total population with the level of community employment opportunities and social services. Optimally, each new town is a compact, self-contained entity in which the need for long-distance commuting is minimized or even entirely eliminated and residents are provided with schools; medical centers; markets; police, fire, and ambulance service; parks and playgrounds; and community centers. Planners also seek to enhance the aesthetic qualities of such environ-

FIGURE 12–22

The new-town movement in Great Britain. Left, new and expanding towns in the London region. Right, new towns in England, Wales, and Scotland.

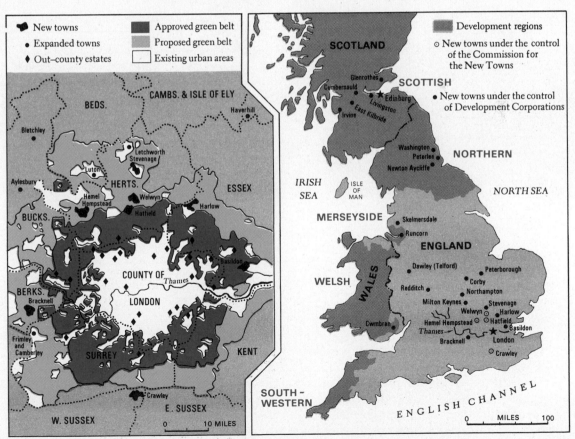

FIGURE 12-23

Southwest over Roosevelt Island, which is located in New York's East River between the boroughs of Manhattan and Queens. Occupied until recently mainly by a few old farmhouses, hospitals, and a prison, the island is now the site of a modern housing development that seeks to combine apartment living and easy access to open land and recreational facilities. (Roosevelt Island Development Corp.)

ments—for instance, by avoiding the eyesore of rooftop antennas and utility poles. Perhaps most important, most town planners make a conscious effort to harmonize permanent artificial features with the natural environment.

So far, planners have only been able to come close to achieving some of their goals;

none of the existing new towns is ideal. Some critics claim, for instance, that the new communities look too much alike and that they are lacking in color, character, and social facilities; others point out that there is usually an insufficient number and range of jobs and thus a widespread need to commute. Obviously, much more imaginative work must be done by planners and civic leaders before the ideal community can become a reality.

Future Urban Design

To think of the vast possibilities that lie ahead in urban design is a most challenging pursuit (Fig. 12–23). If history is a proper guide, the prospects for the world's urban landscape appear to be centered on a pattern of rise and decline; some urban centers will decline and perhaps even die (become defunct), while others will continue to grow. Further, while some future urban developments may be totally new, most urban growth will occur around sites already established as urban centers.

Given the population explosion, a continuing growth in both the population and the areal extent of most metropolises is inevitable. The United Nations World Health Organization predicts that, by the year 2000, the world's total urban population will nearly triple in size, from the present estimated total of about 1.5 billion to over 4 billion. In this same period, the number of urban dwellers in the United States, about 150 million in 1970, is expected to nearly double, to somewhere around 250 million. A significant percentage of this additional urban population is expected to live in the larger urban centers. This will mean that, for many newcomers to already overcrowded cities, the move will be literally upwards; for

ever-increasing population will bring about the construction of more and taller skyscrapers, even in areas where they now are prohibited. This utilization of vertical space will no doubt bring about many societal changes; for one, much of the home-to-office commuting done in the next century may require only an elevator, with many future skyscrapers including both offices and apartments as well as shopping and health facilities.

However, trends in the United States since 1970 indicate that most of the expected increase in the nation's population will concentrate not in the cities but in the suburbs. As a result, many predict that the most likely basic urban form of the future will be horizontal, with a rather poorly defined nucleus, suggesting the present configuration of Los Angeles. Most people, it seems, prefer to live in detached houses that have a bit of open land associated with them.

As cities and their suburbs continue to expand they will eventually coalesce, forming replicas of the megalopolises that already exist in several parts of the world; these current ones will also expand. It is very possible, for example, that by the year 2000 the megalopolis along the northeastern seaboard of the United States will grow to include such midwestern cities as Chicago and Detroit. Thus, for better or for worse, the megalopolis will probably become the dominant unit of urban development for generations to come —not only in the United States but throughout the world.

REVIEW AND DISCUSSION

1. Discuss and evaluate the contention that there is a correlation between degree of urbanization and level of socioeconomic development.
2. Explain, in general terms, the difference between *urbanization* and the *growth of cities*. Evaluate the geographic significance of these two concepts.

3. Within your own frame of reference, what are the principal causes and consequences of the phenomenal growth of cities in recent decades?

4. What is a Standard Metropolitan Statistical Area? What is its value in urban analysis?

5. Identify and evaluate, in as much detail as possible, the three major types of urban renewal.

6. Describe, in as much detail as possible, the structure and operation of the city government under which you live or by which you are most often affected.

7. What seems to be the reasons for the recent rebirth of urban planning? What problems were created by the trial-and-error approach to urban development commonly used in the past?

8. Discuss and evaluate: some of the legal methods by which city governments can implement their master developmental plans, and some of the ways in which beauty, recreational opportunities, and a sense of openness can be added to metropolitan areas.

9. Explain, in general terms, the basic assumptions inherent in the *new town* concept. Discuss the origin and diffusion of new towns on a worldwide basis and evaluate their impact and record of success.

10. What do you envision will be the major changes in urban design during the next several decades? Through what means are these changes likely to occur?

SELECTED REFERENCES

Adams, R. McC. *The Evolution of Urban Society*. Chicago: Aldine, 1966.

Babcock, R. *The Zoning Game*. Madison: University of Wisconsin Press, 1966.

Blumenfeld, H., and P. D. Spreiregen, eds. *The Modern Metropolis: Its Origins, Growth, Characteristics, and Planning*. Cambridge: Massachusetts Institute of Technology Press, 1967.

Borchert, J. R. "American Metropolitan Evolution." *Geographical Review,* Vol. 57 (July 1967), 301–32.

Chapin, F. S., Jr. *Urban Land Use Planning*. Urbana: University of Illinois Press, 1965.

Down, A. *Urban Problems and Prospects*. Chicago: Markham, 1970.

Eldredge, H. W. *Taming Megalopolis,* 2 vols. New York: Doubleday, 1967.

Gans, H. J. *People and Plans*. New York: Basic Books, 1968.

Goodman, W. I., and E. C. Freund. *Principles and Practice of Urban Planning*. Chicago: International City Managers' Association, 1968.

Gottmann, J. *Megalopolis: The Urbanized Northeastern Seaboard of the United States*. Cambridge: Massachusetts Institute of Technology Press, 1964.

Howard, E. *Garden Cities of Tomorrow*. Cambridge: Massachusetts Institute of Technology Press, 1965.

International Urban Research. *The World's Metropolitan Areas*. Berkeley: University of California Press, 1959.

Linsky, A. S. "Some Generalizations Concerning Primate Cities." *Annals of the Association of American Geographers,* Vol. 55 (September 1965), 506–13.

McGee, T. G. *The Southeast Asian City: A Social Geography of the Primate Cities of Southeast Asia*. New York: Praeger, 1967.

Meyer, J. R., J. F. Kain, and M. Wohl. *The Urban Transportation Problem*. Cambridge, Mass.: Harvard University Press, 1965.

Michelson, W. *Man and His Urban Environment: A Sociological Approach*. Reading, Mass.: Addison-Wesley, 1970.

Milgram, G. *The City Expands: A Study of the Conversion of Land from Rural to Urban Use, Philadelphia, 1945–62.* Philadelphia: Institute for Environmental Studies, University of Pennsylvania, 1967.

Mumford, L. *The Culture of Cities.* New York: Harcourt Brace Jovanovich, 1970.

Muth, R. *Cities and Housing.* Chicago: University of Chicago Press, 1969.

Natoli, S. "Zoning and the Development of Urban Land Use Patterns." *Economic Geography,* Vol. 47 (April 1971), 171–84.

Osborn, F. J., and A. Whittick. *The New Towns: The Answer to Megalopolis.* Cambridge: Massachusetts Institute of Technology Press, 1969.

Owen, W. *The Metropolitan Transportation Problem.* Garden City, N.Y.: Doubleday, 1966.

Perloff, H. "New Towns Intown." *Journal of the American Institute of Planners,* Vol. 32 (May 1966), 155–61.

Putnam, R. G., F. J. Taylor, and P. G. Kettle, eds. *A Geography of Urban Places.* Toronto: Methuen, 1970.

Schaffer, F. *The New Town Story.* London: MacGibbon and Kee, 1970.

Simmons, J. W. "Changing Residence in the City: A Review of Intra-Urban Mobility." *Geographical Review,* Vol. 58 (October 1968), 622–51.

Stouffer, S. A. "Intervening Opportunities and Competing Migrants." *Journal of Regional Science,* Vol. 2 (Spring 1960), 1–26.

Strole, L. "Urbanization and Mental Health: Some Formulations." *American Scientist,* Vol. 60 (September–October 1972), 576–83.

Timms, D. W. G. *The Urban Mosaic.* Cambridge, England: Cambridge University Press, 1971.

Vernon, R. *Metropolis 1985.* Cambridge, Mass.: Harvard University Press, 1960.

Wilson, J. Q., ed. *Urban Renewal: The Record and the Controversy.* Cambridge: Massachusetts Institute of Technology Press, 1966.

Sikhs fleeing West Pakistan after the partition of British India.
(Margaret Bourke-White/Time-Life Picture Agency, © Time, Inc.)

13

Population Trends and Spatial Linkages

Since their beginnings, human beings have been very much a part of the natural environment. At first they accepted the bounty of nature as they found it, changing the environment little in satisfying their need for food and physical security. Later, as a means to improved food supplies, they learned to domesticate plants and various animals, and thus were able to make more extensive use of plant and animal products for clothing and shelter. As human groups learned more effective ways of adapting nature to their simple but expanding needs, their own numbers began to increase—sometimes exceeding the largess of the immediate environment. Many groups so taxed their surroundings that it became necessary for some members, or even all, to seek new living sites. Repeated through the millennia, this pressure for more abundant living space eventually brought about the spread of human beings to most of the present habitable world.

It is estimated that, for three million years or more, the number of humans on earth grew very slowly, reaching no more than a quarter billion by the first century A.D. (Fig. 13–1). During the next dozen or more centuries, until about 1650, the number of humans doubled, to approximately one-half billion; by 1830, less than two centuries later, the total had again doubled, giving the world its first billion human population. The population spiral continued to gather momentum, and, by 1925, the human total reached two

FIGURE 13–1

Estimated millennial world populations, from 4000 B.C. to A.D. 2000.

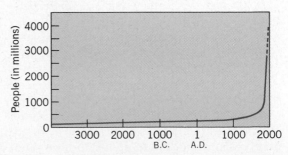

billion; by 1960, three billion; and, by 1975, four. Should this population explosion continue, there will be five billion human beings on the earth by 1985—and close to seven billion by the year 2000, less than a generation from now (Fig. 13–2).

FIGURE 13–2

The accelerating pace of world population increase. Humankind's first 1 billion population required close to 3 million years of human reproduction; the latest 1 billion was added in less than 15 years.

Time periods	World population	Time lapses
3,000,000 B.C.–A.D. 1	Under 250 million	3 million years
A.D. 1–1650	500 million	1,650 years
1650–1830	1 billion	180 years
1830–1925	2 billion	95 years
1925–1960	3 billion	35 years
1960–1975	4 billion	15 years
1975–1985	5 billion	10 years
1985–2000	7 billion	15 years

Population Distribution and Density

The spatial distribution of population over the earth, perhaps the most significant of the major cultural patterns, is, and has always been, extremely uneven. The entire Antarctic continent, as well as many large, isolated islands scattered throughout the oceans and seas, is still virtually uninhabited, while, for instance, the small tropical island of Java supports a population of over 60 million people and Singapore over 2 million—giving these areas statistical densities of 1,000 and 9,000 per square mile, respectively (Plate VII).

The spatial irregularity of human population can be effectively represented by means of a *dot distribution map,* which gives a clear visual impression of gross areal distribution; the right-hand map in Figure 13–3 contains such a graphic device. But a more common and certainly more useful method of representing population distributions and densities is by means of an *isopleth map,* through which one can indicate with greater precision the number of people living on a given unit of land. This is a quantitative approach—showing the ratio of total population to total unit area—and is known as the *arithmetic density,* or *man–land ratio* (Plate VII).

Both of these graphic devices have inherent limitations. The dot map details spatial distribution, but it makes few quantitative distinctions and therefore shows little in the way of man–land ratios. The density map, on the other hand, shows man–land ratios but suggests only generally the actual geographic, or areal, distribution of charted populations. Thus, where possible, the two types of map should be used together to obtain an adequate representation of distribution and density, concepts closely interrelated in all population studies.

Gross Distributions

On either a distribution or a density map of the world's present population, several major regional differences are discernible. First, the vast majority of the world's people is concentrated in the Northern Hemisphere, this owing to the incidence of birth as well as to migration; less than 10 percent of today's population lives in areas south of the equator. Second, the East is more heavily populated than the West; more than 85 percent of humanity lives in the Old World. Still another distributional pattern is discernible in the concentration of population along coastal lowlands and fertile river valleys inland; at least two-thirds of the world's people lives within 300 miles of the sea. The effect of these disparities is that about 80 percent of all the world's people is found within less than one-third of its land area.

Four areas of the world stand out as major population centers: eastern Asia, southern Asia, western Europe, and eastern North America (Fig. 13–4). And these major population centers share certain environmental conditions: moderately level terrain with low elevations, coastal and riverine plains, relatively high to moderate rainfalls, and temperature regimes of considerable range (see Fig. 13–3). Further, they are all major resource production centers.

In marked contrast to these four population centers, many other regions of the world are nearly, or even completely, empty of human beings. They include the vast arctic fringes — where a total human population of only a few thousand people is scattered widely over a landscape five times the areal

FIGURE 13–3

The terrain and population patterns of Japan. Dense populations crowd the small and scattered plains areas, which are favorable to human occupance; whereas, the mountains and hilly areas are sparsely populated.

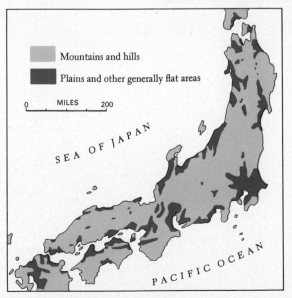

Mountains and hills

Plains and other generally flat areas

MILES 0 200

SEA OF JAPAN

PACIFIC OCEAN

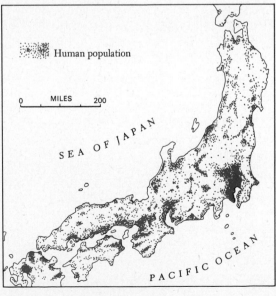

Human population

MILES 0 200

SEA OF JAPAN

PACIFIC OCEAN

FIGURE 13-4

The beach at Coney Island, New York, on a summer's day. This forest of people is temporary, but it is a reminder that individuals in a megalopolis experience overcrowding on a daily basis—in housing, traffic, public transportation, and recreation. (Ben Ross)

extent of India, which contains over 600 million—and the vast continental interiors of South America, northern Africa, central Asia, northern North America, and central Australia.

National Arithmetic Densities

Population density is usually expressed as a ratio derived by dividing the number of people in a given area by the number of square miles in that area. In 1975 the average world population density was about 70 per square mile, the earth's 57.3 million square miles of land containing nearly 4 billion people. However, since the arrangement of peo-

ple over the earth is far from uniform, this ratio has very limited uses. National density ratios are much more revealing, and they range from fewer than one to several thousand persons per square mile. For example, French Guiana averages 1.1 persons per square mile; the United States about 59; China about 200; Czechoslovakia about 300; Trinidad about 500; Belgium about 800; Bermuda about 2500; Hong Kong over 10,000; Monaco over 40,000; and Macao over 41,000. Even this sort of national figure is not without distortion, however, for it reflects all the land within the areal unit, inhabited as well as uninhabited areas, and therefore tells little about how the population is arranged within the nation. Thus, as an example, if one computes Hong Kong's population density in terms of its total area, the ratio obtained is slightly over 10,000 persons per square mile —although, in fact, the Mong Kok district within Hong Kong's city of Kowloon itself has a population density of over 400,000 persons per square mile (Fig. 13–5). Despite such inherent handicaps, the concept of arithmetic density is one of the best means of amplifying general population patterns.

Other Densities

In detailed studies of small areas, measures of population other than arithmetic density may be of greater service. In attempts to understand the effects of overpopulation, for instance, it is frequently useful to know how many people there are in a given area per unit of arable land; the arithmetic expression of this relationship is sometimes known as an area's *nutritional density*. Other frequently used population ratios include *agricultural density*, the number of agriculturally occupied people per unit of arable land; *rural density*, the number of people carrying on rural activities in addition to agriculture and living in rural settlements per unit area; and, its companion, *urban density*.

The major difficulty in these more specific types of population ratios, especially in international regional comparisons, is the inadequacy of the contributing data. While fairly accurate general population figures are available for most local areas, at least in the more advanced countries, a woeful lack of data on arable land and individual economic activities exists almost universally. It is therefore usually impossible to establish valid local population ratios on these subjects, and hence most international comparisons deal only with arithmetic densities.

Age Structure

Age structure, or breakdown by age group, is one of the most basic and meaningful ways of describing a population. Data on the size of different age groups have multiple uses in assessing population resources and planning socioeconomic development, for the age make-up of a society largely determines its domestic priorities. A predominantly youthful society has economic and psychological needs that differ from those of a predominantly old-age society, and both sets of needs will be at some variance with those of a predominantly middle-age culture. The populations of most societies are mixtures of the old, the middle-aged, and the young; but these mixtures are seldom even or unchanging through a long period of time.

FIGURE 13–5

A narrow side-street market in Kowloon, Hong Kong. (Paul Conklin from Monkmeyer)

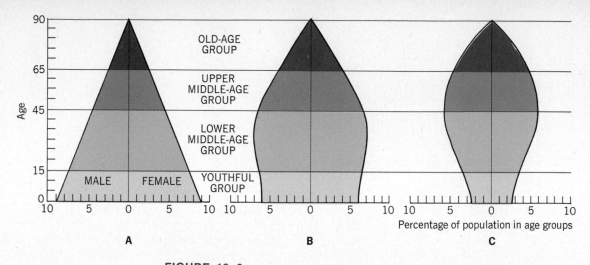

FIGURE 13–6

Some age structure models. A. Youthful population. B. Middle-aged population. C. Old-aged population.

Even barring major migrations and such catastrophes as war and famine, the age composition of a society changes with its birth and death rates; of the two, birth rate is usually the more influential factor.

The division of a population into age groups in any demographic study is usually quite arbitrary. An adequate selection of age boundaries has not been standardized for such purposes; however, some broad age ranges do seem to prevail in most international studies: *young* is normally applied to members of the population below the age of 16; *old* to all persons over 65 years of age; and *middle-aged* to all those between 16 and 65 years (Figs. 13–6 and 13–7).

In countries where crude birth and death rates are high, the youthful group is apt to be the largest of the three, as it is in most underdeveloped societies. Worldwide, the youthful group accounts for perhaps as much as three-fourths of the total population. It is generally an economically unproductive segment, and its housing, food, and educational needs represent a major societal burden—sometimes an overwhelming one.

The oldest group, which comprises a larger percentage of the population in developed societies than it does elsewhere, also requires expenditures that exceed its economic productivity. The middle-age group is the most economically productive of these broad groups, and it is largely responsible for the support of all three.

Population Change

The three principal components of population change in modern societies—mortality, fertility, and migration—tend to be variably influenced by the same factors. Most high national death rates, for example, are fostered by such factors as poverty, illiteracy, low national health standards, and fatalistic religious attitudes, while, to an almost equal extent, these same factors contribute to high national birth rates.

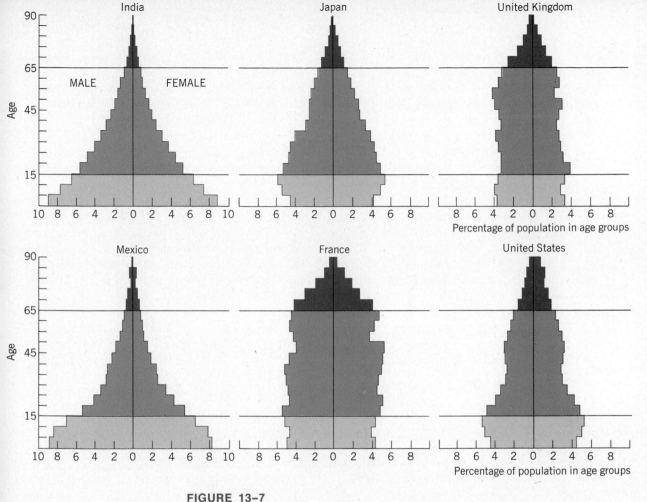

FIGURE 13–7

The age profiles for some selected countries showing their male-female population divisions in the present decade.

Mortality

Throughout most of history the death, or mortality, rates among human groups exceeded those known today in even the least advanced societies. It is estimated that the average human life span in Western societies nearly doubled between prehistoric times and the end of the Middle Ages, after which it remained almost constant until the nineteenth century. During the last century and a half, and especially in recent decades, the death rate in the Western world has declined by 50 percent or more. The first of these spectacular increases in the human life span, from 18 to 35 years, is traceable to a host of socioeconomic changes largely associated with the political consolidation of new territories into powerful states. The more recent doubling, from 35 to 75 years, reflects mainly technological advancements affecting agrarian activities and advancements in the

325

fields of medical practice and public health. Medical innovations and the spread of improved public health services have been so extensive that marked declines in death rates have been effected in many societies even in the absence of the usual contributing rises in socioeconomic well-being (Fig. 13–8). The declining death rate in Asia in the twentieth century is due not so much to the continent's own recent industrialization as to discoveries of Western science and medicine that have been diffused into Asia (Fig. 13–9).

Technology and the Death Rate. Humankind's contest with lesser forms of life, a substantial cause of high human mortality through the millennia, has been largely won through technological advancement: from the turn to agrarian activities in lieu of the hunt to the gradual dominance of science over disease-carrying varmint and insects. But in its contest with the parsimony of nature, humankind has not been as successful, for hunger still challenges human ingenuity throughout much of the world. Improved storage and distribution systems have virtually ended the persistent danger of local famines; but such disasters still occur, and when they do, political considerations and xenophobia often prevent or greatly impede their relief.

There are other, active hindrances to the decline in death rates as well. For countering the victories over disease and famine, humans have applied their technology to the deliberate extermination of their own kind. Indeed, armed conflict seems to be an expected and increasingly large-scale feature of human life, rather than a declining remnant of a barbaric past. Deaths in the First World

FIGURE 13–8

A clinic for the families of copper miners in Chinoala, Zambia. (Marc and Evelyn Bernheim from Woodfin Camp and Associates)

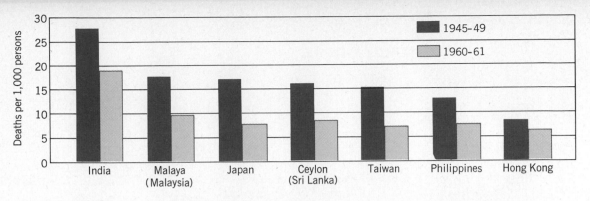

FIGURE 13–9

Death rates for several Asian countries in the periods 1945 to 1949 and 1960 to 1961.

War totalled nearly ten million, and the Second World War produced five times that many. If the present knowledge of nuclear science were applied in another world war, the death toll would possibly include most of the human population.

Measures of Mortality. The *crude death rate,* or the number of deaths within a population unit per year, is the most commonly used measure of mortality and the one most readily available on a worldwide basis. However, since it does not consider the age or sex of the dead, it tends to understate international differences in mortality; for instance, in general, the more advanced societies have a larger portion of their population in the higher age groups, where the probability of death is greatest. A more sophisticated measure of mortality is the *age-specific death rate,* which calculates the number of deaths within each age group, making international comparisons more meaningful. It is difficult to employ either measure of mortality comprehensively on a country-by-country basis, however, since death records for many parts of the world are either nonexistent or very unreliable—those societies with the higher mortality generally having the poorer recording of vital statistics.

Mortality Comparisons. On the continents of Asia and Africa, although reliable, objective measures of population have been made in only a very few countries, death rates have apparently declined considerably since mid-century; but they are still quite high (see Fig. 13–9). The world death rate is estimated at about 15 persons per 1,000—or about half the world birth rate. In the most underdeveloped countries of Asia, Africa, and Latin America, the death rate exceeds this average, ranging from 20 to 30 persons per 1,000. Most of the heavily industrialized countries have death rates below the world average (Fig. 13–10).

Fertility

Estimates made by the United Nations suggest that the world average birth rate has not declined significantly since the mid-twentieth century—while the world average death rate has decreased by a third in the same period. The index such organizations and independent researchers most often use for measuring the reproductive level of a society is its *crude birth rate,* or the number of live births within each unit of population per

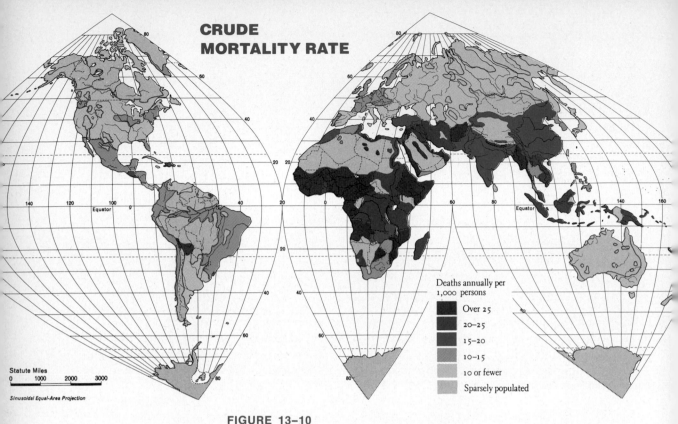

CRUDE MORTALITY RATE

Deaths annually per 1,000 persons

- Over 25
- 20–25
- 15–20
- 10–15
- 10 or fewer
- Sparsely populated

Statute Miles
0   1000   2000   3000

Sinusoidal Equal-Area Projection

FIGURE 13–10

The world average annual mortality rate is currently about 15 per 1,000 persons.

year. Of course, this index is most easily prepared when the subject country is one in which births are normally registered; but, even supported by reliable data, it has some significant limitations, for, like the crude death rate, it does not consider the population's age distribution and sex ratios.

Determinants of Fertility. If birth rates were determined only by biological factors, the average number of live human births would probably range between 10 and 15 per couple. But since socioeconomic factors tend to intervene in many societies, the number of live births averages no more than 5 or 6 per couple. One increasingly influential social determinant of fertility is the development of medical birth control, but setting the climate for its acceptance, and thus of greater overall

importance, are a host of socioeconomic influences of which potential parents are often largely unaware. Among these is the decreasing need for large numbers of offspring as farm helpers and a protection against hardship in one's old age, due primarily to the spread of industrialism and relative economic prosperity. A shift to urban living, with its distractions and spatial restrictions, has also contributed to the slow but persistent reduction in childbearing in many societies. Operating more specifically than such worldwide trends, religious sanctions, marriage practices, levels of education, age and sex ratios, and political and psychological considerations are also important general fertility controls. Political intervention, for example, can be seen to have affected the fertility of major countries both positively and negatively in the present era: the government of Nazi Germany promoted high birth rates in the pre–Second World War period; the government of postwar Japan encouraged low birth rates.

Fertility Trends. The present crude birth rates of the world's countries range from lows of about 15 per 1,000 persons to highs of around 60 per 1,000, with 30 per 1,000 the accepted but arbitrary division between low and high (Fig. 13–11). Future birth rates are difficult to predict, since birth trends are basically products of changing socioeconomic factors. However, the United

Nations estimates a "possible drop" in the crude birth rate of most underdeveloped societies, from the current 40 or more per 1,000 to about 35 per 1,000 population by the 1980s and even 28 per 1,000 by the 1990s.

But fertility decreases are not necessarily permanent. In the 1920s and '30s Canada and the United States showed declining birth rates, with the latter reaching its all-time low rate of about 17 per 1,000 in the late 1930s, the receding years of the Great Depression. The marked rise in United States births following the Second World War produced high national rates of 25 per 1,000 in both 1950 and 1957; but birth rates closer to

FIGURE 13–11

The world annual fertility rate is currently about 30 per 1,000 persons — that is, about twice the annual mortality rate.

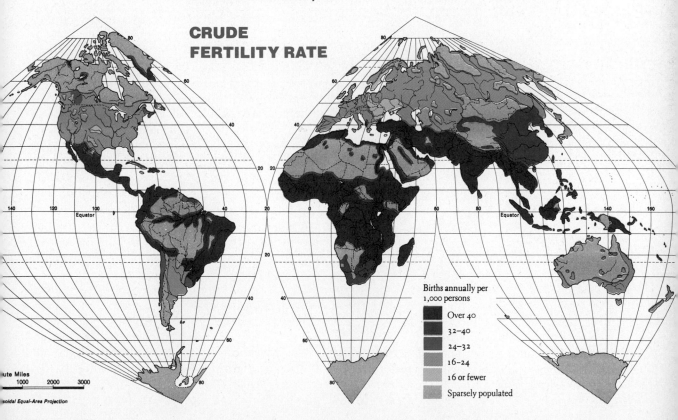

CRUDE FERTILITY RATE

Births annually per 1,000 persons

Over 40
32–40
24–32
16–24
16 or fewer
Sparsely populated

those of the Depression years have characterized the nation in subsequent years. Somewhat similar postwar ebbs have been typical of Canada, many western European countries, and Australia as well.

The Demographic Transition

The succession of changes in mortality and fertility rates that theoretically accompanies the economic modernization of a given society is referred to as its *demographic transition*. Endorsed by many population geographers and cultural geographers, the contention that such changes will occur is based upon the well-documented history of Western countries during the last two centuries.

In evolving from agrarian societies into strong urban-industrial ones, these and most other modern societies have concurrently moved (usually in four stages) from high mortality and fertility to relatively low mortality and fertility (Fig. 13–12). And in this transition, nearly all have experienced intermediate stages in which death rates markedly below birth rates resulted in relatively large increases in total population and, of course, changes in age distribution.

The time consumed by such demographic transitions varies, involving one-half century to several centuries. For western European societies, as an example, the first stage occurred before 1750, years in which a combination of high mortality and high fertility rates resulted in low-growth populations. The second stage began with the Industrial Revolution, when, as the new societal economies expanded and basic health services became more readily avail-

FIGURE 13–12

A *demographic transition* model, involving major sequential changes. A very large *natural increase* (growth) occurs in a population when its mortality (death) rate declines substantially while its fertility (birth) rate does not, as in stage 2; and natural increase is smaller when death and birth rates approach a common level, as in stages 1, 3, and 4.

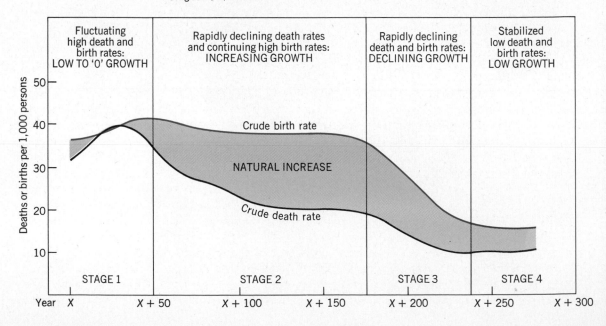

POPULATION INCREASE

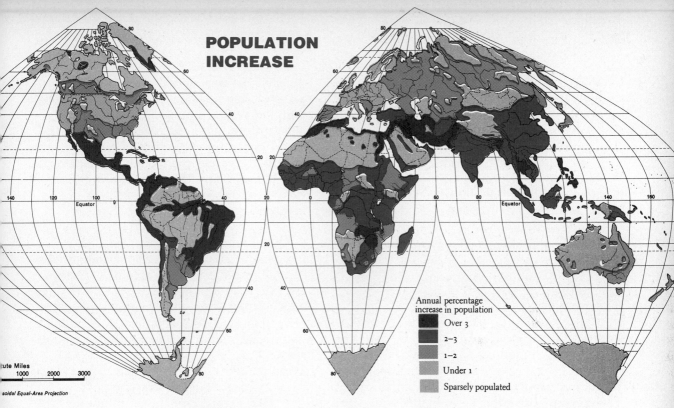

Annual percentage
increase in population

Over 3

2–3

1–2

Under 1

Sparsely populated

FIGURE 13–13

Recent rapid increases in human populations lie at the base of many of modern society's major problems, particularly food and energy shortages and urban sprawl.

able, mortality rates declined and fertility rates maintained their high levels—resulting in major growths in population. The last quarter of the nineteenth century marked the beginning of stage three. Its declines in total growth rates reflect the first acceptances of modern birth control (now known as *family planning*) and a new view of large families as economic handicaps. The demographic transition of these European societies reached stage four toward the mid–twentieth century, when both mortality and fertility rates stabilized at new low-growth levels.

Natural Population Increase

The numerical difference between the crude birth rate of a society and its crude death rate constitutes its rate of *natural popu-lation increase;* this figure will differ from its total rate of increase if there have been net gains or losses through migration. With over 120 million live births and over 50 million deaths annually, the world currently experiences an annual natural increase of about 70 million persons. This represents a growth rate of about 20 per 1,000 persons, or—as demographers usually express it—2 percent, annually. If the world rate of natural increase remains constant at 2 percent, then the human population of the earth will double in about 35 years.

The countries with the highest average annual rates of natural increase—3.0 percent and above—are located in Latin America (Fig. 13–13). Most African countries, with an estimated average of 2.3, and Asian countries, with a 2.2 rate of natural increase, are well below the Latin American levels and only slightly above the world average. The

331

lowest average annual rates of natural increase are found in the heavily industrialized countries of Europe. A half dozen European countries consistently maintain rates of 0.5 percent or lower, while only three such countries have established rates of over 1.0 percent — giving the continent a very low natural growth rate of 0.7 percent. The two largest heavily industrialized societies, the United States and the Soviet Union, and urbanized Australia maintain average annual rates of about 1.1 percent.

Migration

Technological advances in transport and communication linkages in recent times have greatly expanded human capabilities for international migration. The first trips by humans across the Bering land bridge and down the western shores of the Americas undoubtedly represented generations of family and tribal wanderings, with only a few of the strongest members surviving each leg of the journey. In contrast, contemporary human migrations from northern Asia to America, accomplished by ship or by airplane, are matters of but a few days. Today, in technical terms at least, the population of any one continent could be relocated to any other in less time than it once took to travel between New York and California.

But such huge shifts do not occur. Migration has seldom assumed an importance in world population distribution even remotely comparable to that of natural increase; indeed, with more and more countries establishing legal immigration barriers, the relative importance of migration in international demography is probably on the wane. However, the present population of the world is so large that the involvement of even a very small percentage in international migration can constitute a sizable population change. Further, if a society's numerical gains or losses through migration are concentrated within a particular population segment (income level, age range, sex, or professional group) — as they seldom are through natural processes — the socioeconomic effects may be discernible for generations and may even alter the course of the society permanently.

European Colonial Emigrations. Among the most extensive international migrations of modern times is the migration of Europeans to overseas colonial territories during the early sixteenth to mid-twentieth centuries. Over this long period probably 70 million Europeans took up residence abroad, and at least 50 million of them resettled permanently — about 35 million making their new homes in the United States.

This great international migration did not occur as a continuously large and steady stream, however. Until the early nineteenth century, the numbers involved were relatively small, with less than two million immigrants to the Americas throughout the previous three centuries. The more massive migrations from Europe began about 1830 and, by the beginning of the First World War, included more than a million people per year. At first the principal countries of origin were those in northwestern Europe; but by the early twentieth century, most of the new immigrants came from Europe's Mediterranean and Slavic countries.

United States Immigrations. The long period of heavy immigration to the United States, the late nineteenth and early twentieth centuries, reflected the extensive European emigrations (Fig. 13–14). Before 1890 the major countries of origin were Great Britain and Germany, with smaller numbers of immigrants coming from the Scandinavian countries, Italy, Russia, and the Austro-

Hungarian Empire; by the end of the nineteenth century, 70 percent of the immigrants to the United States were natives of Mediterranean and Slavic Europe (Fig. 13–15).

Many less recent Americans became alarmed at the rising number and new ethnic make-up of the European immigrants, and they clamored for some sort of restrictive measure—presumably, something similar to the 1882 act that had curbed Chinese immigration to the west coast states. Thus in 1921 and 1924, the United States Congress enacted immigration laws designed "to maintain the cultural and racial homogeneity of the United States by the admission of immigrants in proportions corresponding to the composition in the present population." In addition, the worldwide Depression of the 1930s reduced all immigration into the country, and, war continuing the reduction, the average annual levels sunk to little more than a quarter million by the middle of the next decade.

For much of this century, therefore, immigration to the United States has not reflected European "population pressures," as it once did. The extension of a selective immigration policy in the 1920s established a set of annual quotas that favored Great Britain, Ireland, and Germany—who never used more than half their allotments. In 1966 the United States Congress abolished the quota system, but it also reduced the maximum number of immigrants and attempted to bar those who would take jobs sought by Americans; the growing prosperity in western Europe has also affected immigration. Thus, in the years following the quota system's abolition, nationality ratios among new immigrants changed substantially; by the late 1960s, over 40 percent of all immigrants to the United States were from Latin America, mainly Mexico and the Central American countries.

Some Post–World War II Migrations.
Migration in response to political turmoil did not come to an end with the signing of peace

FIGURE 13–15

European emigrants traveling steerage on the *SS Pennland* in the late 1800s as it headed for the United States. (Byron Collection, Museum of the City of New York)

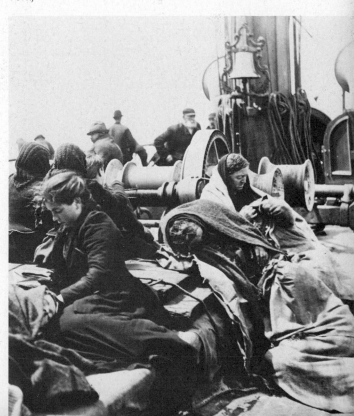

FIGURE 13–14

The origins of most immigrants to the United States between 1831 and 1910. During this period, over 90 percent of the new settlers in the United States were from northwestern and southern Europe.

Origin	U.S. Immigrants
Europe	25,500,000
Canada	1,200,000
Latin America	300,000
Asia and the Pacific	700,000
Total	27,700,000

FIGURE 13–16

Migration in the Middle East. Top, Jewish immigrants arriving in Israel soon after the establishment of the new state. (Consulate General of Israel) Bottom, children of a Palestinian refugee camp bringing home their family's rations. The camp shown is near Amman, Jordan; many similar encampments exist elsewhere in Jordan and in the adjoining nations. (Katrina Thomas from Photo Researchers)

treaties ending World War II. Indeed, as independence came to European colonies in Asia and Africa in the postwar years, one of the results was often the uprooting and forced migration of millions of people from these areas.

The partition of British India, in 1947, into Moslem Pakistan and Hindu India, set in motion a vast, two-way migration. The total number of people uprooted has been estimated at about 17 million, representing, in almost equal numbers, Moslems who fled

India for Pakistan and Hindus and Sikhs who fled Pakistan for India. Another major postwar migration began in 1948, with the establishment of the State of Israel. In subsequent years over 600,000 Jews migrated to the new state from Europe, North Africa, the United States, and other parts of the Middle East. Unfortunately, nearly an equal number of Arabs were uprooted as a result; and many who fled their ancestral lands found that their hardships continued, and sometimes multiplied, elsewhere (Fig. 13–16). Almost simultaneously, Communist victories in China sent millions of Chinese into permanent exile in Taiwan, Hong Kong, and other Southeast Asian centers; these precursors of the 1949 takeover also dislodged the country's large European population, many of whom had come to China as refugees during the First World War.

Unlike European refugees of the post–World War II years, Asian migrants of the same era remain largely unsettled, with little being done to alleviate their misery. The human casualties of Asia's "forced" migrations are still visible in the streets and alleys of such great cities as Calcutta and Bombay, Bangkok and Saigon, and Hong Kong and Taipei.

The Rush to the Cities.   One of the most striking population changes of modern times is the rural exodus in search of urban opportunities. If demographic predictions are correct, urban populations will account for over 50 percent of the earth's total population by the year 2000, which is above the present ratio. A universal trend, this rush to the cities is particularly strong in newly developing societies, where, unfortunately, there are few resources to deal with the resultant array of social, economic, and political problems. In Colombia, for example, the rural sector's rate of growth is about 1.0 percent, while the urban sector's is 5.0 percent. And such disparities exist in many other Latin American and African societies. And Israel, in southwest Asia, has one of the highest urban population ratios in the world: with nearly 85 percent of all Israelis living in towns and cities, and with an even higher percentage within the Jewish population. Tel Aviv alone accounts for about 30 percent of Israel's total population.

Twentieth-Century Spatial Linkages

The present world *circulation,* or transportation–communication, network has evolved bit by bit throughout the long course of human history. Its configuration reflects humankind's successes and failures in overcoming the distances and barriers of nature, and thus the progress of the species from primitive isolationism to complex group associations and interrelationships.

The spatial linkages of early human groups were few and irregular, perhaps radiating from each group's crude shelters to its hunting grounds or water sources, and limited by the distances the average adult could travel afoot in the hours of daylight. With the domestication of large animals, human spatial ranges increased—pathways becoming established trails, and hunting and fishing sites developing into temporary rest stations. Local road networks grew and joined those of neighboring peoples, and water bodies provided paths to more distant sites. Always the intent and result were the extension of each group's "known world."

Today, the socioeconomic level of a society determines the nature of its circulation network and the intensity of that network's use. To the subsistence sawah farmer of southern Asia, superhighways and airports are of little significance; southern Asia's circulation network consists largely of paths and cart tracks leading from village to field to town. They are not heavily or speedily traveled by people or goods. By contrast, in such industrial societies as western Europe and the United States, superhighways and a web of air, water, and surface feeders are essential. Along these routes flow the products upon which the livelihoods of an industrial people are based.

The spatial arrangement of any circulation system is subject to strong influences from both physical and cultural elements of the environment. Since the basic function of any route is to link together two points in space, and since the shortest distance between two points is a straight line, it follows that the ideal route is a straight line. However, this ideal rarely occurs, for many obstacles force deviations from its course. Some of these obstacles are physical, such as terrain slope, elevation, and surface condition; others are cultural, such as political boundaries, zoning limitations, and property lines.

Road Systems

In early times, roads were developed and operated primarily on a local basis. Perhaps the earliest major departure from this tendency was the extensive road system created by the ancient Romans. Under the Roman emperors, surfaced roads were built throughout much of southern and western Europe, all leading eventually to Rome itself. Main trunk lines linked Rome with all parts of its empire, and especially with strategic points on the frontier; the primary purpose of this system was to facilitate troop movements. With the decline of the Roman Empire, this road system contributed to its defeat, for it gave invading armies easy access to lands formerly under strong Roman control and, later, to Rome itself. In modern times, both France and Germany have built national road systems that, like the Roman, center on the capital city and fan out to strategic points on the frontier (Fig. 13–17). And in both countries, in times of war, the road system served invading armies all to well.

During the Middle Ages the impetus for roadbuilding was lost, and existing road systems declined. It was not until the end of the fifteenth century, and then only in France, that organized road systems again became national interests. Further, it was not until the age of the automobile that such systems showed major improvements over the Roman models. As it answered the need for

FIGURE 13–17
The principal roads of France, a network centered on Paris.

FIGURE 13–18

Contrasting road systems. Left, a primitive road in central Africa. (United Nations) Right, heavy traffic on the Harbor Freeway, one of the many freeways that help to make sprawling Los Angeles a functioning unit. (Southern California APCD)

high-speed circulation between centers of industry and commerce, the automobile created a demand for new and better road systems; these were provided throughout much of the United States and Europe by the mid–twentieth century, and they have since been a feature of national development plans in nearly all parts of the world.

Today, among the world's small to medium-sized countries, the highest road density occurs in Japan, which is followed closely in this respect by the United Kingdom, Denmark, France, Germany, and Belgium—the latter all highly industrialized countries of western Europe, the most densely road-crossed multinational region. Among large countries, the United States has the highest road density, but some sizable

areas of northeast China and peninsular India have fairly dense road systems as well. India's rather extensive road system, acquired largely under British colonial rule, has benefited from good road maintenance and bridge-building programs since the country obtained independence in 1947. Today, India has over 200,000 miles of good hard-surfaced roads.

The road systems of most other countries and regions suffer by comparison with those mentioned above. South America, Africa, eastern Europe, and Southeast Asia are not characterized by elaborate road systems. Thus for the most part, the density and quality of a society's road system seems to vary directly with its level of economic development (Figs. 13–18 and 13–19).

337

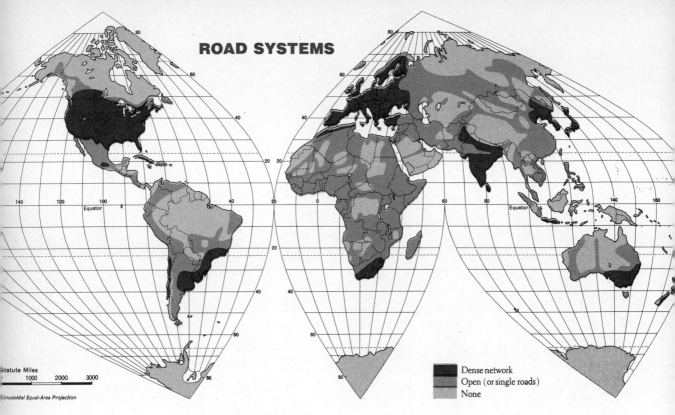

ROAD SYSTEMS

Dense network
Open (or single roads)
None

Statute Miles
1000   2000   3000

Sinusoidal Equal-Area Projection

FIGURE 13–19

Dense road networks, which occur over relatively little of the earth's landmass, are found, for the most part, in heavily industrialized nations and in some of their former colonies.

Rail Systems

While most of the world's societies have road systems of some kind, railways are almost exclusively features of industrial societies and some of their client states (Fig. 13–20). The dense rail systems of the eastern United States and northwestern Europe mirror the heavy concentrations of industry in these regions (Fig. 13–21). Most other societies of the world are but lightly served by railroads. Tremendous expanses in Asia are little touched by rail traffic. Some loosely connected railroads extend across Soviet Europe, but the Trans-Siberian is the lone railway across the vastness of Soviet Siberia to the Pacific coast. And elsewhere in Asia, as in Africa, Latin America, and Australia,

vast stretches of moderate to densely populated lands have little rail service.

While rail travel has a rather short history—the world's first railway was put into operation in England in 1825—railroads have been so vital to urban society that it is difficult to understand how major cities once existed without them. In the development of the United States, they have influenced the location of major population centers, the outcome of a civil war, and reams of folklore and fantasy. Nevertheless today, at least in both the United States and Europe, other modes of transportation have taken over much of the local and transcontinental traffic of the railways. Automobiles, trucks, buses, and airplanes have largely displaced railroads in the moving of passengers and freight.

RAIL SYSTEMS

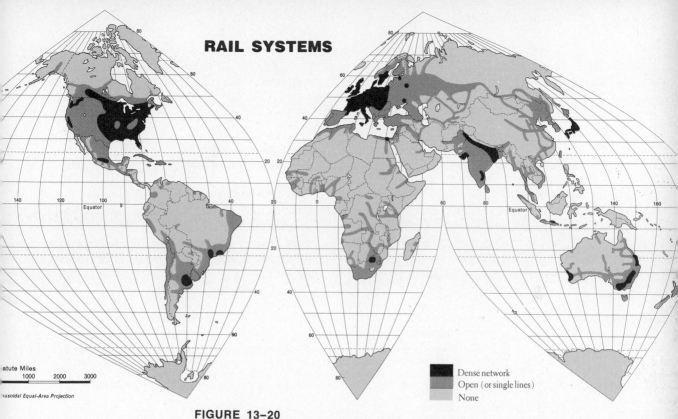

Statute Miles
1000   2000   3000

Sinusoidal Equal-Area Projection

■ Dense network
▨ Open (or single lines)
□ None

FIGURE 13–20

Dense rail networks are features principally of Western Europe and the eastern half of the United States, the world's most highly industrialized areas.

FIGURE 13–21

An automated classification yard of the Louisville and Nashville Railroad. (Association of American Railroads)

Other Circulation Systems

Existing along with the world's road and rail systems are many other means of societal circulation, most obviously water (Fig. 13–22) and air vehicular routes, but also power lines and pipelines and such communication tools as telephonic and telegraphic lines, radio and television networks, and radar and satellite-tracking stations. Like dense rail and road networks, these communication systems are found largely in urban-industrial societies; yet they too are stretching out to touch practically every individual in every society of the world (Fig. 13–23).

Transport and Western Culture

That the many fragments of world populations and societies have come to be more closely interlinked as a result of the development and spread of Western culture is a fact of record. During an early period of history, the people of a small south European tribe

FIGURE 13–22
Barge traffic near Bonn on the Rhine River, one of the world's busiest water routes. (Lufthansa Archiv)

FIGURE 13–23

The use of closed-circuit educational television in Niger, where experiments in television teaching have been made since 1964. (United Nations)

gradually expanded throughout the Italian peninsula, as well as eastward and southward into the Middle East and Africa and northwestward across Europe beyond the English Channel. They took all this vast territory under their political control and, welding it together with a farflung system of roads and waterways, formed the Roman Empire.

Eventually this vast empire declined as a political society, but its descendant societies later brought even more European peoples into the dynamic and expanding sphere of Western culture. These societies underwent radical economic growth and expansion and, in time, became highly industrialized. Their ever-increasing needs for goods and markets required their contact with more and more of the world's people. The linkages between industrial cores of European societies and their client regions were at first roadways and waterways and later the railways, airways, and early long-distance communication networks.

Imperfect though this intricate circulation system still is today, its transportation and communication networks have profoundly affected humankind's concepts of the physical environment and the human role therein. For most individuals and societies today, the world is no longer a simple collection of small scattered societies and activities, separated one from another by xenophobic barriers. Rather, it is a complex mosaic of societies, interrelated and interfunctioning by means of a vast matrix of transportation and communication linkage systems.

REVIEW AND DISCUSSION

1. What caused the pressures for more abundant living space that eventually brought about the diffusion of human beings beyond their original centers of origin?
2. Cite some specific "empty" areas of the world and explain why they remain "empty." Distinguish between the following types of density: nutritional, agricultural, rural, and urban.
3. The three principal components of population change in modern societies — mortality, fertility, and migration — tend to be variably influenced by the same cultural factors. Substantiate this statement with facts and examples.
4. Discuss the extent and consequences of the death-rate decline in the Western world during the last 150 years. In what ways is technology related to this decline?
5. Discuss the effects of trends in crude birth rates and death rates during the twentieth century.
6. What is the meaning of the term *demographic transition?* Discuss its application to several contrasting societies.
7. What is the meaning of *natural population increase?* What are the uses and limitations of this measurement?
8. How does migration compare with natural population increases as an influence on world population?
9. Discuss some of the socioeconomic consequences of the major post–World War II migrations. How did some of these migrations set the stage for many of today's social and political problems?
10. Contrast the national and international rail system linkages in developed societies with those of developing societies. What is the role of rail transportation in modern socioeconomic development? What major changes will probably take place in the rail system of the United States by the end of the present century?

SELECTED REFERENCES

Barbour, K., and R. Prothero, eds. *Essays on African Population.* New York: Praeger, 1962.

Becht, J. *A Geography of Transportation and Business Logistics.* Dubuque, Iowa: Brown, 1970.

Borah, W. "America as a Model: The Demographic Impact of European Expansion upon the Non-European World." *Actas y Memorias, XXXV Congreso Internacional de Americanistas.* Vol. 3 (1964), 379–87.

Carr-Saunders, A. M. *World Population: Past Growth and Present Trends.* Oxford: Clarendon, 1966.

Cipolla, C. M. *The Economic History of World Population.* Harmondsworth, England: Penguin, 1962.

Clarke, J. *Population Geography.* Oxford: Pergamon, 1965.

Cook, R. "Israel: Land of Promise and Perplexities." *Population Bulletin,* Vol. 21 (November 1965), 101–34.

Cootner, P. "The Role of the Railroad in United States Economic Growth." *Journal of Economic History,* Vol. 23 (December 1963), 477–521.

Demko, G., H. Rose, and G. Schnell. *Population Geography: A Reader.* New York: McGraw-Hill, 1970.

Drake, M., ed. *Population in Industrialization.* London: Methuen, 1969.

Durand, J. "The Modern Expansion of World Population." *Population Problems, Proceedings of the American Philosophical Society,* Vol. 3 (June 1967), 133–93.

Ehrlich, P. R., and J. P. Holdren. "Impact of Population Growth." *Science,* Vol. 171 (March 1971), 1212–17.

Eliot Hurst, M. E. *Transportation Geography: Comments and Readings,* Part 1. New York: McGraw-Hill, 1973.

Farris, M., and P. McElhiney, eds. *Modern Transportation: Selected Readings.* Boston: Houghton Mifflin, 1967.

Kindleberger, C. "Mass Migration, Then and Now." *Foreign Affairs,* Vol. 43 (July 1965), 647–58.

Kosinski, L. *The Population of Europe: A Geographic Perspective.* London: Geographical Publications, Longman, 1970.

Learmonth, A. "Medical Geography in India and Pakistan." *Geographical Journal,* Vol. 127 (March 1961), 10–26.

Murphey, R. "The Population of China: An Historical and Contemporary Analysis." *Geography of Population,* 1970 Yearbook of the National Council for Geographical Education, Palo Alto, Calif., 117–34.

O'Dell, A., and P. Richards. *Railways and Geography,* 2nd ed. London: Hutchinson University Library, 1971.

O'Flaherty, C. *Highways.* London: Arnold, 1967.

Peterson, W. *Population,* 2nd ed. New York: Macmillan, 1969.

Schechtman, J. B. *Postwar Population Transfers in Europe, 1945–1955.* Philadelphia: University of Pennsylvania Press, 1962.

Sealy, K. *The Geography of Air Transport,* 3rd ed. London: Hutchinson University Library, 1966.

Stamp, L. D. *The Geography of Life and Death.* London: Collins, 1964.

Taaffe, E., et al. "Transport Expansion in Underdeveloped Countries: A Comparative Analysis." *Geographical Review,* Vol. 53 (October 1963), 503–29.

Taaffe, E., and H. Gauthier. *Geography of Transportation.* Englewood Cliffs, N.J.: Prentice-Hall, 1972.

Taft, D., and R. Robbins. *Internation Migrations: The Immigrant in the Modern World.* New York: Ronald Press, 1955.

Thomlinson, R. *Population Dynamics.* New York: Random House, 1965.

Trewartha, G. *A Geography of Population: World Patterns.* New York: Wiley, 1969.

Wolpert, J. "Migration as an Adjustment to Environmental Stress." *The Journal of Social Issues,* Vol. 22 (October 1966), 92–102.

Wrigley, E. *Population and History.* New York: McGraw-Hill, 1969.

Zelinsky, W. "Toward a Geography of the Aged." *Geographical Review,* Vol. 56 (July 1966), 445–47.

Zelinsky, W., L. Kosinski, and R. Prothero, eds. *Geography and a Crowding World.* New York: Oxford University Press, 1970.

The effluent takeoff of a jet airplane. (Harbrace Photo)

14

Emerging
Environmental Realities

As burgeoning societies exert unprecedented pressure on their environments and as increasing numbers of people seek more living space, greater food supplies, and ever more uses of energy resources, great injury has frequently been done to the earth's air, waters, and land. Today, some people still boast of "man's conquest of nature," seemingly unmindful of the feat's high cost. But among a growing number of people there is a deepening awareness that, if the conquest continues recklessly, the cost will be more than the species or the environment can long stand. Most societies today are thus attempting to achieve a better understanding of nature and carrying out or planning a more careful utilization of their environments.

Movements to check environmental damage, in existence for the past two hundred years, met with some success in Europe and the United States prior to World War I and experienced a brief revival after the war. But most early environmental movements were overshadowed by other concerns during the years of economic depression, World War II, and the cold war that followed.

During those demanding decades, however, world environmental problems grew more serious, more complex, and practically impossible for societies to continue to ignore.

Thus the Western world's present-day environmental movements, for the most part creations of the late 1960s, have heritages that date back to the early industrial revolution. Those who today urge Americans and Europeans to "clean up the environment" while there is still time echo the voices of such concerned figures of the past as American naturalists John James Audubon (1785–1851) and John Burroughs (1837–1921), Theodore Roosevelt (1858–1919), German biologist Ernst Heinrich Haeckel (1834–1919), American forester Gifford Pinchot (1863–1946), and Sir Arthur George Tansley (1871–1955), a British ecologist (Fig. 14–1).

In too many instances today, environmental problems have progressed far beyond being local nuisances. Many have already become progressive maladies that threaten the socioeconomic strengths of whole societies. As countries with an urban-industrial base and the attendant environmental pollu-

Today, *environmental pollution* has taken on a broad meaning; for in general the term now incorporates all the ways in which humans pollute, damage, and endanger the environments in which they live and work. Everyone on earth who eats, drinks, and works contributes a small share to today's worldwide environmental pollution. In the production-exchange-consumption complex in which most people are involved, contaminants of various types are dumped into the environment. The day-to-day production of food, clothing, shelter, vehicles, energy, roads, books, and the host of other necessities and luxuries involves the concurrent production of unusable and unwanted by-products that become pollutants and solid wastes. To this there is but one practical alternative. Some of today's abundant technologies must be redirected toward the development of pollution-free methods of producing the luxuries and necessities of life.

tion and waste problems become increasingly numerous, many environments are being turned into cores of pollution. Such environmental decline, if unabated, may soon create international "disaster areas," seriously threatening the health and welfare of millions of people.

Air Pollution

Human Impacts

Although contaminated air has been a problem in most industrial centers since the early nineteenth century, only within the past two decades have people begun to view air pollution as perhaps the most serious threat to the environment. Most prevalent where population is concentrated and societal activities highly developed, air pollution

has many harmful effects on human health and welfare, some temporary and others long-range. Many manufactured gases and minute airborne wastes are debilitating to human beings, often seriously damaging their respiratory systems. Airborne wastes, or *particulates,* more than most other pollutants, collect in the lungs and cause or contribute to such respiratory diseases as asthma and bronchitis. Research indicates that particulates may also be contributory factors in many cases of cancer, pneumonia, and emphysema.

Although usually a debilitator rather than an immediate killer, air pollution has sometimes become so intense in specific locations that only a few hours or days demonstrated its lethal potential. In 1930, for example, in the Meuse Valley of Belgium, many people were stricken with respiratory illnesses during a few-hour period of extreme air pollution, and 63 pollution-related deaths were recorded. Some years later, in 1948, a similar period of intense air pollution struck the town of Donora, in the Monongahela Valley of western Pennsylvania, resulting in 17 deaths (Fig. 14–2). And in 1952, during two weeks of severe air pollution in the area, London experienced approximately 4,000 "excess deaths."

During the nearly half century since those tragedies, air pollution problems have received increasing attention among scientists, the general public, and politicians of many countries. Much has been learned and put into practice in the area of pollution abatement during the past two decades, but there is still much work to be done before we can control air pollution. For example, explicit evaluations of the origins and effects of the pollutants in smog are still not yet available, although this atmospheric condition is an old and ever-present health hazard in many areas of the world.

Local meteorological conditions of any sort are almost entirely beyond the control of human beings and, despite radar and satellites, remain largely unpredictable even from day to day. But just as naturalists and environmental planners consider watersheds, or river basins, operational units, it may well be possible to study, plan, and act upon the inherent nature of large atmospheric regions, or "air sheds."

FIGURE 14–2

A smog-shrouded intersection in the central business district of Donora, Pennsylvania, on October 30, 1948. (Wide World Photos)

Thermal Inversion

Precipitation and wind tend to disperse air pollutants and remove them from their source areas. At times, however, weather conditions are such that air pollutants are concentrated over a region instead of being cleared away. One such major weather condition, one that occurs almost anywhere and in many areas repeatedly, is known as a *thermal inversion*. During a thermal inversion, a layer of warm air settles over a layer of cool air that lies nearer, and perhaps in contact with, the ground. The warm upper layer acts as a natural cap and stalls, or minimizes, air currents within the lower layer of air; in so doing it prevents the usual dispersal of air pollutants by means of rising air currents. When, by a continuous build-up, stagnated pollutants are concentrated at or near ground level, the condition is called *smog*. If the air pollution is severe, a thermal inversion that lasts a few days or even a few hours will have noticeable harmful effects upon the comfort of even the healthiest human beings (Fig. 14–3).

Los Angeles County, where *smog* has been a household word since World War II, is topographically and meteorologically ideal for thermal inversions, for it occupies a large basin that is open to the sea and encircled landward by a chain of hills and mountains. Warm air from the interior deserts can slip over the encircling mountains and settle over low, cool air from the Pacific. As the thermal inversion keeps the area's abundant automobile and industrial pollutants from escaping upward, light prevailing breezes from the ocean may exert just enough pressure to keep them from drifting out to sea. And so

FIGURE 14–3

The layering of air over a hypothetical metropolis. A. Under normal conditions. B. During a thermal inversion.

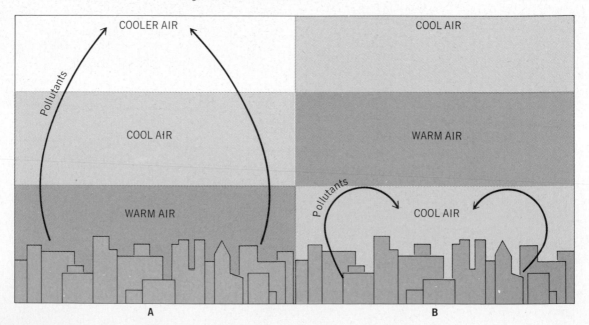

FIGURE 14–4

Downtown Los Angeles in 1956. Above, on a clear day with no inversion layer. Below, on a smoggy day with an inversion layer at about the 300-foot level. (Southern California Air Pollution Control District)

they remain trapped within the basin until a change of weather brings either sea breezes strong enough to carry them over the mountains, or land breezes strong enough to carry them out to sea (Fig. 14–4). During the stagnation, a series of chemical reactions brought on or accelerated by solar radiation, as provided by the area's abundant sunshine, changes some of the air pollutants into *photochemical smog*. Composed mainly of hydrocarbons and nitrogen oxides, pollutants derived mainly from automobiles, this type

of smog often smarts the eyes of millions of Los Angeles County residents and damages many of the basin's numerous crops and its natural vegetation.

Major Air Pollutants

The air people breathe, every minute of every day, is their most continuously vital environmental resource. Nevertheless, they pollute that very same resource by using it as a waste disposal. Backed by tradition, many still assume that the air can remain beyond societal regulation, free for all to use and misuse without peril. Land and waterways have been at least partially regulated and protected since early in human history. Air, the most vital environmental resource, is the last to come under societal protection.

There have always been natural emissions, from volcanoes and the like, that temporarily overloaded, or polluted, the atmosphere, but the more harmful air pollutants have usually come from human activities. Since the first human control of fire, technological progress and social development have steadily increased the levels of harmful materials in the air.

From Transport Sources. When the components of air pollution in the United States are estimated by weight, those from transportation devices—automobiles, airplanes, trucks and buses, and trains—comprise the most dominant category, accounting for some 42 percent of the total. Such motorized vehicles spew into the atmosphere vast quantities of *carbon monoxide* and lesser quantities of *hydrocarbons, sulfur oxides, particulates, nitrogen oxides,* and *tetraethyl leads*—automobiles are the primary offenders (Fig. 14–5).

Of these air pollutants, carbon monoxide is probably the most toxic to human beings. It can cause sudden death when it reaches 1,000 parts per million (ppm) in the air, and even levels of carbon monoxide below 50 ppm are thought to be damaging to many people. Nevertheless, in many traffic-congested cities the level of carbon monoxide in the air must be as high as 100 ppm, 200 ppm, or even 400 ppm before a pollution alert is declared.

Only major modifications of the engines and the fuels used in automobiles will produce meaningful improvements in

FIGURE 14–5

Air-pollution emissions in the United States in 1968. A. Their types. B. Their sources. (Both in percentages by weight)

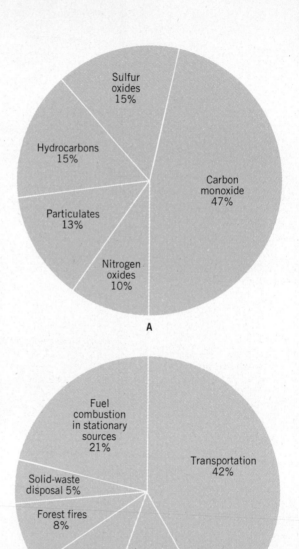

the quality of the atmosphere over most large metropolitan areas. *Catalytic exhaust converters* and similar emission control devices have been developed to help automobiles meet the present and impending government restrictions on harmful vehicular emissions. However, the transition to nearly pollution-free gasoline engines, requiring the cooperation of industry, government, and consumers, will probably proceed at a very slow pace.

The present alternatives to the gasoline-fueled internal-combustion engine are very promising in theory but much less so in operation. The electric car, for example, has a limited driving range between rechargings, and these rechargings take several hours. Moreover, the electrical energy required must be generated somewhere. A switch to the electric car may represent only a shifting of pollutants to someone else's backyard—say,

from Los Angeles to Black Mesa, where local low-quality coals would fuel the large electric power plants necessary to charge the metropolis's cars.

With only minor changes most of today's gasoline engines could operate on natural gas. But the threatened condition of natural-gas supplies since the mid-1970s makes this alternative to the gasoline engine somewhat impractical. Among the other alternatives are the steam, gas-turbine, and diesel engines. The diesel already powers most of the world's trucks and buses, but it remains a less than ideal substitute for the gasoline engine in the family automobile because of its greater emissions of nitrogen oxides.

From Stationary Sources: Power Plants. Thermoelectric power plants (Fig. 14–6), domestic and institutional space-heating systems, community incinerators, and mining

FIGURE 14–6

Air pollution from power plants, air conditioners, and space-heating units—in a typical North American city. (Elliot Erwitt, © 1966 Magnum)

operations are commonly grouped together as *nonindustrial stationary sources* of air pollution. They all involve the "burning" of coal, oil, and gas to create steam to operate turbines—a contrast to the "explosion" of fuels in internal-combustion engines. As a consequence, the operation of most motor vehicles and the running of these stationary systems are almost the reverse of each other in terms of pollutants. Whereas vehicular emissions are high in carbon monoxide and hydrocarbons, the stationary systems emit very little of these toxins; but while motor vehicles emit low sulfur oxides, the stationary sources produce emissions in which the level of sulfur oxides is high. As Middle East oil policies stimulate greater use of coal-fueled steam in thermoelectric power plants, it is projected that the percentage of sulfur oxides in the emissions from these plants will increase (Fig. 14–7).

From Industrial Sources. The world's developed societies and many of the developing ones have been so involved in industrial planning and growth that they have ignored the social and environmental problems created by their economic progress. Frequently the industries that are most vital to their economic infrastructures also contribute most of the gases and particulates that pollute their environments. According to the United States Public Health Service, the principal industrial polluters are the manufacturers of iron and steel and other metals; refined petroleum; petrochemicals, including fertilizers, plastics, and pesticides; and organic chemicals, such as synthetic rubber, pulp, and paper (Fig. 14–8).

Industry in the United States accounts for about 20 percent of the country's atmospheric sulfur oxides and one-third of its airborne particulates, but only about 10 percent

FIGURE 14–7

Estimated electrical generation in the United States through major energy sources, from 1965 to 2000.

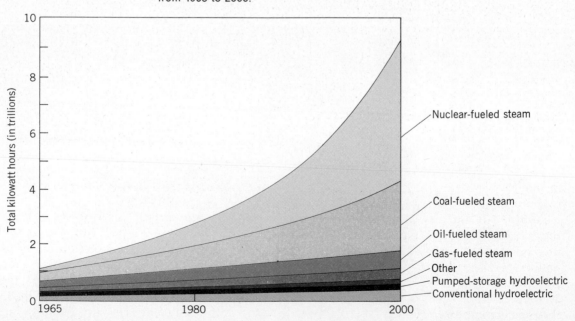

FIGURE 14–8

Industrial air pollution. Above, a chemical plant in Mexico City. (United Nations) Below, lumber mills east of Salt Lake City, Utah. (Grant Heilman)

of the environment's carbon monoxide and hydrocarbons. Thus, while it often receives most of the blame and publicity for the nation's air pollution, industry actually contributes only about 14 percent of the total air pollutants; as suggested earlier, over 42 percent comes from transportation devices and 21 percent from such stationary sources as thermoelectric power plants.

The Atmosphere's Self-Purification

There are natural elements or processes that tend to reduce the levels of most atmospheric pollutants. Precipitation washes large quantities of gaseous pollutants and particulates from the atmosphere into the soils and water of the earth. And the oxygen of the air itself combines with many pollutants, creating compounds that are more readily removed from the air. *Sulfuric acid* droplets, which probably contributed heavily to the London smog tragedy of 1952, and the photochemical smog of many west coast areas are but stages in the atmosphere's own natural process of self-purification. But nature's "scrubbing" processes can no longer keep pace with humankind's environmental polluting.

United States Air Pollution Controls

The United States government's first legislative involvement in meaningful air pollution control did not occur until 1955, when Congress appropriated $5 million for air pollution research and assistance to state and local air-pollution-control programs. And it was not until the passage of the Air Quality Act, in 1967, that further substantial federal action was taken against air pollution. With the passage of this act, the United States government assumed a large part of the responsibility for the improvement and maintenance of the nation's air (Fig. 14–9). Although the act encourages action at state and local levels, federal intervention is assured if lower-level agencies fail to function effectively.

As a step toward fulfilling its responsibility for the atmosphere, the federal government has demanded that all new automobiles produced domestically comply with specific limitations on emissions of carbon monoxide, hydrocarbons, and nitrogen oxides. While these limitations represent a 90 percent improvement over the norm in the recent past, additional restraints on automobiles and their use will probably be instituted by local government in some cities. Those that have exceptionally congested traffic conditions—Los Angeles, New York, Chicago, Philadelphia, and others—may well find it necessary to initiate minimum passenger requirements and limit access to particular streets and highways.

Some Global Aspects of Air Pollution

The relationships between air pollution and urban growth are recognizable today in most countries of the world—in both the highly developed industrial societies and in the newly industrializing ones. Urban populations and industrial activities are increasing the atmospheric pollution in so many metropolitan centers and to such an extent that nature's self-purification processes cannot cope with the problem. And since they are not "scrubbed" or converted by the overtaxed natural processes, urban air pollutants are scattered and deposited over larger areas by the winds and precipitation, eventually

1. Pittsburgh	11. Washington	21. Salt Lake City	31. Portland, Oreg.
2. Detroit	12. Phoenix	22. Toledo	32. Seattle
3. Chicago	13. Atlanta	23. Denver	33. Fresno
4. Springfield, Mass.	14. Philadelphia	24. San Diego	34. San Francisco
5. Los Angeles	15. Milwaukee	25. Cincinnati	35. Kansas City, Mo.
6. Baltimore	16. Newark	26. Syracuse	36. Houston
7. Cleveland	17. Minneapolis	27. Birmingham	37. Buffalo
8. St. Louis	18. Boston	28. Rochester	38. Miami
9. Fairbanks	19. Bridgeport	29. El Paso	39. Dallas
10. New York	20. Indianapolis	30. New Haven	40. New Orleans

FIGURE 14–9

The forty most-polluted cities of the United States, according to air-quality tests by the Environmental Protection Agency.

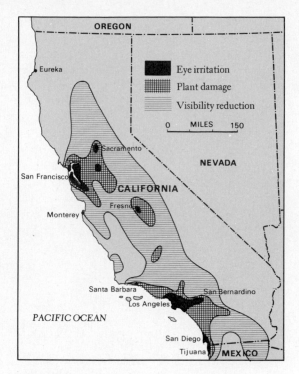

FIGURE 14–10

The extent and some effects of air pollution in California in the early 1960s.

tochemical smogs, created largely by the increasing emissions of nitrogen oxides and hydrocarbons from the engine fuels of transportation systems.

In other instances, and to varying degrees, the rapid increases in urban air pollution in many locations are due to local terrain and weather conditions, which are as yet largely beyond human control (Fig. 14–10 and Plates II, III, and IV). Winter air pollution in the Great Salt Lake basin of Utah, for example, is caused as much by the poor air drainage over the Wasatch mountain range as it is by the high seasonal use of local coals for industrial purposes and home heating. The wind and temperature patterns over the Hudson Valley and neighboring land and water bodies contribute in a large way to the trapping of heavy concentrations of pollutants over New York City for protracted periods. And the cities of Santiago and Lima, on the west coast of South America and backed by the high slopes of the Andes, are also periodically subject to trapped pollution conditions because of the limited ventilation of their situations (Plates II–IV). Tokyo, Hong Kong, and Sydney are each situated amid terrain that resembles, to varying degrees, the mountain-girdled Los Angeles basin, and each is similarly beset by almost constant heavy air pollution.

plaguing even remote rural areas where few air pollutants are ever created (Plate IV). Probably most common are the worldwide photochemical air pollutants, or pho-

Water Pollution

The problems created by water pollution are not new. History is replete with accounts of streams and lakes despoiled by culturally induced land erosion and foul-smelling urban sewers, of garbage-laden harbors, diseased water wells, and sludge-choked rivers. The problem has existed for centuries, but it is now progressing at a much faster rate than in the past (Fig. 14–11). The seriousness of its present state is being acknowledged in many parts of the world; there is increasing public interest in additional antipollution laws and in more stringent enforcement of existing water-use regu-

FIGURE 14–11

Pollution within the Great Lakes water system. Left, an aerial view of pollutants flowing into Lake Michigan along the Chicago lakefront. (NASA, Grant Heilman) Right, some effects of water pollution in Pennsylvania, which borders Lake Erie. (Grant Heilman)

lations. Unfortunately the chemistry and mechanics of water pollution are so complicated that there is still wide disagreement among the experts as to its causes and long-range effects.

The "Water Budget"

Water is vital to all the earth's living things; adequate supplies of it have always been deciding factors in the distribution of plant and animal life, including human populations. For most human uses, and some commercial ones as well, the quality of water is as important as is its supply; to be suitable for human consumption, water must be sub-

stantially free from brackishness, plant and animal wastes, and bacterial contamination. Such unpolluted, or "fresh," water supplies are known as *potable waters.* Early human migration routes and settlement sites were certainly much influenced by the availability of drinkable water, and today—despite advances in drilling, irrigation, and purification—the location, quality, quantity, ownership, and control of potable waters remain major human concerns.

For all practical considerations, the earth's total estimated water supply, or "water budget," is constant. Moreover, the planet's various water forms—vapor, liquid, and solid—have been maintained in practically constant proportions over thousands of years. Significant variations in their proportions occur only during periods of widespread glaciation or deglaciation, when there is a marked change in the amount of water "locked up" in the continental ice sheets. The constancy of the earth's water forms results from an environmental system called the *hydrologic cycle,* which involves the continuous natural processes of evaporation, movement, condensation, precipitation, runoff, and percolation. But with about 97.2 percent of the world's water composed of oceanic brines, and about 2.2 percent locked up in polar ice caps and glaciers, only a meager 0.6 percent of the water budget consists of continental fresh waters—and most of these are subsurface rather than easily accessible to humans in lakes and rivers.

Major Water Pollutants

"Pure water" is a rare substance. Because of its abilities as a solvent, many dissolved substances are usually present in *natural water.* The most common of these natural pollutants are harmless compounds of such chemicals as sodium, calcium, iron, and magnesium. But humans further pollute the surface and subsurface waters of most of the inhabited world by adding an infinite variety and quantity of alien compounds. Wastes from industrial processes, agricultural processes, and human life processes are all dumped sooner or later onto the land and into the waters, and, either indirectly or directly, find their way into the earth's supply of fresh water.

From Industrial Sources. Industrial chemicals and biological matter often reach streams and lakes and subsurface waters as parts of municipal sewage (Fig. 14–12). The principal contributors of such pollutants include food processing plants, textile mills,

pulp and paper plants, iron and steel plants, and synthetic rubber and plastics plants. The effluents of iron and steel plants, an abundant and potent variety of acids, alkalies, and wastes, play a major role in the pollution of streams and lakes in the northeastern United States, northwestern Europe, the Soviet Union, and a score of other large iron and steel centers around the world (Fig. 14–13). Utilizing superheated water, they are also the cause of extensive *thermal pollution* in these waters; today's iron and steel technology uses as much as 12,000 to 14,000 gallons of water per ingot-ton produced, largely for the cooling of high-temperature blast furnaces. As long as the penalties for polluting

FIGURE 14–12
Nondegradable detergent foam covering Conestoga Creek, in Lancaster County, Pennsylvania. (Grant Heilman)

FIGURE 14–13

Water-polluting effluents from industrial sources. Left, at Sparrows Point, Maryland, a large steel mill spewing wastes into Chesapeake Bay. Right, the wastes of a paper mill at Cloquet, Minnesota, flow into the St. Louis River. (Both, Grant Heilman)

public waters are not swift, certain, and high, industry will have little incentive to discover ways to control its pollution. Some efforts are being made, however. A California steel mill located where deep wells must be used to obtain an adequate water supply has developed new cooling technologies that require only about 2 percent of the water used in comparable operations by other steel manufacturers. And pulp and paper plants, traditionally heavy users of public waters for washing and processing, have largely shifted from traditional high-waste (sulfite) production processes to a relatively low-waste (kraft) process—thereby reducing their chemical and wood effluents by as much as 95 percent in the pulping stages.

From Agricultural Sources. For millennia there has been a certain amount of water

pollution from agriculture and animal husbandry, the forces of erosion carrying minerals and biotic materials from soils and grazing lands to nearby streams and lakes. But modern agricultural activities, expanding constantly to feed an additional billion people every generation or less, present an increasingly complex pollution problem. If washed from the soils in sufficient quantities, some of the very chemical fertilizers and pesticides that make possible record crop yields can pollute both surface and subsurface waters and render them unfit for human and animal use.

From Human Sources. But despite the harm done by manufactured substances, the most dominant water pollutant, especially in densely populated developing countries, is still human waste. Raw and undertreated sewage is allowed to flow into the waters that supply tens of thousands of communities throughout the world. More extensive and more effective treatment of sewage is necessary in many urban areas of even the most developed societies.

Oil Pollution of the Oceans. Combining ignorance with hope, past generations have treated the great oceans as limitless waste disposal systems. Even today, it is a bit difficult for most people to understand that the vast oceanic system can be overtaxed by human-induced pollutants; nevertheless, two major appendages to the system, the Mediterranean and the Great Lakes, are already at least partially polluted. Because it is so visible to the naked eye, oil pollution may be one of the major factors in the growing but limited public recognition that even the mighty oceans must be guarded from human abuse. Many of the world's harbors are already choked with harmful oils and debris, and oil spills have scarred beaches and destroyed marine life. The *Torrey Canyon* oil-tanker wreck off the coast of Cornwall, England, in 1967; the Louisiana offshore drilling platform blowout in 1969; and the Santa Barbara, California, offshore drilling platform leaks, in 1969 and 1970, are but some of the disasters that have made oceanic oil pollution a reality to the general public (Fig. 14–14). Unfortunately, such mishaps have also contributed to the vast floating films of oil that now persist over parts of the oceans for extended periods. And with the world energy crisis worsening, offshore drilling and the voyages of supertankers will no doubt be on the increase.

Water Regeneration

There are natural processes that work to absorb limited amounts of natural and human-induced pollutants in all surface and subsurface waters. In this *water regeneration,* which takes much longer than most pollution, natural chemical actions convert many waste pollutants into harmless, sometimes even useful, substances. These processes are very similar to the regenerative powers of the human body in counteracting poisons and eliminating harmful substances.

Degradable Pollutants. The aerobic bacteria in a large body of water use oxygen to transform both natural and culturally induced wastes into chemical *nutrients*— usually nitrates, phosphates, and carbon dioxide—that do no harm to fish or sea plants. Human wastes, kitchen garbage, food processing wastes, wood pulp, and other

FIGURE 14–14

Clean-up operations along a pier in Oakland, California, in 1973 following a 50,000-gallon oil spill into the Oakland estuary. (Wide World)

degradable substances are all transformed by natural chemical decomposition, to the limit of the water's regenerating capacity. The chemical nutrients produced in the process are used as food by *algae* and other green water plants—which become the food of microscopic aquatic animals called *zooplankton*. Small fish eat the zooplankton and are eaten in turn by larger fish, and they by still larger ones. The decomposition of dead animals and fish allowed to remain in water begins the *food chain* anew.

But the natural regenerative processes of water can become overburdened. When excessive waste pollutants are dumped into a body of water, maximum quantities of oxygen are used up in their decomposition; the more oxygen thus used, the less the amount available for use by aquatic animals and plants. These animals and plants begin to suffocate and die, adding even more waste pollutants to the water and increasing the depletion of its oxygen content. Not dependent on a supply of oxygen, *anaerobic* bacteria (rather than aerobic) take over the water body and its waste decay and transformation process; they are effective, but emit noxious gases that give off strong odors.

Eutrophication. The addition of nutrients to a water body through cultural activities and the water's natural processes is usually referred to as *eutrophication*, or nutrient enrichment (Fig. 14–15). Heavy eutrophication greatly increases algae growth. Produced beyond the needs of their water's zooplankton, algae will die and become waste themselves. Their increasing decomposition uses up more and more of the water's oxygen. Thus a stream or lake that is artificially stocked with nutrients—as in the runoff of chemical fertilizers or the dumping of industrial detergents—may eventually choke on its own plant growth. It may take thousands of years for a large water body to

succumb to this evolutionary process, but a small pond can be transformed into a swamp or marsh within a few decades. Even the downfall of a lake can occur within a human lifetime.

Lake Erie, over 200 miles long, is considered a *dead lake* by some scientists, a century or more of abuse by humans having made it a mammoth cesspool. Human and industrial pollutants have been dumped directly into Lake Erie from all directions: Detroit; Windsor, Ontario; Toledo; Cleveland; Erie; Buffalo; and smaller communities have all contributed their wastes. The Cuyahoga River, which flows into Lake Erie's south side at Cleveland, has at times demonstrated a bacterial count near that of raw sewage; and the Detroit River dumps pollutants into the lake from the whole upper Great Lakes basin. The regeneration of Lake Erie is possible, but it will require the joint efforts of nature and human beings for years or even decades.

FIGURE 14–15

A diagrammatic representation of the eutrophication, or excess fertilization, of large water bodies. The process is caused when heavy pollution promotes a cycle of algae growth and decay.

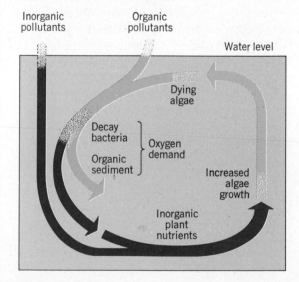

Land Pollution

Humankind's early plant and animal production may have disturbed the upper layers of the cultivated soils and grazing lands, but probably did little to permanently upset their natural processes and formations. The effect of agriculture in recent centuries has been much more harmful; and, in the last three decades, doubling and quadrupling world food demands have placed unparalleled pressures on the world's cultivable soils. Although human understanding of soil exhaustion has progressed markedly in this period, land in many parts of the world is still being overworked and misused.

Throughout most of history, animal manures, night soil, and "green fertilizers" (legumes and grasses plowed under) were the farmer's chief sources of *soil enrichment*. Not until well into the twentieth century did American and European farmers make the first extensive uses of chemical fertilizers and acid neutralizers. As food-production demands have continued to spiral upward, more and better commercial fertilizers have been produced. And along with the wide array of fertilizers, science has provided an equally varied assortment of pesticides and fungicides. Their effects on food production have been phenomenal, but it is becoming clear that they offer unwelcome repercussions as well; some of the new wonder fertilizers and pesticides are now thought to be harmful to human health, both when encountered directly and when ingested through the products and tissue of plants and animals. Excessive use of fertilizers and pesticides is even being discouraged as harmful to the humus layer of soil, for it apparently decreases the layer's natural nutrient production and thus makes the soil more dependent on continuous artificial enrichment.

Agriculture and Mining

Soil erosion has always been a problem in world agriculture and gardening. But the seriousness of the problem has increased greatly since the introduction of deep-plowing a century ago and the marked increase, since the beginning of this century, of clean-row cultivation—the cultivation in even, weeded rows of such crops as cotton, potatoes, and cabbage. Both these techniques generate increases in crop yields, by allowing for better utilization of natural soil moistures, but they also contribute to extensive erosion (Fig. 14–16). All the topsoil of a

FIGURE 14–16

Oddly shaped islands of cultivated land in an extensive area of Kansas once covered by wheat fields. Abetted by noncontour planting and serious droughts, soil erosion has gullied most of the area and made it useless for farming. (Grant Heilman)

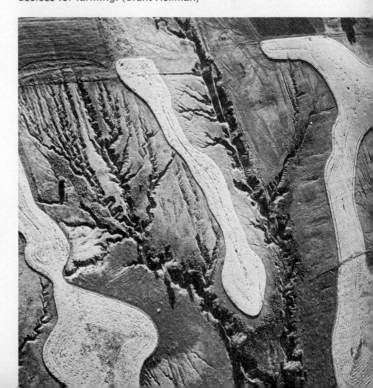

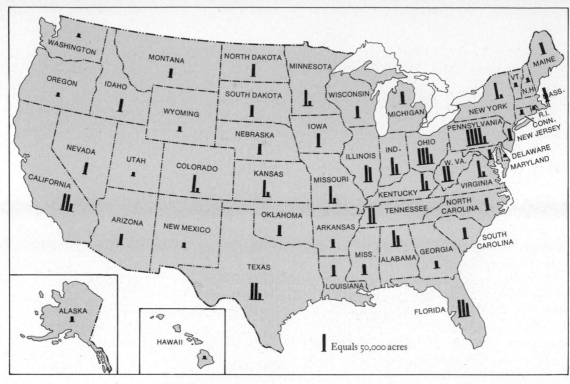

FIGURE 14-17

Above, the extent of strip mining in the United States; by the mid-1970s over 3.5 million acres had been laid waste by surface mining. Below, random absorptions of farmland due to the strip mining of coal, near Appleton City, Missouri. (Grant Heilman)

clean-cultivated field may be washed away by *sheet erosion* within a few years or even a single season. Since the first pioneers made their way across the United States, the fertile topsoils of its agricultural lands have been eroded away in many places by as much as one-third of their original depths—mainly through *eolian erosion,* which carries away soil denuded by excessive cropping and overgrazing (see Chapter 2, section entitled "The Dust Bowl"). Irresponsible farming practices are the basic cause of this and much of the world's soil erosion, but they can now be avoided relatively easily and cheaply.

Ranking second to agriculture as a source of erosion is the extraction of minerals from the earth's surface by means of strip mining, a process that will probably become even more extensive in response to the recent energy crisis. By the beginning of the 1970s, over three and a half million acres of United States land—over 5,000 square miles —had been cut and ridged by strip mining (Fig. 14–17). Strip mining to extract coal accounts for over half of these distressed areas, and the extraction of precious metals, such as gold, and sand and gravel is the cause of most of the rest.

A Positive Geomorphic Step

As geomorphic agents, with relatively superior skills and highly advanced technologies, people in a developing society can reshape the earth's surface in a variety of ways and with varying degrees of permanence. Some of this geomorphic activity is environmentally constructive, and some is extremely destructive.

One of the most constructive, and extensive, of all artificial landforms is found in the Zuider Zee region of the Netherlands, where the Dutch government has drained

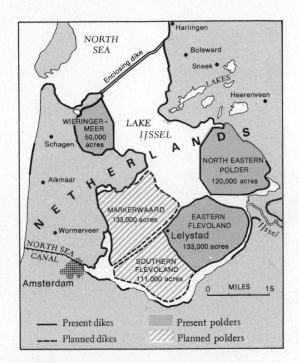

FIGURE 14–18

The diked and drained new lands in the Netherlands.

the sea water from 950 square miles of land in large sectors called *polders* (Fig. 14–18). The first polder, 50,000 acres facing the North Sea, was drained in 1930. A 20-mile-long dike was then completed across the remaining mouth of the estuary, in 1932, to permanently separate the entire bay area from the sea. More of the Zuider Zee now has been diked and drained, and more is being readied; the deepest part has been converted into Lake IJssel. The second polder, 120,000 acres, was drained in 1942; and the third, 133,000 acres, in 1957. Two remaining areas, one 111,000 acres and the other 133,000 acres, are being readied for draining. After each polder is drained of its sea water, the new lands are worked and flushed extensively for several years under government supervision; when they are suitable for cultivation, they are leased to private farmers.

Comparable landform changes in other parts of the world include the creation of vast agricultural terraces throughout most of south and east Asia—especially in China, Japan, India, Sri Lanka, Nepal, the Philippines, and Indonesia—and the enormous excavations necessary in the building of the Suez and Panama canals (Fig. 14–19).

FIGURE 14–19

One of modern society's major geomorphic feats, the building of a canal across the Isthmus of Panama was both useful to humans and environmentally sound. Above, Panama Canal construction at Culebra Cut in 1904. Below, the Pacific entrance to the canal, through Miraflores Locks, in 1953. (Panama Canal Official Photo)

Other Forms of Pollution

Noise

Another rapidly growing environmental problem in most societies of the world is *noise*. While the dangers of human exposure to intense sound and vibration are usually most severe in highly urbanized, heavily industrialized centers, serious noise problems also exist in suburban, commercial, and entertainment areas. And with the proliferation of television sets, dishwashers, vacuum cleaners, and food blenders, the noise levels in the modern home are beginning to approach those of factories, airports, and discotheques. Prolonged exposure to certain intense noises can cause hearing impairments and, probably, adverse effects on the human nervous system (Fig. 14–20).

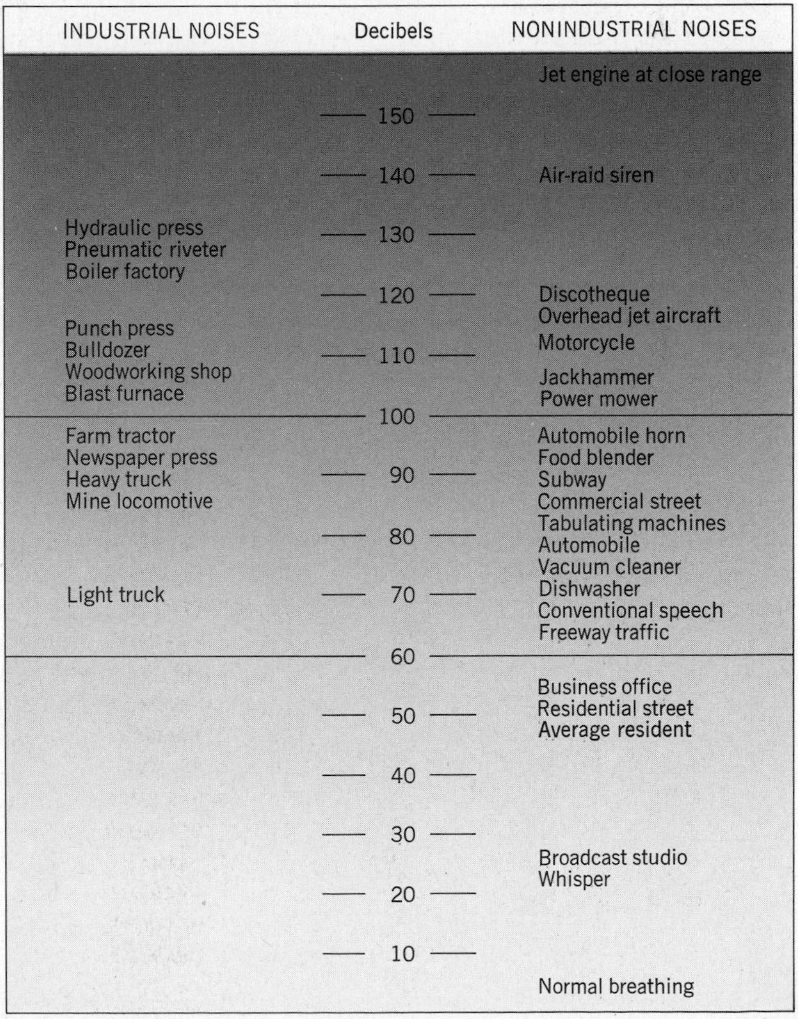

INDUSTRIAL NOISES	Decibels	NONINDUSTRIAL NOISES
		Jet engine at close range
	— 150 —	
	— 140 —	Air-raid siren
Hydraulic press Pneumatic riveter Boiler factory	— 130 —	
	— 120 —	Discotheque Overhead jet aircraft
Punch press Bulldozer	— 110 —	Motorcycle
Woodworking shop Blast furnace		Jackhammer Power mower
	— 100 —	
Farm tractor Newspaper press		Automobile horn Food blender
Heavy truck Mine locomotive	— 90 —	Subway Commercial street
	— 80 —	Tabulating machines Automobile Vacuum cleaner
Light truck	— 70 —	Dishwasher Conventional speech Freeway traffic
	— 60 —	
	— 50 —	Business office Residential street Average resident
	— 40 —	
	— 30 —	Broadcast studio
	— 20 —	Whisper
	— 10 —	
		Normal breathing

FIGURE 14–20

A comparison of industrial and nonindustrial noise levels. Such levels are measured in decibels: those below 60 decibels are considered acceptable to human sensibilities; those between 60 and 100 generally annoying; and those above 100 frequently damaging to human health.

Noise levels are expressed in units called *decibels*, which represent the intensity of sounds on a scale from 0 to 160. Least perceptible sounds are low on the scale, and there is a multiplying intensity with each decibel rise. The perceived sound intensity of any noise source at 160 decibels is about four times that of the same noise source at 140 decibels. Most noises that register between 0 and 60 decibels are considered to be of little physical or psychological danger to human beings; those that register between 60 and 100 are generally annoying and at least mildly hazardous if prolonged; and all those noises that register above 100 decibels are probably both physically and psychologically dangerous to most people subjected to them for extended periods.

FIGURE 14–21

Comparative estimates of solid wastes in the United States. (After U.S. Bureau of Solid Waste Management)

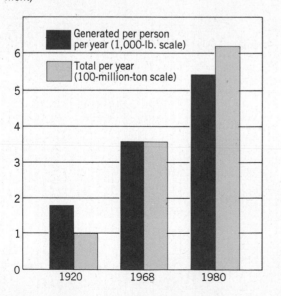

Heavy Metals

Heavy metals, such as mercury and lead, are introduced into the air and water daily, both through the normal processes of nature and the varied activities of human beings. Most of the additions for which humans are responsible are made by means of energy-combustion processes—in factories, power-generation plants, and automobile engines. As solids, liquids, and gases, most heavy metals are highly poisonous to human beings and, consumed in large amounts, can affect the nervous system adversely and permanently. Due in large part to the widespread use of pesticides, these poisonous metals have been diffused throughout large portions of the earth's atmosphere, water, and soil. They are particularly menacing because they collect in the organs and tissue of animals and, unchanged in food preparation, can pass through an entire food chain, with each order in the chain acquiring the accumulations of all preceding orders.

Radiation

Although necessary for all life on earth, *radiation* can also destroy all forms of earthly life. To the radiation that comes directly from the sun, science has added large amounts from radioactive materials—through nuclear fallout, waste from nuclear power plants, and such electronic equipment as X-rays, laser beams, color television, and microwave ovens. Research on the effects of radiation is as yet inconclusive, but exposure to unusual amounts is thought to result in cancer and other harmful changes in animal cells. International agreements banning most testing of nuclear devices in the atmosphere have been signed by many nations of the world, but the atmospheric testing by abstaining nations and all underground testing are without official restrictions. Moreover, even unanimous agreement to the present nuclear treaties would not be a guarantee against large-scale accidental contaminations.

Solid Wastes

Of all the pollutants created in the name of societal progress, *solid wastes* are probably among the most serious environmental threats, and the most difficult to handle. Early societies were not very subtle in disposing of their solid wastes—for the most part bones, bowls, broken tools, and charcoals—but nature was able to cooperate in fairly effective cover-ups, now known as *middenheaps* and considered valuable anthropological records. Modern societies often seem nearly as inept in disposing of their solid wastes, and the composition and volume of these materials sometimes seems to defy nature as well (Fig. 14–21).

Sources and Disposal. Each day the people of the United States throw away great quantities of solid wastes, or trash, their cast-offs reaching a total of over 4 billion tons a year. Fortunately, over 90 percent of this discarded material is associated with agricultural and mining activities and is thus widely dispersed through sparsely populated rural and mountain areas, where, tending to blend with the natural landscape, it offends or threatens relatively few people. The remaining 10 percent of the country's rubbish develops within more heavily populated areas, where it is highly concentrated, highly visible, and a virtual plague on everyone's doorstep—householders, institutions, and businesses alike (Fig. 14–22).

The federal Bureau of Solid Waste Management estimates that household and commercial sources contribute about 6 percent of the country's annual total of solid wastes. Wastepaper represents about one-half of this figure, with bottles, cans, textiles, and lawn rubbish accounting for most of the re-

FIGURE 14–22

While solid wastes are ever becoming a more visible problem of the countryside, the greater portion of every nation's solid wastes, or rubbish, is amassed within heavily populated urban areas. Mounds comparable to the one shown here exist in many urbanized areas of the world, and their varying contents tell much about the interests and socioeconomic levels of different societies. (Bayer from Monkmeyer)

FIGURE 14–23

A shorefront dumping area in New Jersey. Some countries have prohibited such dumps within densely populated areas, but prohibition is futile unless accompanied by effective reclamation and recycling programs. (Bruce Davidson, © 1969 Magnum)

mainder. Industrial solid wastes, though only about 3 percent of the total, represent a much greater threat to the environment than household and commercial wastes.

Until recently, many small commercial and industrial establishments disposed of their solid wastes mainly by burning or merely dumping them in open lots. But federal and state regulations now place heavy restrictions on open burning at dump sites. Sanitary landfill-dumps have been introduced in many progressive communities, but they are only small first steps in a much needed long-range federal solid-waste-management program (Fig. 14–23).

Reclamation and Recycling. There are materials in most solid wastes that can be reclaimed and put to new uses, or recycled.

Often among them are such valuable natural resources as iron, copper, and bauxite ores, from slag piles and old tailings; iron and steel, copper, aluminum, and tin, from old machinery, cans, and automobiles; glass, from old bottles and jars; and paper pulp, from old newsprint. An increasing number of less valuable materials is also being recycled in order to avoid the problems of their collection and disposal. With aggravated collection and disposal problems impending, it is likely that even greater importance will have to be given to recycling, especially as it involves the reuse of depletable natural materials, such as lumber or nondegradable substances. Conservation is in style again, and one hopes that societal attitudes toward balanced resource management will continue their present upward trend.

REVIEW AND DISCUSSION

1. Write a short, well-organized essay on the major aspects of environmental damage and conservation attempts during the nineteenth and twentieth centuries.
2. Cite briefly several harmful impacts of air pollution on living beings in either your specific local community or geographical region.
3. Describe *thermal inversions* and indicate where such conditions frequently occur within the United States.
4. Compare and contrast the impacts of air pollutants from the three major sources: transportation devices, power plants, and industry. What are the "atmosphere's self-purification" processes? Discuss one major example.

5. For most human uses, and some commercial ones as well, the quality of water is as important as is its supply. Comment on the relationship of this important fact to water pollution. Discuss the world's "water budget" and its significance in the understanding of water pollution.

6. Discuss the differing distributions and consequences of water pollutants from industrial sources, from agricultural sources, and from human sources, on an international basis.

7. What is meant by *water regeneration?* How is it affected by nondegradable pollutants? What is *eutrophication?* How does this process proceed?

8. Research and write a short essay on one of the world's many polluted water bodies—for example, the Rhine River, Lake Tahoe, the Danube River, the Monongahela River, the Mediterranean Sea, Lake Baikal, the Dead Sea, or the Ganges River. How did this water body become polluted? What is being done to restore it or to keep it from additional harm?

9. What is the status of noise pollution as an ever-growing environmental problem? How widespread is this type of pollution? What serious encounters with it have you had? What were their effects?

10. Of all the pollutants created in the name of societal progress, solid wastes are probably the most aesthetically undesirable. How can solid wastes also do physical damage to the environment?

11. What are the principal sources of solid wastes? What have been the usual means of solid waste disposal in the past, and what may be the best means of disposing of solid wastes in the future? What roles do you think reclamation and recycling can and will play in future environmental protection?

12. Would there be environmental pollution if human beings did not exist? Explain and provide examples to support your argument.

SELECTED REFERENCES

American Chemical Society. *Solid Wastes.* Washington, D.C., 1971.

Andrassy, J. *International Law and the Resources of the Sea.* New York: Columbia University Press, 1970.

Baron, R. A. *The Tyranny of Noise.* New York: St. Martin's, 1971.

Bates, M. "The Human Ecosystem." *Resources and Man.* San Francisco: Freeman, 1969.

Benarde, M. A. *Our Precarious Habitat,* rev. ed. New York: Norton, 1973.

Brady, N. C., ed. *Agriculture and the Quality of Our Environment.* Washington, D.C.: American Association for the Advancement of Science, 1967.

Bryson, R. A., and J. E. Kutzbach. *Air Pollution.* Washington, D.C.: Commission on College Geography, Resource Paper No. 2, Association of American Geographers, 1968.

Bullard, F. M. *Volcanoes in History, in Theory, in Eruption.* Austin: University of Texas Press, 1962.

Carr, D. E. *The Breath of Life.* New York: Norton, 1965.

Clark, J. R. "Thermal Pollution and Aquatic Life." *Scientific American,* Vol. 220 (March 1969), 18–27.

Commoner, B. *The Closing Circle: Nature, Man and Technology.* New York: Knopf, 1971.

Detwyler, T. R., ed. *Man's Impact on Environment: Selected Readings.* New York: McGraw-Hill, 1971.

Doerr, A., and L. Guernsey. "Man as a Geomorphological Agent: The Example of Coal Mining." In F. E. Dohrs and L. M. Sommers, eds., *Physical Geography: Selected Readings.* New York: Crowell, 1967.

Dorst, J. *Before Nature Dies.* Baltimore: Penguin, 1971.

Ehrlich, P., and A. Ehrlich. *Population, Resources, Environment.* San Francisco: Freeman, 1970.

Fenner, D., and J. Klarman. "Power from the Earth." *Environment,* Vol. 13 (December 1971), 19–26, 31–34.

Friedman, W. *The Future of the Oceans.* New York: Braziller, 1971.

"Great Lakes Water Use: Population, Land Use, Power, Waste Disposal, Commodity Flow" (Map). Ottawa: Department of Energy, Mines and Resources, 1971.

Greenwood, N., and J. Edwards. *Human Environments and Natural Systems.* Belmont, Calif.: Wadsworth, 1973.

Hamblim, L. *Pollution—The World Crisis.* New York: Barnes & Noble, 1971.

Hannon, B. M. "Bottles, Cans, Energy." *Environment,* Vol. 14 (March 1972), 11–21.

Hare, F. K. "How Should We Treat the Environment?" *Science,* Vol. 167 (23 January 1970), 352–55.

Hines, L. G. *Environmental Issues: Population, Pollution, and Economics.* New York: Norton, 1973.

Hubschman, J. "Lake Erie: Pollution Abatement, Then What?" *Science,* Vol. 171 (12 February 1971), 536–40.

Kromm, D. E. "Response to Air Pollution in Ljubljana, Yugoslavia." *Annals of the Association of American Geographers,* Vol. 63 (June 1973), 208–17.

Malin, H., and C. Lewicke. "Pollution-Free Power for the Automobile." *Environmental Science and Technology,* Vol. 6 (1972), 512–17.

Marine, G. *America the Raped.* New York: Simon & Schuster, 1969.

Mecklin, J. M. "It's Time to Turn Down All That Noise." *Fortune,* Vol. 80 (October 1969), 130–33, 188–95.

Miller, G. *Replenish the Earth.* Belmont, Calif.: Wadsworth, 1972.

Shepard, P. *Man in the Landscape.* New York: Random House, 1967.

Small, W. E. *Third Pollution: The National Problem of Solid Waste Disposal.* New York: Praeger, 1971.

Steinhart, J., and C. Steinhart. *Blowout: A Case Study of the Santa Barbara Oil Spill.* Belmont, Calif.: Duxbury Press, 1972.

Stern, A., ed. *Air Pollution,* 2nd ed., 3 vols. New York: Academic Press, 1968.

Strobble, M. *Understanding Environmental Pollution.* St. Louis, Mo.: Mosby, 1971.

Turk, A., et al. *Ecology, Pollution and Environment.* Philadelphia: Saunders, 1972.

Warren, C. *Biology and Water Pollution Control.* Philadelphia: Saunders, 1971.

Weinberg, A. "Social Institutions and Nuclear Energy." *Science,* Vol. 177 (March 1972), 27–34.

Wexler, H. "Volcanoes and World Climate." *Scientific American,* Vol. 186 (April 1952), 74–80.

Willrich, T., and N. Hines, eds. *Water Pollution Control and Abatement.* Ames: Iowa State University Press, 1967.

Wilson, C., ed. *Man's Impact on the Global Environment.* Cambridge: Massachusetts Institute of Technology Press, 1970.

Wolozin, H., ed. *The Economics of Air Pollution: A Symposium.* New York: Norton, 1966.

Graphic Representations
of the Earth

Modern field and laboratory work in geography employs both traditional devices, such as maps and globes, and many recently discovered techniques, such as aerial and color photography and remote sensing—a highly sophisticated system involving the use of high-altitude aircraft or space vehicles. Thus, today's geographer is able to record earth phenomena with much greater facility and speed than his predecessors. The wealth of data gathered by these new means has led to increasingly sophisticated hypotheses concerning the total earth environment.

The Geographic Grid

The *globe* is the closest approximation of the earth yet devised by humankind. A scale model of the entire earth, it is usually small enough to be scanned in a few glances. The ancient Greeks—who, more than 1,600 years before the time of Columbus, postulated that the earth was approximately spherical—were the first to reproduce the earth in the form of a globe. (The oldest existing globe, however, is of German origin and was completed in 1492; it is now in the Germanic Museum at Nurenberg, Germany.)

A glance at any globe reveals a system of intersecting lines. This network consists of the *meridians*—north-south lines connecting the north and south poles—and the *parallels*—east-west lines crossing the meridians at right angles (Fig. A–1).

The meridians are used to measure distances and to designate positions that are east or west of a particular line of reference. Arbitrarily chosen and later confirmed by international agreement, this line of reference is the meridian that passes through Greenwich (London), England, and is designated the *prime meridian*. Measurements that are east or west of the prime meridian are designated by the term *longitude,* and are expressed in degrees and fractions thereof. *East longitude* extends halfway around the earth to the east; *west longitude* extends halfway around the earth to the west. Since all circles are comprised of 360 degrees, the east and west longitudes each encompass 180 degrees (Fig. A–2). For further refinement of measurement and loca-

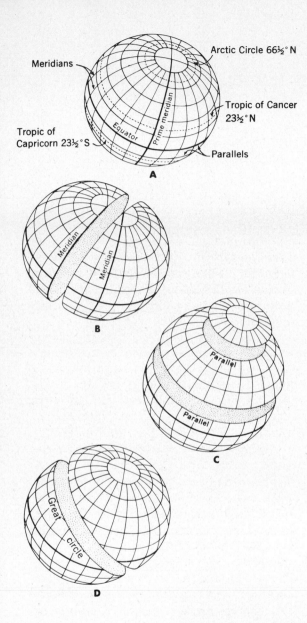

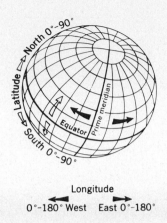

FIGURE A–2

Reference lines. The measurement of *longitude east* and *west* of the prime meridian, and the measurement of *latitude north* and *south* of the equator.

FIGURE A–1

The Globe. A. The most important *lines* on the globe. B. The *meridians.* Any meridian is one half of a great circle. C. The *parallels.* Of these, only the equator is a great circle. D. The *great circles.* Any circle drawn on the earth's surface whose center coincides with the center of the globe is a great circle.

tion, each degree (°) is divided into 60 minutes ('), and each minute may itself be divided into 60 seconds ("). Thus, for example, Colombo, Sri Lanka is said to be located at 79°52′ E and Hilo, the largest island of Hawaii, at 155°01′ W (Plate II).

Parallels are used to measure distances and to designate positions north or south of the equator. These north-south positions, or distances, are called *latitudes,* and, like longitudes, are expressed in degrees, minutes, and seconds. The distance from the equator to either pole is one-fourth of the circumference of a circle, or 90 degrees. Thus, north and south latitudes each encompass 90 degrees (Fig. A–2). In terms of latitude, Colombo, Sri Lanka is located north of the equator at 6°58′ N and Hilo, Hawaii at 19°44′ N.

The full coordinates of Colombo, Sri Lanka are thus 6°58′ N, 79°52′ E; and the full coordinates of Hilo, Hawaii are 19°44′ N, 155°01′ W.

Time Systematization

Standard Time Zones

Time is determined with respect to the average rotation period of the earth on its axis. One rotation period of the earth is designated a day. Since every point on the earth rotates in a 360° circle around the earth's axis once every 24 hours, every point on the earth moves through 15° of the arc every hour of time. This simple space-time relationship provides the working basis for the system of *standard time zones*—a system devised during the last century in response to humanity's urgent need to keep track of time on a global basis.

If the earth rotated in such a fashion as to present the same face—the same half—to the sun at all times (as is almost the case with the planet Mercury), then that half would have constant daylight, and the other half would be in constant darkness. This does not occur, however, because, as noted before, the speed of rotation is such that, for each 24-hour period, the earth presents a steadily changing face to the sun. Thus, there is an infinite succession of mornings, noons, evenings, and midnights, no one of which can possibly occur over the entire earth at the same time. If it is noon in Los Angeles, it is midnight at an *antipodal* (opposite) location somewhere in the Indian Ocean (Plate IX).

Because the earth rotates toward its own east, each morning approaches from the east, as does each noon, sunset, and midnight. Thus, when it is noon in Chicago, it is approximately 1:00 P.M. in New York, but only about 11:00 A.M. in Denver (Fig. A-3). Actually, there are as many noons—that is, noon positions of the sun—as there are longitudinal positions on the earth. Clocks set according to the noon positions of the sun would even show slightly different times for east and west Chicago. Thus, a century ago, with the development of cross-country rail travel in the United States, a more uniform time system became mandatory—time had to be standardized.

In 1883, the railroads of the United States agreed upon a system of standard time zones. In ensuing years, the entire country followed suit. Today, the coterminous United States is divided into four standard time zones established by the Interstate Commerce Commission (Fig. A-3). Each zone is 15° of longitude in width, or, in other words, "one hour of time" in width. All localities within each zone are governed by the time of the zone's *central meridian;* and each zone is one hour earlier than its neighboring zone to its east. The longitudinal boundaries of these zones are irregular lines, for they were drawn so as to avoid splitting major population agglomerations into different zones.

The world standard time zone system is simply an extension of the system developed in the United States. The earth is divided into 24 time zones, each covering 15° of longitude, or one hour of time (Fig. A-4). The "0" time zone is based on the prime meridian, and both to the west and to the east of it are zones consecutively numbered from 1 to 12, indicating the number of hours to be subtracted from (if to the west), or added to (if to the east), *Greenwich Mean Time* in order to get the given zone's *standard time*. The boundaries of these zones also are purposely irregular to avoid, as much as possible, the splitting of major national and economic areas into two or more time zones.

The International Date Line

From the above discussion, it follows that comparisons of the "day" at distant places on the earth can become somewhat complex. One might assume that it is noon on Wednesday in London and that it is midnight on the other side of the earth (at the 180° meridian). But the question is, what midnight?

The answer is relatively simple. By inter-national agreement, each new calendar day begins at midnight at the *International Date Line,* which, in general, follows the course of the 180° meridian: from pole to pole through the central Pacific (Fig. A–4). Every day of the week begins at midnight at the International Date Line, travels westward around the earth, and arrives (and ends) at the date line 24 hours later. Thus, there is a westward procession of the "days," just as there is a westward procession of the "hours" of the day; and, just as it is not the same time all over the earth, it also is not the same calendar day. When crossing the international date

FIGURE A–3

The *standard time zones of the United States.* The meridians shown are the so-called *central,* or *standard,* meridians. Standard time for Alaska was set by Congress as that of the 150°W meridian; but actually, as indicated in Figure A–4, four different times are used.

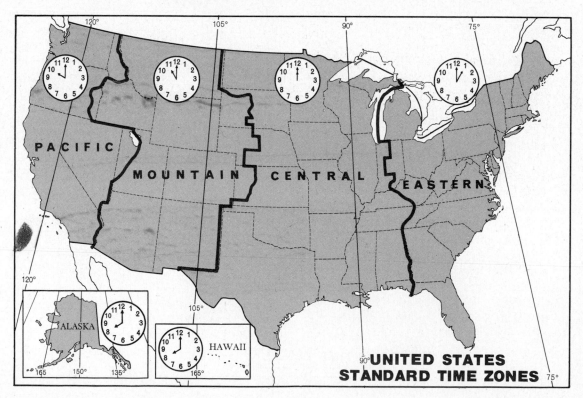

UNITED STATES
STANDARD TIME ZONES

line going westward, a person loses a day—for example, Wednesday morning immediately becomes Thursday, even though only moments have passed. When crossing the date line going eastward, a person repeats the same day—for example, one Wednesday is followed by a second Wednesday (Fig. A–4).

The arbitrary positioning of the International Date Line in the mid-Pacific has proven to be highly convenient, for, in that area, there are few lands and people to be affected by the collision of different days. The slightly irregular trace of the date line is an attempt to place entire island groups to one side or the other of the line for added simplicity and the convenience of the islands' inhabitants.

FIGURE A–4

The *standard times zones of the world*. The earth is divided into twenty-four time zones, each covering 15° of longitude. The time of the "0" zone is based on the 0° meridian (located at Greenwich, England), and it is generally adopted as *standard time* for 7°30′ eastward and westward. Each of the zones beyond is *designated* by a number representing the hours to be added to, or subtracted from, that zone's standard time to get *Greenwich Mean Time*. Irregularities in the zonal pattern are due to adjustments made for national and economic convenience.

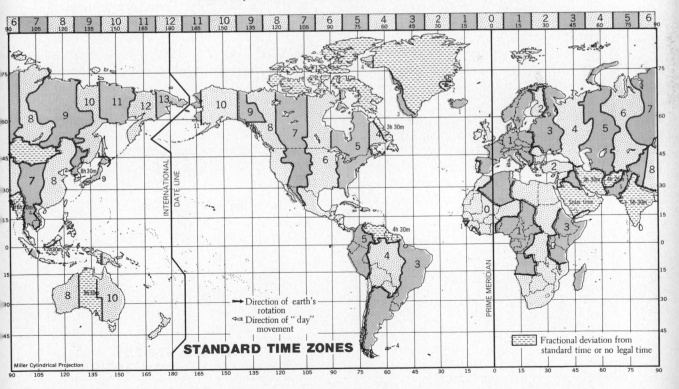

Maps

Planimetric Maps

Today, maps are virtually infinite in purpose, design, scale, and origin; and they continue to be the principal tools or devices for geographic investigation and exposition. The term *map* derives from the Latin word *mappa,* meaning cover. By today's definition, a map is a scaled representation of all, or some portion, of the earth, constructed on a flat, or plane, surface. The earliest map still in existence is a clay tablet that shows a part of Mesopotamia and that dates from about 2,500 B.C.

For clarity and easy reference, modern maps generally include certain standard components. These are *title, date, legend,* and some identification of the *scale, latitude, longitude, direction,* and *projection* involved. One or more of these components are sometimes omitted, especially when maps appear in close relation to textual materials.

A concise but full *title* that identifies the purpose and extent of a map is an aid in its documentation, cataloguing, and use in subsequent research; this is true both of an intricate map of world vegetation (Plate V) and of a much simpler map of, say, drainage patterns. Many maps also carry a *date* and,

sometimes, both the date of the data portrayed and, if different, the date of the map's publication. Very large maps of relatively small areas are frequently self-explanatory in regard to the data they portray, but most maps are of such small size in proportion to their area of coverage that it is necessary to include appropriate symbolization in a *legend* (Plate IV).

Since maps are flattened out globes, or parts of globes, they all have *scale* relationships with the earth, or with whatever segment of it they portray. Several methods, or devices, are commonly used to indicate the scale of a map. One means of scale identification is the *printed word*—as in "one inch equals one mile," or, "one inch equals 315 miles." More frequently, however, the scale of a map is indicated *graphically* by a measured line, graduated to show the relationship between map-distances and corresponding earth-distances (Plate II). This type of graphic, or *bar,* scale is frequently accompanied, or replaced, by a *representative fraction* (RF), or fractional scale—such as 1:24,000. The following listing provides some of the map scales most commonly used on an international basis.

Map scale (RF)		Equivalents on the earth's surface to one inch on the map (in feet and miles)
1:	10,000	833 feet
1:	24,000	2,000
1:	50,000	4,166
1:	62,500	5,208
1:	63,360	1.00 mile
1:	100,000	1.58
1:	500,000	7.89
1:	1,000,000	15.78
1:	50,000,000	789.00

Small- and large-scale maps differ not only in the quantity of detail that can be incorporated but also in the quality of such detail, and in the effectiveness of the generalizations that can or must be made.

A map that indicates latitude and longitude data, either along the margins or by showing parallels and meridians, indicates the precise position of the map area on the face of the earth. This same data may also be a reference to the direction shown on the map, since parallels always extend east-west and meridians north-south. *Direction* is also indicated on some maps by means of a *north arrow,* which may refer to and be marked either *true north* or *magnetic north.* A true north arrow is in alignment with a meridian and thus points to the *geographic* (true) north pole. A magnetic north arrow is in alignment with the flows, or lines, of the magnetic forces that course through the earth. At any point on the earth, the angle between true north and magnetic north is known as the *magnetic declination.* The lines of magnetic force follow wavy paths, not the meridians, and they flow not from geographic pole to geographic pole but between the earth's magnetic poles. They also fluctuate and shift gradually through the years. The *north magnetic pole* is presently at approximately 75° N, 101° W (Fig. A–5); and the *south magnetic pole* is located near the fringe

FIGURE A–5

Magnetic declinations (variations of the compass) in part of the Northern Hemisphere. The solid and dashed lines are *isogonic lines* (lines of equal magnetic declination). The heavy line is the *agonic line* (line of no magnetic declination). The dashed lines are in areas where the magnetic compass points west of *true north;* the solid lines are in areas where it points east of true north. The *north magnetic pole* is located approximately at 75° N, 101° W. (Adapted from U.S. Hydrographic Chart No. 1706, for 1965)

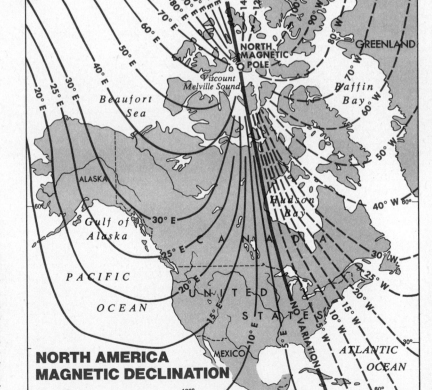

NORTH AMERICA MAGNETIC DECLINATION

of Antarctica, south of New Zealand. To allow for corrections of magnetic north to true north, detailed maps showing magnetic declination are prepared by various hydrographic agencies. Each line on such maps is called an *isogonic line;* and all points on a given isogonic line have the same declination. The line along which there is no magnetic declination is called the *agonic line.* In southern California, the magnetic compass points about 15° east of true north, which thus requires a 15° correction to the west. In central Maine, the magnetic compass points about 20° west of true north, which thus requires a 20° correction to the east (Fig. A–5).

Topographic (Contour) Maps

The most useful and most exact of the various relief, or three-dimensional, maps is the *contour map.* In the United States, this type of map is used for the standard topographic maps issued by the United States Geological Survey, Department of the Interior. A portion of such a topographic map, showing part of the Saticoy Quadrangle (contour map 1:24,000) appears inside the back cover of this book. Close examination of this map will show patterns of approximately paralleling fine brown lines bending and curving over its land areas. Each of these fine lines is a *contour line,* and the presence of a sufficient number of them enables one to perceive the third-dimension (depth) of minor landform features. To the trained observer, a contour map takes on the appearance of a relief model.

A contour line connects, or extends through, points that are the same elevation above sea level (Fig. A–6). In reading a contour map, one must know the *contour interval* —that is, the *vertical distance* between the contour lines, or the *vertical difference in elevation* between two adjacent contours.

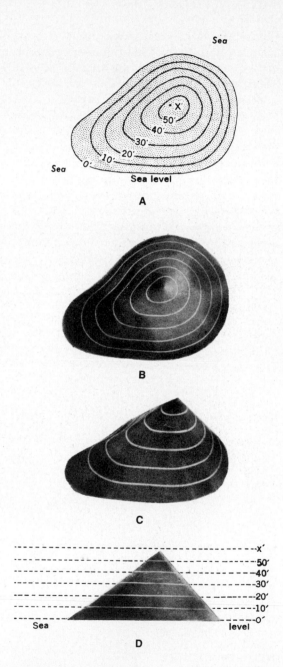

FIGURE A–6

Contour lines as they appear on a *contour map,* and as the same lines appear on views of a model of the same conically-shaped landform. The contour interval used here is 10 feet. A. Contour map. B. Vertical view. C. Oblique view. D. Side view.

With a considerable number of such lines arranged closely over an area, one can generally visualize the varying relief represented. Whatever the nature of the terrain features represented—plains, hills, cliffs, or even mountains—the spacings of their contours indicate their surface *gradients*. (Gradient is the degree of *slope steepness*, as measured in amount of *vertical change* in a given horizontal distance.) The closer the contour lines crowd together, the steeper the gradient; and the wider apart they spread, the flatter the gradient. Contours spread far apart on level areas and crowd together, and even merge, along steep slopes and sheer cliffs.

The stylized contour map in Figure A–7 illustrates several elementary characteristics common to all contour maps, regardless of the scales or terrain types involved. Most contour maps indicate a number of *bench marks*, which are precisely located spots on the earth's surface for which exact elevations have been determined. A permanent bench mark is usually a post that is set into a concrete base and then topped by a small bronze plate. This plate has several important functions. It serves to indicate the area's latitude and longitude, elevation and direction, the plate's date of installation, and the name of the agency that erected it.

FIGURE A–7

A simple and stylized contour map, illustrating the behavior of contours, the types of bench marks, and the determination of elevations and slopes. The contour interval used here is 25 feet. Contour lines wide apart indicate gentle slope. Contour lines close together indicate steep slope.

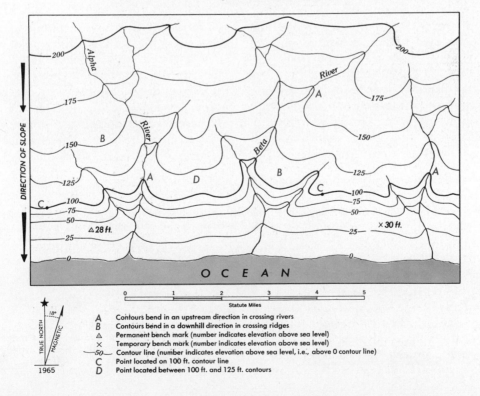

Map Projections

The ideal way to represent the total earth, its components, and its many changing surface aspects is by means of a globe — the only "true representation." But, the globe has several distinct disadvantages, mainly its limited portability, and production and reproduction difficulties. So people depend largely on maps that are flat, and on the projections that make it possible to construct flat maps for extensive areas.

A *map projection* is any orderly realignment of the spherical earth's *grid*, or *graticule*, of meridians and parallels onto a flat or level surface. Every map projection has its own peculiar version of this linear network; some are simple, others more complex and irregular (Fig. A–8). But there is no perfect, or all-purpose, map projection. The construction of every projection involves some distortion of the earth's grid. Each projection thus has its own particular limitations and should be used only for the purposes for which its design is well suited.

The two major properties of map projections (never found together in the same projection) are *equivalence*, or *equal-area*, and *conformality*, or *true shape*; and the two significant secondary properties are *azimuth*, or *true direction*, and *equidistance*, or *true distance*.

Equivalent, or equal-area, map projections portray all of their subject areas in proportion to their true sizes on the earth — but the shapes of these areas are badly distorted. Among such projections are the sinusoidal equal-area projection (Plates II–VIII) and the Mollweide projection (Fig. A–9).

Conformal, or true shape, map projections portray all small features of a small area in their true shapes, but their areas are distorted; one example is the Mercator projection (Fig. A–10). (Unfortunately, no projection can show the true shapes of such large areas as Asia or America — only a globe can do this.) Conformal map projections are designed especially for use in navigation and surveying.

Azimuthal, or true direction, map projections show the correct directions of an area from a stated point on the map. Equidistance, or true distance, map projections show the correct distances of an area from a stated point on the map.

These four groups of map projections include most of the maps in general use today. A few map projections do not fall within any

FIGURE A–8

Map projections. At the left, the relatively simple grid of one type of *cylindrical projection.* In the center, the globe. At the right, the relatively complicated grid of the *sinusoidal projection.*

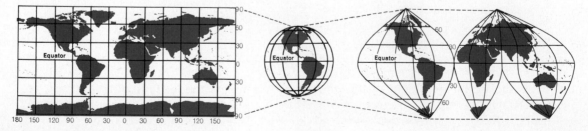

one of these groups; for there are some that distort area, shape, direction, and distance all at the same time — however the degree of distortion may be small in one or all of the properties.

This brief discussion should provide a sufficient basis for an understanding of map projections, why they are necessary, and their major and secondary properties. Further consideration of the above subjects, as well as information on the construction of map projections can be found in most standard textbooks on cartography.

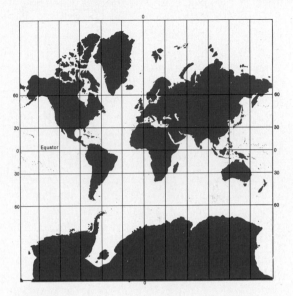

FIGURE A–10
A *conformal projection*. The earth as it appears on the Mercator projection (one of several conformal projections). Note how Greenland and other high-latitude areas assume sizes out of proportion to actual sizes (compare with Figure A–9).

FIGURE A–9
An *equivalent*, or *equal-area*, *map projection*. The earth as it appears on the Mollweide projection, one of several equal-area projections (compare with Figure A–10).

Remote Sensing

Remote sensing is the obtaining and analyzing of an image of a portion of the earth's surface from some position detached from that surface. In a sense, even a photograph taken with a hand-held camera by a person standing on the ground is a form of remote sensing, since the camera is raised above the surface to the height of the photographer's eye. In common usage, however, the term is restricted to images obtained from vehicles detached from the earth and at considerable heights above it.

The simplest and most common form of remote sensing is the *aerial photograph,* or *air photo,* taken by a camera from an airplane. Air photos fall into several classes based upon the kind of film used, the angle photographed, and the altitude of the aircraft.

Black-and-white film is most commonly used, but use is also made of color film (which utilizes the ordinary visible spectrum of light waves), and of both black-and-white and color infra-red film (which utilizes spectra ranging into the shorter heat-transmitting wave lengths). The latter have the advantage of being usable at night, when ordinary light is at a minimum.

Aerial photographs taken from directly overhead are termed *verticals*. They are often used as map substitutes and are invaluable in map-making. When two verticals are taken just moments apart from the same moving airplane, the area of overlap portrayed on each of them can be viewed stereoscopically, producing a three-dimensional image. From this image, landforms can be mapped in detail, and contours can be drawn with great accuracy. Groups of adjacent overlapping verticals can be fitted together to form a *photomosaic*, which, when annotated with place names, becomes a *photo map*. Air photos taken at any angle other than a vertical one are termed *obliques*. Scale varies greatly in an oblique, and only by complex methods of *scale readjustment (resolution)* can such photos be used as a basis for mapping. However, since they have a more realistic appearance to the layman than do verticals, obliques are often preferred for some types of public presentation.

A special type of oblique is produced by *low angle side scanning radar*. Radar beams are emitted from an airplane at right angles to its line of flight and, reflected back in varying strengths from the terrain, are received by a receptor on the same airplane. The receptor records the reflected beams and produces a continuous strip photograph of the landscape to one side of the flight path.

Continuously orbiting satellites and manned space missions are providing us with images of the earth taken from altitudes far greater than those attained by conventional aircraft. Some of these images become available only after the return of the spacecraft to the earth, but many others are transmitted from the vehicle in flight to receptors on the earth's surface. Some of these latter images show areas of cloud cover as they develop from hour to hour, and they are therefore proving quite useful in weather forecasting.

Still very much in its infancy, remote sensing offers great possibilities for the gathering of information without the hardships of field expeditions. Thus, it will be an invaluable aid in the charting of areas that cannot be easily penetrated on foot or safely traversed by low-flying aircraft. Combined with the geographical data obtained on the earth's surface (*ground truths*), the information obtained through remote sensing will make the human capacity for extrapolating environmental data almost endless.

One Hundred Contour Maps
that Illustrate Specific Landforms
and Drainage Conditions

The list of maps given below has been adapted from "A Set of One Hundred Contour Maps That Illustrate Specified Physiographic Features," as issued by the United States Geological Survey, Washington, D.C. The list contains many maps that are already available in college and university libraries or in separate map collections in such institutions. Others may be obtained from the Director of the United States Geological Survey. A few titles are out of print and are not scheduled for reissue.

The following listing is divided into two parts, List A and List B. List A contains contour maps, by name, in alphabetical arrangement. Under the name of each contour map is a list of landforms and drainage features that appear on the map. List B is arranged according to specific landform and drainage features (for example, fiord, hanging valley, terminal moraine, tidal flat, and so on), and the maps on which each feature appears are listed alphabetically by name below the name of the feature.

List A

Antietam, Md.–Va.–W.Va.
Braided stream
Dissected peneplain
Intrenched meander
Intrenched stream
Mature topography
Ridges due to hard rocks
Valley excavated in soft rocks
Water gap or narrows
Wind gap or pass

Aransas Pass, Tex.
Barrier beach
Beach, abandoned
Lagoon or coastal lake
Offset barrier beach
Recurved or hooked spit
Sand dunes
Tidal marsh
Truncated headland
Wave-cut cliff
Winged headland

Atlanta, Ga.
Consequent stream (southeast part)
Dissected peneplain
Dome of crystalline rock
Early mature drainage
Early mature topography
Intrenched stream (Chattahoochee)
Migrating divide (between Chattahoochee and Atlantic drainage)
Monadnock
Rock sculpture controlled by exfoliation

Avon, Ill.
Cut-off meander or oxbow lake
Ground moraine (plain)
Plain (of ground moraine)
Stream meander
Stream prematurely aged by valley filling
Youthful drainage
Youthful topography

Ballarat, Calif.–Nev.
Alluvial slope, possibly including planed rock slope
Alluvium-filled valley (all valleys)
Bolson basin (same as above)
Canyon or gorge
Mountain not glaciated
Nonglaciated or v-shaped valley
Playa
Rugged or youthful mountain
Sand dune (Saline and Death valleys)
Sand wash
Valley due to dislocation of the rocks

Baton Rouge, La.
Floodplain
Lateral drainage diverted by floodplain deposits (Bayou Fountain)
Natural and artificial levees
Plain (of erosion)
Stabilized stream (Mississippi River)
Stream meander
Swamp or marsh

Bright Angel, Ariz.
Canyon or gorge

Cliff
Contrast among surfaces formed in different cycles of erosion
Dissected plateau
Encroachment of younger upon older drainage
Hanging valley
Intrenched stream
Mesa (Shiva Temple)
Migrating divide (south of the river)
Nonglaciated or v-shaped valley
Old drainage (on plateau)
Old topography (on plateau)
Plateau
Rejuvenated stream
Rock sculpture controlled by fractures (Bright Angel Creek Valley)
Rock terrace
Stream piracy (on plateau)
Waterfall or rapid
Youthful drainage
Youthful topography

Buck Hill, Tex.
Alluvial slope, possibly including planed rock slope
Canyon or gorge
Escarpment
Mesa
Plain
Youthful drainage

Cape Henry, Va.
Barrier beach
Drainage blocked by barrier beach

Drowned valley
Estuary (Lynnhaven Bay)
Foreland (Cape Henry)
Sand dune
Swamp or marsh
Wave-formed plain
Youthful drainage
Youthful topography
Capitola, Calif.
Barrier beach
Beach, abandoned (about 200 feet in altitude)
Drainage blocked by barrier beach
Lagoon or coastal lake
Sand dune
Thorofare or tidal runway
Tidal marsh
Wave-cut cliff (at Capitola)
Wave-cut cliff, abandoned (Capitola to Port Watsonville)
Wave-formed terrace (north of Pajaro River)
Castlegate, Utah
Alluvial slope
Canyon or gorge
Dissected alluvial slope
Dissected plateau (Porphyry Bench, etc.)
Early mature topography
Escarpment (Book Cliffs)
Floodplain
Mature topography (northern part)
Nonglaciated or V-shaped valley
Stream meander
Cherry Ridge, Mont.
Cut-off meander or oxbow lake
Esker
Glacial lake and pond
Kame
Kettlehole
Stream meander
Stream prematurely aged by valley filling
Terminal moraine
Underfit stream
Youthful drainage
Chico Landing, Calif.
Alluvial slope (eastern part)
Alluvium-filled valley
Cut-off meander or oxbow lake
Development or shifting of meander
Floodplain
Meander migrating downstream
Natural and artificial levees
Stream meander
Chisos Mountains, Tex.
Alluvial fan or cone (Heath Creek)
Alluvial slope, possibly including planed rock slope
Canyon or gorge
Cuesta
Intrenched meander (Rio Grande)
Intrenched stream (Rio Grande)
Ridges due to hard rocks
Valley excavated in soft rocks
Cincinnati. *See* EAST CINCINNATI
Crater Lake National Park, Oreg.
Caldera (basin of Crater Lake)
Cliff (on rim of caldera)
Contrast among surfaces formed in different cycles of erosion (on rim of caldera)
Crater Lake
Glaciated or trough valley
Mesa
Truncated volcanic cone (ancient Mount Mazama)
Volcanic cone

Youthful drainage
Cross Plains, Wis.
Alluvium-filled valley
Contrast between glaciated and nonglaciated surfaces
Dissected plain
Glacial lake and pond
Ground moraine (on right)
Infantile drainage (on right)
Mature drainage (on left)
Mature topography (on left)
Stream prematurely aged by valley filling
Swamp or marsh
Valley train
Cumberland Island, Ga.
Barrier beach
Beach, abandoned (ridges back of beach)
Offset barrier beach
Recurved or hooked spit
Sand dune
Thorofare or tidal runway
Tidal marsh
Cut Bank, Mont.
Canyon or gorge (Cut Bank Creek)
Dissected alluvial slope (west of Cut Bank Creek)
Escarpment
Glacial lake and pond
Infantile drainage
Kettlehole
Terminal moraine (northeastern part)
Youthful drainage
Youthful topography
Cuyuna, Minn.
Cut-off meander or oxbow lake
Glacial lake and pond
Infantile drainage
Infantile topography
Intrenched stream
Kame
Kettlehole
Lake plain (southeastern part)
Stream meander
Swamp or marsh
Terminal moraine
De Queen, Ark.–Okla.
Consequent stream (southward-flowing streams)
Dissected peneplain (middle part)
Early mature topography (same as above)
Intrenched meander
Intrenched stream
Late mature topography
Mature topography
Ridges due to hard rocks
Subsequent stream (eastward-flowing and westward-flowing streams)
Trellis drainage
Valley excavated in soft rocks
Water gap or narrows
East Cincinnati, Ohio–Ky.
Alluvium-filled valley (Little Miami)
Canyon or gorge
Dissected peneplain
Dissected plateau
Drainage deranged by ice sheet
Early mature drainage
Early mature topography
Floodplain (Little Miami)
Intrenched stream
Meander scar (at Cincinnati and Newport)
Stream terrace (Terrace Park)
Elk Point, S.D.–Neb.–Iowa
Cut-off meander or oxbow lake

Dissected plain
Floodplain
Lateral drainage diverted by floodplain deposits (Big Sioux River)
Mature topography (upland)
Meander, migrating downstream (down to Elk Point)
Plain
Stream meander
Stream prematurely aged by valley filling (Big Sioux River)
Stream terrace
Swamp or marsh
Underfit stream (Big Sioux River)
Erie, Pa.
Beach, abandoned (700- and 740-feet altitude)
Delta
Drainage deranged by ice sheet
Ground moraine (southern part)
Intrenched stream
Lagoon or coastal lake
Recurved or hooked spit
Sand dune
Wave-cut cliff
Wave-formed terrace (about 740-feet altitude)
Youthful drainage
Everett, Pa.
Anticlinal valley (between Evitts-Dunning and Tussey Mountains)
Floodplain
Intrenched meander
Intrenched stream
Ridges due to hard rocks
Ridges due to the erosion of an anticline (Warrior Ridge)
Ridges due to the erosion of a syncline (ridges in Dunning Cove)
Valley excavated in soft rocks
Water gap or narrows (Bedford and Mount Dallas)
Zigzag ridges
Fargo, N.D.–Minn.
Intrenched meander
Intrenched stream
Lake plain (Glacial Lake Agassiz)
Youthful drainage
Youthful topography
Fayetteville, W.Va.
Canyon or gorge
Cliff (top of gorge)
Dissected plateau (northwestern part)
Intrenched meander
Intrenched stream
Mature drainage (northwestern part)
Mature topography (northwestern part)
Plateau
Waterfall or rapid (Kanawha Falls)
Fond du Lac, Wis.
Delta
Drumlin (southeastern part)
Escarpment
Glacial lake and pond
Ground moraine
Infantile drainage
Swamp or marsh
Terminal moraine
Fort Payne, Ala.–Ga.
Anticlinal valley (Big Wills Creek)
Canyon or gorge (Little River Gulf)
Escarpment (east front of Lookout Mountain)
Old drainage (Coosa Valley)
Old topography (Coosa Valley)
Plateau
Ridges due to hard rocks
Stream meander

Genoa, N.Y.
  Delta
  Dissected plateau modified by glaciation
  Ground moraine
  Spit
  Youthful drainage (parallel)
  Youthful topography
Gilbert Peak, Utah–Wyo.
  Comb ridge or cleaver
  Disappearing stream
  Glacial cirque
  Glacial col
  Glacial lake and pond
  Glaciated or trough valley
  Hanging valley
  Kettlehole
  Matterhorn peak
  Mountain modified by alpine glaciation
  Solution basin and sinkhole
Glacier National Park, Mont.
  Alpine or valley glacier
  Canyon or gorge
  Cliff (bordering glacial cirques)
  Comb ridge or cleaver
  Continental or subcontinental divide
  Delta (St. Mary)
  Dissected alluvial slope (Milk River Ridge)
  Fault-line scarp (east front of mountains)
  Glacial cirque
  Glacial lake and pond
  Glaciated or trough valley
  Glacier
  Hanging glacier
  Hanging valley
  Matterhorn peak
  Mountain modified by alpine glaciation
  Mountain range
  Nonglaciated or V-shaped valley, (southwestern part)
  Rugged or youthful mountain
  Waterfall or rapid
  Wind gap or pass (Gunsight, Swiftcurrent, etc.)
Grass Creek Basin, Wyo.
  Anticlinal valley (Grass Creek Basin)
  Cuesta
  Dissected alluvial slope
  Mature topography
  Ridges due to hard rocks
  Ridges due to the erosion of an anticline
  Stream terrace (Cottonwood Creek)
Greylock, Mass.–Vt.
  Canyon or gorge
  Escarpment
  Glacial lake and pond
  Ground moraine
  Hanging valley
  Mountain modified by continental glaciation
  Mountain peak, isolated
  Plateau
  Valley excavated in soft rocks
Henderson, Ky.–Ind.
  Alluvium-filled valley
  Development or shifting of meander
  Dissected plain
  Floodplain
  Lateral drainage diverted by floodplain deposits
  Mature topography
  Stream meander
  Underfit stream (Canoe Creek)

Youthful drainage
Hollow Springs, Tenn.
  Contrast among surfaces formed in different cycles of erosion
  Dip slope (Plateau of the Barrens)
  Dissected plateau
  Early mature drainage
  Early mature topography
  Encroachment of younger upon older drainage
  Migrating divide (western edge of plateau)
  Nonglaciated or V-shaped valley
  Old drainage (on plateau)
  Old topography (on plateau)
  Plateau
  Solution basin and sinkhole
Honomu, Hawaii
  Canyon or gorge
  Consequent stream (all streams)
  Hanging valley
  Rock stack
  Volcanic cone
  Waterfall or rapid
  Wave-cut cliff
  Youthful drainage
  Youthful topography
Hot Springs and vicinity, Ark.
  Dissected peneplain
  Intrenched stream
  Mature topography
  Ridges due to hard rocks
  Ridges due to the erosion of an anticline
  Ridges due to the erosion of a syncline
  Valley excavated in soft rocks
  Water gap or narrows
  Zigzag ridges
Houghton, Mich.
  Delta (Sturgeon and Pilgrim Rivers)
  Drainage deranged by ice sheet
  Glacial lake and pond
  River valley, abandoned
  Sand dune
  Swamp or marsh
  Terminal moraine
  Wave-cut cliff
  Youthful drainage
  Youthful topography
Interlachen, Fla.
  Lake in solution basin
  Lake plain
  Meander scar
  Solution basin and sinkhole
  Stream prematurely aged by valley filling (Oklawaha River)
  Swamp or marsh
Joplin district, Mo.–Kan.
  Alluvial slope
  Dissected plateau
  Early mature topography
  Floodplain
  Intrenched meander
  Intrenched stream
  Waterfall or rapid (Grand Falls)
Kaaterskill, N.Y.
  Beheaded stream (Gooseberry and Schoharie creeks and Beaver Kill)
  Escarpment
  Glacial lake and pond
  Ground moraine
  Late mature topography (lowland)
  Mature topography (upland)
  Migrating divide
  Mountain modified by continental glaciation
  Rock terrace (on escarpment)
  Stream piracy (*see* Beheaded stream)

Trellis drainage (lowland)
Wind gap or pass
Kalamazoo, Mich.
  Drainage deranged by ice sheet
  Glacial lake and pond
  Infantile drainage
  Infantile topography
  Kame
  Kettlehole
  Pitted outwash plain
  Stream prematurely aged by valley filling (Kalamazoo River)
  Stream terrace
  Swamp or marsh
  Terminal moraine
  Underfit stream (Kalamazoo River)
Kilmarnock, Va.
  Bay bar
  Beach, abandoned
  Cut-off meander or oxbow lake
  Dissected plain (upland)
  Drowned valley
  Estuary
  Land-tied island or tombolo
  Meander scar (Meachim Creek)
  Recurved or hooked spit
  Tidal marsh
  Wave-formed plain (upland)
  Wave-formed terrace
Kimmswick, Mo.–Ill.
  Contrast among surfaces formed in different cycles of erosion
  Cut-off meander or oxbow lake
  Development or shifting of meander
  Dissected plateau (upland)
  Floodplain
  Lateral drainage diverted by floodplain deposits
  Mature topography (upland)
  Meander scar
  Natural and artificial levees
  Solution basins and sinkhole
  Stream terrace (Meramec River and Sandy Creek)
  Unsymmetrical stream (upland in Missouri)
Knoxville, Iowa
  Cut-off meander or oxbow lake
  Dissected plain
  Early mature drainage
  Early mature topography
  Floodplain
  Stream meander
Lake Placid, N.Y.
  Glacial lake and pond
  Ground moraine (in valley)
  Mountain modified by continental glaciation
  Stream prematurely aged by valley filling (Saranac River)
  Swamp or marsh
  Water gap or narrows (Wilmington Notch)
  Wind gap or pass
  Youthful drainage
Lake Providence, La.
  Cut-off meander or oxbow lake
  Development or shifting of meander
  Floodplain
  Natural and artificial levees
  Swamp or marsh
La Porte, Tex.
  Drowned valley
  Infantile drainage
  Intrenched stream
  Meander scar
  Mud spring (mud volcano), extinct
  Natural and artificial levees

Medial and lateral moraines (on gla-
ciers)
Nunatak
Recurved or hooked spit
Tidal flat
Tidewater glacier (Shoup Glacier)
Quincy, Wash.
Cliff
Dip slope
Escarpment
Infantile topography (lake plain)
Lake plain
Stream terrace
Waterfall, abandoned
Ravenswood, W.Va.–Ohio
Dissected peneplain
Floodplain
Intrenched meander
Mature drainage
Mature topography
Meander migrating downstream (Ohio
River)
Meander scar (at Letart)
River valley, abandoned (at Racine)
Stream terrace
Redlands, Calif.
Alluvial slope
Alluvium-filled valley
Braided stream (Santa Ana, Wash.)
Canyon or gorge
Contrast among surfaces formed in
different cycles of erosion (northern
part)
Encroachment of younger upon older
drainage (northern part)
Fault-line scarp (front of mountain)
Mountain not glaciated
Nonglaciated or V-shaped valley
Rugged or youthful mountain
Sand wash
Reelfoot Lake, Tenn.–Mo.–Ky.
Delta
Dissected peneplain
Early mature topography
Earthquake lake
Floodplain
Natural and artificial levees
Stream meander
Rehoboth, Del.
Barrier beach
Drowned valley
Estuary
Lagoon or coastal lake
Offset barrier beach
Plain
Sand dune
Solution basin and sinkhole
Thorofare or tidal runway
Tidal marsh
Truncated headland (Rehoboth
Beach)
Rochester east, N.Y.
Barrier beach
Bay bar
Beach, abandoned (Ridge Road)
Canyon or gorge
Delta (Irondequoit River)
Drowned valley
Intrenched stream
Kame
Kettlehole
Lagoon or coastal lake
Swamp or marsh
Terminal moraine
Waterfall or rapid (Rochester)
Youthful drainage
Youthful topography

St. Albans, Vt.
Bay bar
Beach, abandoned (east of lake)
Delta (Missisquoi River and Mill
Run)
Distributary stream (Missisquoi delta)
Intrenched stream
Natural and artificial levees
Spit (Stephenson Point)
Swamp or marsh
Waterfall or rapid (Highgate Falls)
Wave-formed terrace
St. Croix Dalles, Wis.–Minn.
Canyon or gorge
Glacial lake and pond
Infantile drainage
Infantile topography
Kame
Kettlehole
Stream terrace (at Taylors Falls)
Swamp or marsh
Terminal moraine
Waterfall or rapid (St. Croix Falls)
Seattle, Wash.
Cut-off meander or oxbow lake
Delta
Distributary stream
Floodplain
Glacial lake and pond
Spit
Stream meander
Stream prematurely aged by valley
filling
Tidal flat
Wave-cut cliff
Standingstone, Tenn.
Disappearing stream
Dissected peneplain (1,000 and 1,900
feet altitude)
Dissected plateau (edge of plateau)
Intrenched meander
Intrenched stream
Plateau (Cumberland Plateau)
Solution basin and sinkhole
Stockton, Utah
Alluvial fan or cone (of Ophir Creek)
Alluvial fan or cone, abandoned (of
Soldier Creek)
Alluvial slope
Alluvium-filled valley
Bay bar, abandoned (north of Stock-
ton)
Beach, abandoned (northeast of
Stockton)
Bolson basin (Rush Valley)
Canyon or gorge
Cliff (in Dry Canyon)
Lake plain (all below 5,250 feet)
Mature topography (mountain)
Mountain not glaciated
Nonglaciated or V-shaped valley
Playa (floor of Rush Lake)
Playa lake (Rush Lake)
Recurved or hooked spit, abandoned
(Stockton)
Rugged or youthful mountain
Swamp or marsh
Valley due to dislocation of the rocks
Wave-cut cliff, abandoned (northeast
of Stockton)
Wave-formed terrace (northeast of
Stockton)
Stryker, Mont.
Comb ridge or cleaver
Drumlin
Escarpment
Glacial cirque
Glacial col

Glacial lake and pond
Glaciated or trough valley
Matterhorn peak
Mountain modified by alpine glacia-
tion
Swamp or marsh
Tehama, Calif.
Alluvial fan or cone (Mill and Ante-
lope creeks)
Alluvial slope
Alluvium-filled valley
Canyon or gorge
Contrast among surfaces formed in
different cycles of erosion (north-
eastern part)
Distributary stream (on fans)
Fault-line scarp (base of mountain)
Floodplain
Infantile topography
Nonglaciated or V-shaped valley
Valley due to dislocation of the rocks
Youthful topography
Van Horn, Tex.
Alluvial fan or cone (Victoria Can-
yon)
Alluvial slope
Alluvium-filled valley
Block mountain (Sierra Diablo)
Bolson basin (Salt Flat)
Canyon or gorge
Cliff (eastern face of Sierra Diablo)
Cuesta (Sierra Diablo)
Escarpment (eastern front of Sierra
Diablo)
Fault-line scarp (eastern foot of Sierra
Diablo)
Mountain not glaciated
Playa (floor of Salt Lake)
Playa lake (Salt Lake)
Valley due to dislocation of the rocks
Washington and vicinity, D.C.–Md.–
Va.
Braided stream
Canyon or gorge
Delta (creeks below Alexandria)
Delta, abandoned
Dissected peneplain (east of Potomac
and Anacostia rivers).
Drowned valley
Early mature topography
Estuary (Potomac River)
Fall line (through Washington, from
northeast to southwest)
Floodplain
Intrenched meander
Intrenched stream
Meander scar
Rejuvenated stream (Potomac River)
Stream terrace (below Great Falls)
Swamp or marsh
Tidal flat
Waterfall or rapid (Great and Little
Falls)
Waukegan, Ill.–Wis.
Extended stream (streams east of Chi-
cago & Northwestern Ry.)
Kame
Kettlehole
Lake plain (higher part of Waukegan
and Zion City)
Stream prematurely aged by valley
filling
Swamp or marsh
Terminal moraine
Terrace formed by silted-up lake
basin, partly excavated later (same
as lake plain)
Wave-cut cliff (south of Waukegan)

Wave-cut cliff, abandoned (north of Waukegan)
Wave-formed terrace (lower part of Waukegan and Zion City)
Youthful drainage
White Mountains, Calif.–Nev.
Alluvial fan or cone (Montgomery, Marble, and Milner creeks)
Alluvial slope
Alluvium-filled valley
Bolson basin (Fish Valley)
Contrast among surfaces formed in different cycles of erosion
Distributary stream (on fans)
Early mature topography (mountain)
Fault-line scarp (western foot of White Mountains)

Glacial cirque (summit of White Mountains)
Mountain range
Playa (Fish Valley)
Rugged or youthful mountain
Sand dune
Valley due to dislocation of the rocks (west of White Mountains)
Yosemite Valley, Calif.
Alluvial fan or cone (below Rocky Point)
Alluvial slope
Alluvium-filled valley
Canyon or gorge
Cliff (El Capitan and others)
Contrast among surfaces formed in different cycles of erosion

Distributary stream (on alluvial slope)
Dome of crystalline rock (Half Dome and others)
Glaciated or trough valley
Hanging valley (Bridalveil Valley and others)
Lake plain (bottom of Yosemite Valley)
Roches moutonnées (Liberty Cap and Mount Broderick)
Rock sculpture controlled by fractures
Rock sculpture controlled by exfoliation
Rock slide and talus (foot of cliffs)
Waterfall or rapid

List B

(*Asterisks* [*] *indicate that a particular feature is well shown on the map.*)

COASTAL FEATURES
Barrier beach
* Aransas Pass, Tex.
* Cape Henry, Va.
* Capitola, Calif.
* Cumberland Island, Ga.
  Oyster Bay, N.Y.
  Point Reyes, Calif.
* Rehoboth, Del.
  Rochester east, N.Y.
Bay bar
  Kilmarnock, Va.
* Montpelier, Idaho–Wyo.–Utah
* Oyster Bay, N.Y.
  Point Reyes, Calif.
  Port Valdez district, Alaska
* Rochester east, N.Y.
  St. Albans, Vt.
Bay bar, abandoned
* Stockton, Utah
Beach, abandoned
* Aransas Pass, Tex.
  Capitola, Calif.
  Cumberland Island, Ga.
  Erie, Pa.
* Kilmarnock, Va.
* Niagara River and vicinity, N.Y.
* Oberlin, Ohio
  Palmyra, N.Y.
  Rochester east, N.Y.
  St. Albans, Vt.
* Stockton, Utah
Delta
  See VALLEYS
Drowned valley
* Cape Henry, Va.
* Kilmarnock, Va.
* La Porte, Tex.
  Oyster Bay, N.Y.
* Point Reyes, Calif.
* Rehoboth, Del.
  Rochester east, N.Y.
* Washington and vicinity, D.C.–Md.–Va.
Estuary
* Cape Henry, Va.
* Kilmarnock, Va.
  Point Reyes, Calif.
* Rehoboth, Del.
* Washington and vicinity, D.C.–Md.–Va.
Fiord
* Mount Desert, Maine
* Port Valdez district, Alaska
Foreland
* Cape Henry, Va.

Lagoon or coastal lake
* Aransas Pass, Tex.
  Capitola, Calif.
  Erie, Pa.
  Point Reyes, Calif.
  Rehoboth, Del.
  Rochester east, N.Y.
Land-tied island or tombolo
  Kilmarnock, Va.
  Oyster Bay, N.Y.
Offset barrier beach
* Aransas Pass, Tex.
  Cumberland Island, Ga.
  Point Reyes, Calif.
  Rehoboth, Del.
Recurved or hooked spit
  Aransas Pass, Tex.
  Cumberland Island, Ga.
* Erie, Pa.
  Kilmarnock, Va.
  Mount Desert, Maine
  Oyster Bay, N.Y.
  Port Valdez district, Alaska
Recurved or hooked spit, abandoned
* Stockton, Utah
Rock stack
  Honomu, Hawaii
* Point Reyes, Calif.
Spit
  Genoa, N.Y.
  Mount Desert, Maine
* Oyster Bay, N.Y.
  St. Albans, Vt.
* Seattle, Wash.
Thorofare or tidal runway
  Capitola, Calif.
* Cumberland Island, Ga.
  Rehoboth, Del.
Tidal flat
  Port Valdez district, Alaska
* Seattle, Wash.
* Washington and vicinity, D.C.–Md.–Va.
Tidal marsh
  Aransas Pass, Tex.
  Capitola, Calif.
* Cumberland Island, Ga.
  Kilmarnock, Va.
  Rehoboth, Del.
Truncated headland
  Aransas Pass, Tex.
* Point Reyes, Calif.
  Rehoboth, Del.
Wave-cut cliff
  Aransas Pass, Tex.
  Capitola, Calif.

* Erie, Pa.
* Honomu, Hawaii
* Houghton, Mich.
  La Porte, Tex.
* Oberlin, Ohio
* Oyster Bay, N.Y.
* Point Reyes, Calif.
  Seattle, Wash.
* Waukegan, Ill.–Wis.
Wave-cut cliff, abandoned
* Capitola, Calif.
* Stockton, Utah
* Waukegan, Ill.–Wis.
Wave-formed plain
* Cape Henry, Va.
  Kilmarnock, Va.
Wave-formed terrace
  Capitola, Calif.
* Erie, Pa.
* Kilmarnock, Va.
  Point Reyes, Calif.
* St. Albans, Vt.
* Stockton, Utah
  Waukegan, Ill.–Wis.
Winged headland
* Aransas Pass, Tex.
* Oyster Bay, N.Y.
MOUNTAINS
Alluvial fan or cone
  See VALLEYS
Alluvial slope
  See VALLEYS
Alluvial slope, possibly including planed rock slope
  See VALLEYS
Block mountain
  Olancha, Calif.
  Point Reyes, Calif.
* Van Horn, Tex.
Dissected alluvial slope
  See VALLEYS
Dome of crystalline rock
* Atlanta, Ga.
* Yosemite Valley, Calif.
Landslide
  See VALLEYS
Matterhorn peak
  See FEATURES DUE TO GLACIATION OF MOUNTAINS
Monadnock
  See RESULTS OF EROSION IN VARIOUS STAGES OF THE CYCLE
Mountain modified by alpine glaciation
* Gilbert Peak, Utah–Wyo.
* Glacier National Park, Mont.
* Manitou, Colo.

Valley excavated in soft rocks
  Antietam, Md.–Va.–W.Va.
  Chisos Mountains, Tex.
* De Queen, Ark.–Okla.
* Everett, Pa.
* Greylock, Mass.–Vt.
* Hot Springs and vicinity, Ark.
* Loveland, Colo.
* Meriden, Conn.
  Natural Bridge, Va.
* Pawpaw, Md.–W.Va.–Pa.
Water gap or narrows
* Antietam, Md.–Va.–W.Va.
  De Queen, Ark.–Okla.
* Everett, Pa.
  Hot Springs and vicinity, Ark.
  Lake Placid, N.Y.
  Loveland, Colo.
  Pawpaw, Md.–W.Va.–Pa.
STREAMS
Beheaded stream
* Kaaterskill, N.Y.
Braided stream
  Antietam, Md.–Va.–W.Va.
* Lower Matanuska Valley, Alaska
  Mount Hood, Oreg.–Wash.
* Mount Rainier National Park, Wash.
* Ogallala, Neb.
* Passadumkeag, Maine
* Port Valdez district, Alaska
* Redlands, Calif.
* Washington and vicinity, D.C.–Md.–
  Va.
Consequent stream
* Atlanta, Ga.
  De Queen, Ark.–Okla.
* Honomu, Hawaii
* Loveland, Colo.
* Mesa Verde National Park, Colo.
  Montpelier, Idaho–Wyo.–Utah
Cut-off meander or oxbow lake
  Avon, Ill.
  Cherry Ridge, Mont.
* Chico Landing, Calif.
  Cuyuna, Minn.
  Elk Point, S.D.–Neb.–Iowa
  Kilmarnock, Va.
  Kimmswick, Mo.–Ill.
* Knoxville, Iowa
* Lake Providence, La.
  Loveland, Colo.
  Marysville Buttes and vicinity, Calif.
  Montpelier, Idaho–Wyo.–Utah
* Nashua, Mont.
  Peeples, S.C.–Ga.
  Seattle, Wash.
Development of shifting meander
* Chico Landing, Calif.
* Henderson, Ky.–Ind.
  Kimmswick, Mo.–Ill.
  Lake Providence, La.
Disappearing stream
* Gilbert Peak, Utah–Wyo.
* Standingstone, Tenn.
Distributary stream
  Marysville Buttes and vicinity, Calif.
* Point Reyes, Calif.
* Port Valdez district, Alaska
* St. Albans, Vt.
* Seattle, Wash.
* Tehama, Calif.
* White Mountains, Calif.–Nev.
* Yosemite Valley, Calif.
Drainage blocked by barrier beach
* Cape Henry, Va.
* Capitola, Calif.
  Point Reyes, Calif.
Drainage deranged by faulting

* Point Reyes, Calif.
Drainage deranged by ice sheet
  East Cincinnati, Ohio–Ky.
  Erie, Pa.
* Houghton, Mich.
* Kalamazoo, Mich.
  Meriden, Conn.
  Monadnock, N.H.
* Naples, N.Y.
  Palmyra, N.Y.
  Passadumkeag, Maine
Early mature drainage
  Atlanta, Ga.
  East Cincinnati, Ohio–Ky.
* Hollow Springs, Tenn.
  Knoxville, Iowa
  Monticello, Ky.
Encroachment of younger upon older
  drainage
  Bright Angel, Ariz.
* Hollow Springs, Tenn.
  Mount Mitchell, N.C.
* Olancha, Calif.
  Redlands, Calif.
Extended stream
* Waukegan, Ill.–Wis.
Infantile drainage
  Cross Plains, Wis.
* Cut Bank, Mont.
* Cuyuna, Minn.
* Fond du Lac, Wis.
* Kalamazoo, Mich.
  La Porte, Tex.
* Marysville Buttes and vicinity, Calif.
* Palmyra, N.Y.
* Passadumkeag, Maine
* St. Croix Dalles, Wis.–Minn.
Intrenched stream
  Antietam, Md.–Va.–W.Va.
  Atlanta, Ga.
  Bright Angel, Ariz.
  Chisos Mountains, Tex.
* Cuyuna, Minn.
  De Queen, Ark.–Okla.
* East Cincinnati, Ohio–Ky.
  Erie, Pa.
* Everett, Pa.
* Fargo, N.D.–Minn.
* Fayetteville, W.Va.
  Hot Springs and vicinity, Ark.
  Joplin district, Mo.–Kan.
* La Porte, Tex.
  Lower Matanuska Valley, Alaska
* Milton, W.Va.
* Monticello, Ky.
  Mount Mitchell, N.C.
* Natural Bridge, Va.
* Oberlin, Ohio
  Pittsburgh, Pa.
  Point Reyes, Calif.
* Rochester east, N.Y.
  St. Albans, Vt.
  Standingstone, Tenn.
  Washington and vicinity, D.C.–Md.–
  Va.
Lateral drainage diverted by floodplain
  deposits
  Baton Rouge, La.
* Elk Point, S.D.–Neb.–Iowa
  Henderson, Ky.–Ind.
  Kimmswick, Mo.–Ill.
Mature drainage
  Cross Plains, Wis.
* Fayetteville, W.Va.
* Milton, W.Va.
  Monticello, Ky.
  Oelwein, Iowa
* Pawpaw, Md.–W.Va.–Pa.

* Pittsburgh, Pa.
* Ravenswood, W.Va.–Ohio
Meander migrating downstream
  Chico Landing, Calif.
* Elk Point, S.D.–Neb.–Iowa
  Milton, W.Va.
* Monticello, Ky.
  Natural Bridge, Va.
* Pawpaw, Md.–W.Va.–Pa.
* Ravenswood, W.Va.–Ohio
Old drainage
  Bright Angel, Ariz.
* Fort Payne, Ala.–Ga.
* Hollow Springs, Tenn.
* Loveland, Colo.
Rejuvenated stream
  Bright Angel, Ariz.
* Washington and vicinity, D.C.–Md.–
  Va.
Stabilized stream
* Baton Rouge, La.
* La Porte, Tex.
Stream meander
  Avon, Ill.
  Baton Rouge, La.
  Castlegate, Utah
  Cherry Ridge, Mont.
* Chico Landing, Calif.
  Cuyuna, Minn.
  Elk Point, S.D.–Neb.–Iowa
  Fort Payne, Ala.–Ga.
* Henderson, Ky.–Ind.
* Knoxville, Iowa
  Loveland, Colo.
  Marysville Buttes and vicinity, Calif.
  Montpelier, Idaho–Wyo.–Utah
* Nashua, Mont.
  Peeples, S.C.–Ga.
  Peever, S.D.–Minn.
  Pittsburgh, Pa.
  Reelfoot Lake, Tenn.–Mo.–Ky.
* Seattle, Wash.
Stream piracy
  Bright Angel, Ariz.
* Kaaterskill, N.Y.
* Milton, W.Va.
Stream prematurely aged by valley fill-
  ing
  Avon, Ill.
  Cherry Ridge, Mont.
  Cross Plains, Wis.
  Elk Point, S.D.–Neb.–Iowa
  Interlachen, Fla.
* Kalamazoo, Mich.
  Lake Placid, N.Y.
  Naples, N.Y.
* Nashua, Mont.
* Peeples, S.C.–Ga.
* Seattle, Wash.
  Waukegan, Ill.–Wis.
Subsequent stream
* De Queen, Ark.–Okla.
  Montpelier, Idaho–Wyo.–Utah
Superposed stream
  Montpelier, Idaho–Wyo.–Utah
Synclinal stream
* Natural Bridge, Va.
Trellis drainage
* De Queen, Ark.–Okla.
* Kaaterskill, N.Y.
  Pawpaw, Md.–W.Va.–Pa.
Underfit stream
  Cherry Ridge, Mont.
* Elk Point, S.D.–Neb.–Iowa
  Henderson, Ky.–Ind.
* Kalamazoo, Mich.
  Malaga, Wash.
  Milton, W.Va.

Kaaterskill, N.Y.
Kimmswick, Mo.–Ill.
* Milton, W.Va.
Monticello, Ky.
Mount Hood, Oreg.–Wash.
Naples, N.Y.
Nashua, Mont.
Oelwein, Iowa
* Pawpaw, Md.–W.Va.–Pa.
* Pittsburgh, Pa.
* Ravenswood, W.Va.–Ohio
* Stockton, Utah
Monadnock
* Atlanta, Ga.
Manitou, Colo.
* Monadnock, N.H.
Monticello, Ky.
Old drainage
See STREAMS
Old topography
Bright Angel, Ariz.
* Fort Payne, Ala.–Ga.
* Hollow Springs, Tenn.
* Loveland, Colo.
Prematurely old stream
See STREAMS
Rejuvenated stream
See STREAMS
Rock sculpture controlled by exfoliation
* Atlanta, Ga.
* Yosemite Valley, Calif.
Rock sculpture controlled by fractures
Bright Angel, Ariz.
* Meriden, Conn.
* Mount Desert, Maine
* Mount Rainier National Park, Wash.
* Yosemite Valley, Calif.
Rugged or youthful mountain
See MOUNTAINS
Subdued or old mountain
See MOUNTAINS
Youthful drainage
See STREAMS
Youthful topography
Avon, Ill.
Bright Angel, Ariz.
* Cape Henry, Va.
Cut Bank, Mont.
* Fargo, N.D.–Minn.
* Genoa, N.Y.
* Honomu, Hawaii
* Houghton, Mich.
Nashua, Mont.
* Oberlin, Ohio
Oelwein, Iowa
Ogallala, Neb.
Rochester east, N.Y.
* Tehama, Calif.
GLACIERS
Alpine or valley glacier
Glacier National Park, Mont.
* Mount Hood, Oreg.
* Mount Rainier National Park, Wash.
* Port Valdez district, Alaska
Glacier
* Glacier National Park, Mont.
Lower Matanuska Valley, Alaska
* Mount Hood, Oreg.–Wash.
* Mount Rainier National Park, Wash.
* Port Valdez district, Alaska
Hanging glacier
* Glacier National Park, Mont.
Mount Hood, Oreg.–Wash.
* Mount Rainier National Park, Wash.
* Port Valdez district, Alaska
Tidewater glacier
* Port Valdez district, Alaska

FEATURES DUE TO
CONTINENTAL GLACIATION
Contrast between glaciated and non-
glaciated surfaces (1), or between
a surface deeply covered with drift
and one that has only a slight cover
of much older dissected drift (2)
* (1) Cross Plains, Wis.
* (2) Oelwein, Iowa
Drainage deranged by ice sheet
See STREAMS
Drumlin
* Fond du Lac, Wis.
* Palmyra, N.Y.
Stryker, Mont.
Esker
Cherry Ridge, Mont.
* Passadumkeag, Maine
Glacial outwash plain
* Port Valdez district, Alaska
Ground moraine
* Avon, Ill.
Cross Plains, Wis.
Erie, Pa.
Fond du Lac, Wis.
Genoa, N.Y.
Greylock, Mass.–Vt.
Kaaterskill, N.Y.
Lake Placid, N.Y.
Monadnock, N.H.
Naples, N.Y.
Niagara Falls and vicinity, N.Y.
Oelwein, Iowa
* Palmyra, N.Y.
Kame
* Cherry Ridge, Mont.
Cuyuna, Minn.
* Kalamazoo east, Mich.
Rochester east, N.Y.
* St. Croix Dalles, Wis.–Minn.
* Waukegan, Ill.–Wis.
Kettlehole
* Cherry Ridge, Mont.
* Cut Bank, Mont.
Cuyuna, Minn.
Gilbert Peak, Utah–Wyo.
* Kalamazoo, Mich.
Lower Matanuska Valley, Alaska
Meriden, Conn.
Peever, S.D.–Minn.
Rochester east, N.Y.
* St. Croix Dalles, Wis.–Minn.
Waukegan, Ill.–Wis.
Mountain modified by continental gla-
ciation
See MOUNTAINS
Pitted outwash plain
* Kalamazoo, Mich.
Terminal moraine
* Cherry Ridge, Mont.
* Cut Bank, Mont.
* Cuyuna, Minn.
Fond du Lac, Wis.
Houghton, Mich.
* Kalamazoo, Mich.
Lower Matanuska Valley, Alaska
Manitou, Colo.
Meriden, Conn.
* Naples, N.Y.
Oyster Bay, N.Y.
Peever, S.D.–Minn.
Rochester east, N.Y.
* St. Croix Dalles, Wis.–Minn.
Waukegan, Ill.–Wis.
Valley train
* Cross Plains, Wis.
FEATURES DUE TO
GLACIATION OF MOUNTAINS

Comb ridge or cleaver
* Gilbert Peak, Utah–Wyo.
Glacier National Park, Mont.
* Mount Rainier National Park, Wash.
* Stryker, Mont.
Glacial cirque
* Gilbert Peak, Utah–Wyo.
* Glacier National Park, Mont.
Lower Matanuska Valley, Alaska
* Manitou, Colo.
Mount Hood, Oreg.–Wash.
* Mount Rainier National Park, Wash.
Olancha, Calif.
* Stryker, Mont.
White Mountains, Calif.–Nev.
Glacial col
* Gilbert Peak, Utah–Wyo.
Mount Rainier National Park, Wash.
* Stryker, Mont.
Glaciated or trough valley
See VALLEYS
Matterhorn peak
* Gilbert Peak, Utah–Wyo.
Glacier National Park, Mont.
* Mount Rainier National Park, Wash.
Stryker, Mont.
Medial and lateral moraines
* Mount Rainier National Park, Wash.
* Port Valdez district, Alaska
Mountains modified by alpine glaciation
See MOUNTAINS
Nunatak
* Mount Rainier National Park, Wash.
* Port Valdez district, Alaska
Roches moutonnées
* Yosemite Valley, Calif.
VOLCANIC FEATURES
Caldera
* Crater Lake National Park, Oreg.
Dissected volcanic cone
* Marysville Buttes and vicinity, Calif.
Truncated volcanic cone
* Crater Lake National Park, Oreg.
Volcanic cone
* Crater Lake National Park, Oreg.
* Honomu, Hawaii
* Mount Hood, Oreg.–Wash.
* Mount Rainier National Park, Wash.
* Mount Riley, Ariz.
Wedge segments of volcanic cone out-
lined by erosion
* Marysville Buttes and vicinity, Calif.
* Mount Rainier National Park, Wash.
SOLUTION FEATURES
Natural bridge
* Natural Bridge, Va.
Solution basin and sinkhole
Gilbert Peak, Utah–Wyo.
Hollow Springs, Tenn.
* Interlachen, Fla.
Kimmswick, Mo.–Ill.
* Monticello, Ky.
Montpelier, Idaho–Wyo.–Utah
Natural Bridge, Va.
Pawpaw, Md.–W.Va.–Pa.
* Peeples, S.C.–Ga.
Rehoboth, Del.
* Standingstone, Tenn.
MISCELLANEOUS
Continental or subcontinental divide
* Glacier National Park, Mont.
* Mount Mitchell, N.C.
Peever, S.D.–Minn.
Fall line
* Washington and vicinity, D.C.–Md.–
Va.
Mud spring (mud volcano), extinct
* La Porte, Tex.

Climatic Classification
and Statistics

The Köppen Classification of Climates

Origin

The most commonly used classification of climates is that devised by a Russian meteorologist, Wladimir Köppen (1846–1940). As early as 1900, Köppen suggested a climatic classification based on plant cover. It was in 1918, however, that he first formulated the actual scheme. In its major aspects, this original plan has not been altered markedly, although there have been many minor modifications. The final form specified by Köppen himself appeared in 1936 as a section of a five-volume work, *Handbook of Climatology,* of which Köppen was one of the authors and an editor.

General Features

The Köppen classification deals with the two climatic elements that are most obviously significant to human beings as they live and make a living on the face of the earth. These two elements are temperature and precipitation. Long-time records of each are available for numerous and widely scattered places on the earth. When these records are analyzed, it is found that certain outstanding combinations regularly occur. For example, some places show a combination of "hot and moist"; others are "hot and dry"; still others are "cold and moist"; and so on, through many temperature and moisture combinations. It is such recognized combinations, or types, that constitute the Köppen system of climatic classification.

This system recognizes five *major* categories. To each of these a letter symbol is given. One of the major categories, for example, is expressed by the letter **A,** which signifies moist climates that are perennially hot. Subdivisions are made within each of the major classes, and each of these in turn is given a letter symbol. One of the subdivisions of the **A** climates is **Af.** The addition of the **f** indicates one special type of **A** climate, one that is not only moist and hot, but moist to the degree that there normally is no season of true drought at any time during the year.

The type of climate, or the *climate-formula,* to use Köppen's designation, is expressed as a combination of two or more letters. The letters are defined both specifically and generally. In the use of the complete system, many detailed differences can be indicated by the addition of as many letter symbols as apply to the measurements at hand. For purposes of a general world survey, the subdivisions of the climatic types usually involve at least a third letter. Thus, a given climate may be symbolized as **Cfa.** The third letter in this instance signifies hot summers, and it, too, is capable of exact, quantitative definition.

Significance of Classification

The Köppen classification of climates is extremely useful, first, because it is a quantitative and wholly objective device for the categorization of observed climatic phenomena. As has been indicated, it makes use of temperature and of precipitation amounts and of temperature and precipitation distribution throughout the year. These are measurable facts that are commonly observed over a large part of the earth's surface. When the Köppen definitions are applied to the observed facts, there is no question as to which category those facts represent. Given a set of climatic statistics, any individual, no matter from what part of the world she or he may come, can arrive at the proper climate-formula for her/his own, or any other, climate. The classification thus provides a sort of international climatic shorthand.

Second, the Köppen classification is an extremely useful geographic tool for world or continental study. The definitions are stated in exact amounts that are capable of accurate representation on maps. It is therefore possible to construct maps on which the areas of different climatic types may be specifically delimited. From these maps, direct comparisons between one part of the world and another, or between one part of a continent and another, may be made. Further, these comparisons are standardized by the quantitative nature of the definitions. On a worldwide or on a continental scale, the patterns disclosed by a map of climatic types are basic to an understanding of the variety

that exists. It must here be noted, however, that the classification is of much less value in disclosing significant patterns within small areas.

Third, the Köppen classification is easy to apply. It does not require any special knowledge, either of meteorological details or of mathematical processes. It can, therefore, be used by nonspecialists fully as easily as it can by professional meteorologists.

Finally, the Köppen classification has come into such common use throughout the world that it may now be considered a standard. Nearly all of the many current classifications of climate are variants of the Köppen system. In some variants, names have been substituted for combinations of letter symbols. Thus, it is fairly common to speak of an **Af** climate as a tropical rainforest climate, of a **BW** climate as a desert or saharan climate, and of a **Cs** climate as a Mediterranean climate. In other variants, there have been different definitions proposed for those of Köppen while the main framework remains unaltered. Whether they be descriptive-type variations or definition variations, no one of the alternative classifications has had the worldwide acceptance that has been accorded the Köppen system as a useful geographic tool. This is not to suggest that there are no weaknesses in the Köppen system—for example, the definitions specify types that are far too broad for purposes of climatological research. But, despite difficulties of this sort, the system remains an extremely useful and a widely accepted tool for geographers.

Plan of Classification

Major categories. The five major categories of climate are given the letter symbols **A, B, C, D,** and **E.** Climates that are humid and are always hot, showing no appreciable seasonal changes of temperature, are designated the **A** climates. Dry climates, in which potential evaporation exceeds precipitation, are given the symbol **B**. Humid climates in which there is a definite, though mild, winter are called **C** climates. Humid climates with severe winters use the letter **D**. And climates that have, essentially, no summer season are known as **E** climates. For convenient reference, a tabular summary of general meanings of all symbols is given in Figures C–1 and C–2, in this part of the appendix. In addition, exact definitions for each symbol are given in the second section. The method of determination of the climatic symbol represented by any set of temperature and precipitation statistics is included in the following part of the appendix.

The choice of the particular letters is purely arbitrary. It should be noted that the first letter symbol in the classification is always a capital letter. This is important because, in the definition of subdivisions of the major categories, some of the letters are used again, but they are always written or printed as lower case letters.

The **A, C,** and **D** climates are humid; that is, they are climates in which, regardless of the temperature, there is normally no problem of insufficient precipitation. The **E** climates are so cold that the problem of moisture is not significant. Only in the **B** climates does one find, as a normal condition, the problem of moisture deficiency.

Moisture deficiency, or dryness, must be defined on a sliding scale. Efficiency of precipitation, from the point of view of the cover of vegetation that it produces, is closely related to the rate of evaporation. More water will evaporate at high temperatures than at low ones. If evaporation is high, water available for plants is decreased. Hence, the amount of precipitation that is adequate for plant growth in a cool area is altogether insufficient in an area of constantly high temperatures. Likewise, an area that receives

FIGURE C–1

Twenty-five main climatic types of the Köppen system.

Af	Always hot, always humid climate
Am	Always hot, seasonally excessively humid climate
Aw	Always hot, seasonally droughty climate
BSh	Semiarid, hot climate
BSk	Semiarid, cool or cold climate
BWh	Arid, hot climate
BWk	Arid, cool or cold climate
Cfa	Mild winter, always humid climate with long, hot summers
Cfb	Mild winter, always humid climate with short, warm summers
Cfc	Mild winter, always humid climate with very short, cool summers
Cwa	Mild winter, humid summer climate with long, hot summers
Cwb	Mild winter, humid summer climate with short, warm summers
Csa	Mild winter, humid winter climate with long, hot, droughty summers
Csb	Mild winter, humid winter climate with short, warm, droughty summers
Dfa	Severe winter, always humid climate with long, hot summers
Dwa	Severe winter, humid summer climate with long, hot summers
Dfb	Severe winter, always humid climate with short, warm summers
Dwb	Severe winter, humid summer climate with short, warm summers
Dfc	Severe winter, always humid climate with very short, cool summers
Dwc	Severe winter, humid summer climate with very short, cool summers
Dfd	Severe winter, always humid climate with short summers and excessively cold winters
Dwd	Severe winter, humid summer climate with short summers and excessively cold winters
ET	Polar climate with very short period of plant growth
EF	Polar climate in which plant growth is impossible
H	Undifferentiated mountain climates

most of its precipitation during the warm growing season when the evaporation rate is high must have more water available than an area where most of the precipitation comes during the cooler season when evaporation is low. If evaporation records were kept as frequently and as accurately as are those of temperature and precipitation, it would be possible to determine directly the location of the line along which evaporation equals precipitation. This would permit exact definition of the boundary between climates that are humid and those that are dry. Unfortunately, records of evaporation are comparatively few in number and the points of observation are widely scattered. For these reasons, it has been necessary to introduce into the classification a definition that is not predicated upon a single amount of precipitation, but is in reality a crude estimate of evaporation. This definition makes allowance for temperature, for yearly precipitation, and for seasonal distribution of precipitation.

Subdivisions of the major categories. The B climates are subdivided into arid climate, which is represented by the secondary symbol W, and semiarid climate, which is represented by the secondary symbol S. These are written as capital letters when they are used with B and they have no tie with the letters w and s as those are used with the A, C, and D types. Beyond the classification as arid or semiarid, a further difference within the B climates is made in terms of temperature: those dry climates that are always hot use the symbol h, and those that are cold or have a pronounced winter season use the symbol k.

In each of the A, C, and D types the second symbol is one that specifies the nature, the amount, and the distribution of precipitation throughout the year. There are three possibilities so far as the distribution of precipitation during the year is concerned:

the precipitation is rather evenly spread throughout the year, is concentrated in the cooler part of the year, or is concentrated in the warmer part of the year. The symbol that indicates an even spread throughout the year is f; the one that indicates concentration in the cooler part of the year is s; and the one that shows concentration in the warmer part of the year is w. Theoretically, any of the three might be used following the first letter of the climate-formula. Actually, s occurs so infrequently with either A or D that it may be omitted so far as those two major categories are concerned. Within the A climates, another letter, m, is used to indicate an intermediate position between f and w.

In the C and D climates a third symbol commonly is used. Since in those two categories the nature of the winter and of the summer have great effect upon the vegetation, the symbols should indicate the nature of each of those seasons. The first letter does this in part; the third letter completes the statement. Three of the letters used in third place characterize the summer and one of them, the winter. Where the summers are long and hot, the symbol a is used; for short and warm summers, b is used; for very short and cool summers, c is the symbol; and where winters are excessively cold and severe, the symbol d is used.

Within the climates that, in an ordinary sense, have no summer, E, a distinction can be made between areas of practically continuous frost, F, and those in which temperatures are high enough to permit the growth of tundra vegetation, T.

Summary of Types

Generalized description. In summary, twenty-five climatic types are recognized. These are listed in Figure C–1 in this part

FIGURE C–2

The relationship between the major categories of climate and their subdivisions.

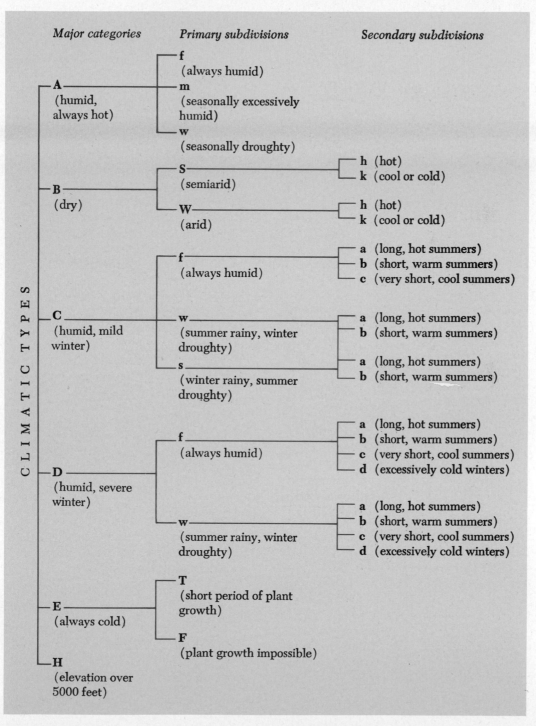

FIGURE C–3
Some climatic type equivalents.

Type name used in this text	Köppen type	Place name example
Tropical wet	**Af**	Upper Amazon
Tropical monsoon	**Am**	Malabar
Tropical dry-winter	**Aw**	Southern Sudan
Semiarid	**BSh** and **BSk**	Lower Rio Grande and Northern Great Plains
Arid	**BWh** and **BWk**	Sahara and Tarim Basin
Humid subtropical	**Cfa**	Gulf states
Midlatitude marine	**Cfb** and **Cfc**	Northwestern Europe
Subtropical dry-winter and tropical upland	**Cw**	South China and Ethiopia
Mediterranean	**Csa** and **Csb**	Mediterranean countries
Humid continental with hot summers	**Dfa** and **Dwa**	Iowa and North China
Humid continental with warm summers	**Dfb** and **Dwb**	Northern Great Lakes and Northern Manchuria
Subarctic	**Dfc, Dwc, Dfd,** and **Dwd**	Central Canada, Amur Lowland, and Northeastern Siberia
Tundra	**ET**	Northern Alaska
Icecap	**EF**	Antarctica

of the appendix, each with a generalized résumé of its major features. Figure C–2 shows the relationship between the major categories and their subdivisions. It also indicates the relative position of each of the types within the whole scheme.

Equivalent climatic types. It is common practice to refer to climatic types by descriptive names, as has been done in the body of this text, or by names of places in which the climates occur. For convenience, certain of these equivalent names are listed in Figure C–3 of this part of the appendix. It should be pointed out that, even though they are rough equivalents, the descriptive or place-name climatic types lack the uniformity and convenience of detailed, standard definition that the Köppen types possess.

Definitions of Climatic Symbols

Primary Types

A Average temperature of the coolest month 64.4° F. or over.

B Precipitation less in inches than the amount $.44t - 8.5$ when it is evenly distributed throughout the year; or less than the amount $.44t - 14$ when it is concentrated chiefly in winter; or less than the amount $.44t - 3$ when it is concentrated chiefly in summer. In all of these amounts, *t* equals average annual temperature in degrees F. These amounts are worked out in Figure C–4. See note regarding meaning of "concentrated" in Figure C–4.

C Average temperature of the warmest month over 50° F. and of the coldest month between 64.4° F. and 32° F.

D Average temperature of the warmest month over 50° F. and of the coldest month 32° F. and below.

E Average temperature of the warmest month below 50° F.

Secondary Types

As they occur with **A**
f Precipitation of the driest month of the year at least 2.4 inches.
w Precipitation of the driest month of the year less than the amount shown in Figure C–5.
m Precipitation of the driest month of the year less than 2.4 inches, but more than the amount shown in Figure C–5.

As they occur with **B**
W Precipitation for the year less than half the amount shown in the definition for **B**. See Figure C–4.
S Precipitation for the year less than the amount shown in the definition for **B**, but more than half that amount. See Figure C–4.

As they occur with **C** *and* **D**
s Precipitation for the driest month of the summer half of the year less than 1.6 inches and less than ⅓ the amount that falls in the wettest month of the winter half of the year.

w Precipitation of the driest month of the winter half of the year less than 1/10 the amount that falls in the wettest month of the summer half of the year.
f Precipitation not satisfying the definitions for **s** or **w**.

As they occur with **E**
T Average temperature of the warmest month of the year between 50° F. and 32° F.
F Average temperature of the warmest month 32° F. or below.

Tertiary Types

As they occur with **B**
h Average annual temperature 64.4° F. or above.
k Average annual temperature below 64.4° F.

As they occur with **C**
a Average temperature of the warmest month 71.6° F. or above.
b Average temperature of the four warmest months 50° F. or above, and average temperature of the warmest month below 71.6° F.
c Average temperature of from one to three months 50° F. or above, and average temperature of warmest month below 71.6° F.

As they occur with **D**
a Same as with **C**.
b Same as with **C**.
c Same as with **C**.
d Average temperature of the coldest month below −36.4° F. (*Note:* **a**, **b**, and **c** do not specifically exclude **d**, *but* when **d** can be used, do *not* use **a**, **b**, or **c**.)

FIGURE C–4

The amount of precipitation (in inches) at the boundary between the **B** climates and the other primary types for each average annual temperature from 32°F. to 90°F., and for the three possible distributions of rain throughout the year.

Average annual temperature	Precipitation concentrated chiefly in winter (.44t − 14)	Precipitation evenly distributed throughout the year (.44t − 8.5)	Precipitation concentrated chiefly in summer (.44t − 3)	Average annual temperature	Precipitation concentrated chiefly in winter (.44t − 14)	Precipitation evenly distributed throughout the year (.44t − 8.5)	Precipitation concentrated chiefly in summer (.44t − 3)
32	.08	5.58	11.08	62	13.28	18.78	24.28
33	.52	6.02	11.52	63	13.72	19.22	24.72
34	.96	6.46	11.96	64	14.16	19.66	25.16
35	1.40	6.90	12.40	65	14.60	20.10	25.60
36	1.84	7.34	12.84	66	15.04	20.54	26.04
37	2.28	7.78	13.28	67	15.48	20.98	26.48
38	2.72	8.22	13.72	68	15.92	21.42	26.92
39	3.16	8.66	14.16	69	16.36	21.86	27.36
40	3.60	9.10	14.60	70	16.80	22.30	27.80
41	4.04	9.54	15.04	71	17.24	22.74	28.24
42	4.48	9.98	15.48	72	17.68	23.18	28.68
43	4.92	10.42	15.92	73	18.12	23.62	29.12
44	5.36	10.86	16.36	74	18.56	24.06	29.56
45	5.80	11.30	16.80	75	19.00	24.50	30.00
46	6.24	11.74	17.24	76	19.44	24.94	30.44
47	6.68	12.18	17.68	77	19.88	25.38	30.88
48	7.12	12.62	18.12	78	20.32	25.82	31.32
49	7.56	13.06	18.56	79	20.76	26.26	31.76
50	8.00	13.50	19.00	80	21.20	26.70	32.20
51	8.44	13.94	19.44	81	21.64	27.14	32.64
52	8.88	14.38	19.88	82	22.08	27.58	33.08
53	9.32	14.82	20.32	83	22.52	28.02	33.52
54	9.76	15.26	20.76	84	22.96	28.46	33.96
55	10.20	15.70	21.20	85	23.40	28.90	34.40
56	10.64	16.14	21.64	86	23.84	29.34	34.84
57	11.08	16.58	22.08	87	24.28	29.78	35.28
58	11.52	17.02	22.52	88	24.72	30.22	35.72
59	11.96	17.46	22.96	89	25.16	30.66	36.16
60	12.40	17.90	23.40	90	25.60	31.10	36.60
61	12.84	18.34	23.84				

NOTE: Precipitation is said to be concentrated in summer when 70 percent or more of the average annual amount is received during the warmer six months. It is concentrated in winter when 70 percent or more is received in the cooler six months. If neither season receives 70 percent of the annual total, the precipitation is considered to be evenly distributed. Division of the year into six-month periods is made between March and April on the one hand and between September and October on the other.

FIGURE C–5

The amount of precipitation (in inches) during the driest month of the year along the boundary between **Am** and **Aw** climates for differing amounts of yearly precipitation. If the amount in the driest month is 2.4 inches or more, the symbol **f** is used; if the amount in the driest month is between 2.4 and the amount shown in this table, the symbol **m** is used; and if the amount in the driest month is less than that shown in this table, the symbol **w** is used.

Total yearly precipitation	Precipitation in driest month	Total yearly precipitation	Precipitation in driest month	Total yearly precipitation	Precipitation in driest month	Total yearly precipitation	Precipitation in driest month
38.5	2.40	54	1.78	69.5	1.15	85	.54
39	2.38	54.5	1.77	70	1.13	85.5	.51
39.5	2.36	55	1.75	70.5	1.11	86	.50
40	2.34	55.5	1.73	71	1.10	86.5	.48
40.5	2.32	56	1.70	71.5	1.08	87	.46
41	2.30	56.5	1.68	72	1.06	87.5	.44
41.5	2.29	57	1.66	72.5	1.03	88	.42
42	2.26	57.5	1.64	73	1.02	88.5	.40
42.5	2.24	58	1.63	73.5	1.00	89	.37
43	2.22	58.5	1.60	74	.98	89.5	.36
43.5	2.20	59	1.58	74.5	.96	90	.34
44	2.18	59.5	1.56	75	.94	90.5	.32
44.5	2.16	60	1.55	75.5	.92	91	.29
45	2.14	60.5	1.53	76	.90	91.5	.28
45.5	2.12	61	1.51	76.5	.88	92	.26
46	2.10	61.5	1.48	77	.86	92.5	.24
46.5	2.08	62	1.47	77.5	.84	93	.22
47	2.07	62.5	1.45	78	.81	93.5	.20
47.5	2.04	63	1.42	78.5	.80	94	.18
48	2.02	63.5	1.41	79	.78	94.5	.16
48.5	2.00	64	1.38	79.5	.76	95	.14
49	1.98	64.5	1.36	80	.74	95.5	.11
49.5	1.96	65	1.34	80.5	.72	96	.09
50	1.94	65.5	1.33	81	.70	96.5	.07
50.5	1.92	66	1.30	81.5	.68	97	.06
51	1.90	66.5	1.28	82	.66	97.5	.04
51.5	1.88	67	1.26	82.5	.63	98	.02
52	1.86	67.5	1.24	83	.61	98.5	.00
52.5	1.85	68	1.22	83.5	.59		
53	1.82	68.5	1.20	84	.58		
53.5	1.80	69	1.18	84.5	.56		

NOTE: If the total yearly precipitation is 197 inches, there can be two whole months without rain and the symbol m used; if the yearly amount is 295.5 inches, three months may be dry and the symbol m used; etc. The symbol m signifies that the dry period is compensated by excess rain at another time whereas w indicates a lack of compensating amounts. Hence, the dividing amount in the driest month becomes smaller as the total for the year becomes larger.

The Determination of Climatic Types

General Procedure

Primary types. In order to determine the climatic type at a given place, it is necessary to have available average temperatures for each month and for the year, as well as average precipitation for each month and for the year. With these statistics at hand, the actual classification can most easily be accomplished by following the routine procedure stated below. It is essentially a process of elimination.

To determine the first letter of the climate-formula, proceed according to the following questions.

1. Is the average temperature of the warmest month below 50° F.? If it is, the climate is of the **E** type; if it is not, proceed to the second question.
2. Is the amount of precipitation less than the amount specified as the limit of the **B** climates in Figure C–4? If it is less, the climate is of the **B** type; if it is not, proceed to the third question.
3. Is the average temperature of the coolest month 64.4° F. or above? If it is, the climate is of the **A** type; if it is not, proceed to the fourth question.
4. Is the average temperature of the coldest month between 64.4° F. and 32° F.? If it is, the climate is of the **C** type; if it is not, or, in other words, if the average temperature of the coldest month is below 32° F., the climate is of the **D** type.

Thus by following through a sequence of, at most, four questions, it is possible to determine which one of the five primary climatic types is represented by any set of temperature and precipitation statistics.

Secondary types. Once the primary type is determined, similar routines are followed to obtain the second and third letters of the climate-formula. Secondary characteristics of each of the main types are most easily determined by applying the following questions.

1. If the climate is of the **E** type, is the average temperature of the warmest month over 32° F.? If it is, the secondary symbol is **T**, if it is not, the secondary symbol is **F**.
2. If the climate is of the **B** type, is the yearly precipitation over one half the amount specified as the limit of the **B** climates in Figure C–4? If it is, the secondary symbol is **S**; if it is not, the secondary symbol is **W**.
3. If the climate is of the **A** type:
   a. Is the precipitation of the driest month 2.4 inches or more? If it is, the secondary symbol is **f**; if it is not, refer to the next question.
   b. Is the precipitation of the driest month more than the amount specified in Figure C–5? If it is, the secondary symbol is **m**; if it is not, the secondary symbol is **w**.
4. If the climate is of the **C** or **D** type:
   a. Is the driest month of the year in the summer six-month period and is its precipitation less than 1.6 inches? If both conditions are satisfied, proceed to question b; if either is not satisfied, proceed to question c.
   b. Is the precipitation of the driest month of summer less than ⅓ that of the wettest month of winter? If it is, the secondary symbol is **s**; if it is not, the secondary symbol is **f**.

c. Is the precipitation of the driest month of winter less than $1/10$ that of the wettest month of summer? If it is, the secondary symbol is **w;** if it is not, the secondary symbol is **f.**

Tertiary types. Tertiary characteristics of each of the **C** and **D** climates are determined most easily as follows. If the climate is of the **C** or **D** type, apply the following questions.

1. Is the average temperature of the coldest month below $-36.4°$ F.? If it is, the symbol is **d;** if it is not, proceed to the next question.
2. Is the average temperature of the warmest month $71.6°$ F. or above? If it is, the symbol is **a;** if it is not, proceed to the next question.
3. Are the average temperatures of the four warmest months $50°$ F. or above? If they are, the symbol is **b;** if they are not, the symbol is **c.**

Application of Classification Procedure

First example. The first example is Maracaibo, Venezuela. The statistics are given on the following page.

Beginning with the primary types, we must first ask the question, "Is the average temperature of the warmest month below $50°$ F.?" The warmest month is August, with an average of $84.4°$. This is well above $50°$ and hence the type cannot be **E.** We have eliminated one of the primary types.

Second, we must ask the question, "Is the amount of precipitation less than the amount specified by definition as the limit of the **B** climates?" It is simplest here to refer to Figure C–4. To use the table, we must know three things about the place in question.

These are: (1) the average annual temperature, (2) the average annual precipitation, and (3) the distribution of the precipitation throughout the year—for example, does 70 percent or more of the precipitation come in the winter six months? Does 70 percent or more come in the summer six months? Or does 70 percent come in neither season?

Items 1 and 2 are given in the statistics: Maracaibo has an average annual temperature of $82.3°$ F. and an average annual precipitation of 18.2 inches. To secure the necessary third item requires the application of simple arithmetic.

The warmer six months at Maracaibo are April through September. During these months, the precipitation in inches is as follows: April, .5; May, 2.4; June, 1.6; July, 1.4; August, 1.3; and September, 3.3. The total for this season is 10.5 inches. Since the total for the year is 18.2 inches and that for the warmer six months is 10.5 inches, the amount that falls in the cooler six months must be 18.2 minus 10.5, or 7.7 inches. The summer, or warmer season, precipitation is 10.5 inches; the winter, or cooler season, precipitation is 7.7 inches. Is either of these amounts equal to or more than 70 percent of the total for the year? Seventy percent of 18.2 is 12.74. Since neither the warmer season precipitation nor that of the cooler season is equal to or greater than 70 percent of the total, the precipitation is considered to be evenly distributed throughout the year.

Now, the three items necessary for the use of Figure C–4 are available: average annual temperature, $82.3°$ F.; average annual precipitation, 18.2 inches; and evenly distributed precipitation. Consulting Figure C–4 we find in the first column average annual temperatures in whole numbers. The nearest to 82.3 is 82. The third column is headed "Precipitation evenly distributed throughout the year." We follow down this column until

	J	F	M	A	M	J	J	A	S	O	N	D	YEAR
Maracaibo													
TEMP.	80.7	81.0	81.2	82.5	83.2	83.5	84.1	84.4	83.5	82.0	81.3	81.0	82.3
PREC.	0.1	0.1	0.3	0.5	2.4	1.6	1.4	1.3	3.3	4.3	2.5	0.4	18.2

we come to the figure on the same line as 82 in the first column. That figure is 27.58. Now we can answer the question, "Is the amount of precipitation less than the amount specified by definition as the limit of the **B** climates?" The precipitation at Maracaibo (18.2 inches) is less than the limit figure (27.58 inches). Hence, Maracaibo has a **B** climate.

We need go no further with the primary types for no set of statistics will fulfill the requirements for more than one. The task is now to determine the secondary symbol.

For the second symbol, only one question is necessary: "Is the yearly precipitation over one half the amount specified in Figure C–4?" The amount specified in Figure C–4 in this instance is 27.58. One half of that is 13.79. Is the annual precipitation at Maracaibo (18.2 inches) over one half the amount (13.79 inches) specified in Figure C–4? It is, so the secondary symbol is **S**. Maracaibo thus has a **BS** climate.

Second example.   As a second example of the application of the procedure of classification, the statistics for Iloilo in the Philippine Islands may be examined on the next page.

We follow the same order as in the example of Maracaibo. First, is the average temperature of the warmest month below 50° F.? It is not; therefore the type is not **E**. Is the precipitation for the year less than the amount specified for the limit of the **B** climates? We must know three things to answer this question: (1) the average annual temperature; (2) the average annual precipitation; and (3) the distribution of precipitation throughout the year. The warmer six months at Iloilo is the period of April through September. In

that season, 60.8 inches of rain fall. Since 88.7 inches fall during the whole year, the amount in the cooler season is 88.7 minus 60.8, or 17.9 inches. Seventy percent of 88.7 is 62.09. Neither the amount that falls in the warmer season nor that which falls in the cooler season is equal to or more than 62.09. Therefore, the precipitation may be considered to be evenly distributed throughout the year. Referring to Figure C–4, we find 81 in the first column. Opposite it in the third column is 27.14. This represents the amount of precipitation that, under these conditions of temperature, limits the **B** climates. The amount of precipitation at Iloilo is more than 27.14; therefore, the climate at Iloilo is not **B**.

We proceed to the next question. "Is the average temperature of the coolest month 64.4° F. or above?" The coolest month at Iloilo has an average temperature of 78.0° F. Therefore, Iloilo has an **A** climate.

There is a threefold division within the **A** climates. We must now discover into which of these three Iloilo fits. The first question asks "Is the precipitation for the driest month 2.4 inches or more?" The driest month at Iloilo has 1.3 inches of rain. The answer to the question is in the negative and consequently the symbol **f** does not apply. The second question asks "Is the precipitation of the driest month more than the amount specified in Figure C–5?" In order to use that table, we must know the average annual precipitation and the precipitation of the driest month. At Iloilo, the average annual precipitation is 88.7 inches; the precipitation of the driest month is 1.3 inches. On Figure C–5 in the column headed "Total yearly precipitation," the figure 88.5 can be found. This is the figure closest to 88.7. Oppo-

	J	F	M	A	M	J	J	A	S	O	N	D	YEAR
Iloilo													
TEMP.	78.0	78.5	80.0	80.7	82.3	81.3	80.5	80.7	80.0	80.0	79.7	78.8	81.0
PREC.	2.4	1.8	1.3	1.6	5.9	10.5	16.3	13.8	12.7	10.3	7.7	4.4	88.7

site it in the column headed "Precipitation of the driest month" is the figure .40. Returning to the question, we can see that the precipitation of the driest month at Iloilo (1.3 inches) is more than the amount specified in Figure C–5 (.40 inch). Therefore, the symbol **m** can be used. The climate at Iloilo is of the **Am** type.

The World Distribution of Climate Types

Since climatic types represent quantitative measurements of temperature and precipitation, it is easy to erect a simplified plan, indicating diagrammatically the place of occurrence of the major types. One such plan is shown in Figure C–6. Each of the corners of the rectangle represents extreme combinations of the two elements, temperature and precipitation. The upper left-hand corner indicates the extreme of cold and dry; the lower left-hand corner indicates the extreme of hot and dry; the upper right-hand corner, cold and wet; and the lower right-hand corner, hot and wet.

The Generalized Continent Diagram

The very simple pattern shown on Figure C–6 takes into account only the factor of quantity for both of the basic climatic elements. To get at the pattern for the world, there must be included some indication of the distribution of land and water, which is so powerful a control of distribution for both temperature and precipitation.

It will be remembered that there are two great "world islands," the Americas on the one hand and the Europe–Asia–Africa land mass on the other. These "world islands" are roughly triangular in broad outline. Their widest extent occurs at about 60° North latitude and they taper into the Southern Hemisphere where both of them pinch out in the middle latitudes. After a short break, land appears again in the circumpolar continent of Antarctica. In the Northern Hemisphere, the continents fray out poleward toward the Arctic Ocean and do not extend to the Pole.

This very generalized distribution of land in each hemisphere is represented diagrammatically in Figure C–7. The outline circle represents the outer edge of a hemisphere. The top-shaped figure upon it represents the outline of land. The continent thus delineated indicates simply land as opposed to water. No attempt is made to show generalized differences of elevation, nor is any attempt made to show detailed position of any actual coastline. The smaller triangular figure is a generalization of the Antarctic continent. The whole figure is called the *generalized continent diagram,* or the *ideal continent.*

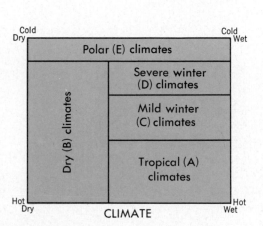

FIGURE C–6

The relationship of temperature and precipitation to major classifications of climate.

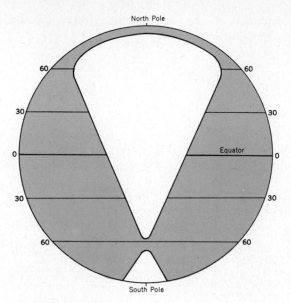

FIGURE C–7

Generalized continent diagram—distribution of land and water.

Distribution of Major Climatic Categories

The zone of greatest heating and of highest precipitation for the world as a whole occurs along the equator, and the greatest cold, whether dry or wet, occurs in the higher latitudes near, but not at, the poles. In the higher latitudes coastal positions are wet and continental positions are comparatively dry. The remaining combination, hot and dry, is found within the tropics extending inland from the continental west coasts. These facts can be placed upon the generalized continent diagram as in Figure C–8.

Now, instead of the pattern that appeared on the rectangular diagram (Fig. C–6), a new pattern can be drawn. A line must appear between the hot-wet and the hot-dry focal points. Lines must be drawn between the hot-dry and the two cold-wet locations. Finally, there must be indicated the limit, in the continental interior, where dryness becomes less significant than coldness. There are thus formed, on the generalized continent diagram, curving loops that extend from the west coasts between about 20° and 30° latitude both North and South into the continental interiors of the higher middle lati-

tudes (Fig. C–9). The areas within the loops
are distinguished by their dryness; everything outside, by wetness. The loops, then,
outline the areas of dry (**B**) climate. Outside
them lie the tropical humid (**A**); the humid
mild-winter (**C**); the humid severe-winter
(**D**); and the polar (**E**) climates.

Across the polar reaches in both hemispheres perennial cold is so dominant that
relative wetness and dryness are not significant. Lines may be drawn (Fig. C–10) in both
hemispheres to indicate the equatorward
limit of the polar (**E**) climates. The portion
of the generalized continent not yet subdivided includes now only tropical humid
(**A**); humid mild-winter (**C**); and humid severe-winter (**D**) types.

Temperatures characteristic of the tropical
humid (**A**) climates occur only within the low
latitudes. On the generalized continent, the

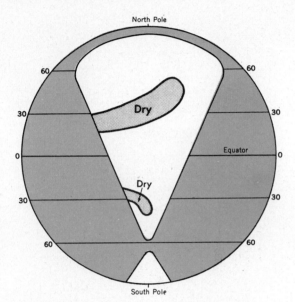

FIGURE C–9

Generalized continent diagram—dry (**B**) climates.

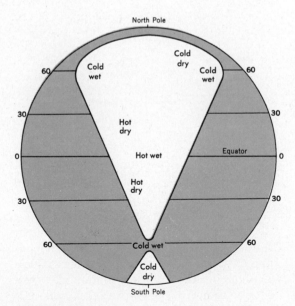

FIGURE C–8

Generalized continent diagram—distribution of descriptive climatic terms.

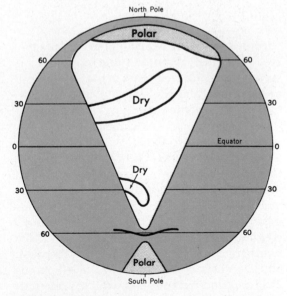

FIGURE C–10

Generalized continent diagram—polar (**E**) and dry (**B**)
climates.

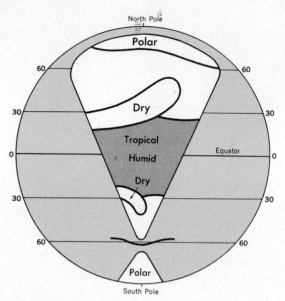

FIGURE C–11

Generalized continent diagram—tropical humid (**A**), polar (**E**), and dry (**B**) climates.

severe-winter (**D**) climates must cross the diagram from east to west. Latitude for latitude, west-coast temperatures in the middle latitudes are higher for winter than are those of the east coast. Hence, the limit between the humid mild-winter (**C**) and the humid severe-winter (**D**) climates begins on the west coast at approximately 60° North latitude, curves equatorward across the continent, and leaves the east coast at about 45° North. In the section where it crosses the dry (**B**) climate, its significance is lost, for the climates are dry on either side of it. In that section, the line is omitted from the diagram. The *generalized* distribution of the five major categories of climate as they occur over the land thus appears in Figure C–12.

It must be thoroughly understood that Figure C–12 is not a detailed map of climatic distribution over the world. It is simply a

only portion of these latitudes remaining unspecified is that between and east of the two areas of dry (**B**) climate. A line in each hemisphere from the east coast to the dry interior approximately at the edges of the low latitudes provides the remaining boundaries for the tropical humid (**A**) climates (Fig. C–11).

There remain only the humid mild-winter (**C**) and humid severe-winter (**D**) climates to delimit. There is not sufficient continentality in the Southern Hemisphere to allow the development of the humid severe-winter (**D**) type. Hence, it is only necessary to indicate the separation between the two in the Northern Hemisphere. To the east, the west, and the north of the dry (**B**) zone, climate is characterized as humid or wet. As one proceeds away from the equator, coldness increases. Therefore, the boundary between the humid mild-winter (**C**) and the humid

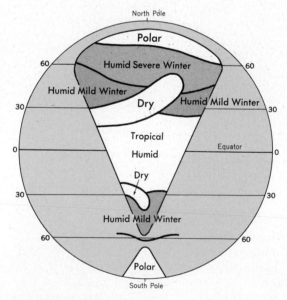

FIGURE C–12

Generalized continent diagram—five major climatic types.

key to the *relative* position assumed by each major category on any one land mass. Variations from this pattern are induced first by irregularities of land surface and secondly by the detailed position of the coastline.

The effects of irregularities of surface can be seen in many places on the map showing the world distribution of all climatic types (Plate IV). For example, consider the African portion of that map. The tropical humid (**A**) climates do not extend to the east coast of that continent north of the equator. On the generalized continent diagram (Fig. C–12), the tropical humid (**A**) climates extend the whole breadth of the tropics along the east coast. Eastern Africa is a plateau region with hills and mountain masses upon it. The surface character is not the whole reason for the absence of tropical humid (**A**) climates along the east coast, but it is a strong contributory factor. Another instance occurs in South America. On the generalized diagram (Fig. C–12), the tropical humid (**A**) climates extend along the equator unbroken from east coast to west coast. In South America, a break occurs near the west coast (Plate IV). The break is located where the towering Andes stretch north-south across the equator. Their high elevations produce temperatures lower than those that characterize the tropical humid (**A**) climates.

The effect of irregularities of coastline are well illustrated in the Caribbean region of the Americas. The climatic map (Plate IV) shows that the dry (**B**) climate comes to the east coast near the boundary between Mexico and the United States. On the generalized continent diagram (Fig. C–12), the dry (**B**) climates are seen to be well inland from the east coast. The apparent contradiction results from the fact that the coastline on the generalized continent omits the large indentation of the Gulf of Mexico.

Again, part of the reason for the lack of tropical humid (**A**) climate on the African east coast north of the equator is the actual position of the coastline, this time in relation to wind directions. Prevailing winds are parallel to this coast no matter what the season. Consequently, little moisture is carried onshore from the Indian Ocean. The precipitation necessary to the tropical humid (**A**) climates is therefore lacking from that source. When this is coupled with the control induced by the surface, which was stated above, the greater part of the dryness of the African east coast is explained and the absence of tropical humid (**A**) climate is reasonably well understood.

Distribution of Climatic Types

The use of the generalized continent diagram may be further enhanced by the addition to it of the facts of seasonal distribution of precipitation. On the continental west coasts between approximately 25° and 40° latitude both North and South, there is a zone in which such precipitation as falls is concentrated in the winter half of the year.

This zone extends inland to form rough half ovals, as in Figure C–13. Within the shaded areas, precipitation occurs mainly during the winter and the summer is droughty.

The opposite condition, summer rain and winter drought, is characteristic of truly continental locations. As has been explained previously, there is a tendency toward an

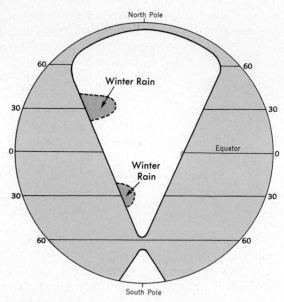

FIGURE C–13
Generalized continent diagram—areas of winter precipitation.

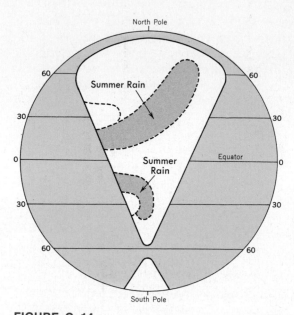

FIGURE C–14
Generalized continent diagram—areas of summer precipitation.

indraft of air into continents in summer and an outdraft in winter. This means that more moisture is available for precipitation in summer than in winter. The indraft is pronounced only when there is a very considerable land mass, but the characteristic tendency toward summer precipitation concentration is everywhere prominent away from coastline locations. Generalization of the regions in which this condition prevails is indicated on Figure C–14.

The only other possibility is that precipitation be relatively evenly spread throughout the year. When the zone of winter concentration (Fig. C–13) and the zone of summer concentration (Fig. C–14) are plotted, that which is left in the area of year-round precipitation. Figure C–15 shows the characteristic location of each of the three possible

rainfall regimes.

We now have one diagram (Fig. C–12) showing the generalized pattern of the five major categories of climate: tropical humid (**A**), dry (**B**), humid mild-winter (**C**), humid severe-winter (**D**), and polar (**E**); and one diagram (Fig. C–15) showing the generalized pattern of precipitation types. By superposition (Fig. C–16), we secure the key to the expected location of the major climatic types on the generalized continent. As has been stated previously, departures from this design result primarily from the controls emphasized by irregularities of surface and by details of coastline position.

Further subdivision of the humid mild-winter (**C**) and humid severe-winter (**D**) climates is made on the basis of the character of the summers. Without discussing this

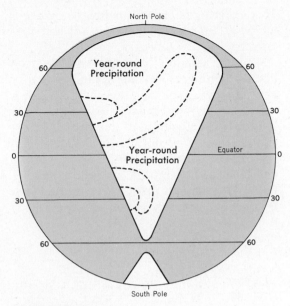

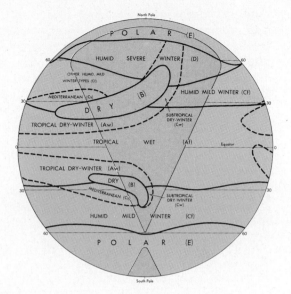

FIGURE C-15

Generalized continent diagram—areas of year-round precipitation.

FIGURE C-16

Generalized continent diagram—distribution of climatic types over both land and ocean.

breakdown in detail, the generalized pattern is shown in Figure C–17. In this diagram, part of the Northern Hemisphere portion of the generalized continent has been enlarged so as to show the relationship of the types more clearly.

Climate of the Oceans

Largely because human beings live permanently on the land masses, climate over the oceans is generally neglected. Nevertheless, the same major types are found there as on land. The pattern is shown on Figure C–16.

Two specific features should be noted. First, the area of dry (**B**) climate is greatly reduced over the ocean. This is to be expected, for the existence of dry (**B**) climate is based primarily on two conditions: (1) the absence of large amounts of water vapor in the air and (2) the absence of some means of forcing the condensation of such vapor as is present. Over the oceans both of these deficiencies are generally restricted to sections close to the continental west coasts. Second, the area of humid severe-winter (**D**) climate is likewise very small in proportion to that over the continent. By definition, the humid severe-winter (**D**) climates have very large temperature ranges. In other words, they are continental. As we have seen, the presence of large water bodies tends to reduce temperature range. The result of this tendency is to produce insufficient range over the oceans to satisfy the definition of the humid severe-winter (**D**) type in all except two small areas off the coasts of the higher middle latitudes in the Northern Hemisphere.

Finally, it should be noted that there is a much more regular belted arrangement of climates over the oceans than over the land.

This reflects the facts already pointed out in the discussion of temperature and precipitation.

Though climatic maps may show the distribution over the oceans, the boundaries between one type and another are much more broadly generalized than those over the land. Realization of the fact that the climatic types are not confined to the land is essential; so also is the realization of the generalized distribution of those types, for knowledge of their precise distribution over the sea is neither possible nor would it be considered particularly vital.

FIGURE C–17

Northern Hemisphere portion of generalized continent diagram, showing in greater detail the distribution pattern of the subdivisions of humid mild-winter (**C**) and humid severe-winter (**D**) climates.

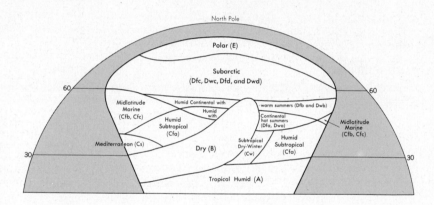

Selected Climatic Statistics

North and Middle America and the Caribbean Area

	J	F	M	A	M	J	J	A	S	O	N	D	YEAR
1. San Juan, PUERTO RICO													
TEMP.	75	75	75	77	79	80	80	80	80	80	78	76	78
PREC.	4.1	3.0	3.0	4.1	5.2	5.4	5.8	5.9	6.0	5.7	7.0	5.4	60.6
2. Miami, FLORIDA													
TEMP.	66	68	72	74	79	81	82	82	81	77	73	69	75
PREC.	3.3	2.5	2.8	3.1	5.9	7.9	7.2	7.3	9.9	9.2	2.4	2.2	63.7
3. Port-au-Prince, HAITI													
TEMP.	78	78	79	80	81	83	84	84	82	81	80	78	81
PREC.	1.2	2.7	4.1	6.7	8.0	4.0	2.7	4.8	7.7	7.4	4.2	0.9	54.4
4. Acapulco, MEXICO													
TEMP.	78	78	79	80	83	83	83	81	81	83	80	79	81
PREC.	0.6	0	0	0	1.7	16.5	6.0	6.3	14.7	5.9	1.9	0.7	54.3
5. Veracruz, MEXICO													
TEMP.	70	71	74	78	81	81	81	81	80	78	75	71	77
PREC.	1.0	0.6	0.5	0.6	1.7	11.4	13.0	10.7	12.0	5.7	3.1	1.0	61.3
6. Medicine Hat, CANADA													
TEMP.	13	16	28	45	55	63	69	67	56	45	30	19	42
PREC.	0.6	0.6	0.6	0.7	1.6	2.5	1.8	1.4	1.2	0.6	0.7	0.7	13.0
7. Goodland, KANSAS													
TEMP.	29	33	40	50	59	70	77	74	66	54	41	30	52
PREC.	0.3	0.6	1.0	1.8	2.5	2.8	2.7	2.5	1.6	1.0	0.6	0.6	18.0
8. San Diego, CALIFORNIA													
TEMP.	54	55	56	58	61	64	67	69	67	63	59	56	61
PREC.	1.8	2.0	1.5	0.6	0.3	0.1	0.1	0.1	0.1	0.3	0.9	1.8	9.6
9. Mexico City, MEXICO													
TEMP.	54	57	61	63	65	64	62	62	61	59	57	55	60
PREC.	0.2	0.3	0.5	0.7	1.9	4.1	4.5	4.3	4.1	1.6	0.5	0.3	23.0
10. Phoenix, ARIZONA													
TEMP.	50	54	60	67	75	84	90	88	82	70	59	52	69
PREC.	1.0	0.7	0.6	0.4	0.1	0.1	1.3	1.0	0.7	0.5	0.8	0.7	7.9
11. La Paz, MEXICO													
TEMP.	63	65	68	71	74	78	82	84	82	79	72	66	74
PREC.	0.2	0.1	0	0	0	0	0.4	1.2	1.4	0.6	0.5	1.1	5.5

	J	F	M	A	M	J	J	A	S	O	N	D	YEAR

12. Cairo, ILLINOIS

	J	F	M	A	M	J	J	A	S	O	N	D	YEAR
TEMP.	44	47	57	67	76	85	88	87	81	70	56	46	67
PREC.	3.9	3.2	4.1	3.9	3.8	3.9	3.0	3.0	2.9	2.8	3.6	3.3	41.4

13. New York, NEW YORK

	J	F	M	A	M	J	J	A	S	O	N	D	YEAR
TEMP.	30	31	38	49	59	69	75	73	66	55	44	34	52
PREC.	3.3	3.3	3.5	3.3	3.5	3 4	4.1	4.4	3.4	3.4	3.6	3.3	42.5

14. Washington, D.C.

	J	F	M	A	M	J	J	A	S	O	N	D	YEAR
TEMP.	33	35	42	53	64	73	77	75	68	57	45	36	55
PREC.	3.1	3.1	3.5	3.3	3.7	3.7	4.3	4.1	3.3	3.1	2.6	3.0	40.8

15. San Antonio, TEXAS

	J	F	M	A	M	J	J	A	S	O	N	D	YEAR
TEMP.	53	55	63	69	75	81	83	83	79	70	61	54	69
PREC.	1.4	1.6	1.8	2.7	3.2	2.7	2.5	2.6	3.5	2.0	2.2	1.8	28.0

16. Montgomery, ALABAMA

	J	F	M	A	M	J	J	A	S	O	N	D	YEAR
TEMP.	48	51	58	65	73	80	82	81	76	66	56	49	66
PREC.	5.1	5.5	6.4	4.3	3.8	4.2	4.7	4.2	2.9	2.4	3.1	4.5	51.1

17. Sitka, ALASKA

	J	F	M	A	M	J	J	A	S	O	N	D	YEAR
TEMP.	30	32	35	40	46	51	55	55	51	44	37	33	42
PREC.	7.1	6.8	5.6	5.4	4.3	3.5	4.0	7.1	9.7	11.7	8.8	7.4	81.4

18. St. Paul, MINNESOTA

	J	F	M	A	M	J	J	A	S	O	N	D	YEAR
TEMP.	12	15	28	46	58	67	72	70	61	48	31	19	44
PREC.	0.9	0.8	1.4	2.4	3.4	4.1	3.5	3.5	3.4	2.0	1.4	1.0	27.8

19. Albany, NEW YORK

	J	F	M	A	M	J	J	A	S	O	N	D	YEAR
TEMP.	23	24	33	47	59	68	72	71	63	50	39	28	48
PREC.	2.6	2.5	2.7	2.7	3.5	4.0	4.1	3.8	3.4	3.4	3.0	2.7	38.4

20. Dubuque, IOWA

	J	F	M	A	M	J	J	A	S	O	N	D	YEAR
TEMP.	20	23	35	49	60	70	75	72	64	52	37	25	48
PREC.	1.5	1.4	2.2	2.6	3.9	4.5	3.7	3.4	4.0	2.5	1.9	1.5	33.1

21. Edmonton, CANADA

	J	F	M	A	M	J	J	A	S	O	N	D	YEAR
TEMP.	6	12	22	40	51	57	61	59	50	41	26	14	37
PREC.	0.8	0.7	0.8	0.9	1.7	3.1	3.2	2.4	1.3	0.7	0.7	0.8	17.1

22. Toronto, CANADA

	J	F	M	A	M	J	J	A	S	O	N	D	YEAR
TEMP.	22	23	30	42	53	63	69	67	60	48	37	27	45
PREC.	2.8	2.7	2.4	2.5	2.8	2.7	2.9	2.8	3.1	2.4	2.8	2.6	32.5

23. Halifax, CANADA

	J	F	M	A	M	J	J	A	S	O	N	D	YEAR
TEMP.	23	23	30	39	49	58	65	65	58	49	39	28	44
PREC.	5.5	4.9	4.9	4.6	4.1	3.7	3.8	4.5	3.6	5.2	5.5	5.3	55.6

24. Duluth, MINNESOTA

	J	F	M	A	M	J	J	A	S	O	N	D	YEAR
TEMP.	10	13	24	38	48	58	66	65	57	45	29	17	39
PREC.	1.0	1.0	1.5	2.1	3.4	4.4	3.9	3.5	3.7	2.7	1.5	1.2	29.9

25. Norman, CANADA

	J	F	M	A	M	J	J	A	S	O	N	D	YEAR
TEMP.	−19	−13	−2	19	41	54	59	54	41	24	−1	−15	20
PREC.	0.4	0.5	0.6	0.5	1.1	1.3	1.8	1.9	1.0	0.8	0.4	0.4	10.7

26. Churchill, CANADA

	J	F	M	A	M	J	J	A	S	O	N	D	YEAR
TEMP.	−21	−17	−2	17	30	44	54	52	41	27	6	−11	18
PREC.	0.6	1.1	1.1	1.0	0.9	2.0	1.8	2.4	2.6	1.3	1.2	0.8	16.8

	J	F	M	A	M	J	J	A	S	O	N	D	YEAR

27. Father Point, CANADA

	J	F	M	A	M	J	J	A	S	O	N	D	YEAR
TEMP.	9	10	22	34	44	53	58	56	49	41	30	17	36
PREC.	2.5	2.4	2.4	1.9	3.0	3.6	2.9	3.2	3.1	3.3	2.9	2.8	34.0

28. Upernivik, WEST GREENLAND

	J	F	M	A	M	J	J	A	S	O	N	D	YEAR
TEMP.	−7	−10	−7	6	25	35	41	41	34	25	14	1	17
PREC.	0.4	0.4	0.6	0.5	0.6	0.6	1.0	1.1	1.0	1.2	1.1	0.5	9.0

29. Angmagssalik, EAST GREENLAND

	J	F	M	A	M	J	J	A	S	O	N	D	YEAR
TEMP.	18	16	19	25	34	41	45	43	38	30	23	20	29
PREC.	3.3	2.0	2.4	2.4	2.4	2.1	1.9	2.4	3.7	5.7	3.3	2.8	34.4

South America

30. Medellín, COLOMBIA

	J	F	M	A	M	J	J	A	S	O	N	D	YEAR
TEMP.	71	72	71	71	71	71	71	71	71	69	69	70	71
PREC.	2.7	3.5	3.3	6.6	7.7	5.5	4.1	4.6	6.2	6.9	5.2	2.5	58.8

31. Santos, BRAZIL

	J	F	M	A	M	J	J	A	S	O	N	D	YEAR
TEMP.	76	78	76	73	69	66	66	66	67	69	73	76	71
PREC.	10.4	9.2	8.1	6.8	6.1	2.4	4.4	4.6	5.6	6.1	7.8	7.0	78.5

32. Manaus, BRAZIL

	J	F	M	A	M	J	J	A	S	O	N	D	YEAR
TEMP.	80	80	80	80	80	80	81	82	83	83	82	81	81
PREC	9.2	9.0	9.6	8.5	7.0	3.6	2.2	1.4	2.0	4.1	5.5	7.7	69.8

33. Rio de Janeiro, BRAZIL

	J	F	M	A	M	J	J	A	S	O	N	D	YEAR
TEMP.	79	79	78	75	72	70	69	70	70	72	74	77	74
PREC.	4.9	4.8	5.2	4.3	3.1	2.3	1.7	1.7	2.6	3.2	4.1	5.4	43.3

34. Coquimbo, CHILE

	J	F	M	A	M	J	J	A	S	O	N	D	YEAR
TEMP.	64	64	62	59	57	54	54	54	55	57	59	62	58
PREC.	0	0	0	0	1.1	1.5	1.1	0.5	0.2	0	0	0	4.4

35. Lima, PERU

	J	F	M	A	M	J	J	A	S	O	N	D	YEAR
TEMP.	73	74	74	70	66	63	61	61	61	63	66	70	67
PREC.	0	0	0	0	0	0.1	0.2	0.4	0.4	0.4	0.2	0.1	1.8

36. Buenos Aires, ARGENTINA

	J	F	M	A	M	J	J	A	S	O	N	D	YEAR
TEMP.	74	73	69	61	55	50	49	51	55	60	66	71	61
PREC.	3.1	2.8	3.9	4.8	2.8	2.0	2.1	2.2	2.9	3.3	4.0	4.0	37.9

37. Puerto Montt, CHILE

	J	F	M	A	M	J	J	A	S	O	N	D	YEAR
TEMP.	60	58	56	52	50	46	46	46	47	51	54	57	52
PREC.	4.6	4.4	5.9	7.4	10.6	10.0	10.8	9.3	6.3	5.5	5.5	5.4	85.7

38. Mar del Plata, ARGENTINA

	J	F	M	A	M	J	J	A	S	O	N	D	YEAR
TEMP.	67	66	64	59	53	47	46	47	50	53	59	64	56
PREC.	2.1	3.1	3.1	3.1	1.9	2.4	2.1	1.8	2.6	2.4	2.6	2.7	29.9

39. Santiago, CHILE

	J	F	M	A	M	J	J	A	S	O	N	D	YEAR
TEMP.	69	67	62	57	51	46	46	49	52	57	62	67	57
PREC.	0	0.1	0.2	0.6	2.4	3.3	2.8	2.1	1.3	0.5	0.2	0.2	13.7

40. Tucumán, ARGENTINA

	J	F	M	A	M	J	J	A	S	O	N	D	YEAR
TEMP.	77	75	72	66	60	54	54	57	64	69	73	75	66
PREC.	6.3	7.5	5.5	3.1	1.2	0.6	0.3	0.5	0.6	2.3	4.2	5.9	38.0

Europe

41. Astrakhan, U.S.S.R.

	J	F	M	A	M	J	J	A	S	O	N	D	YEAR
TEMP.	19	21	32	49	64	73	78	75	64	50	38	26	49
PREC.	0.5	0.3	0.4	0.5	0.6	0.7	0.5	0.5	0.5	0.4	0.4	0.5	5.8

	J	F	M	A	M	J	J	A	S	O	N	D	YEAR

42. Turin, ITALY

	J	F	M	A	M	J	J	A	S	O	N	D	YEAR
TEMP.	33	37	46	54	61	69	74	73	65	54	43	35	54
PREC.	2.2	1.6	2.3	4.4	4.8	4.2	2.3	2.6	2.8	3.6	2.6	1.6	35.0

43. Trieste, ITALY

	J	F	M	A	M	J	J	A	S	O	N	D	YEAR
TEMP.	39	41	47	54	62	69	74	73	66	58	49	43	56
PREC.	2.2	2.3	2.8	2.9	3.7	4.1	3.7	3.7	4.0	4.7	3.6	3.4	41.1

44. Paris, FRANCE

	J	F	M	A	M	J	J	A	S	O	N	D	YEAR
TEMP.	37	39	43	51	56	62	66	64	59	51	43	37	51
PREC.	1.4	1.1	1.4	1.5	1.9	2.1	2.0	1.9	1.9	2.1	1.9	1.6	20.8

45. Dublin, IRELAND

	J	F	M	A	M	J	J	A	S	O	N	D	YEAR
TEMP.	40	41	42	45	49	55	58	57	54	48	44	41	48
PREC.	2.2	1.9	1.9	1.9	2.1	2.0	2.6	3.1	2.0	2.6	2.9	2.5	27.7

46. Reykjavik, ICELAND

	J	F	M	A	M	J	J	A	S	O	N	D	YEAR
TEMP.	30	30	31	36	43	49	52	51	46	39	34	30	39
PREC.	3.9	3.3	2.7	2.4	1.9	1.9	1.9	2.0	3.5	3.4	3.7	3.5	34.1

47. Frankfurt am Main, WEST GERMANY

	J	F	M	A	M	J	J	A	S	O	N	D	YEAR
TEMP.	32	36	41	49	57	63	66	64	58	49	41	35	49
PREC.	1.5	1.4	1.7	1.2	1.9	2.2	2.6	2.2	1.9	2.1	1.8	2.0	22.5

48. Edinburgh, SCOTLAND

	J	F	M	A	M	J	J	A	S	O	N	D	YEAR
TEMP.	38	39	40	45	49	55	58	57	54	47	42	39	47
PREC.	2.0	1.8	1.7	1.5	1.9	2.4	2.7	3.0	2.5	2.4	2.3	2.3	26.5

49. Athens, GREECE

	J	F	M	A	M	J	J	A	S	O	N	D	YEAR
TEMP.	48	50	53	58	66	74	80	80	73	66	57	52	63
PREC.	2.1	1.8	1.3	0.9	0.8	0.6	0.3	0.6	0.7	1.4	2.9	2.5	15.9

50. La Coruña, SPAIN

	J	F	M	A	M	J	J	A	S	O	N	D	YEAR
TEMP.	49	50	52	55	58	62	64	64	62	57	53	50	57
PREC.	2.7	3.5	3.2	2.9	2.0	1.4	0.9	1.1	1.7	3.1	3.5	3.5	29.5

51. Granada, SPAIN

	J	F	M	A	M	J	J	A	S	O	N	D	YEAR
TEMP.	44	48	52	58	63	70	77	77	70	60	51	44	59
PREC.	2.0	1.7	2.2	2.1	1.8	0.8	0.1	0.2	1.1	1.8	1.9	1.9	17.6

52. Lisbon, PORTUGAL

	J	F	M	A	M	J	J	A	S	O	N	D	YEAR
TEMP.	51	52	55	58	62	67	71	72	69	63	57	51	61
PREC.	3.4	3.3	3.4	3.1	1.8	0.6	0.2	0.2	1.3	2.4	3.6	4.3	27.6

53. Bucharest, RUMANIA

	J	F	M	A	M	J	J	A	S	O	N	D	YEAR
TEMP.	26	31	41	52	62	69	73	72	64	53	40	31	51
PREC.	1.2	1.1	1.5	1.7	2.3	4.3	2.2	2.2	2.0	1.6	1.6	1.2	22.9

54. Odessa, U.S.S.R.

	J	F	M	A	M	J	J	A	S	O	N	D	YEAR
TEMP.	25	28	35	48	59	68	73	71	62	52	41	31	49
PREC.	0.9	0.7	1.1	1.1	1.3	2.3	2.1	1.2	1.4	1.1	1.6	1.3	16.1

55. Oslo, NORWAY

	J	F	M	A	M	J	J	A	S	O	N	D	YEAR
TEMP.	25	26	31	41	51	60	63	60	52	42	33	27	43
PREC.	1.1	1.1	1.3	1.3	1.7	1.9	2.8	3.5	2.4	2.5	1.9	1.7	23.2

56. Moscow, U.S.S.R.

	J	F	M	A	M	J	J	A	S	O	N	D	YEAR
TEMP.	12	15	23	38	53	62	66	63	52	40	28	17	39
PREC.	1.7	0.9	1.2	1.5	1.9	2.0	2.8	2.9	2.2	1.4	1.6	1.5	21.6

	J	F	M	A	M	J	J	A	S	O	N	D	YEAR

57. Stockholm, SWEDEN

| TEMP. | 27 | 26 | 30 | 38 | 48 | 57 | 62 | 59 | 53 | 43 | 35 | 29 | 42 |
| PREC. | 1.4 | 1.3 | 1.3 | 1.5 | 1.5 | 1.7 | 2.4 | 2.9 | 1.9 | 1.8 | 1.9 | 1.9 | 21.5 |

58. Tromsö, NORWAY

| TEMP. | 26 | 24 | 27 | 32 | 39 | 47 | 52 | 51 | 44 | 36 | 30 | 27 | 36 |
| PREC. | 4.3 | 4.4 | 3.1 | 2.3 | 1.9 | 2.2 | 2.2 | 2.8 | 4.8 | 4.6 | 4.4 | 3.8 | 40.8 |

59. Archangel, U.S.S.R.

| TEMP. | 7 | 9 | 19 | 30 | 41 | 54 | 60 | 57 | 47 | 35 | 22 | 12 | 33 |
| PREC. | 0.8 | 0.7 | 0.8 | 0.7 | 1.0 | 1.5 | 2.2 | 2.1 | 2.0 | 1.5 | 1.1 | 0.8 | 15.2 |

60. Vardö, NORWAY

| TEMP. | 22 | 21 | 23 | 30 | 35 | 42 | 48 | 48 | 43 | 35 | 28 | 24 | 33 |
| PREC. | 2.6 | 2.8 | 2.1 | 1.7 | 1.4 | 1.6 | 1.7 | 2.0 | 2.4 | 2.5 | 2.5 | 2.6 | 25.9 |

Africa

61. Nouvelle-Anvers, REPUBLIC OF THE CONGO

| TEMP. | 79 | 80 | 79 | 78 | 78 | 78 | 77 | 78 | 78 | 77 | 77 | 77 | 78 |
| PREC. | 4.1 | 3.5 | 4.1 | 5.6 | 6.2 | 6.1 | 6.3 | 6.3 | 6.3 | 6.6 | 2.6 | 9.3 | 67.0 |

62. Freetown, SIERRA LEONE

| TEMP. | 81 | 82 | 82 | 82 | 82 | 80 | 78 | 77 | 79 | 80 | 81 | 81 | 80 |
| PREC. | 0.6 | 0.5 | 1.1 | 5.4 | 14.8 | 21.3 | 36.8 | 39.6 | 32.5 | 15.2 | 5.3 | 1.3 | 174.4 |

63. Banana, REPUBLIC OF THE CONGO

| TEMP. | 80 | 81 | 82 | 80 | 79 | 75 | 73 | 73 | 76 | 79 | 80 | 80 | 78 |
| PREC. | 2.1 | 2.3 | 3.7 | 6.1 | 1.9 | 0 | 0 | 0.1 | 0.1 | 1.6 | 5.9 | 4.7 | 28.5 |

64. Mombasa, KENYA

| TEMP. | 80 | 80 | 82 | 81 | 78 | 77 | 75 | 76 | 77 | 78 | 79 | 80 | 79 |
| PREC. | 0.8 | 0.9 | 2.3 | 7.8 | 13.7 | 3.6 | 3.5 | 2.2 | 1.9 | 3.4 | 5.0 | 2.2 | 47.3 |

65. Kimberley, SOUTH AFRICA

| TEMP. | 76 | 75 | 72 | 64 | 56 | 50 | 51 | 56 | 62 | 68 | 73 | 76 | 65 |
| PREC. | 2.8 | 3.0 | 2.8 | 2.0 | 0.7 | 0.5 | 0.1 | 0.3 | 0.2 | 0.8 | 2.1 | 2.9 | 18.2 |

66. Gorée, SENEGAL

| TEMP. | 69 | 66 | 68 | 69 | 72 | 78 | 81 | 82 | 82 | 82 | 78 | 72 | 75 |
| PREC. | 0 | 0 | 0 | 0 | 0 | 0.9 | 3.6 | 9.9 | 5.2 | 0.7 | 0.1 | 0 | 20.4 |

67. Cairo, EGYPT

| TEMP. | 54 | 57 | 63 | 70 | 77 | 82 | 84 | 83 | 78 | 75 | 66 | 59 | 71 |
| PREC. | 0.3 | 0.2 | 0.2 | 0.2 | 0 | 0 | 0 | 0 | 0 | 0.1 | 0.1 | 0.2 | 1.3 |

68. Swakopmund, NAMIBIA

| TEMP. | 61 | 63 | 63 | 60 | 61 | 59 | 57 | 55 | 56 | 58 | 59 | 62 | 59 |
| PREC. | 0 | 0.1 | 0.2 | 0 | 0 | 0 | 0 | 0 | 0 | 0.1 | 0 | 0.2 | 0.6 |

69. Cape Town, SOUTH AFRICA

| TEMP. | 69 | 70 | 68 | 63 | 59 | 56 | 55 | 56 | 57 | 61 | 64 | 67 | 62 |
| PREC. | 0.7 | 0.6 | 0.9 | 1.8 | 3.9 | 4.4 | 3.5 | 3.3 | 2.2 | 1.6 | 1.1 | 0.8 | 24.8 |

70. Algiers, ALGERIA

| TEMP. | 53 | 55 | 58 | 61 | 66 | 71 | 77 | 78 | 75 | 69 | 62 | 56 | 65 |
| PREC. | 4.2 | 3.5 | 3.5 | 2.3 | 1.3 | 0.6 | 0.1 | 0.3 | 1.1 | 3.1 | 4.6 | 5.4 | 30.0 |

71. Pretoria, SOUTH AFRICA

| TEMP. | 72 | 71 | 68 | 63 | 57 | 53 | 52 | 57 | 63 | 68 | 69 | 71 | 64 |
| PREC. | 5.5 | 3.9 | 3.5 | 1.1 | 0.6 | 0.2 | 0.1 | 0.2 | 1.1 | 1.8 | 3.7 | 4.2 | 25.9 |

Asia and Adjacent Islands

	J	F	M	A	M	J	J	A	S	O	N	D	YEAR
72. Legaspi, PHILIPPINES													
TEMP.	78	78	80	82	83	82	81	81	81	81	80	79	81
PREC.	15.2	13.0	7.7	5.4	5.3	8.8	10.1	7.2	10.2	13.0	17.3	18.7	131.9
73. Manokwari, NEW GUINEA													
TEMP.	78	78	79	79	79	79	79	79	79	80	80	79	79
PREC.	10.8	10.7	13.0	11.1	7.8	8.3	6.0	5.3	5.1	4.2	6.6	10.6	99.5
74. Medan, INDONESIA													
TEMP.	75	77	78	79	79	78	78	78	77	77	76	76	77
PREC.	5.4	3.9	4.1	5.2	7.0	5.2	5.2	6.9	8.7	9.8	10.1	8.9	80.4
75. Yap, CAROLINE ISLANDS													
TEMP.	80	80	80	81	81	81	80	80	80	81	81	81	81
PREC.	7.0	6.8	4.9	5.2	9.6	10.8	16.6	16.2	13.4	11.8	10.1	8.9	121.3
76. Djakarta, INDONESIA													
TEMP.	78	78	79	80	80	79	79	79	80	80	79	79	79
PREC.	11.9	13.4	7.9	5.6	4.1	3.7	2.6	1.6	2.8	4.5	5.7	7.6	71.4
77. Moulmein, BURMA													
TEMP.	76	79	84	85	83	80	79	79	80	81	79	76	80
PREC.	0.2	0.2	0.5	2.8	20.0	37.8	45.2	42.8	28.1	8.5	2.2	0.3	188.6
78. Colombo, SRI LANKA													
TEMP.	79	80	81	82	82	80	80	81	80	79	80	79	80
PREC.	3.2	1.9	4.7	11.4	12.1	8.4	4.5	3.8	5.0	14.4	12.5	6.4	88.3
79. Bombay, INDIA													
TEMP.	75	75	78	82	85	82	80	79	79	81	79	76	79
PREC.	0.1	0	0	0.1	0.5	20.6	24.6	14.9	10.9	1.8	0.5	0.1	74.1
80. Tehran, IRAN													
TEMP.	34	42	48	61	71	80	85	83	77	61	51	42	62
PREC.	1.2	0.9	2.4	0.9	0.4	0	0.4	0	0.1	0.1	1.2	1.3	8.9
81. Tashkent, U.S.S.R.													
TEMP.	30	34	47	58	70	77	81	77	67	54	43	36	56
PREC.	1.8	1.4	2.6	2.6	1.1	0.5	0.1	0.1	0.2	1.1	1.4	1.7	14.6
82. New Delhi, INDIA													
TEMP.	58	62	74	86	92	92	86	85	84	79	68	60	77
PREC.	1.0	0.6	0.7	0.3	0.7	3.2	8.4	7.4	4.4	0.4	0.1	0.4	27.6
83. Karachi, PAKISTAN													
TEMP.	65	68	75	81	85	87	84	82	82	80	74	67	78
PREC.	0.6	0.3	0.1	0.1	0	0.4	3.2	1.8	0.7	0	0.2	0.2	7.6
84. Tokyo, JAPAN													
TEMP.	37	38	44	54	62	69	75	78	72	61	50	41	57
PREC.	2.0	2.6	4.3	5.3	5.9	6.3	5.6	4.6	7.5	7.2	4.3	2.3	57.9
85. Shanghai, CHINA													
TEMP.	38	39	46	56	66	73	80	80	73	63	52	42	59
PREC.	2.2	2.3	3.4	3.8	3.7	6.5	5.5	5.9	4.7	3.2	1.7	1.2	44.1
86. Wuhan, CHINA													
TEMP.	39	40	49	61	71	78	84	83	76	65	54	43	62
PREC.	2.1	1.1	2.8	4.8	5.0	7.0	8.6	4.6	2.2	3.9	1.1	0.6	43.8

	J	F	M	A	M	J	J	A	S	O	N	D	YEAR

87. Varanasi, INDIA

	J	F	M	A	M	J	J	A	S	O	N	D	YEAR
TEMP.	60	65	77	87	91	89	84	83	83	78	68	60	77
PREC.	0.7	0.5	0.3	0.1	0.6	5.5	12.5	11.2	6.5	2.2	0.2	0.2	40.5

88. Darjeeling, INDIA

	J	F	M	A	M	J	J	A	S	O	N	D	YEAR
TEMP.	40	42	50	56	58	60	62	61	59	55	48	42	53
PREC.	0.8	1.1	2.0	4.1	7.8	24.2	31.7	26.0	18.3	5.3	0.2	0.2	121.7

89. Peking, CHINA

	J	F	M	A	M	J	J	A	S	O	N	D	YEAR
TEMP.	24	29	41	57	68	76	79	77	68	55	39	27	53
PREC.	0.1	0.2	0.2	0.6	1.4	3.0	9.4	6.3	2.6	0.6	0.3	0.1	24.8

90. Irkutsk, U.S.S.R.

	J	F	M	A	M	J	J	A	S	O	N	D	YEAR
TEMP.	−5	1	17	35	48	59	65	60	48	33	13	1	31
PREC.	0.6	0.5	0.4	0.6	1.2	2.3	2.9	2.4	1.6	0.7	0.6	0.8	14.6

Australia and New Zealand

91. Darwin, AUSTRALIA

	J	F	M	A	M	J	J	A	S	O	N	D	YEAR
TEMP.	84	84	84	84	82	79	77	79	83	85	86	85	83
PREC.	15.2	13.5	9.6	4.1	0.6	0.1	0.1	0.1	0.5	2.0	4.7	9.8	60.3

92. Hall's Creek, AUSTRALIA

	J	F	M	A	M	J	J	A	S	O	N	D	YEAR
TEMP.	86	85	83	78	71	66	64	69	76	84	87	87	78
PREC.	5.7	4.8	3.0	0.8	0.4	0.2	0.2	0.1	0.2	0.6	1.5	3.3	20.8

93. Alice Springs, AUSTRALIA

	J	F	M	A	M	J	J	A	S	O	N	D	YEAR
TEMP.	83	82	77	73	60	54	53	58	66	74	79	82	70
PREC.	1.7	1.7	1.2	0.7	0.6	0.6	0.4	0.4	0.4	0.7	1.0	1.5	10.9

94. Marble Bar, AUSTRALIA

	J	F	M	A	M	J	J	A	S	O	N	D	YEAR
TEMP.	93	92	90	84	75	68	67	71	78	84	90	92	82
PREC.	2.6	3.2	1.9	0.9	0.7	1.1	0.6	0.2	0	0.2	0.4	1.3	13.1

95. Auckland, NEW ZEALAND

	J	F	M	A	M	J	J	A	S	O	N	D	YEAR
TEMP.	66	66	64	61	57	54	52	52	55	57	60	63	59
PREC.	2.6	3.3	3.0	3.5	4.6	5.0	5.0	4.2	3.7	3.6	3.4	2.9	44.8

96. Melbourne, AUSTRALIA

	J	F	M	A	M	J	J	A	S	O	N	D	YEAR
TEMP.	68	68	65	59	54	50	49	51	54	58	61	65	59
PREC.	1.8	1.8	2.1	2.2	2.1	2.0	1.8	1.8	2.4	2.6	2.2	2.2	25.0

97. Hobart, TASMANIA

	J	F	M	A	M	J	J	A	S	O	N	D	YEAR
TEMP.	62	62	59	55	51	47	46	48	51	54	57	60	54
PREC.	1.8	1.6	1.7	1.9	1.8	2.2	2.1	1.8	2.1	2.2	2.4	1.9	23.5

98. Adelaide, AUSTRALIA

	J	F	M	A	M	J	J	A	S	O	N	D	YEAR
TEMP.	74	74	70	64	58	54	52	54	57	61	67	71	63
PREC.	0.7	0.8	1.0	1.7	2.7	3.1	2.6	2.4	2.1	1.7	1.1	0.9	20.8

99. Mackay, AUSTRALIA

	J	F	M	A	M	J	J	A	S	O	N	D	YEAR
TEMP.	80	79	77	74	68	64	62	64	68	73	77	79	72
PREC.	15.0	13.7	15.4	7.3	4.4	2.7	2.3	0.9	1.1	2.4	2.7	7.3	75.2

Indian Ocean

100. KERGUELEN ISLANDS

	J	F	M	A	M	J	J	A	S	O	N	D	YEAR
TEMP.	44	45	39	39	35	37	33	34	33	34	39	41	38

Conversion Tables

Conversion of Degrees Fahrenheit (°F) and Degrees Centigrade (°C)

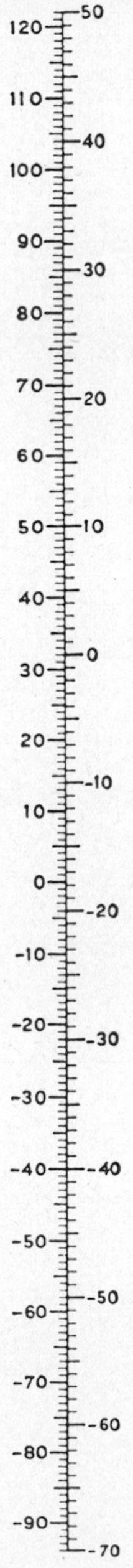

One °F = $\frac{5}{9}$ths °C
Freezing °F = 32° F

To change °*F to* °*C,* and *if the* °*F figure is* above *freezing, subtract* 32 and then multiply by $\frac{5}{9}$.

EX. If the °F figure is 50° F, subtract 32 from 50 and then multiply by $\frac{5}{9}$ ($50 - 32 = 18$; $18 \times \frac{5}{9} = \frac{90}{9} = 10$). Thus, 50° F = 10° C.

To change °*F to* °*C,* and *if the* °*F figure is* below *freezing,* determine the number of degrees below freezing in °F and then multiply that number by $\frac{5}{9}$.

EX. If the °F figure is −20° F, this means 52 Fahrenheit degrees below freezing. Multiply 52 by $\frac{5}{9}$ ($52 \times \frac{5}{9} = \frac{260}{9} = 28.88$). Thus, −20° F = 28.88° C.

One °C = $\frac{9}{5}$ths °F
Freezing °C = 0° C

To change °*C to* °*F,* and *if the* °*C figure is* above *freezing,* multiply by $\frac{9}{5}$ and then *add* 32.

EX. If the °C figure is 30° C, multiply 30 by $\frac{9}{5}$ and add 32 ($30 \times \frac{9}{5} = \frac{270}{5} = 54$; $54 + 32 = 86$). Thus, 30° C = 86° F.

To change °*C to* °*F,* and *if the* °*C figure is* below *freezing,* multiply by $\frac{9}{5}$ and then *subtract* 32.

EX. If the °C figure is −20° C, multiply 20 by $\frac{9}{5}$ and subtract 32 ($20 \times \frac{9}{5} = \frac{180}{5} = 36$; $36 - 32 = 4$). Thus, −20° C = −4° F.

COURTESY AMERICAN GEOGRAPHICAL SOCIETY

Conversion of Inches, Millimeters, and Centimeters

1 inch = 25.4 millimeters = 2.54 centimeters

To convert *inches to millimeters,* multiply the number of inches by 25.4.
    EX.   21.4″ × 25.4 = 543.56 mm.

To convert *millimeters to inches,* divide the number of milli-meters by 25.4.
    EX.   650.2 mm. ÷ 25.4 = 25.598″

To convert *millimeters to centimeters,* point off one more place to the left on the millimeter figure.
    EX.   299.72 mm. =29.972 cm.

To convert *inches to centimeters,* multiply the number of inches by 2.54.
    EX.   16.2″ × 2.54 = 41.148 cm.

To convert *centimeters to inches,* divide the number of centi-meters by 2.54.
    EX.   65.28 cm. ÷ 2.54 = 25.70″

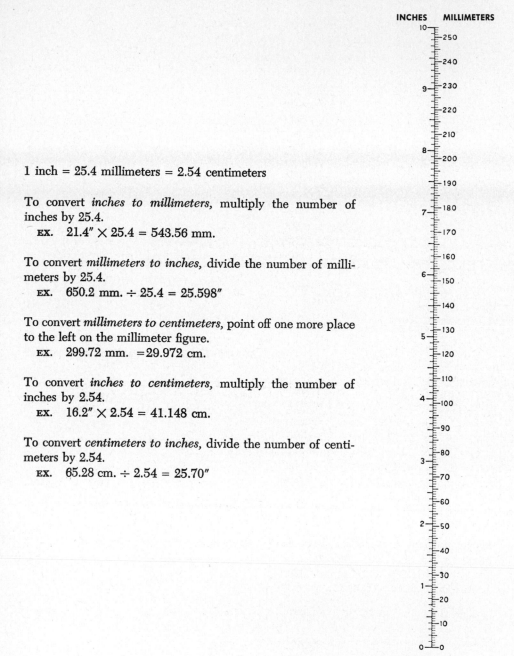

COURTESY AMERICAN GEOGRAPHICAL SOCIETY

Comparative Measurement of Atmospheric Pressure

1 inch of mercury = *25.4 millimeters* = *33.86395 millibars*
1 millibar = *.02953 inches* = *.75006 millimeters*

INCHES	MILLIBARS		INCHES	MILLIBARS		INCHES	MILLIBARS
27.0	= 914		28.6	= 968		30.1	= 1019
27.1	= 918		28.7	= 972		30.2	= 1023
27.2	= 921		28.8	= 975		30.3	= 1026
27.3	= 924		28.9	= 979		30.4	= 1030
27.4	= 928		29.0	= 982		30.5	= 1033
27.5	= 931		29.1	= 985		30.6	= 1036
27.6	= 935		29.2	= 989		30.7	= 1040
27.7	= 938		29.3	= 992		30.8	= 1043
27.8	= 941		29.4	= 996		30.9	= 1046
27.9	= 945		29.5	= 999		31.0	= 1050
28.0	= 948		29.6	= 1002		31.1	= 1053
28.1	= 952		29.7	= 1006		31.2	= 1057
28.2	= 955		29.8	= 1009		31.3	= 1060
28.3	= 958		29.9	= 1013		31.4	= 1063
28.4	= 962		30.0	= 1016		31.5	= 1067
28.5	= 965						

Some Linear Measurement Equivalents

1 statute *mile* = 5280 *ft.* = 1.6093 *km.* = 1609.3 *m.*
1 nautical *mile* (international) = 6076.1033 *ft.* = 1.852 *km.* = 1852 *m.*
1 *furlong* = 660 *ft.* = 220 *yds.* = ⅛ statute *mile* = 201.162 *m.*
1 *rod* = 16.5 *ft.* = 5.5 *yds.* = ¹⁄₃₂ statute *mile* = 5.029 *m.*
1 *yard* = 36 *in.* = 3 *ft.* = ¹⁄₁₇₆₀ statute *mile* = .9144 *m.*
1 *foot* = 12 *in.* = 30.48 *cm.* = .3048 *m.*
1 *inch* = 2.54 *cm.* = 25.4 *mm.*

1 *chain* (surveyor's) = 100 *links* = 66 *ft.* = 792 *in.* = ¹⁄₈₀ statute *mile*
1 *fathom* = 8 *spans* = 72 *in.* = 6 *ft.* = 1.8288 *m.*

1 *kilometer* (km.) = 3280.8399 *ft.* = .62137 statute *mile*
1 *meter* (m.) = 39.37 *in.* = 3.28 *ft.*
1 *centimeter* (cm.) = .3937 *in.* = .0328 *ft.*
1 *millimeter* (mm.) = .03937 *in.*

(1 km. = 1000 m.; 1 m. = 100 cm.; 1 cm. = 10 mm.)

Some Area Measurement Equivalents

1 *square mile* (sq. mile) = 640 *acres* = 258.999 *hectares*
1 *acre* = 43,560 *sq. ft.* = .4046 *hectares* = 4046.8564 *sq. m.*
1 *hectare* = 2.471 *acres* = .01 *sq. km.*

1 *square kilometer* (sq. km.) = 247.1054 *acres* = .3861 *sq. miles*
1 *square meter* (sq. m.) = 10.7639 *sq. ft.*

1 *survey township* = 36 *sq. miles* = 36 *survey sections*
1 *survey section* = 1 *sq. mile* = 640 *acres* = 258.999 *hectares*

Some Time Measurement Equivalents

1 *minute* = 60 *seconds*
1 *hour* = 60 *minutes* = 3600 *seconds*
1 *day* = 24 *hours* = 1440 *minutes* = 86,400 *seconds*
1 *year* = 365.2422 *days*

Some Circular Measurement Equivalents

1 *circle* = 360 *degrees* = 4 *quadrants* = 1 *circumference*
1 *quadrant* = 90 *degrees* = ¼ *circle*
1 *degree* = 60 *minutes*
1 *minute* = 60 *seconds*
1 *radian* = 57 *degrees,* 17 *minutes,* 44.8 *seconds* (57°17′44.8″)

Some Longitude—Time Measurement Equivalents

360 *degrees of longitude* = 24 *hours of time* = 1 *day*
 15 *degrees of longitude* = 1 *hour*
  1 *degree of longitude* = 4 *minutes*
  1 *minute of longitude* = 4 *seconds*
  1 *second of longitude* = ⅟₁₅ *second*

Some Weight Measurement Equivalents

1 *short ton* = 2000 *pounds* = 907.18 *kilograms*
1 *long ton* = 2240 *pounds* = 1016.05 *kilograms*
1 *metric ton* = 2204.623 *pounds* = 1000 *kilograms*

1 *pound* = 16 *ounces* = 453.5923 *grams* = .4536 *kilograms*
1 *ounce* = 28.3495 *grams* = 16 *drams*

1 *kilogram* = 35.274 *ounces* = 2.2046 *pounds*
1 *quintal* = 100 *kilograms* = 220.4623 *pounds*
10 *quintals* = 1 *metric ton*

Geologic Time Scale

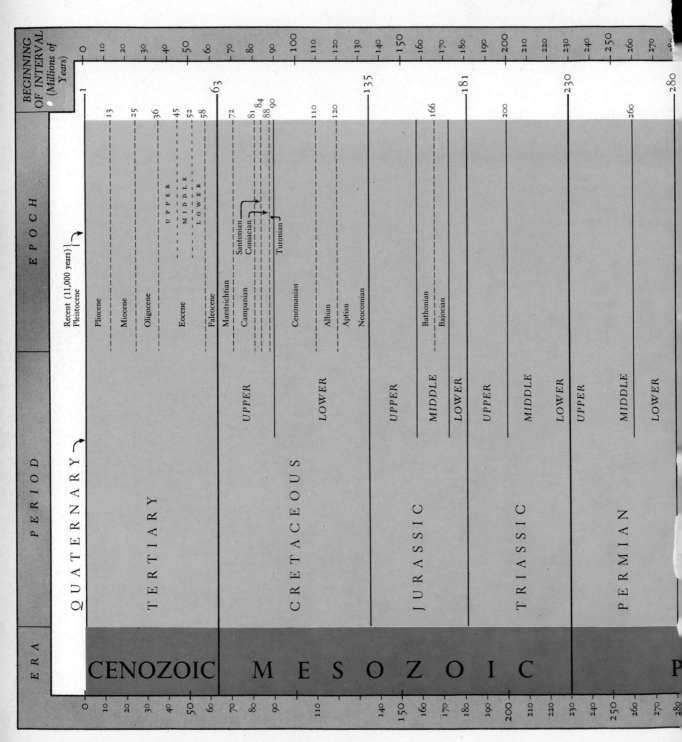

ERA	PERIOD	EPOCH		BEGINNING OF INTERVAL (Millions of Years)
CENOZOIC	QUATERNARY	Recent (11,000 years)		
		Pleistocene		1
	TERTIARY	Pliocene		13
		Miocene		25
		Oligocene		36
		Eocene	UPPER	45
			MIDDLE	52
			LOWER	58
		Paleocene		63
MESOZOIC	CRETACEOUS	UPPER	Maestrichtian	72
			Campanian	81
			Santonian	84
			Coniacian	88
			Turonian	90
			Cenomanian	
		LOWER	Albian	110
			Aptian	120
			Neocomian	135
	JURASSIC	UPPER		
		MIDDLE	Bathonian	166
			Bajocian	
		LOWER		181
	TRIASSIC	UPPER		200
		MIDDLE		
		LOWER		230
P	PERMIAN	UPPER		260
		MIDDLE		280
		LOWER		

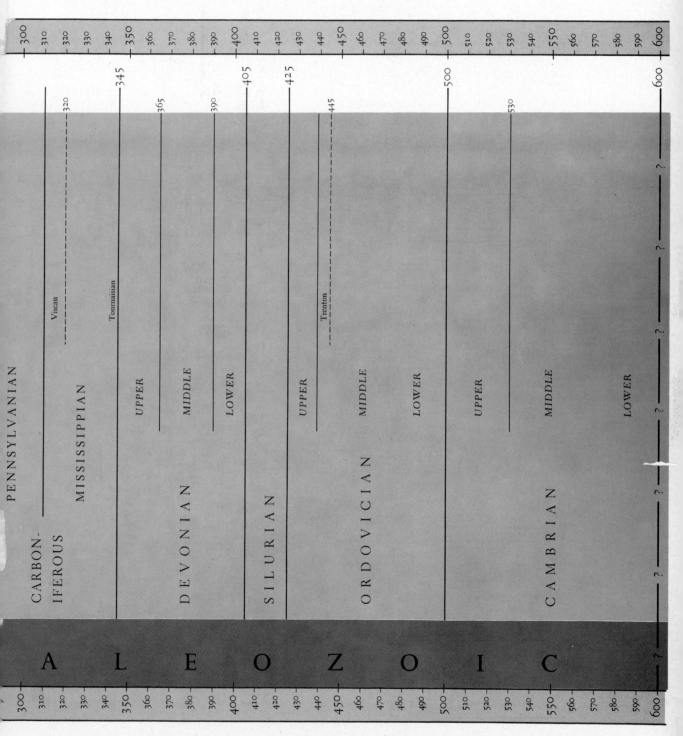

The Seventh Approximation (7A):
A Classification of Soils

In addition to the great soil groups, the widely accepted classification of soils used in this and most other geography texts, various other classifications have been developed. The basic objectives of all of these classifications are essentially the same, however, despite differences in soil categories and nomenclature. One of the most recent and comprehensive of these classifications is known as the *7th Approximation,* or *7A.* When this new system was presented to the Seventh International Congress of Soil Science in 1960, it had already undergone a series of developmental stages. Since the 1960 presentation represented the seventh stage of its development, the classification has been designated the 7th Approximation.

The 7th Approximation has ten major *orders* of soils, all of which are strictly defined and limited—as are the lower *suborders* and *great groups.* The terminology used is much more rigorous than a simple compounding of geographic names with textural classes. This is because the system attempts to describe the morphology of a soil, as well as to delineate its quantitative dominances of type. The ten orders of soil are: *entisols* (recent); *vertisols* (mixed); *inceptisols* (new surfaces); *aridisols* (desert); *mollisols* (calcified); *spodosols* (podzolized); *alfisols* (pedalfers); *ultisols* (weathered); *oxisols* (laterized); and *histosols* (organic).

There are twenty-nine suborders, within which the oxisols and histosols are as yet undivided. The suborder name is derived by the compounding of one of fifteen prefixes (for example, *aqu* = wet) with the root of one of the order terms; thus, *aquent* stands for a *waterlogged recent soil.* The great groups are designated by adding short suffixes (for example, *hal* = salty) to the suborder names. The great groups are further subdivided into *subgroups, families,* and *series,* according to soil texture, mineral form, and so on.

The 7th Approximation has had some impact on soil science and soil geographers. Reactions to it have been varied, to say the least; but, the genetic directness of 7A may, in time, balance the initial impact caused by its curious nomenclature.

Indexes

Index of Geographical Terms

General Index

Back Endpaper

Left page, a color infrared photograph of the New York City area that was obtained by a NASA U-2 aircraft at an altitude of 65,000 feet. (NASA—Ames Research Center)

Right page, a color photograph of Manhattan Island taken with a KA-56 horizon-to-horizon aerial camera at an altitude of about 2,000 feet. (Howard Sochurek)